Unlocking Cousin Daisy's Cabinet

Unlocking Cousin Daisy's Cabinet

Published by The Conrad Press Ltd. in the United Kingdom 2022

Tel: +44(0)1227 472 874

www.theconradpress.com

info@theconradpress.com

ISBN 978-1-914913-63-1

Crossing I, a painting by Nila Rusnell Oakes, 1999, owned by the author is used on the book cover. Typesetting and Cover Design by: Charlotte Mouncey, www.bookstyle.co.uk

The Conrad Press logo was designed by Maria Priestley.

Printed and bound in Great Britain by Clays Ltd, Elcograf S.p.A.

Unlocking Cousin Daisy's Cabinet

— personal recollections —

Thomas C. Brutting

For Michael, who I sincerely wish could have heard
these recollections directly from me...
and to Mrs. Robinson, a Kindergarten teacher
at PS 112 in Long Island City, NY,
who changed the course of my life in 1960.
Finally, to the person bringing me the most joy, Ed.

Contents

Introduction

L ife takes many twists and turns. What we do with our lives, the adventures we have, and the experiences that influence our sense of self: all these add up in the most unpredictable and remarkable ways to create who we are.

I have always been amazed how people, especially some Americans, are able to live and stay in one place their entire lives. That certainly has not been my reality. I have made six major moves in my life, always to a different geographic place in the United States. My experiences in each had a lasting impact.

This is a compilation of excerpts and recollections from my life, all true-life events. The places, people and names are genuine, as are all the experiences. The chapters can be read individually as short narratives; yet they all are interrelated in various ways. They are purposely not in any chronological order. This is meant to mix things up a bit; to be reflective of the individuality and uniqueness of the event or person discussed.

We can never control where we were born and I figure myself privileged to have been born in New York City, a leading city of the world; and to have lived in the South, Midwest, and the West. My time in those places will be outlined with what made each region interesting and special in their own way, and the influence each one had on me.

Life, for me, has been a fascinating mix of many people, places, insights, and encounters. I feel very fortunate to have been exposed to so many unique things, although some tragic too. I have always tried to move beyond whatever unforeseen circumstances may arise putting an unpleasant twist in my life. Yet there has been a richness in my life with the unexpected events that occurred along the way, both good and bad.

I apologize in advance for any disagreement over cultural observations as they are merely taken from my perspective at the time. Keeping in mind, as well, that what I observed at age eleven or twelve might be observed quite different at age forty or fifty, just from maturity.

I reflect on my sixty-five years, a lifespan I view in segments, phases and small books that open and close as the years progress. The enormous joy and pain over time has resulted in my appreciation of the importance of having values and integrity in one's life, a foundation gifted from my parents.

I have found that treasures are not in financial assets, but rather in the people we meet, the friends and family we have, and the many wonderful experiences one can discover in the world.

Let's take the journey together.

Thomas C. Brutting, February 2022

Chapter I

Unlocking Cousin Daisy's cabinet

Let us get right to the crux of explaining about Daisy, and her cabinet.

Daisy is the cousin of my mother's best friend, Marguerite. My mother had moved to San Francisco from Florida in 1996 after my father died of cancer in the fiftieth year of their marriage. They had retired to Florida and lived there for fifteen years before his passing. My mother was quite brave to make such a significant move to California while in her late seventies. Her prime reason was to be closer to me, her only child. She moved with three boxes and a suitcase of clothes.

In starting her new San Francisco, California life I convinced her to give up driving and her big Florida car. After arriving we had to get her a California I.D. card in lieu of a driver's license which required presenting her birth certificate. Low and behold with all the carefully stored and organized documents my father had put together there was no birth certificate for her.

I wrote to the Bureau of Records in New York City where she was born, noting her birth date, and they came up with nothing. Following many attempts for conversation she refused to discuss it, but then one day she blurted out, 'they can send me back if they want!'. That led me to wonder if she hadn't been born in this country and had been hiding it. I finally enlisted a friend in New York to go to the Bureau and investigate it.

They said they could search further, for an additional fee, and comb through previous and subsequent years from the date given. Well, low and behold, we found a birth certificate for her three years prior to her claimed birth year! She refused to acknowledge it, and asserted it wasn't hers since the first name was slightly different, Dora in lieu of Dorothy. Yet the parents' names lined up. She had also claimed to be younger than her brother, which turned out to not be true as well.

Getting an I.D. was not easy, even with the birth certificate we now had in hand, as none of her other legal documents lined up with the same year. I enlisted the office of Senator Quentin Kopp who with an explanation of the circumstances got it done. With her California I.D. issued, she never wanted to talk about it again. Yet a couple of years later during a lunch she finally decided to unravel the mystery. She told that when she married my father in 1945, he decided to change the year to put it in alignment with the year he was born! It wasn't vanity, or being an older woman, or anything of that nature, just his whim which apparently you could easily do in those days! Case closed.

In her new San Francisco home, she met Marguerite, a widow of approximately the same age, in the high-rise apartment building where they both lived, and developed a truly good friendship. She was very much like my mother in many ways, including her demeanor, and held secrets too. They called each other every morning to check in and be sure everything was OK. Marguerite, of Greek heritage, was a native San Franciscan and took my mother under her wing to accumulate her to life in the city. Since I convinced my mother against driving in the city, and Marguerite didn't drive either, instead of cabs they rode public transportation everywhere. It was almost a daily outing, a treat, for them to ride long distances by bus or subway.

Marguerite lived on the fourth floor in a two-bedroom apartment while my mother lived on the twelfth, top floor, in a one bedroom that she so eloquently called 'the penthouse'. The apartments were large, and my mother's place had a great view out to the ocean. She kept it sparsely furnished, yet comfortable for her needs.

I typically telephoned her at seven thirty each morning for a check-in call. During one of these calls, I found out that the elevators, for whatever reason, weren't working the day before. She discovered it after returning home from shopping. I asked her what she did as living on the twelfth floor at her age presented some challenges. The possibility of the elevators being inoperable was one thing she feared when first looking at the apartment. Well, it happened periodically, and she proudly told me that she walked up the stairs. Yes, twelve flights. I asked why she did not stop at Marguerite's place on the fourth floor, at least until the elevators worked again, and she quickly responded, 'I wanted to be home'. She was an avid walker and no need to discuss it further. End of story.

She and Marguerite made friends with the bus drivers who came to know them from their frequent excursions. Going food shopping at the farthest place possible, just for the ride, made their day. There is an infamous Safeway in San Francisco's Marina neighborhood known for decades where people cruised for a pickup or a date. Guess where they went? Right there! It was way out of their way, but they went, nonetheless. I used to tease my mother about it.

Marguerite had a cousin, Daisy, who was quite wealthy and lived in an enormous Pacific Heights mansion. From the story I heard Daisy's husband made money by building and owning one of the primary parking garages in downtown San Francisco. I guess parking is quite profitable. In any case they lived quite lavishly.

On occasion Marguerite would go check on the place while Daisy was away; or stay there for short stints. She apparently was not fond of it; and disliked the vastness of each floor with a multitude of rooms on each. Sometimes my mother would accompany Marguerite to check on the place during Daisy's absence.

Eventually Daisy passed away. Marguerite received an ornate Chinese cabinet from the mansion. From recollection it stood about four to five feet high, about two feet deep, quite beautiful and was permanently locked; no key.

Well, of course, this locked cabinet that Marguerite received, without really wanting it from what I understood, became a great fascination and frustration to know what was inside.

She was totally perplexed and very anxious to get it open, so over many days she tried with everything from toothpicks to bobby pins to old keys, nothing worked. The lock was LOCKED. Discussing it with my mother she was certain something must be inside if indeed it had been locked. Why lock it otherwise?

My husband, Ed, and I were visiting my mother one afternoon, and the phone rang. It was Marguerite. When she learned we were visiting she asked if we'd come down to look at the cabinet and lock, so we went to her apartment.

The cabinet was beautiful, ornate, and obviously a fine antique. Both Ed and I picked, poked, shook and tugged the lock. Nothing moved or budged. In total bewilderment Ed finally took a bobby pin from Marguerite and just went at it, jiggling and doing whatever possible to get it open. Our last resort would be to cut it somehow, but we did not want to break anything or ruin the integrity of the cabinet. Perhaps it had been locked many years, if not decades, and even rusted inside.

After about an hour of frustrated yanking and jiggling, pronto! IT OPENED. We all stood there in amazement and in total awe opening the cabinet. Treasure? Money? Asian antiquities? Linens? Clothes? No.

NOTHING! ABSOLUTELY NOTHING. It was completely empty.

We all went into a roaring laughter, yet it was one of those moments where you just must wonder. Marguerite tossed the lock into the cabinet and closed the doors. So much time spent for so little, yet in the end we made Marguerite very happy, and Ed became her newest hero.

No one will ever know why the cabinet was locked, perhaps simply because it could be locked. And whatever happened to the key? In any case the mystery will remain; and is one of those life experiences, albeit a small one, that makes one ponder.

The lesson, I guess, is never assume anything until the unknown is revealed in fact. Like my mother's birth certificate some things come to light, and then others not. In life, as you'll read in subsequent chapters, the unknown unfolds, in some cases opening full of treasure, and in others emptiness.

I miss Marguerite and my mother as they both passed away not too many years later, and their adventures in their senior years ended too.

CHAPTER 2

Unprecedented times

The world went upside down in the early part of 2020.

Late in December 2019, a serious virus outbreak in Wuhan, China left everyone speculating. The virus continued into the new year growing exponentially within that city. People were dying, and supposedly it started in a 'wet market' within the city, transmitted from some animal of unknown origin to people. It spread rapidly to other regions.

At first the Western world took a not so cautious outlook figuring China was locked down and it would be isolated within that country, not realizing that people from there were traveling the world and spreading the virus across the globe. Soon the numbers of infected people began increasing and it was found popping up beyond China.

Then a cruise ship pulled into a port in Japan and people were getting sick. The ship with passengers and crew from around the world had to be isolated. No one quite knew what to make of it, but one thing was certain it was the same deadly virus, Coronavirus or Covid-19.

Soon it became evident that something beyond a localized menacing outbreak was occurring and a pandemic was truly opening on the world. Although we had known for decades that this type of thing could happen, especially the United States, we were not prepared. As with other types of potential disasters we recognize the risks yet hide under the covers, so to speak, to adequately handle it should it occur. This is very similar to when Hurricane Katrina hit New Orleans... for decades they knew it was coming yet the fallout from being ill prepared was profound.

This pandemic, however, was quite unique and crossing the globe quickly and without much understanding of it. After China then Italy became the next epicenter of the virus. That country completely shut down and went into total quarantine; unprecedented for a country to completely stop all business. Other places in Europe began seeing outbreaks, and it was eventually traced to a ski resort as ground zero for transmission.

In the U.S. the first case was found in a man in Washington State, that then was disproven by evidence of an earlier case, from 2019, in a woman in California who had died and was later autopsied. The rate of infection where she resided was rapidly increasing.

Just before this all started to unfold my good friend, Mary Ruth, and I attended a comedy theatrical performance at the Berkeley Rep. It was excellent and included scenes of life in the present day as an interviewer went around talking with everyday folks. At one point the Coronavirus was noted in the play; and was met with consternation in reviews afterwards. Apparently, no one wanted to hear about it, and/or joke about it.

Our County, Alameda, issued a 'Shelter-In-Place' order on Monday, March 16, effective at midnight. It was to last until April 7, yet later got extended much further on, and on. It was scary and surreal. The order came by text message, and by landline phone message. It was quite clear that everyone was to get home and stay there.

When the order was issued, I thought it would be a good time for me to high tail it up to our little grocery a couple of blocks away, but by time I got there the place was packed with people. The checkout line was all the way down an aisle. I decided not to buy anything and left, especially when we were supposed to be social distancing six feet apart from each other, yet that wasn't happening. The store owner was frantically telling people to distance themselves.

Outside I saw our neighbors, the Rubin-Walners, who were also attempting to get last minute things before the order went into effect. It was one of those crazy times, similar to a sci-fi movie, where the world is about to be upended, and everyone was preparing for their lives to be in imminent danger. The sky was crystal clear and quite beautiful, yet you knew clouds would gather and doom was looming close.

The days to come would be quite challenging.

At the time I write this, May 2020, we have no idea how or when this will end. In a matter of fact this is the first time in my life to have a very unusual anniversary; I have not been in a store in two months! Getting home deliveries for everything has become routine, including all groceries. Sanitizing everything before it enters the house is mandatory. Only my husband, Ed, and I have been together while living in total isolation. Email, telephone, and an occasional meeting, at a distance, with a neighbor as we take a daily walk are the possible outside connections. 'ZOOM' live internet contacts with friends, family and business associates are ubiquitous.

In early May 2020, the United States saw 81,000 deaths

from this virus. By the end of May it grew to 100,000, more than those who died in the Vietnam War, and the number will continue to grow. It is speculated we may be in this for months, or even a couple of years to come.

It has been amazing how certain food supplies, basic staples, have been unavailable at various times over the past couple of months. First eggs, then bleach, flour, vinegar and now garlic has been out of stock. They are predicting serious meat shortages as the meat processing plants face large numbers of employees infected with Coronavirus.

Starting retirement this year, I have had two and a half months of freedom before the pandemic escalated, and now two months of quarantine. Cooking everyday has become routine and so long as the food supplies flow, we are being as creative as possible with everything from preparing Viennese Chicken Schnitzel to our own concoction, 'Mexican Surprise', a bit of everything in the frig that mimics Mexican cuisine.

People really want to get back to work and probably by time you read this our economy will be in the worst state since the Great Depression.

I was supposed to go to Washington DC the week of the Shelter-In-Place order to attend the opening of a longtime friend and college buddy, Alan Karchmer, for his photography exhibit at the National Building Museum. His architectural photography is internationally recognized, and his entire collection is being donated to the museum. He and his wife, Sandra Ann, his photography stylist, are wonderful, dear friends and we have shared many great, fun times together. We enjoy it so much when we visit as they are food connoisseurs, and we like sharing that with them too. Plus, they have a fabulous sense of humor.

Because of work responsibilities Ed would not be able to attend Alan's exhibit opening so I planned to fly there myself. However, a couple of weeks before something in me told me not to go, so I called and regretfully declined. The plan was for both Ed and I to go there a couple of weeks later. Although saddened it would not have happened anyway as the opening was ultimately cancelled due to the pandemic as well as all travel plans for the foreseeable future.

As the weeks progressed the obvious stress and uncertainly of where the pandemic was heading was very disconcerting.

On May 24, 2020, the *New York Times* published the names, ages, places, and something about all 100,000 Americans that have died to date. Most sobering to say the least. It is a good reminder on this Memorial Day Weekend the tragedy we have faced so far.

There were some rather interesting, unexpected moments during this time; some made light of the situation that did help in surviving it.

Ed and I were walking through the neighborhood one day and a car came down the road behind us. It stopped, the window came down, and two nuns who live in a house within the neighborhood gleefully extolled the fact that they had bought margaritas and were heading home with them in their trunk to enjoy. It was so fun and really made us chuckle.

If anything, I hope the result of this terrible event is that we learn to live slower, simpler lives and that we finally recognize the damage we have done to the environment. There have been some amazing and inspiring comparison photos, before and after, of the pollution in New Delhi and the disappearance of it after the country went into lockdown!

And as if the world wasn't strained enough in late May 2020 a black man named George Floyd was killed by a police officer during an arrest in Minneapolis. That sparked a national outcry and outrage leading to peaceful protests across the nation, yet also accompanied by unprecedented riots and looting. One pronounced difference, compared to previous riots, was that they now occurred in affluent, upscale neighborhoods. Major upmarket retail stores, Nieman Marcus, Saks, Cartier, were being vandalized along with smaller shops and restaurants.

The heightened crisis of racial inequality went global adding another level of stress everywhere.

By September 2020 there was a somber tone engulfing the nation. Riots, unrest, a national election of consequence, unrelenting pandemic. All of it was fueling a sense of despair and uncertainty. It was debated if schools should open, along with some businesses, now failing by the droves. Resuming operations, and then closing again; uncertain if those without jobs would ever get one, and on and on. During this time, I had many messages from friends expressing that they felt 'morose' and 'depressed'. Families couldn't get together as usual, weddings were cancelled or postponed indefinitely, limited travel, countries closed to visitors, and all types of typical events just didn't take place, some for the first time in many decades or even a century or more, mostly cancelled.

During this time my dear cousin, Cynthia Hicks, died unexpectedly from a brain aneurysm. She lived with her husband in Florida, and I had hope to reunite with her soon as we hadn't seen each other in over forty years. She had emailed me on a Friday to see if we were faring well with the recent events and by Tuesday she was gone. A wake and funeral occurred the following week on Long Island in New York, and I truly wondered how they would do it during this pandemic time. I did not attend but it did make me ponder how at this time one couldn't even mourn as usual.

The sentiment of our times was indeed morose and depressing.

Frugality became the mantra of the day. Food wasn't wasted; nothing was wasted. Very little was thrown away, and most household items, especially food storage items including aluminum foil, were reused again and again when possible.

Our endurance was further tested when during the end of August an unprecedented and highly unusual thunder and lightning storm hit one Sunday. This started a rash of serious fires around California, and especially in the Bay Area. That led to weeks of smoke, ash, and incredibly bad air quality. As if we hadn't taken on enough, we now had to live without fresh air.

People tended to keep their wits about them, but one morning on September 9, when the sun did not rise, there was nothing but an ominous orange glow in the sky. Speculation of apocalypse and impending doom was expressed by everyone. Our neighbor, Dan, had his outdoor funeral on this day. Regretfully, we did not attend due to the severely poor air quality. It seemed things could not get worse.

The fires, severe smoke, and loss of homes and life continued through September, and it was relentless. Just as everything seemed to improve a couple of new fires broke out in Napa County and near Santa Rosa in Sonoma County. Of course, smoke followed and again the air quality diminished; plus, the temperatures went up to the high nineties. If anyone denies 'global warming' they are kidding themselves.

There are those endearing, humorous instants that would punctuate it all and become memorable. In our case it was a blue jay that lived somewhere in our yard. We named him Franklin. Franklin was quite mischievous and would follow us around everywhere we went on the property. Every time you'd turn around there would be Franklin. If he lost sight of me or Ed he'd start squawking like a maniac. He, we presume a 'he', made a high-pitched bird noise. Every time we stepped outside, for days on end, there would be Franklin.

It is now December and nearing the end of 2020. We have no idea how this will all end, however, vaccines are now being slowly distributed. After having a raucous Presidential election next year will be a new dawn, hopefully.

We are nearing 400,000 deaths from Covid-19 as the year ends with predictions for many more to come.

This once in a century event, if not a millennial one, will never be forgotten. It is my hope that it makes us appreciate our world more, and the smaller, simpler things we should appreciate. Things were moving so quickly and nearly out of control that stopping for a minute to reflect is not necessarily a bad thing. We also learned a lot about human nature.

If there has been one lesson, the pandemic has taught us endurance and appreciation of the blessings we have in life, no matter how insignificant they may have seemed beforehand.

Chapter 3

The greatest show on earth

I had the distinct pleasure of witnessing and experiencing five Mardi Gras seasons in New Orleans. Having decided to attend Tulane University it was inevitable to become a part of it. As a 'Northerner' I had no idea what to expect, and oh my, what a wild ride it is to see it firsthand.

The festive season lasts several weeks culminating with 'Fat Tuesday', or *Mardi Gras* in French. It is a time of overindulgence before the beginning of Lent. The weeks of festivities with parades, celebrations, parties, and events seems endless. All during the season the Krewes, or social organizations, keep precise schedules for their parades using a designated route through the city, along with other events, and customarily with a Mardi Gras ball. The only exception would be the Krewe of Zulu, a black Krewe, that never reveals the route or location of their parade, although it occurs on the same day, and approximately the same time of day, each year. Generally, the parades are on St. Charles Avenue or Canal Street, primary streets of New Orleans, with several using alternate, lesser prominent routes.

In the years before the 1970s, some of the parades went through the French Quarter but were later banned as being too dangerous. The tightly packed streets, with a dense number of closely attached wood buildings were particularly vulnerable to the intensity of the parades. Some Krewes use 'flambeaux' which are flaming torches employed since the 1850s in their parades. These wood torches, originally meant to light the parade route, are spun, and tossed by the men carrying them and present a particular challenge in an area like the French Quarter.

Some of the most well-established Krewes, Momus, Comus, Rex, are some of the oldest and most prominent social organizations. Momus and Comus are secret societies from exclusive, private, men's only clubs, and most often the members names and identities are concealed as they are also masked in the parade. These all-white organizations date back to the middle 1800s and have only recently met with resistance to their exclusive membership rules. Some do not 'parade' any longer due to cries and legal cases of discrimination.

Bacchus is perhaps the most popular and the 'King' is typically a major entertainment figure. The Mardi Gras colors of Green, for faith, Gold, for power, and Purple, for justice come from Bacchus.

Rex is the most civic in prestige and typically includes local politicians. Neither Bacchus or Rex are secret societies and being the 'King and Queen of Rex' essentially makes one the 'King and Queen of Carnival'. Each 'king' receives a Mardi Gras flag with the year they are bestowed with the honor on it, that then is traditionally displayed and flown outside their homes thereafter during the season.

Alternative Krewes of women, LGBTQ+, Latinos, neighborhoods, and others have grown in popularity too.

The Krewe of Momus traditionally parades the Thursday before Mardi Gras day. Bacchus is the Sunday before it. Rex and Comus parade on Mardi Gras day. They then go to the Civic

Auditorium for their balls, one on each side, with a partition down the middle separating them. At midnight, the partition is opened, and one King invites the other to join the ball. They come together while marching around the Auditorium to the song, 'If I Ever Cease to Love'. This part is televised.

That ends Mardi Gras for the year. Mardi Gras, or Carnival, abruptly ends at midnight on Fat Tuesday. Ash Wednesday, or the day to repent along with Lent, begins.

There is a definite hierarchy to Mardi Gras, especially for New Orleanians. The prominent secret membership Krewes have members from the city's elite. As with French royalty and culture, from which Mardi Gras partly originated, there exists a royal order within each Krewe. Each year a King and Queen are chosen, along with Dukes and other royal figures. It is a big deal to become a member of royalty within the Krewe and is a status symbol. There is enormous pride in belonging to a Krewe, and it comes with enormous financial expense. With most of the balls, should someone outside the Krewe be invited to attend, you only sit and watch.

A parade is also a big deal, usually with elaborate floats and costumed Krewe members who throw things like beads and doubloons from the floats. People gather and stand along the parade route and shout, 'throw me something, Mister'. Usually that results in a rain of beads and doubloons tossed into the crowd. Children are placed on ladders with seats built on top of them so they can see over the heads of the crowd to the floats, and perhaps catch anything coming their way. Glass beads used to be common; and are now collectable since being replaced by cheaper plastic ones, with less potential of injury from a flung glass set of beads directly hitting your face.

Excessive drinking is a big part of Mardi Gras. If New Orleans is already a drinking town, Mardi Grad just ramps it up. As it gets closer to Mardi Gras day millions of people pour into the city from all corners of the US and the world. The downtown, and especially the French Quarter, become nearly impassable. Bourbon Street becomes the epicenter of debauchery and drinking.

Mardi Gras is infectious, and once bitten by the 'Fat Tuesday' bug there is never escaping it. You will remember it your entire life.

There are certain French phrases that stand out during Mardi Grad season, '*Joie de Vivre*', the Joy of Life and '*Laissez Les Bons Temps Rouler*', Let the Good Times Roll; phrases that exist the entire year in New Orleans.

Because Ash Wednesday, the day after Mardi Gras, is the beginning of the Lenten Season, predicated on Easter, the date changes each year. It can be as early as February 3 to as late as March 9 and the partying begins right after the Epiphany on January 6. This can make for a very long holiday season after Christmas and New Year's! When the kickoff of the season begins it accelerates with countless parades and celebrations day after day; and the pandemonium continues up until the weekend before Mardi Gras day and culminates on Tuesday.

Most people who are not from New Orleans, or Louisiana, do not realize that Mardi Gras is a sanctioned holiday, everything closes for it.

There are many unique customs and traditions that come with Mardi Gras, besides finding a costume for the day it occurs. There is King Cake. The cake is a super sweet ring cake with frosting and sprinkles in the colors of Mardi Gras, green, purple and gold. Baked inside is a tiny plastic 'baby' doll, a disgusting little thing that looks like it went through a nuclear attack and was permanently fixed in a seated position. It is served at every party during the season. As people eat the cake the person who gets the baby in their piece is honored, and generally is expected will give the next party. This goes on for days on end. In certain circles the honor includes that person being the 'king' or 'queen' for that event or party.

The festivities, with excessive eating and drinking, is endless. It becomes nearly oppressive after a few days. Regardless, the party always goes on.

Jews have typically been excluded from Mardi Gras as it is considered a Christian event. Many of them leave town, although this has changed too in recent years. What is most amazing is the amount of money people pour into Mardi Gras and the Krewe membership each year. It is a major yearly expenditure. Since Jewish people have been generally excluded from participating, they have poured their resources and money into building civic buildings and funding libraries, museums and contributing to other noteworthy civic minded endeavors. Frankly, if it wasn't for the New Orleans Jewish population few of these civic benefits would exist at the level they do.

My first Mardi Gras, in 1973, was simply magical. I had been to many parades but nothing to the energy level of a Mardi Gras parade. The floats, the bands, the costumes, the beads and commemorative doubloons, the exuberance.

Then there's the downside, especially the drunkenness. Certain things happen, like the cast iron posts holding up the French Quarter balconies are greased so people can't shimmy up them. Yet people try. Getting through the crowd downtown is daunting at best, and at times dangerous, as I recall stories of people with razor blades in their shoes kicking people in the shins, although I never knew anyone who had that happen to them.

There was one time the car I was riding in was overcome by revelers. They got on the car and started pounding and shaking it until deciding to move on. Not fun, and scary. Another noteworthy recollection was having gone to dinner with a group of friends. After leaving the restaurant we could not stay together due to the raucous mob. I got separated with my friend's short, petite mother who grabbed my arm tightly for security. She looked up at me and calmly said, 'don't worry, we'll make it'. Most endearing in the intensity of the moment. I got her back to her hotel safely.

On campus the enormous Tulane Stadium became a makeshift medical center for those who became ill or injured in the city during the final days of Mardi Gras. There they cared for hundreds of injured people, each year, until the stadium was demolished in the mid 1970's.

Streetcars were so packed full of people that when the driver tried to go past a stop, unable to take more passengers, people just precariously hung on the side, or tried to climb through the open windows over those who were seated. One friend had a man take her long hair and began licking it while in a crowded car! After reprimanding him we immediately got off the streetcar in shock and disgust. That was the type of thing that happened during Mardi Gras.

There were fun times too. Once a whole group of us held hands while skipping and singing loudly in jubilation down the entire length of St. Charles Avenue, a bit inebriated. Why?

Who knows! It was fun, and during Mardi Gras you could get away with it.

During one Mardi Gras a group of us went costumed as 'white trash'. We wore large garbage bags stuffed with crumpled paper, so we looked like inverted mushrooms with ribbon tied around the top of the bag near the neck. The words 'white trash' were written with markers on the front and back of the bag. It was a totally tasteless, crass thing to do. Well, we never realized how popular we'd be, or how many people liked it, except for one major drawback. More than several people saw it as a convenient opportunity to pull open the neck and throw their garbage into us! Used drink cups, food wrappers, napkins, all types of waste. YUK! We decided to call it a day sooner than expected.

My last Mardi Gras, 1977, was the most memorable and traumatic.

Since it was my fifth Mardi Gras the special newness and excitement of it had rather worn off at that point. There was little more to expect from it, perhaps a new drink concoction at the most. At the Tulane Student Union I saw, along with a couple friends, a notice posted for a tour company looking for students to help with tours they were conducting for Mardi Gras. They would pay a hundred dollars each to work a tour. Well, I and a couple of my friends thought it would be fun, a different approach to Mardi Gras, and make a bit of money too.

We signed on and got little instruction or preparation other than show up at a particular time for a three-day stint. We were the tour guides for Sunday, Monday, and Tuesday. Initially it seemed like great fun.

The tour company was a well-known, budget level affordable

tour company from the Northeast. They were bringing in buses of visitors to Mardi Gras, primarily from the New York Metropolitan area. We learned many were from Brooklyn and New Jersey, and for many of them it was the one big trip of their lives. Some told us that they had saved for years to come to Mardi Gras. Nearly all were over fifty years old and retired. Unfortunately, we soon learned that the tour company wasn't all that professional or prepared, perhaps reflective of the bargain prices they offered to travel to the event.

Also interesting was they put these folks up in a motel far outside the city, in the suburbs, Metairie, close to the airport. There was no way they could do anything but stay in the motel unless taken by bus to where all the activities took place. This ruled out any exploring on their own, without taking a many mile trek by taxi to get to the heart of New Orleans, and any interesting tourist parts of the city.

Each of us were assigned to our own bus and group of people. We were quickly introduced and given a microphone to tell the visitors what we knew of the city and Mardi Gras. I love being a tour guide, so it was right up my alley! Sometimes the bus driver would talk over the loudspeaker, and I found knew absolutely nothing of the city often giving out incorrect information, mispronouncing names and giving wrong directions! I was shocked and it was awkward to correct him. I also came to learn that the bus driver greatly resented me, although he was friendly; but extremely jealous of me being an 'entitled college kid' at a private university. He kept reminding me that he never had the opportunities afforded to me. To some extent I was empathetic as he was perhaps correct in his assessment of our lives. It made me appreciate what he was saying.

Everything went relatively well until we got downtown on Sunday for the premier parade, Bacchus. When we got into the swarm of the crowd the bus driver turned to me and asked where to park the bus! Let me repeat, where to park the bus! During Mardi Gras! Downtown! Swarms of people and packed parking lots!!!!

I literally cringed and said I had no idea where to park a bus, or anything for that matter. The driver got very irritated with me. It was apparent that was my job, although no one had told me about that until that very minute. Here was a bus load of anxious visitors, late in getting to their first parade, and I wasn't doing what I should do.

I do not recall how we found some place to park, but we did, and the bus driver had to stay with the bus. It was a sketchy proposition for such a big vehicle to be left alone. The driver was not particularly happy as it meant he would miss the parade.

In turn I escorted the 30 or so people through the throngs to Gallier Hall where we would watch the parade. We made it with few problems, and we had a reserved spot to stand or sit on the steps of the building. As our space was extremely limited, I had to wrap my arm around one of the massive columns while standing on the base of it. It was a precarious perch, but I wanted the tourists to be comfortable. The throngs of people on the street were five people deep and the parade was indeed fun, yet the yelling and throwing of beads overwhelming too. The 'King' of the parade was the celebrity Henry Winkler, 'Fonzi', from the TV show *Happy Days*. When his float passed us, he looked directly at me hanging from the column and yelled out in his distinctive accent from the show, '*HEEEY*!'

while shrugging his shoulders. I 'hey'd' back. He smiled.

That evening when my college buds and I got back to together to recollect our first day on the job we were frustrated, angry, exhausted, and exasperated. We felt like quitting and walking away from this tour company; the one hundred dollars was not worth it. Yet, we liked the tourists, and they liked us, so we just decided to carry on and get the job done.

Monday wasn't better and the tour included some side visits to places around New Orleans. The bus driver depended on me for directions and information for everything.

That afternoon we returned everyone to the motel and a couple of the tourists, a very nice older Italian woman from Brooklyn and her traveling companion, another older woman, asked me to lunch. I thought that was a very kind offer and I accepted. They treated me to a McDonald's hamburger and fries next door to the motel. We shared stories of our lives. The Italian woman was very gracious and a bit outspoken, reminiscent of the older Italian women I remembered from my boyhood in New York. We laughed and had a great time together, and they even poked fun at the bus driver.

What I remember most is the Italian woman telling me how much she loved opera. She would save her money for long periods during the spring and summer to attend performances at the Met, either in the cheap seats or standing room only section. I admired her commitment to what she adored so much.

When we finished our meal, the other woman got up immediately and began to collect our refuse and clean the table. As she began to pick up the trash, I got up to help. The Italian woman grabbed my arm and whispered for me to sit down, telling me the other woman was German and 'they like doing that type of thing.'

As we were going out in the evening, I got to spend time in the bus driver's motel room which was more than awkward, to say the least. Not only was it uncomfortable but there was a constant barrage of reminding me about my entitled privilege and how lucky I am in life.

Then came Mardi Gras day, Fat Tuesday!

From what I remember for most of the day we all had a good time. We fortunately got the bus parking figured out. Mind you the tour company had been doing this for some time, so they should have had a clue what to do all along.

Truthfully, I have little recollection of the day other than how it ended which is etched in my memory forever.

Sometime after dusk we were to return everyone back to their motel. I was to be dropped off somewhere along the way, although I forget the exact location. A friend, Greg, from another bus was heading back with me. As we headed out of downtown on Tulane Ave., I was about to get up and thank everyone for coming to New Orleans, and hoped they enjoyed Mardi Gras. The bus came to a stop at an intersection for a red light. Just as I contemplated getting up there was a loud explosion, and everything went momentarily blank. I was dizzy. When I regained composure, I realized the bus had moved to the middle of the intersection. I looked over my shoulder out the window. A man at a gas station was running frantically toward us.

I immediately sensed something was very wrong and there was both a dark silence and some wailing behind me on the bus. Looking back, I saw the back of the bus was severely damaged, and people were dazed, confused, and stunned. I got off the bus with the driver and saw that a large pick-up truck had rear ended us, probably at a high speed, and pushed the bus into the intersection. The rear of the bus was pushed forward and crumpled into a mass of metal.

Getting back on the bus I quickly assisted people to get out. Some were traumatized or shaking. I had never experienced people in trauma before. The man from the gas station was attempting to assist however he could, along with the bus driver and my other friend. There was some fear the bus could explode, and we were near a gas station!

Shortly thereafter when the police and fire trucks arrived with a fanfare of sirens, it was evident some were injured, and there were deaths. The police pried opened the door of the pick-up and the driver fell out dead, along with several empty liquor bottles.

Greg and I were put in charge of helping those in trauma, not sure exactly what to do except to comfort them while ambulances arrived.

After some time, another friend came to pick us up and drove us to his house. We sat totally speechless in the dark for hours. We were quite shaken, and I realized that if I had stood up, like I intended, there was a likelihood I would have been thrown through the front window and run over by the bus. It was not beneficial to speculate the 'what ifs' at that point.

Weeks later there were several calls from insurance agents to get details, as well as reports we had to give to the police.

The incident did make the papers the next day, with a photograph of the wreckage. I did not keep it, yet it was a profoundly unfortunate way to end my days at the greatest show on earth.

I have never returned for Mardi Gras.

Chapter 4

My mantra-motto

Fate is inevitable, yet how we philosophically live our lives may change its course.

Before graduating from elementary school, St. Patrick's School in Long Island City, NY, each student got a little book with a padded cover approximately six inches square called an 'Autograph Book'. It had a couple of introductory pages where we could enter information about ourselves and then many blank pages, in a variety of muted, pastel colors.

The intent of the book was to get many signatures, and well wishes, from everyone. That included fellow classmates, teachers, family, friends, or whomever we had regular contact. They'd write clever or witty messages, sometimes poignant ones, and then sign it. There were even stock messages from an accompanying sheet tucked into the book's jacket to inspire, or just copy.

The introductory page asked you to list such things as your favorite book, sport, and best friend. For me the book I listed was *Shackleton's Valiant Voyage* about the expedition to Antarctica by the explorer, Ernest Shackleton. I loved that book and read it several times. The entire book and story just mesmerized me, and I got to know about South Georgia Island, and the gallant exploration with innumerable challenges to overcome.

Another favorite thing to list was your motto. At age thirteen I wrote the following, 'You can do anything you want if you only try'. That was my special mantra, my motto, and I believed in it.

Being young I reached for the stars with my aspirations. I believed that there was nothing I couldn't do, and I'd strive to be the best at it. Perhaps I was a budding 'over achiever'. In following that motto, I did well; but I never reached the stellar heights I thought possible. Fate did interject some limitations. However, I feel a resigned contentment with what I did achieve.

I do believe that part of my lofty aspirations came from staring at the island of Manhattan during my formative years. Looking at those skyscrapers every day made me think that the ability to succeed had no boundaries.

At first, I thought of being an attorney. It would be a good career for me, but thankfully I got over that quickly. Sometime around age eleven, and perhaps inspired by all those buildings around me, I had an inkling to be an architect. My family didn't know any architects and I never had exposure to any, so who really knows why that occurred, but it did and grew more pronounced with each passing year. With that determination I became an architect.

I am also a firm believer in taking risks, calculated risks. As I've grown older the calculations have become more conservative yet I'm still willing to take a leap of faith. And, it has always worked out for me. I mentor young people to not be afraid of risk, especially if it can potentially enhance their lives knowing that if the calculated risk doesn't pan out there may be a fallback position to keep in mind. So, as I matured into adulthood my motto included 'risk can lead to rewards'.

I have taken three major risks in my life, in terms of where I chose to live. Each time I have leapt and hoped for the best. Each time I moved to a new location, always geographically many miles away, without work. In each case I was determined to make it work, and admittedly through the uncertainty, persistence was key. Career wise each move turned out to be beneficial.

Like any work plan, strategic plan, or master plan consider risk to be a roadmap plan. It is something to follow and guide you; but allow yourself a detour if needed.

I was given a huge opportunity in 1998. Fate came to call. A couple of days before Christmas I was working at my desk when no one was in the office. It was peacefully quiet. The phone rang and it was the business advisor who had been working with my employer doing an extensive evaluation of our operations, including interviews with employees. What came next totally caught me off guard. I was in the middle of checking some documents, and admittedly my mind was not totally focused on the call, at first.

The business adviser/consultant informed me that I was being offered a partnership in the firm. She said I should consider it and a formal offer would be forthcoming. I remember being stunned, overwhelmed, flattered, terrified, and elated, all at the same time. What did it mean? Certainly, it was something I always wanted, yet the responsibility was enormous. It was a well-established firm and opportunities like it did not come along often. I took a breadth, took it in, and gave it a lot of consideration.

The offer did come shortly after Christmas, and it was truly wonderful. Once explained the financial part seemed plausible, and although not without possible risk, it worked. I along with two others within the firm were being given the offer as two of the senior partners were transitioning into retirement. So at least I had companions in the deal and felt the strength to make it happen. And it did. It turned out to be a wonderful thing for me and my career. Risk, along with hard work, again led to rewards as I was able to shape the firm with my partners as we saw fit, and we did successfully.

It wasn't without consequences as there were others in the firm who thought they deserved the partnership- friends, and close associates of mine; so that was difficult. Plus, being a partner meant being different from the other staff, treated differently, and responsible for their livelihoods.

Whether in business or in one's personal life some risk is beneficial, as well as striving to do what you want to do, the best you can.

With risk one must be tenacious, diligent, persistent, enthusiastic, determined, passionate, patient, and diplomatic. Living by a motto or mantra is something I advocate. Like with Shackleton the incentives in overcoming challenges to reach a goal can be most rewarding.

CHAPTER 5

'The Big Apple' to 'The Big Easy'

I had the good fortune of being born and raised in New York City. There are certainly advantages to such a world class urban environment, yet there is also a downside. One learns at an early age about 'street smarts', the ability to stay safe while learning the dangers that exist in large urban environments.

My neighborhood in New York City was Astoria in Queens, just across the Queensboro (59th Street) Bridge from midtown Manhattan. It was very much a 'day and night' situation crossing that bridge as on each side the environment was quite different. Astoria had a small city feel to it compared to the density of Manhattan. Most folks from the outer boroughs, although within the city itself, say they are 'going to the city' when referring to going to Manhattan. Each borough, Manhattan, Brooklyn, Queens, Bronx, and Staten Island are distinctly different in character, as are the microcosms of neighborhoods within each.

Astoria had a much lower scale and density than Manhattan or most of Brooklyn, yet my part of Astoria was denser than many other neighborhoods in Queens. Astoria, and associated Long Island City, was primarily settled in the 1800s and often became a stepping off point for new immigrants coming to the US. First it was the Germans and Irish closely followed by the Italians, Greeks, and many other ethnic groups that arrived subsequently in waves.

When I lived there, in the 1950s and 1960s, it had a very large and significant Greek community. It was often said that there were more Greeks in Astoria than in Athens, which wasn't true at all. Yet it was indicative of the large Greek population that existed then. Greek culture through stores, shops, restaurants, and churches abounded in the area. As a kid I can vividly remember squid and octopus hanging in grocery store windows, something I doubt existed extensively elsewhere. It was frequently mentioned that to get the best pizza in town you went to a Greek establishment, and not an Italian one.

We had many Greek neighbors, and they were outstanding in their outgoing personalities and friendliness. Somehow the Mediterranean culture just blended well with being community. There was a strong adherence to the Greek Orthodox faith. The Orthodox churches thrived; however, I never remember anyone proselytizing superiority for their beliefs.

Italians were a second large group, most recent immigrants, and again very outgoing and community oriented with adherence to Mediterranean culture. Both the Greeks and Italians greatly influenced my upbringing, and they especially embraced children of any ethnic background, including my own German-Lithuanian one. Our one neighbor, Mary Rombone, taught me to sing Italian songs and when hanging out her laundry in the backyard would yell over to me, 'Sing with me Tommy!' At age ten I could sing 'Volare' like a pro with her! When I was a child her husband, Frank, would take my hand and walk me down the street for ice cream. He was like a grandfather. They were like family.

Even though the elementary school I attended was named St. Patrick's, located near Queens Plaza, and run by Irish nuns there was a large Italian street fair every year. There were games of chance, a dime a shot, and lots of wonderful Italian food stalls. My favorite was the Italian 'Hero' sandwiches, or Grinders, on a large bun with sausage, peppers, and onions. Often juice from the sandwich would run down the side of my face. I could go through two of those at a time.

Food was central to all these cultures and the excess of prepared dishes flowed throughout the neighborhood. Everyone shared their food, and I got quickly acclimated to different cuisines, that to this day influences my enjoyment of food. It was amazing how so many culinary dishes of something wonderful were shared and passed across the fences. It was not unusual for me to be playing outside and have a neighbor call me in for a bite of something being cooked, only to return home totally overstuffed and unable to eat my mother's own prepared dinner! Sharing food and culture was the glue that held the neighborhood together. It was a tremendous catalyst for bringing people together.

Community and neighborhood are what I remember and cherish most of those days, and although everyone was identified by their ethnicity, no one particularly cared what it was or how it mattered.

It was a working-class community with some professionals living there. Our house was a brick row house built in 1954 on a major thoroughfare street, Crescent Street, that connected the two main bridges into Queens, the Queensboro and Triboro. At one point, almost at the midpoint, the street did bend in a crescent. We had a single-family house which was rare. There were many apartment buildings and behind our house were the Ravenswood Apartments, a large city-owned public 'projects'.

Some of my friends lived there and it wasn't a bad place for a kid to hang out with other kids as they had playgrounds and open space, including lots of trees and lawn. My one good friend, Doug Coffee, lived there. His parents were teachers. I remember the apartments being small, cramped, and dark without much natural light. It wasn't considered one of the dangerous 'projects' like the Queensboro, near the bridge, where one never went near.

Our house had a front and back yard, quite nice for such an urban setting. The front yards, and stoops, often became places to sit and gather in the heat of summer. It also developed a sense of community. My father bought the house when it was new. It had a place for an apartment to be included, but they never completed it. It remained a large open room, part laundry room, and primarily a playroom for me with a bathroom. My father constructed, by hand, a large model train set for me that was truly amazing. It was approximately eight feet by ten feet in size and had multiple train tracks, mountains, and other interesting topographical elements. It ran by electric and was in the 'HO' model scale that we added components to over time. I loved that 'train set'. It even had one engine with smoke billowing out of it.

There were street gangs and drugs too. Both were something to avoid and I knew how to get around encountering either of them. There were streets I did not go down as they were referred to as 'bad-streets'. Many of them still were paved with cobble stones. Astoria also had a lot of commercial enterprises, warehouses, and in Long Island City near the Queensboro bridge there was considerable light industrial, factories and more warehouses. Sunshine Biscuits was very prominent with a large sign hovering overhead.

43

My bedroom window was the window on the world. I had a direct view of the Queensboro Bridge and midtown Manhattan from my bed. It was awe inspiring for a kid. I could clearly see the Empire State Building, Chrysler Building, The U.N., the Waldorf Towers, and many other iconic structures. It was my OZ, a dreamscape. I dreamt of the day when I would conquer that 'City', becoming a part of it and it a part of me. The energy, vibrance and overwhelming character was something I wanted to taste, live, and ultimately thrive in it. That day would come, years later.

I also could clearly see the Ravenswood apartments. Late at night with the lights on I could see people move from room to room, tiny silhouettes moving about in their apartments, floor upon floor. Similarly, when I sat in my classroom at St. Patrick's School, I could see the elevated subway trains coming and going to the 'City', Manhattan. There was a famous curve near Queens Plaza where the trains leaned at a precarious angle going around it. Those were the trains that would transport me to that magical place I saw from my bedroom every night.

Often, I thought that looking at that view was the inspiration for my becoming an architect. I pondered in amazement how those spectacular structures were created. The design, the massing, the fenestration, and the detail was all so fascinating.

There were famous people of the day that used New York as their playground. Artists like Andy Warhol were coming into their own, and unbeknownst to me Noguchi had his studio just blocks away from us in Astoria, although the museum somewhat later. The Duke and Duchess of Windsor would arrive with great fanfare, staying at the Waldorf Towers which I clearly saw from my bedroom. On my sixtieth birthday I got to stay at the Waldorf Towers, and it was heartfelt as I was able to look back on Astoria from our substantial suite. I was living my childhood dream.

Astoria was also the original home of the movie industry in the U.S. with Paramount Studios located there in the 1920s before moving to Hollywood. The studio buildings still exist and continue to be used for filmmaking. From the early days my grandmother recalled seeing silent film stars like Mary Astor and Mary Pickford milling about between shoots. Her apartment building, a block away, was named Valentino Court.

Of course, there were all the cultural opportunities that a world class city affords, especially for a growing youth. There were the museums that my mother made sure we visited each year, music venues, interesting neighborhoods, restaurants, and parks. My mother also frequently took me and often my cousins to Central Park. It was a giant playground of amazement and exploration. We would visit the zoo and wander the vastness of the park. The bridges, fountains and beauty of a Fredrick Olmstead designed park was unmistakable, and impressionable.

To this day I remember my parents with fondness. They were unassuming, hard-working people who endured their early lives during the Great Depression and World War II. The War gave my father a window on the world as he was drafted and sent to the Pacific front. He loved Hawaii where he was stationed for some time; and wished to stay there when the war ended. He regaled us with stories of Diamond Head and the beauty of the place. The Army, however required that they return soldiers back to their base of deployment, in my father's case New York. He relished and talked of his memories of Hawaii yet never saw it again. Fortunately, years later I was able to take my mother there twice to see it, once to Maui and once to Kauai.

Although my mother claimed she would have liked to have worked and had a profession my father was old fashioned and insisted she remain home as a housewife. In her younger days before WWII, she had worked as a governess/nanny for a wealthy Great Neck family, the Graces. That exposed her to a life of incredible privilege, and one she particularly disliked. She had said that the family always wanted her in the main rooms with them, but she preferred being with the 'downstairs' folks. While being exposed to the grand estates of Long Island with limousines, servants, high style, and fashionable events none of it truly impressed her as she found it a bit shallow and depressing. She said that the two girls she watched over enjoyed taking the limousine with her to visit my grandparents' house, just down the road, in less assuming surroundings.

My mother also said that she was sad in that the two girls she cared for were only allowed to see their mother for an hour each day in her dressing room. She spoke of one time visiting the enormous estate of one of the Grace family in Old Westbury. While being outdoors she could see one of the bachelor sons staring at her from behind the drapes of one of the windows and it made her feel very uneasy. Little could she say or opinionate about any of these things for the possibility of losing her job.

I did enjoy hearing her stories of the nearby Walter P. Chrysler estate with peacocks roaming the property, that later became the Merchant Marine Academy where both her brother and my grandfather eventually enlisted.

During WWII she worked for Hazeltine, a manufacturer

of radar parts, and became a supervisor until she married my father in November 1945, post war.

My father having grown up in Astoria, the home of his family for generations, graduated from Bryant High School and immediately entered the war thereafter. In years later he would attend college and study computer science in its early days of the 1960s. In the Army, as a Staff Sargent, he learned electronics and after the war ended opened a TV/radio repair shop with his brother in Astoria that sold records and appliances. They worked long hours; and did quite well. He went on to go into business with The Hammond Organ Co. and finally with a start-up computer cash register business, Alpex Corporation in Danbury, CT. With that we moved just north of there to New Fairfield in 1968. When Alpex went bankrupt in the 1970s he went on to be absorbed by Pitney Bowes where he worked until he chose retirement in 1981 at age sixty-two.

My mother had an excellent singing voice, but never developed it. She always had the radio playing music in the house and often would sing along with the songs; or would hum while doing chores. A couple of times she was invited to join singing groups and she flatly turned it down.

My parents were wonderful people, and as an only child they taught me well and gave me a sense of values. They never discouraged any of my wild ideas of adventure and growth, but rather encouraged it.

Three things I recall distinctly.

First, while living in Astoria a family we knew had a dad who lost his job. They had ten children. There was no shame in that community and people rallied around to support them through an awful time. My mother made it her mission to not only bring them food but to give the mother all my hand me down clothes. Yet, my mother also took me aside and privately made it clear to me that should I see any of those children wearing my clothes that I was NOT to ever say that item had been mine. She told me it was *their* clothing now; and to allow them the dignity of that.

Second, they knew a couple who were long-time friends, quite affluent living in a Connecticut suburb who had an only child, a son my age, who was developmentally disabled. It was a tremendous burden and shame to them. When we would visit, he would be locked in his room, until my mother would not have it any longer. She had me take charge of Steven, the boy, and play with him as best to his ability. We went on walks together and although we could not effectively communicate in words, he became my friend. We had a very special bond. His mother always profusely thanked me for doing it when we would leave, and I did not understand why. It just seemed right, without apology. Yet I have my parents to thank for that lesson.

Thirdly, when we lived in Connecticut a boy nearby came down with a debilitating disease that could be somewhat alleviated by physical therapy. I do not even remember the type of disease. Nonetheless my mother became a very active part of a group of mothers in the area who agreed to be trained in the therapy and routinely assist in the therapy over a couple of years. I became part of the team. What I recall was the boy would scream in excruciating pain when he moved his body, yet in time he did get better. There was a tremendous celebratory party, and again, it just felt right to have done it.

These are lessons I will never forget.

My mother often took me to the major department stores,

Macy's, Gimbels, Bloomingdales; frequently on Catholic holy days where we would first go to Mass at the small intimate St. Francis of Assisi church just a few blocks south of Macy's. It was a mysterious place of strange statues, relics, and icons; plus, the Franciscan monks who walked around in brown robes and sandals, even in the middle of winter. These same monks would play a role later in my life at the St. Anthony Foundation in San Francisco.

Speaking of religion, it was of prime importance in immigrant communities, although my father's family was somewhat beyond being immigrants. He was raised Lutheran although I do not know how religious they were as a family. His Rodamer side of the family were Lutheran, and some did attend church regularly. Since my mother was Roman Catholic, I was a hybrid. A 'half breed', although because of her we went more in her direction, especially when I attended parochial school. I do, however, give my father a lot of credit as he attended Catholic Mass with us, every Sunday, although sat out most of the kneeling and other ritualistic parts of the Mass. It did draw us together as 'family'.

One thing I do recall when attending Catholic elementary school is that I was once asked to take our class records from my classroom to the principal's office. I will not forget walking down the stairs and stopping to look at mine out of curiosity. After all it was near the top of the pile having a surname beginning with a 'B'. Well, low and behold there were large red letters across the top of my record stating 'child's father is Lutheran. He must be watched'. I was flabbergasted and never told my parents about it.

Being Roman Catholic, we were not allowed to attend any

other denomination of religious service other than our own. My parents did break the rules, as they took me to a neighbor's Greek Orthodox wedding service. But it was awkward for me going to my Lutheran family's funerals and other services. As Catholic kids we were told by the religious to stay away from those other religions. We would run up to the doors of Protestant churches and quickly touch them to see if we'd be instantly obliterated or sent directly to hell.

My father was admirable in the variety of places he exposed me to over the years we lived in New York, from the ballrooms of the Waldorf Astoria to TV studios, and even a jazz club in the basement of a Greenwich Village building where the patrons put out their cigarettes in the stone crevices of the walls and snapped their fingers instead of clapping in enjoyment of a performance. The hippies of the day once saw my family getting out of a car in Greenwich Village and while pointing yelled out, 'Look at the Squares!'

There was also a strange type of phenomena that I can't explain, whispering about seemingly taboo subjects. When Nakita Khrushchev came into New York to attend the United Nations his entourage would travel to a house the Soviets owned on Long Island. Taking the Long Island Expressway, they would always close it to traffic when he traveled it. As kids we would occasionally see the entourage and when telling our friends about it, we would whisper into a friend's ear, 'I saw Khrushchev'. You never wanted to speak it loudly. During that Cold War era of the Soviets being our enemy, out to kill us. It was as if you saw the devil himself. Then there was a cancer treatment hospital in Queens that we'd pass on the highway. When going by it everyone in the car would whisper, 'that's the cancer hospital'. Never would you speak it loudly, or even in a normal voice. Out of respect, or fear?

As a child the airline industry was just taking off. Idlewild Airport, now John F Kennedy Airport (JFK) was in its infancy and my father would take me out to the airfield to watch the planes take off and land. It was very exciting for a kid my age to witness these large mechanical machines leave the earth and return.

The most memorable was when he took me to a classical symphony concert at Carnegie Hall. He had us watch the performance from backstage behind the curtain. I was probably ten years old and totally enthralled, especially being able to see the entire audience. The conductor was Leopold Stokowski, a renowned conductor of the day. He had been married to Gloria Vanderbilt. After the performance there was a roar of applause from the audience with shouts of 'Bravo'. Taking his 'bows' he turned and walked right by us. He looked down at me, smiled and nodded. While standing in awe I was amazed he'd even acknowledge me.

There was a time when I was approximately eight years old that they took me to the Statue of Liberty, the one and only time. It was July and incredibly warm outdoors, yet we climbed the treacherous winding stair to the crown of the statue to look out. It was an amazing view, but a horrendous climb to get there. Today, you can no longer enter the statue.

The one thing I always loved to do; and have done it for years while recommending it to any visitor to the city is to take the Staten Island Ferry from lower Manhattan to Staten Island. It is an amazing ride across New York Harbor. While being out on open water you get the view and true impression of the enormity of Manhattan, and the surrounding city, boroughs, and New Jersey. There was a time when the fare was ten cents, and now it is free. And back in my youth Manhattan was the only place of skyscrapers where they now have been subsequently built in New Jersey, Brooklyn, and Queens too. Some older ones did exist in Brooklyn and Queens but rarely noticeably impacting the skyline.

Before the construction of the Verrazano Narrows Bridge in the 1960s the ferry was the only way to get to Staten Island. Besides being a nice, enjoyable ride in the harbor it was also a necessary means of transportation. Cars were allowed on the ferry and as a child I remember several times going to Staten Island to visit my grandfather who was in a military hospital there. Since I was a child and couldn't go inside, I would wait for my grandfather to wave to me from the window.

Several times my father would purposely drive through The Bowery in lower Manhattan. Often a homeless person would run up to the car while at a stop light and begin to wash the windshield for a tip. It was just to be expected. The Bowery was a depressing place with many people loitering and sleeping on the sidewalks. My dad would say that we should never judge them, belittle them, or look down on them. He said some may have been former attorneys or stockbrokers who fell on bad times. He said anyone could end up on The Bowery and it was our responsibility to do whatever we could to help their situation. I found my place doing that years later at the St. Anthony Foundation in San Francisco.

We also attended baseball games at the new Shea Stadium and occasionally Yankee Stadium. Every year we went to Coney Island and Palisades Amusement Park, along with

'Freedomland', a theme amusement park depicting the U.S., located in the Bronx.

Coney Island in Brooklyn, and its amusement park, was a yearly summer excursion. My mom and her friend would pile a few of us kids together and head out to the boardwalk and Steeplechase. It was hilarious fun, and we enjoyed it greatly. There was this big wooden slide where you'd get on a carpet and slide down a very long chute into a large bowl where you'd be twirled around until you came to a stop. Often an elbow or arm was burned on the wood going down it. My mother always brought Band-Aids.

Once my dad joined us on a weekend day and I insisted on going on a ride called the 'Parachute Jump'. I was seven years old. Nearly twenty stories in the air it was used by paratroopers in WWII for practice and later became a ride. Two people would sit on a precarious bench-type seat and when strapped in you'd be hoisted up in the air to the steel-trellised top of it. When you hit the top of the tower a pin would release you and you'd free fall until the parachute opened and you'd glide gently down to the ground. My mother wasn't sure she wanted me doing it, and when we got to the ride the manager was a bit reluctant too, only because my dad weighed more, and we wouldn't be balanced. But they let me go on. As we ascended the view was amazing. But as we got toward the top and I saw how far down it was to the ground I got a bit squeamish. I looked over to my dad and said, 'I'm not sure I want to do this anymore'. He looked back at me and said, 'grin and bear it', and at that moment we hit the pin and were released into the air at a great speed. Getting back to the ground I was so proud of myself; but swore I'd never do it again. The only other recollection I have of that ride was during inclement weather when the people on it would get stuck mid-air and fire trucks were brought with ladders to rescue them.

There were parades and celebrations too. My mother once took me to see the St. Patrick's Day parade on 5th Avenue. My school, St. Patrick's, closed each year on that day in honor of its namesake Saint. While standing and waiting behind a barricade for the parade to start a well-dressed man approached my mother and gave her two tickets for us to sit in the grandstand! We went and ended up sitting near Mayor Lindsay. What an opportunity to see the parade. Robert Kennedy and other notable people from that time marched by us.

All during the 1950s, 1960s and 1970s I continued to have great experiences in the 'Big Apple'. There were endless opportunities with things to do and experience.

That was my world in the 'Big Apple'. It was home. It was the foundation of who I would become.

In between my time in New York City and my move to New Orleans in 1972, I had a four-year stint living with my parents in Connecticut. That's an entirely different narrative, so let's move on to New Orleans!

New Orleans, 'The Big Easy', is such a unique un-American city that ever existed. I had very little exposure to the South other than knowing something of Florida, if one wants to consider that the 'South'. I often quip that my parents considered Northern Virginia to be the Deep South as we knew little beyond it.

When considering architectural schools, I was limited in my choices. There were none in Connecticut, except for Yale that only had a graduate program. There was no advantage for me with an 'in-state' tuition at a state college, in that a public out-of-state college would cost me nearly the same as a private institution. So, I examined the architecture programs with the highest rankings and applied to four universities, primarily in the Northeast. Tulane, in New Orleans, was the other. It was the only school, and New Orleans the only city I never visited before applying. But it had a great reputation, and seemed alluring in location, so why not? Well, it turned out that Tulane was the first to accept me through 'early admissions.' I got the acceptance letter, stared at it for a little time, and instantly decided to go. I couldn't give up the opportunity of living in such a unique place with enormous history, and a place without snow and cold weather. So, Syracuse and the others went on the back burner.

I told my parents, they winced, and they agreed.

In August 1972 we drove off with my possessions to New Orleans! Our car did not have air conditioning and hitting the deep south in August was most uncomfortable. Needless to say, we were most determined to reach our destination.

Anyone arriving in the outskirts of New Orleans realizes it is rather bland and non-descript. It's entirely spec. houses and strip malls and nothing but flat boredom. It made me a bit anxious. By that point there was silence in the car after the lengthy drive, and at one point, one I will never forget, I said from the back seat, 'it's probably going to be nicer at the campus.' My mother turned around, looked me sternly in the eye and responded, 'You BETTER like it!' OK, got that.

We arrived in Uptown New Orleans near the campus, and it was a whole lot nicer, but still foreign territory to us. Magnolias, mighty oaks with long spindly limbs, and Spanish moss prevailed. When we pulled up in front of my home-to-be, a high-rise dorm called Monroe Hall, we parked and as I was lifting my trunk out of the back of the car several students came to help. Almost immediately I was surrounded by warmth and friendship; and made friends on the spot. I believe we were all somewhat relieved.

I was certainly ready to be independent. My parents finally left for home after getting me settled in, and I was free to start my college life. Well, not everything made immediate sense to me. At my first lunch at the Student Center the woman behind the counter asked if I wanted my hamburger *'dreessed'*. I had no idea what she was referring to so in my bewilderment the person behind me said, 'lettuce, tomato and onion'. OH! I wasn't in the Northeast anymore. There were several adjustments like that, yet all growing and learning experiences.

The City of New Orleans was a treasure trove of experience, and the history just blew me away. As a bit of Europe and the Caribbean in the US I rapidly embraced the beauty and culture of the city in its food, architecture, and music. What could be better?

I learned to appreciate and relish spicy foods, crawfish and other indigenous seafood, and the wonders of jazz. I was surrounded by lush landscapes and palm trees and incredible sense of place. My classmates came from all over the US and places like Panama and Puerto Rico.

Despite the hype of the European influences in New Orleans the culture is also significantly enriched by African, Latin American, and Native Indian cultures too. Its history goes back three hundred years. In the late 1700s and early 1800s the black population far outnumbered the white, and free people of color lived openly in New Orleans before the Civil War.

My five years there were filled with incredible memories and fondness lasting to this day, and what a wonderful place to study the foundation of architecture. Although New Orleans in the 1970s was not known for cutting edge contemporary architecture we had Atlanta and Houston nearby which were booming and full of notable buildings, so we visited both frequently.

The friendships made there last to this day, and I had an exposure to people from all over the country adding to my education. I visited their families and they visited mine during breaks and holidays. And the families that lived there were so open and welcoming. The Trapolins, a large family who lived near campus, became a second home. An Irish Italian family named the McCloskeys literally adopted me and were so very wonderful and kind to me. My classmate, Richard, introduced me into a warm world of ethnic New Orleans that I will always look on fondly. His mother's Italian immigrant family originally lived in the French Quarter and later living in New Orleans East. His grandmother was a portly woman and so energetic and loving. Every Sunday she produced these elaborate pasta dinners in three separate seating times for various parts of the family. I remember her smiling, laughing, always at the stove and giving me a big hug whenever I came over to eat a meal.

That is the New Orleans I remember so well. Unlike New York the 'Big Easy', or 'The City That Care Forgot', New Orleans, was quite different and ultimately molded me into a different man.

Chapter 6

Mangia! Mangia! EAT!

Since design is my area of expertise, I am always curious where and how people live, the environment they enjoy and how they comfortably function within it. Some have said that the hearth is the center of the home, yet I truly believe it is the kitchen. Anyone familiar with farm cultures will know that the kitchen is the heart of the home. It is where cooking and sustenance occurs, gathering happens, and is often the entrance into the house, not the front door. Food and cooking is central to our existence and the kitchen is where it has all happened for millennia.

I've lived in a house built in the 1860's in the Midwest. It wasn't a large house, just two bedrooms and one bathroom, that replaced an original outhouse, on one floor. A simple ranch style home with a wonderful front porch for summer evenings. What was noteworthy was the largest room, the kitchen, allowed for a large table and chairs for gathering, socializing, and of course for eating. There was plenty of space for preparing and cooking food, and even surplus area for a large baker's rack. In San Francisco I lived in a 'Romeo' flat built during the Edwardian era. There, too, the largest room was the kitchen, a very pleasant room with large windows compared to a miniscule living room space.

My point is cooking, and eating, have been central to our

world's culture. Gathering around food is an important factor in bringing people and family together. The essence of 'breaking bread' together is visceral. Sharing food is something I know very well from having grown up in Astoria, Queens in New York City. With a melting pot of nationalities and cultures, many first generation, food transcended everything else. There were Greeks, Italians, Irish, Puerto Ricans, French, Jews, Yugoslavians, Russians, Estonians, Swedes, and Germans.

There is no doubt that I am a 'foodie', perhaps not in an extreme sense, yet I surely love food. When I lived in New Orleans, during my college years, I bought a book entitled, *The New Orleans Underground Gourmet*. The book was divided by types of cuisine, high end, ethnic, and many other categories, including basic cafeterias. In my mission to try as much as I could, I would subsequently return home and write my own review in the margins. That book is chocked full of criticism and the book remains on my bookshelf today. Since New Orleans is such a food centric place, similar to Astoria, I came to develop a real taste for exploring its culinary treasures, from basic to extravagant. Besides much of it was uniquely indigenous to its own cultural roots, expanding my own. There was Creole and Cajun infused with delicious culinary basics from Africa and the Caribbean, plus French, Spanish, and Italian.

I will speculate that my love for food came early in life where cooking, eating, and sharing food was a big part of the culture. New Orleans was a new horizon, and it developed my taste and appreciation of spicy foods. Some dishes originating in Africa and the Caribbean morphed into American Black culture as 'soul food', included peppers, spices, and sauces new to my palate. Southeast Asian influence became prevalent after the

1970s, although I experienced much more than that living on the West Coast later.

I have a humorous recollection of being exposed to Chinese food for the first time at a restaurant in Flushing, Queens, New York City in the early 1960s. You could get a full lunch of egg drop soup, a fried egg roll, chop-suey, and a scoop of ice cream for ninety-nine cents. My grandmother discovered it and occasionally took me there. At the time it seemed so exotic. Not long after we found the more authentic Chinese restaurants in Chinatown in Manhattan. In the 1970s a friend of Chinese ethnicity, a work colleague, wrote out a menu in Chinese on a piece of paper for me to present to any waiter in a Chinese restaurant in lieu of getting an 'American menu'. It was about that time I first heard of Chinese Szechuan cooking, when a person I worked with ordered it for take-out. It was an immediate hit with me, especially for the spiciness.

During my childhood Mexican food was rare, and frankly there weren't many Mexicans living in my area. What substituted, unfortunately, were Mexican TV dinners. They were bland and awful. My first exposure to that specific cuisine was not good, but fortunately I learned later about authentic Mexican cooking, and tasted the best of it in Mexico City.

Being in New York I was also exposed to Jewish cooking, and came to love those New York mainstays of bagels, lox, bliny, pastrami, rye bread, and chopped liver. I will go miles for a good bagel. I will ashamedly admit that when I lived in Manhattan as a young adult, I crossed a picket line for bagels as I wouldn't sacrifice a week without one. When I was previously married my wife and I decided to try an authentic Kosher restaurant near Times Square, and unfortunately it was not a good experience. The food was extremely bland, and we were relegated to the very rear of the restaurant next to a noisy kitchen. We also lived for two years in a predominantly Jewish neighborhood, Forest Hills, Queens, yet I do not recall any specific Jewish food influences there. There existed the typical delicatessens that we didn't frequent much except for good cold cuts, pickles and bread. I do remember, however, that near Passover the supermarkets would clear out an entire aisle just for Kosher foods.

Italian food, hands down, is my favorite food. Perhaps being around such enormous quantities of it as a child contributed to that love. Most of what I knew was southern Italian, the red sauce kind, but truly well done. My very good friend, Andrea Tutrani, and I grew up together, although in different neighborhoods, in Queens. Her mother was truly one of the best Italian cooks ever. Being from Naples her pasta, meat sauce and whatever else she would prepare on Sundays was beyond reproach. It was easy to have two helpings of everything.

When I first encountered the Italian chef and TV show host Lidia Bastianich I was catapulted into total happiness. She is the epitome of the Italians I knew in Astoria, and much to my pleasant surprise lived in Astoria when she came to America in the 1950s. So, we co-existed in the neighborhood at the same time. I subsequently found out she had worked at Walken's Bakery on Broadway in Astoria. That was my family's choice of bakeries, and I spent many a day in that place being sent to buy cookies, cakes, treats and confections of all kinds to bring home. It was an excellent bakery, near a well-known Italian deli with huge jars of pickled vegetables, salted fish, pastas, and giant cans of olive oil.

Walken's was a quintessential neighborhood bakery of the day with beautiful cakes and cookies displayed in the storefront window, and inside long counters of all types of baked goods, including breads. It smelled sweet and delicious. There were typically two to three people in white aprons waiting on patrons from behind those counters. I remember the place always being busy. My mother would often hand me some money and tell me to run down the few blocks to get a cake when we were having company. I loved doing it. Desserts were not a typical part of my family's dining experience, yet this bakery was integral when entertaining.

The bakery was owned by the eminent actor, Christopher Walken's family. So, Lidia Bastianich worked at Walken's before his assent to fame. Meeting her years later at a cookbook signing she had we talked about Walken's. She said that she probably gave me a cookie when I went there as a child. That is very likely. I typically got a cookie as they did that routinely when a child visited. It was another fun reason to go there. Walken's was one of those wonderful, unforgettable family establishments that served the neighborhood and felt like family.

My parents were not 'foodie's. We ate for sustenance, not for cuisine, or dining. Meals were sit down, eat, and get on with it; move on. We did go to restaurants and diners and that might be the only time we took some time to eat. My mother did prepare some Lithuanian and German dishes but most of her cooking was mainstream. She did make extraordinary homemade soups.

There was one restaurant on Long Island, out in Suffolk County, called Links Log Cabin. It was a huge family-type eatery, and we often went there with friends. The enormous room was all wood, a log cabin, and dishes or bowls of food were delivered to the table 'family style'. The energy of the place was fun, and we enjoyed the trip going there.

There was also a diner, somewhere in Nassau County on Long Island, where we often ate when we went to pay a visit to my mother's family cemetery, Holy Rood in Westbury. We also went when they took me to a children's amusement park out that way. I recall us always sitting in a booth and my parents starting off by having an 'Old- Fashioned' cocktail, and getting me a 'Shirley Temple', always with a maraschino cherry.

Surprisingly for the day, my mother was a healthy eating advocate. I believe she got it from being friends with a woman who was a chiropractor and into supplemental vitamins and healthy diets. In any case she did her best to serve healthy meals, including managing portions. When I was growing up portions were much smaller compared to today, including in restaurants. We once had a china service from the 1920s and the dinner plates were indeed smaller than anything we have now, making me ponder if portions were even smaller back then.

Health food stores were a place my mother knew well, and we frequently visited one near our house. The snacks we got there were commonly sesame and honey candies. The inside of the health food store looked, well, healthy. Sugar did not seem to permeate anything they carried. What I found amusing is that in the aforementioned diner, where we ate in Nassau, I would eat the parsley off my plate from my usual dish, Salisbury Steak. My mother would grimace and tell me I shouldn't eat it as it was merely a garnish, but subsequently she learned parsley was quite nutritious. She never chided me again.

Macy's Herald Square in Manhattan had a food hall that my mother and I would visit when shopping. They had food samples to try and the most interesting was when we tried curry for the first time. We didn't have much knowledge of Indian food as it was not particularly known in NYC at that time. We tried it and it was spicy. We laughed because we thought it was disgusting but chalked it up to expanding our food horizons. Because of it I didn't return to have curry for some time, until the 1970s, at a Bangladeshi restaurant on Central Park South called 'Nirvana'. It was on the top floor of a high-rise building with sweeping views of Central Park. This is where I came to learn and develop a taste for curry, and the spicier the better. They had gradations of spiciness and the ultimate, on a lamb dish, gave me quite the jolt! I broke out in a sweat and the waiter smiled.

Eating in some delightful Manhattan restaurants began in my childhood. We ate at such unique places as a Polynesian themed eatery called Luau 400, near Sutton Place. Rather kitschy in atmosphere it was a remnant of restaurants that came about after WWII, reminiscent of the islands visited by the soldiers in the Pacific Theater, of which my father was one.

Later, as an adult I savored the delights of the Russian Tea Room, and it became a favorite for the over-the-top décor and outlandish food. My favored drink there was called the 'Uncle Vanya'. It was quite potent and could knock me for a loop in minutes. On one occasion I could hardly sit through a performance at Carnegie Hall next door after having that drink and a heavy dinner there. I thought I'd either explode or fall out of my seat, and I did unfasten my belt to help some. Noteworthy, however, was before that performance Van Cliburn, the famous classical pianist, came to sit in a box seat to hear the concert. When noticed everyone in the audience began standing and applauded him. He stood, bowed, and it was quite something to experience.

I also enjoyed the energy of Sardi's restaurant in the Theater District where people packed in, ate, left for the theater, emptied the place out, and returned after the shows were out to repack it again. My favorite time being there was between shows when it was near empty. The walls were stacked high with images of celebrities who hung out and ate there, primarily theater folk.

One of the most glamorous restaurants I ever experienced was the Pool Room at The Four Seasons in the Seagram Building on Park Avenue. Designed by Philip Johnson it was a magnificent space in scale and decor, very *Mad Men* mid-century on a grand dimension. It was somber, elegant, and hushed with cuisine that reflected the seasons. The shimmering drapes on the enormously high windows complimented the gentle spray of water in the central pool. My wife and I ate there for her birthday once and we were so amazed by the experience. The waiter even remarked that the mushrooms in one dish were flown in from Japan that morning. It was amazing, although no longer there.

Getting back to Lidia Bastianich… I enjoyed her TV cooking show; and found her cooking style understandable and straightforward. She exudes the glory of cooking, eating, and sharing food together, the foundation of my childhood. Her shows are fun and informative, and she makes them a family affair with her mother, children and grandchildren participating. She's created quite a cooking empire.

We had a lovely chat when she had the book signing in San Francisco. She wanted to know if I enjoyed cooking, and what I like to prepare. We spoke of Astoria, Walken's Bakery, and she even mentioned Most Precious Blood Catholic Church where she attended after emigrating here from Istria, the same church my cousins attended. She's delightful and unpretentious.

I was in New York City for one of my birthdays, when I was in my fifties, and I decided I wanted to have my birthday meal at Lidia's well know restaurant, Felidia, on the East Side of Manhattan. Friends of mine from Connecticut, Paul and Claudia, were invited to come along. Paul is a long-time high school buddy. We arrived by taxi and found the restaurant in a handsome townhouse type building. When we entered sitting right there on the steps was Lidia! I was amazed, surprised; and impressed. So unassuming yet very much in the element of overseeing her establishment, yet ever so friendly and welcoming. Lidia, unlike so many of her fellow TV star chefs, does not have a haughty personality. She is very 'down-to-earth' yet engaging too.

We were expecting a casual red and white checkered tablecloth Italian restaurant, but this was not one. Very high end, professional, and elegant it was beautiful in every detail. The meal was one of the best Italian meals I've had in my life and well-orchestrated. Four waiters would come to deliver our dishes in perfect synchronization to be placed on the table simultaneously. It was so impressive. The highlight was when Lidia came over to chat with us. We complimented her on the meal and had light and jovial conversation. When I reminisced about our Astoria roots, and it being my birthday, she came back with complimentary after dinner drinks for us. Such a professional, and an incredibly good, kind person too.

Breaking bread with people is my joy. I love food. I love restaurants and I love the joy of eating. There is so much to experience through the many cuisines and cooking styles in the world. I've sought out as many as possible.

As noted in other chapters my world of cuisine greatly expanded in New Orleans during the 1970s. Being a college kid my resources were limited, but I spent them wisely while still experiencing a wide array of restaurants from basic to high end. I primarily ate in the college cafeteria where most of my friends had their meals. The campus dining hall was called 'Bruff Commons', otherwise known as 'Barf Hall'. The women who served behind the counters were very fun and interactive. One customarily told me that if I didn't eat my vegetables, she was going to contact my mother; followed by a big grin. After a couple of years, I gave up on Bruff and started eating at Loyola University in another dining hall which had much better food, and it was closer to the Architecture Building where I spent all my time. It was common for Tulane students to eat at Loyola.

Sundays the dining halls were closed, so we were on our own, and that's when we explored the vast array of restaurants in New Orleans. We soon learned that you could eat very well on very little in New Orleans!

If heading to the French Quarter, we gravitated toward either the Fatted Calf or the Steak Pit restaurants. The Fatted Calf was a small intimate place with a gay clientele that didn't much matter to college kids if the food was good and reasonably priced. I especially enjoyed a big juicy hamburger with mushrooms, and fries, that cost one dollar and fifty cents. The burgers were delicious and grilled to perfection. The Steak

Pit, also small and intimate, had a somewhat European flair. It was an entirely different experience. Located at the far end of Bourbon Street it was dark, with lots of brick and wood, inside. A meal cost under two dollars and consisted of a large salad that was brought immediately to the table, followed by a large cauldron of onion soup placed on the table to ladle into bowls while you waited for your entrée to arrive. Being college kids with ample appetites we tried our best to ladle as much soup as possible before the entrée did arrive, usually three or four bowls. My meal was always a hamburger steak, medium rare, and quite filling.

There was another place I frequented in the Quarter, Café Banquette, that later was renamed the Ground Patti. They had hands down the best onion soup anywhere. One of my fondest memories was sitting in this European style café one chilly winter evening, all alone, eating a bowl of the onion soup by the fireplace while both provided warmth. I could see outside through the French doors to the passing crowd, and it was simply delightful.

Then there were the tourist joints, that we typically avoided, although friends and I did occasionally go for beignets and coffee at Café du Monde or Morning Call, then a block away, in the French Market. One evening we got a bit boisterous at Morning Call where you would put your own powdered sugar on the beignets from large shakers. Laughing and carrying on someone energetically put the sugar on the beignet and then blew it toward the others at the table. Unfortunately, it went a little too far and landed on the back of a woman's dark-blue coat! Quite embarrassed, we offered to pay to have it cleaned yet she graciously declined. We did learn a lesson and never did that again.

Which wasn't half as entertaining as the time a group of us went to Pat O'Brien's the famous Quarter bar that has 'Hurricanes', a local tourist drink served in large glasses. One guy in our group had one too many, leaned back in his chair, and fell into the flaming fountain in the middle of the court-yard! We had quite the time rescuing him while disapproving waiters watched.

If we wanted an Italian meal we headed into the outer neigh-borhoods. Most were family owned and operated. Our favorite was a small place called Venezia. Usually the spaghetti, pizza, lasagna, or manicotti were the best bets for dishes to order. There was another place closer to campus, on Maple Street, but I cannot remember the name. What I do remember is a friend and I ordering back-to-back spaghetti dinners after a particularly strenuous day building play equipment for an underprivileged neighborhood school.

There was a very unusual Mexican restaurant downtown, called Poncho's. It was housed within an old classic movie theater that had closed. The voluminous space was enormous, with all the detailing of a 1920s theater, including a ceiling with illuminating sparkling stars in the sky. You went through a cafeteria line to get your food and then sat at an available table. There were small Mexican flags at every table and when you wanted more food you just raised the flag on its pole. A wait person would come and take your order and bring back the food. It was all you could eat for one price, under three dollars.

If you were intending to go upscale there were many options.

Going to Brennan's in the Quarter for brunch on Royal Street was always a special event, with some of the most creative egg dishes anywhere, plus great Bananas Foster. It was a nice place to take a date and I always tried to get a table where one of my classmates was a waiter part time, for exceptional service. We also enjoyed meals at Galatoire's, and Antoine's was very special for an extraordinary celebratory event.

Ed and I celebrated a wedding anniversary at Galatoire's with our good friends, Greg and Mary Alice. I had graduated with Greg from Tulane. Their daughter was the Maitre d' so we got extra preferential treatment. Galatoire's is famous for its Friday lunches by businessmen who go there regularly and spend hours eating in the afternoon. It is located on Bourbon Street, a seedy place indeed, but holds its own in simple New Orleans elegance. It is mainly a tourist place most of the time. For locals there is, however, a hierarchy where you are seated at a table. On this occasion my friend's daughter sat us at a prime table. You could immediately tell the regulars wondered who we were as their gazes lasted for some time. I could tell that Ed felt a bit self-conscience with the stares. The waiter came over to take our order and Ed was very perplexed as we never received menus. What he didn't know, and I failed to tell him, is that regulars never receive a menu, you just know. Mary Alice ordered some appetizers and they brought Ed a menu. It was very cute to watch this truly New Orleans experience unfold. In the end we had an incredible meal, and it was wonderful.

Antoine's was also very hierarchical. Tourists waited in a line outside, but locals had a different method in getting a reservation that the tourists couldn't get; or even knew about. If you had a waiter who customarily waited on you then you would call that person to make a reservation. I had been given two waiters' names, Kietri and Marshal, by a New Orleans family who used either as their exclusive waiter depending on the day each one worked. After making the reservation you would then, at the designated time, walk confidently past the tourist line and go further down the block to a secluded alley. At the end of the alley was a telephone. You picked up the receiver and asked for your waiter who would come to a door in the alley and escort you inside. It felt like a speakeasy. The tourists standing in line saw none of this happen.

Antoine's has a series of back dining rooms where only the locals ate. The main dining room up front was for the tourists, and at that time they had no idea the back rooms existed. When I graduated from Tulane my parents gave me a dinner at Antoine's with our friends from out of town. We did the march down the alley, and everyone was quite impressed as they had never experienced anything like it before then. The meal, with a French menu, was always excellent. And their specialty was Oysters Rockefeller and pompano cooked in parchment which I loved.

Antoine's no longer follows this system, and the last time I visited anyone could make a reservation and sit anywhere.

Speaking of oysters if you visit or live in New Orleans you will be completely overwhelmed with oysters, crab meat and crawfish, when in season. Oyster parties are common, and they are eaten raw, cooked, grilled; all with and without toppings. I have a New Orleans friend, a native, who loved giving oyster parties and that's all he served, nothing else. I once suggested to him that he should at least have an alternative food available as not everyone attending was from New Orleans. He looked at me totally puzzled as though I had lost my mind. There were only oysters served.

The Lakeshore restaurants on Lake Pontchartrain were for

fish and seafood dinners, and we'd go there some Sundays too. Our favorite was Bruning's, now long gone as it, and most West End restaurants, was destroyed in 2005 by Hurricane Katrina. The seafood was fresh and plentiful. There was a big sink in the middle of the room to wash your hands as inevitably you'd get quite messy eating a meal there.

Po Boys and muffulettas were common fare in New Orleans. Because of their size they were sandwiches that could keep one fed for two or more meals. The muffulettas at the Central Grocery in the French Quarter are legendary. We once ordered them for a bus trip we were taking to St. Louis for an exchange program with Washington University. It is a long trip and we nibbled on the muffuletta during the journey. Filled with cold cuts, veggies and a marinade of olives and peppers made into a spread, they are simply delicious. The round loaf of deli goodness was quite satisfying, yet we inadvertently didn't bring anything to drink, and suffered from the dry mouth and thirst it produced.

New Orleans is where I acquired my taste for spicy food, and the spicier the better. I always have a bottle of McIlhenny Tabasco Sauce handy; and use it on nearly everything. The McIlhenny family own Avery Island in Louisiana's Cajun Country where Tabasco Sauce is made. The smell of vinegar permeates everything and is especially noticeable the minute you step out of the car. There is an interesting museum to visit there, and you can also take a tour to see how Tabasco is made, and even try some Tabasco flavored ice cream afterwards.

A particular treat in these parts is a crawfish boil. When visiting New Orleans a few years ago a group of us went to a place on the West Bank for it. Located in Westwego, the restaurant is a Quonset type metal building with an assembly of tables inside, and a large barbeque and smoking room outside. We ordered something equivalent to forty pounds of crawfish. Like any typical boil they toss newspaper across the table and bring out the cooked crawfish, cooked in spices, along with potatoes, corn on the cob and other delights and scatter it on the paper to just grab and munch on whatever is in reach. It is quite a feast, if not a rather messy one. It's best to wear old clothes.

After I moved to San Francisco, another big food town, my living in the three centers of American cuisine was set. Williams Sonoma once put out a three-cookbook set with these cities together, New York, New Orleans, and San Francisco. Of course, I have it.

San Francisco also has an Italian influence, so that has followed me all my life and through the three cities. It is in San Francisco that I came to discover Dungeness crab, Cioppino, Sourdough bread and real Mexican food with a touch of Tex-Mex included, as in the burrito. San Francisco is also known for high end dining, and I've done my fair share of it. There are some exceptional restaurants, and they seem to get better and better every year. I have followed Quince since its humble start in a small place just a couple of blocks away from my Pacific Heights home. Then there are hidden gems, like Acquerello, where they serve exquisite Northern Italian cuisine. I once had a New Year's Eve feast there and the wine flowed so freely that the waiter asked if we wanted a cab at the end of the meal, but we stumbled home a couple blocks walking up a steep hill rather inebriated.

San Francisco also has an amazing array of Asian restaurants of every variety. Going to a Chinese banquet is something not to be missed. But then tasting the differences in Vietnamese to Cambodian to Laotian to Thai to Burmese can really make one's head spin. Sushi is at its prime in San Francisco and for those of you who don't think you'd like it, try it in San Francisco. Los Angeles supposedly had the original corner on that market for quality, but I think San Francisco soon outshone it.

I once had an experience at a bookstore in Berkeley that left me smiling. While perusing through books I saw a woman huddled in a corner wearing a small hat. At one point she got up and turned so I could see her clearly, and it was the famous chef of Chez Panisse, Alice Waters. I was bemused as to the fact that even Alice looked at cookbooks!

My exploration of food continues to this day, and I will try anything once. I have come to love African cuisine, the many variations of Asian food, appreciating the subtle nuances of each, and I am especially fond of Indian food. And I cook attempting to relive meals and try to invent new recipes. I do have a successful recipe I concocted for paella, and one for turkey soup, usually from left over Thanksgiving turkey.

Food is joy, sustenance, and brings people together. Eating together with friends and family is to be treasured and transports us from our everyday lives into something special, perhaps festive. There is nothing better than being in an Italian restaurant or home and hearing the word '*Mangia*!' It radiates- eat, enjoy and be happy.

CHAPTER 7

That amazing 'Ah Ha' moment

My first momentous, 'Ah Ha' moment happened in Monterey, California in October 1985.

It was my first visit to California. I was coming from Wisconsin where I then lived traveling with my wife and sixteen-month-old son. We were on a quasi-vacation, but the prime reason was to determine if it would be a place we would move to after my wife graduated with her doctoral degree in the following year.

Arriving in San Francisco I was just blown away by the beauty of the place. Arriving on a perfect weather day I drove the rental car from the airport down Van Ness Avenue to the hotel; and I thought I was transported to Shangri-La. What I recall most were the imposing Beaux Arts structures of the Civic Center area, an amazing City Hall, Opera House, and other formally planned buildings with a green space of a boulevard down the center of the street. And hills with the topography adding to the interest and uniqueness of this grand city by the Bay.

When we checked in at the hotel the receptionist saw we had rented this full-sized Lincoln Continental. He smiled and said, 'dump the car'. I looked at him rather perplexed. He went on to say 'that's going to be more of an inconvenience than anything. Park it and walk'. He was right. There were times when driving over the crest of a hill, with a roller coaster type slope ahead, that I literally could not see over the hood of the car blocking my view ahead.

It was a particularly unique time to be in San Francisco with its typical temperate Mediterranean climate. The day after we arrived, October 1, the temperatures soared over 100 degrees, almost unheard of there. Usually, the soothing fog and ocean breezes keeps the temperature in check. It was HOT, and the hotel room did not have any air conditioning. To make it comfortable, especially with a young child, I went in search of a fan. Well, that became an interesting endeavor. Many of the Asian owned stores thought I meant a 'fan', like the one you hold, open, and fan yourself. No, I was after the mechanical plug-in type. There were none to be found. I guess everyone knew the heat was coming and bought out those types of fans. After an hour or so, I finally located one and brought it back to create a nice bit of air circulation.

Our intent was to look at San Francisco as a place to live and then drive to San Diego for a comparison look. Los Angeles, although we would drive through it, was not on the short list. It just seemed too large, spread out, and unwieldy; even though I had grown up in New York City. My wife was definitely accustomed to more breathing room, although she did live in New York for a couple of years after we were married.

When we left San Francisco we stopped in Monterey, both to have our son visit the amazing Aquarium there, but also for lunch.

We ate at this little restaurant not far from the Aquarium and it was another one of those clear, beautiful California days and just warm enough to be outdoors. Coming from

Wisconsin, where it is either hot or cold, made this seem even more enticing.

What I remember so vividly was sitting outside eating our meal on a patio with tables under umbrellas and thinking it was heaven on earth. I had ordered an albacore tuna salad and it was fresh and delicious, the perfect lunch. The entire impact of that moment sticks so clearly in my memory.

It was right then that the 'Ah Ha' struck me. California feels like 'home'; and would become my home. There was no going back.

Unfortunately, it did not happen until 1989 due to several things, including a divorce, but ultimately San Francisco became the place I came to adopt and love, and it treated me so very well too.

When I finally arrived in San Francisco the place was in its second Gold Rush period with the high-tech boom. Anything was possible, so I rode the wave! It began with a tuna salad for lunch on a patio of a Monterey restaurant.

Another prophetic 'Ah Ha' moment in my life occurred on the Venetian Island of Torcello. Torcello is in the Venice aquatic basin beyond the islands of Murano and Burano, rather remote and not well visited. It is older than Venice itself and incredibly tranquil and beautiful. Bucolic in appearance it has walking paths and trails and several canals, one crossed by a lovely, curved brick bridge void of sides or railings. It is a truly memorable escape from the activity and crowded existence of Venice.

There's a small number of brick and stone buildings, a village with masonry foot bridges, a small museum and an enormously beautiful Romanesque church, Basilica di Santa Maria Assunta. It has a belfry that you can climb up to, and I once got up there just as the large bells chimed out the noon hour. It was awesome to be up close with them.

I've had the pleasure of visiting Torcello twice. It is only accessible by a ferry ride from Venice and is part of the circuit that also stops at the other nearby islands. It is the furthest away and takes between an hour and a half to two hours to get there, depending on the route and number of intermittent stops.

My first visit there was with someone who I ended up being in an ill-fated relationship. I'm not certain what brought us to Torcello but it made for an interesting excursion. Years later, on the second visit, nothing had changed, and I doubt it has for centuries.

That first visit, however, was a major 'Ah Ha' moment in my life. There is something mystical and magical about Torcello that transcends description. You feel it, and it is quite remarkable. It is almost as though the history and the centuries of its existence, the utter tranquility and contemplative nature of it, encompasses you.

It was during that first visit that something inexplicable overcame me.

While standing at a dock near a small marina just beyond the Basilica I was marveling the scenery and solitude when the theme song from the recent movie *Titanic*, 'My Heart Will Go On' began to play from one of the boats. A middle age Italian couple was standing nearby also admiring the view and beauty. The woman looked at the man and said 'Ah, *Teetanic*' in a vivid Italian accent. I will always remember the way she said it, and that she was inspired to comment on it, perhaps in our mutual admiration of the surroundings.

Yet, right at that moment I felt something incredible

overcome me. I cannot explain it at all, but this remarkable surge of emotion enveloped me, and I felt in my inner heart and soul that Ed York, my now husband, is the man I am destined to spend my life with from then on. That was now twenty-two years ago. The entire experience just overwhelmed me, with both joy and uncertainty as I was in another relationship at the time. Whatever happened transformed my life, and until today I do not regret the force that moved me in that direction.

The prophetic saga of that specific moment was to accelerate forward about three months later over a birthday party, but that is best left for another story. Just know it was life alerting.

Since that time, it was my dream for Ed to see Torcello and to share the experience of that moment with me.

In 2007 that dream came true.

Ed and I were going with friends on an Adriatic-Mediterranean cruise, including Greece and Turkey, that left from Venice, so a perfect opportunity to revisit Torcello arose. Our friends took the ferry out with us, and it was a beautiful, sunny September day. Believe me, there is *something* magical about that island.

We spent a good part of the morning wandering around, and I showed Ed the marina where my 'epiphany' had occurred. I was so glad he was there with me, as if we were meant to be together at that place. It was if our relationship was intended; in that we were truly best friends, soul mates and would be married the next year when it was legal for same sex couples to do so in California.

We continued our exploration of the island and had a simply glorious lunch at a charming restaurant there called Ristorante

Villa 600. It had a covered patio where we sat, and as it was a late lunch, so few people were there. We just luxuriated in the warm breeze of Torcello with our dear friends, JoAnn and Julie, over a delicious meal with wine, thinking life was just grand.

We ordered a whole baked fish, typically on the higher price side, but oh so good, and along with vegetables, dessert, and espresso I'd say we were there for at least two hours, or more.

Torcello is a memorable 'Ah Ha' moment, and I would gladly revisit it any time.

My finding Ed and having him become an integral part of my life is the most amazing and wonderful thing to ever happen for me. I am blessed in so many ways and our compatibility outstanding. We often said that we would have been best friends as kids. In life's trials and tribulations Ed has always been my oasis, my escape from the world, my rock, and my soul mate.

As our relationship developed, I will never forget the day he gave me the key to his house in a beautiful little wooden box for a gift. Or when he said to me 'well, I guess we'll be spending all our time together' in a mention to the growing relationship and both our desires. And finally, the time when he looked at me one day when same sex marriage was legal and said, 'well, we should get married', and we did on October 23, 2008. Every day I wake up and so thankful that he is with me.

There are those moments in our lives that are most profound, groundbreaking and truly momentous. It is good to celebrate them, and to recognize that 'Ah Ha' moment, when it occurs, is to be cherished forever.

CHAPTER 8

Steinway

For some very odd reason the Steinway name has constantly been a part of my life. The famous piano company has its headquarters in Astoria, Queens where I grew up, and because of it there is a major commercial thoroughfare called Steinway Street that played a big part in my early years when I lived nearby.

The Steinway family, Germans, came to Astoria and settled sometime in the 1800s. They opened a piano factory and to this day make one of the finest pianos in the world. The old family mansion still stands as an historic site, as does the factory. The Steinway family was very prominent and influential in the area.

Steinway, the commercial thoroughfare, runs for many blocks through Astoria. I cannot tell you if it's officially a street, avenue, or something else, as everyone just called it 'Steinway'. My grandmother sometimes did refer to it as 'Steinway Street'. It has all types of retail, restaurants, offices, banks and had two large movie theaters from the 1920s, in the Paramount style era. Steinway was essentially the retail heart of Astoria, perhaps second only to Astoria Boulevard that I did not know as well. Steinway also intersects another prime retail street, Broadway, that was closer to my house.

Going to Steinway for Christmas shopping was a big deal. Often my father and I would go there, sometimes in the snow, to find gifts for my mother. There was a variety of clothing stores. My mother frequented a women's store called Lerners. My favorite stop was a large toy store about mid-way down the length of the street. One block had a substantial gift store and what I remember most was a giant cut glass vase, perhaps five feet tall, positioned prominently in the window that I was determined to own one day. That never happened.

The prominence of Steinway in my life, and the love of the piano was a defining factor in my desire to learn an instrument, although I truly favored the organ. I took organ music lessons from 1963 to 1972 with four different teachers. I learned to understand music composition, and it especially increased my appreciation of classical music. My father loved symphonic music, and unfortunately rarely attended concerts. All my teachers, save for one, were quite accomplished and knowledgeable.

The organ my parents purchased for me, a behemoth of a thing, traveled with me to Wisconsin when I moved there in 1980. My parents had just sold their house in Connecticut where it was housed. It was finally sold to a neighbor's sister in 1986, hopefully having a good home somewhere in the wilds of northern Wisconsin.

When I started to learn music, and the organ, my maternal grandfather remembered that my great-grandfather, his father-in-law, was the head organist in the cathedral in Kaunas, Lithuania. That was an interesting revelation, yet I've not been able to track down much about him.

Nonetheless, through my love of the organ and keyboard instruments, the name Steinway hovered over me for many years.

When I returned to New York to look for work as an architect apprentice I ended up with a firm at 111 West 57th Street, the Steinway Building. This was the building where Steinway had their main showroom for displaying and selling pianos, and a concert hall. It was across the street from Carnegie Hall, and it also housed the offices for Metropolitan Life Insurance. The firm I worked for, Russo + Sonder, had the two top floors of the high-rise with direct views to Central Park in the back and from the front onto West 57th Street and the skyline south, including the Empire State Building. The Steinway building was a Beaux Arts classically designed structure with beautiful stone detailing. Outside our conference room there were enormous decorative stone urns and balustrade.

Steinway and Company had a separate entry, prominent and highly elegant, away from the office building entrance. I loved working in that building and the neighborhood was in the heart of everything. The lobby for the offices was marble clad and I remember four elevators, with elaborate bronze doors. As a young man working there it was interesting in that many very attractive young women worked for Metropolitan Life, although they were not terribly worldly. They tried to impress the architects when riding in the elevator together. When a friend and I got on the elevator one day after lunch we were followed by a few 'Met Life' girls. During the ride one said to another, 'Did you watch the Bee Gees concert last night?'. The response was, 'who are they?'. In complete arrogance and assuredness, the other retorted, 'what's the matter with you, do you live in a closet!' while looking at us and smiling. It was 1978. My friend and I did everything possible to hold back from bursting out laughing.

Every morning I would pass the Steinway showroom with these magnificent, stately pianos on display. Highly polished woods, shining keys, and so inviting of a concert hall.

Aside from this piano connection my father's uncle and aunt, Frank and Helen, owned property in Deep River, Connecticut. There were several large greenhouses on the property that stood there for decades. When their daughter, Barbara, who you will read about later, considered selling the property after her parents passed away, she was contacted by the Smithsonian Institute. Apparently one of the greenhouses was significant in the production of pianos! In the mid-1800s elephant tusks were brought there, stored, and dried to eventually make them into piano keys, perhaps many ending up on Steinway pianos. The Smithsonian wanted to have the greenhouse.

So, yet again, this piano legacy followed me around in life.

In 2014 I returned to West 57th Street, this time staying in a new hotel right across the street from the Steinway Building. It was no longer occupied, emptied, shuttered and I feared slated for demolition, not uncommon in this part of Manhattan. But I soon learned that it was not being demolished, rather renovated, with a 100+ story ultra-luxury condo tower to be built on top of it! This one stretch of street is now known as 'Billionaire's Row' made famous for the high-priced condos that only billionaires inhabit, usually as a second, third or fourth residence. I stood in my hotel room looking out the window over to the spaces once occupied by the architectural firm where I worked, the stone urns still standing as prominent and timely as ever, with a layer of dust over them.

Whenever I see a Steinway piano, or even the name, it evokes a great number of memories, and brings me warmth in the things that last.

CHAPTER 9

Being a refugee

Being a refugee, needing to suddenly flee one's home to a new destination caused by strife or prejudice is certainly rather unnerving, frightening, and yet the escape is hugely relieving. My experience of being a refugee is indeed all the above; yet does not approach what people face fleeing from a war torn or politically volatile area to a foreign country for safety. Yet, I can understand the anxiety and feeling of that transition.

I came 'out' as a gay man in 1983. I was married at the time. Being twenty-nine years old it was still at a time when it was illegal in many states and one could either be jailed and/or put in an asylum, lose a job, or be brutally beaten or killed. Nothing about being gay was easy. I had sensed something in myself but denied and suppressed it. My own 'coming out' was precipitated by seeing the movie *An Officer and A Gentleman*, a movie about boldness, integrity, honesty, truth, and honor. I went alone to see it. The movie pulled me to be honest with myself and face something I could no longer deny or escape, nor could I. To not come 'out' would be dishonest about my true identity, and frankly dishonest in my marriage too. And trust me, it's terrifying and not easy. It's not a choice.

Another movie at the time, *Making Love,* addressed my circumstance head on. The plot is about a married doctor who recognizes his being gay and eventually admits it, divorces, and moves on to a happier, honest life. His outcome was much better than mine, initially anyway.

It was indeed a rough period in my life. Sitting down with my wife we had a lengthy discussion where I told her the truth. We attempted to make it work; but after two years or so it was misery for both of us, and understandably in particular for her. I could tell how much it troubled her, although she did try very hard to accept it.

I also met a man who was married, with children, and after confiding with each other we began a relationship, doing our best to balance both sides. Our wives knew about it, were supportive, yet life got very complicated in the process. All of this was very discreet and never mentioned beyond us.

The difficult recognition of the need to divorce was inevitably real and horrible. It wasn't that I didn't love the person I married, yet there was something missing, just not right, and impacting us. It was tearing us apart as much as we hoped it would not.

Without any intent of living with anyone I moved into an apartment and intended to do the best possible to make our lives move forward positively, with little discord or harm. We also had a son, a young boy, at this time. His welfare was important to me. I will keep the details brief, but the divorce turned bitter, with contested custody of the child, and was a grueling experience for the following two and a half years. I had resentment as I do believe an underlying factor of the difficult divorce, perhaps not fully realized, was my being gay. In the eyes of the court, and the phony liberalism of a sector of Wisconsin, gays were not suitable to be around children at that time.

It wasn't a long time thereafter that I was indeed living with the man I had met, as he divorced as well. I moved into his place in Des Moines, Iowa having his two young children live with us, quite ironic based on the facts of my divorce.

If truth be known, I was never compelled that much to want or raise children. Yet the two children I ultimately helped raise through my new family, Matthew and Sarah, were a godsend for me. They were such wonderful kids and fully adopted and embraced me as their 'parent' from the minute I moved in. Having known me for a couple years or more I am sure helped the situation as I was not completely a new person thrust upon them. I was very fortunate to be with these children and they were my rock, especially under the issues around having contact with my own son.

Matthew had Muscular Dystrophy and was wheelchair bound when I came into his life. His struggles, yet endurance, was incredibly powerful. He was gentle, kind, loving, and enjoyed good stories and good humor. Because of his condition he also was very lonely. What impressed me was his sense of 'self', yet he also felt very vulnerable. He was indeed dependent on others to sustain him. He literally could do nothing without some assistance. We finally got him a motorized wheelchair and then a device to use, a contraption really, enabling him to pick up food and eat on his own, yet it was a struggle and he hated it. We ended up feeding him every meal. He was so appreciative of anything I did for him, and it was done out of care and love for the person he was in my life. He gave me strength. Matthew also enjoyed my forays into experimental cooking on Sundays and looked forward to it.

Every summer we drove him to a camp for children with Muscular Dystrophy transporting his heavy electric powered wheelchair. It was a time he seemed to enjoy and was happy being with others.

I was so impressed when for his high school senior prom, the most beautiful girl in his class asked to be his date. He was so honored and proud, and beamed with excitement. We got him a tuxedo to wear. It was such a delightful experience for all of us, and it meant so much to him.

Sarah, his sister, was another delight in my life. I will always remember her sitting on the steps waiting for me to arrive with my furniture to move in. She was outgoing, fun, and as a child, full of playful mischief. Yet, she respected me as a parent, and I am forever grateful for her love and kindness.

She once, in her adult life, told me about things she and her brother did that we never knew about. I had to wonder how many kids did this type of revelation years later with their parents. One was how she would swing from the top of the doors to amuse Matthew. OK, it could have been worse.

One of the most endearing moments I recall was when we both had bad colds and stayed home, me from work and she from school. Waking up from an afternoon nap I went to check on her and she was gone! I looked around, but nowhere to be found. A bit concerned I looked out the glass doors of the living room and saw her sledding in the snow with a friend! I opened the door and called out to her, and her face turned shocked. She came right back, and I did admonish her, but she forlornly returned to her bed having been caught. Nonetheless her attempt at playfulness made me smile.

We led a rather quiet, background existence in Des Moines. It was not really a comfortable place for gay people to be 'out' and this hidden existence was something new to me. I always characterized it like being vampires. We all knew one other; but would never reveal anyone's identity to the outside world. There were a couple of gay bars that we visited on occasion. One popular one was the 'Brass Rail' that we called the 'Brass Ass'. I have no idea how that alternate name came about.

We belonged to a social group of professional gay men who gathered for potlucks and other get-togethers occasionally. Again, it was all very quiet and not advertised, just heard about through word of mouth, primarily for the fear of losing one's job if found out.

During my divorce, these men were enormous emotional support for me, very concerned and caring. This was also true of a 'Gay Fathers' group I belonged to in Madison, Wisconsin. We all stuck together through everyone's trials and tribulations. Sometimes at a gathering there would be a 'check in' just to see how everyone was doing, and it was not uncommon for someone to be going through some upset in life.

The craziness of my divorce overshadowed a lot else going on in my life. It absorbed a lot of time and effort. I was in therapy and my therapist, a family counselor, was amazed by the insanity of the Dane County court system where the divorce took place. Things took on an unexpected, bizarre twist nearly every other day. At one hearing it came up that I was probably 'unstable' because I had nailed the double hung windows in our Madison house shut for safety reasons. We did not exactly live in the safest part of town. However, people in the Midwest didn't know about New York City crime and how safety precautions become ingrained. In New York many folks nail their windows shut by drilling a small hole slightly larger than a nail in size and then inserting the nail between the frames, which can easily be removed from the inside when you want to open the window; but it keeps an intruder from opening the window from the outside. I guess that simple safety technique is proof of craziness outside of New York.

Saturday, February 13, 1988, was a day that changed everything… forever.

On that day Ken Eaton, a forty-one-year-old teacher, was murdered in his apartment. Ken lived in our neighborhood and was a good friend. He was gay and had recently broken up with his partner of many years and was feeling forlorn. The breakup hit him suddenly and hard. Yet through his own sadness Ken supported me in my efforts in tackling the difficult divorce. Just days before his murder he sent me a plant as a gift hoping for a good result to one of my upcoming divorce hearings.

The day after Ken's murder, Sunday, February 14, Valentine's Day, was a day of no return.

That morning our daily newspaper, the *Des Moines Register*, was delivered and on the front page was the news of Ken's death. It was not reported as a murder, merely suspicious, at the time and we speculated possibly a suicide, knowing Ken's recent sorrows. But soon word started floating around the tight knit gay community that Ken had indeed been murdered, and that it was gruesome.

It sent everyone into a panic. We wondered who did it? That same day my partner left for work saying that he hoped the police would not call us. Well, they did. I got the first phone call in the early afternoon, and they asked that I come in for questioning, and then subsequently my partner did too. We became slightly alarmed and uncomfortable; yet had to do what we had to do. At the time, the police did not link us as being partnered and living together.

I went down to the police station and in a room that I passed they had an array of Ken's personal items strewn across the floor: envelopes, pictures, boxes of things. Investigators were pouring through it methodically. The questions they posed to me seemed routine, about where I was at the time of the murder, etc. They initially told me they just considered me a 'neighbor'. Then they pulled out a piece of paper with a list of names. My name was on the list and a few of the names, including mine, had an asterisk next to it. The police said they found it in Ken's apartment and did not yet know the source or what it meant. They then warned me to be careful as the perpetrator could very well be a mass murderer out to kill gay men in Des Moines. They also said that the asterisk may have meaning, possibly who would be the next victims. It was apparent they assumed, or knew, I was gay. Just what I did not want to hear.

My partner went in later, and they did not show him the list, but did ask him additionally a few questions about the type of car I drove, which seemed peculiar to us.

At the time I was traveling 400 miles once or twice a month to handle matters with the divorce and to see my son during the proceedings. I was only allowed supervised visitation, which was unpleasant and controlled. I also knew that being questioned in a murder investigation would not bode well for where I was in the divorce.

A very good friend, Jack, opened his house for me to stay over the weekend in Madison, Wisconsin during these trips. It was a godsend, and he was extremely gracious in his hospitality and care.

Let us just say it was a tumultuous time, and my partner and I had enough on our hands being responsible for raising two children, one of whom was physically handicapped.

Ken's sudden and untimely death sent shock waves across the typically hidden, quiet lives of the professional gay men in Des Moines. Phone calls of speculation circulated. It came out that Ken was murdered in his bedroom. The most shocking part was his teenage daughter was sleeping in the next bedroom when it occurred. She was the one who found him in the morning.

During a conversation with one of my friends, a gay accountant who knew Ken well, I relayed what the police told me about the possibility of this being a mass murderer of gay men, and my concern over it; especially the asterisk on the list of names and what it might mean. I also shared with him the fear I felt, and uncertainty around all of it. In mentioning the 'list' with my name on it Bruce said the police showed him the list as well and he reassured me that I should not be concerned as he knew it was Ken's Christmas card list and he had put an asterisk next to names he especially wanted to get cards out to first. That was an enormous relief. The police now knew that, yet never followed up with me or anyone else they might have worried over it.

Then the worst consequence occurred, rather overshadowing the fear of the infamous 'list'.

My partner came home and told me he had been fired from his job. We were in complete shock. He was a teacher and librarian at a local high school and the principal called him in to discuss his living situation. One of the investigating officers, a friend of the principal, called to tell him that one of his teachers is homosexual and living with a man, me. They had pieced it together by comparing our address and phone number from the multitude of people interviewed; and found us in Ken's address book listed together. Plus, they uncovered a photo of us sitting on Ken's couch with Ken and his partner. In their estimation, proof of our being gay.

The principal gave my partner an immediate ultimatum, either I move out that day or he's fired. He took the latter. I have to say in retrospect I have immeasurable admiration for his decision, especially since his two children were at risk in that decision too.

Fortunately, I was still working, but this event would impact our lives, especially since my partner realized he would never do education work in Iowa again. It was the ultimate fear all of us had in being 'outed'.

Word spread of the firing, and we received a lot of support from our friends. Ten days after the Ken's murder the perpetrators were apprehended! Two men, one nineteen years old and the other age twenty were arrested. The murder weapon, a seven-inch long kitchen knife, with Ken's blood had been tossed in a garbage bin outside their apartment. They were discovered as they had stupidly worn some of Ken's most identifiable clothing, tee shirts with slogans, some of the many things they stole from his apartment after the murder. It was a robbery that went bad. It was determined that Ken had met the men downtown and invited them back to his place. The exact details of what transpired never came out, although I do believe the police knew and never made it public, including at the trials.

There was a sense of relief in the community, yet the repercussions would continue to ripple onward.

A gay lawyer who heard of my partner's firing called him

and suggested we come in to meet with him. We did. He said a wrongful termination should not be pushed aside, that we should fight it; and he'd be willing to take the case to assist us. We spoke it over and decided to pursue it. Unfortunately, we never realized the implications that we would face in that decision.

After the case was filed my partner's mother called from a remote part of Northwest Iowa greatly concerned and to ask if we had read the morning *Des Moines Register*, the state newspaper. We hadn't; but did immediately. There on the front page was a news report about our case with our names listed and all the pertinent information. We never expected this would reach the press or have any notoriety, but apparently it was big news in Iowa.

That started a new set of uncertainties. The news spread rapidly. We were doing all we could to shield the children from all the gory details of Ken's murder, since they knew him and his daughter, and now from this new phase directly involving us. We kept newspapers and news reports away from them to not upset or alarm them, yet we also told them to be cautious with the recent events. They obviously knew that their father had been fired. We also told them not to answer the telephone.

That last part was a good decision because what happened next was unbelievable. We started getting phone calls with very direct threats. The callers called us names that were ugly and inflammatory. One man asked if our fire insurance was paid up since our place would not be around much longer. Another advised us to watch our children because something might happen to them. Just hearing that someone knew we had children sent chills through us. Whether these were real threats or merely intimidation it sent us into a tailspin of fear.

We assumed our immediate neighbors knew of our lives, and no one ever questioned or looked down on us. We were treated like anyone else, and their kids even played with ours, including in our home. One woman, our next-door neighbor, a professional photographer, said to us at one point that we should seriously consider leaving. She believed that we were in definite danger staying in Des Moines, and Iowa for that matter, not even knowing of the phone calls.

During our considering what to do Ken's murderers went on trial, each separately. I attended both trials. The evidence was graphic and hard to look at; and comprehend. Ken was bludgeoned brutally with the kitchen knife, including directly through his heart. Blood was splattered everywhere in the room, on the walls and ceiling. The evidence seemed clear and absolute. Each man blamed the other. It was ugly.

Both received life sentences.

During the trial it struck me as I overheard one of the men's grandmothers, sitting behind me, say to some relatives that she couldn't understand the big deal as they had only killed a gay man. It was very telling of their upbringing and values.

In between all the chaos Ken's memorial service took place. The outpouring of sympathy for him and his family was outstanding. Nearly one thousand people attended the service. He was a loved teacher and educator and that prevailed over all else. Ken's father gave the eulogy, and I was so moved by his ability to stay steady and calm through his entire time speaking. Ken's long-time partner did not attend. I took it very hard because of the good friend Ken had been to me. I couldn't hold back my tears when they played a recording of

Ken singing 'New York, New York', his hometown. It all was a fitting tribute for someone taken brutally and too young.

None of this ever came to bear any significance in my divorce proceedings, and that came to finality in the coming weeks.

The psychological impact of a friend being brutally murdered is profound. To this day I cannot leave a kitchen knife out on a countertop. And each time I reach in the drawer for a seven-inch kitchen knife I think of Ken, the weapon used to kill him. These things last a long time, if not forever.

We decided to leave Iowa, permanently. In discussion with the children's mother, she agreed to take them for a year while we got settled somewhere else. We had a couple of large garage sales to sell our things. Everything happened quickly.

Our destination- San Francisco.

It seemed the only 'safe-haven' for us and we were tired of the hiding, the fear, the homophobia. We wanted to be free to live our lives, and our love, in peace.

I will never forget the freezing February day we woke up at four o'clock and kissing the kids goodbye as they slept. We drove in two separate cars with all our lifelong possessions in each, driving as quickly as possible to leave the Midwest. The early morning air was extremely cold and crisp, and the landscape looked like Siberia with everything encased in ice. It would be quite the contrast to where we were heading. We had no idea what we'd find, or what would ultimately happen when we arrived. We had no jobs. And we knew what it was like to suddenly leave our home and flee.

Although we made reservations to stay in a motel in San Francisco a friend of ours, a Presbyterian minister and a closeted gay man, in a rural Iowa community, contacted friends of his in San Francisco who agreed to take us in until we could get settled. Like so many immigrant and refugee community experiences, when you flee your home your community watches after you, whether they know you or not. And these two men did.

We wound our way along the 'Southern' route across the country since it was winter, and we wanted to avoid Colorado and Utah. We did hit snow in Flagstaff, Arizona, but not a large amount. We went through Missouri and Kansas; then through the panhandle of Oklahoma seeing topography that looked like moonscape, and our first stop was Dalhart, Texas; not exactly a 'gay friendly' place. So, we keep down low the entire time. It is amazing how in 1989 you did not need to worry about leaving all your worldly possessions in your car overnight!

My car, a Crown Victoria my parents had given to me, was beginning to have mechanical problems, yet it endured. West Texas had nothing but enormous ranches with cattle packed in as far as the eye could see. Driving through New Mexico I was amazed to find American Indian, Apache, radio stations. It was alluring and somewhat exotic.

Spending our second night near Flagstaff it was restful as we took a deep breath knowing were getting closer to California. We drove in tandem in the entire way, rarely did we break apart for the hundreds of miles traveled.

Getting to the border of California was as much a relief as it was a little worrisome. There is a border crossing between it and Arizona, and just like refugees entering from a foreign country you are stopped and asked many questions. It exists primarily to check for any plants or pests that can impact California agriculture. When I stopped the guard asked me several questions, especially why my car was stacked with boxes, and where I was going. I was not about to tell him I had a heritage plant from my father's New York store, given to him as a gift when he opened in 1947, carefully concealed under my seat. Not examining the interior of the car further, the guard did ask me to open the trunk and after a quick look at the multitude of items compactly stuffed in it, he sent me on my way.

Across the border in Needles, we stopped to fill up for gas as we were approaching open land, the desert. While at the gas station an attendant ran out to tell me he saw my back tire was not balanced and looked dangerous; crossing the desert would be a terrible risk. He offered to check and fix it for an exorbitant sum of money. Fortunately, my partner had been driving behind me for many miles; and came to me indicating that it was hogwash. He saw no signs of any trouble. We later found that this is a common ploy in Needles to make money, scamming long distance drivers with similar scare tactics about mechanical issues.

After my partner cleared the crossing station, we headed into the Mojave Desert. That drive is not for the faint of heart, especially for someone from New York City. There are several warning signs about having enough gas to transverse the desert, and even in winter the heat is intense. It's simply a surreal landscape, complete nothingness except for sand and occasional cacti for miles. At one point I saw a small settlement way off in the distance that I thought could be a mirage.

The seemingly endless straight road through the desert took a few hours and ends at Barstow, California, a middle of nowhere forbidden place without much character.

We headed on, into another place and land. Getting off

the main highway we traversed the San Juaquin Valley, the breadbasket of California, to head toward the coast. It was lush, emerald-green from recent rains and exactly as characterized-paradise! Such a change from the icy cold winter of Iowa of white and grey. It seemed like heaven driving among the hills as we got closer to the coast, eventually spending the night in Paso Robles.

Like so many of the crop farmers during the Dust Bowl of the 1930s we had made our way from the forbidding mid-west to the beauty and richness of California! It was such a breadth of fresh air.

Although our exodus and journey in no way mimicked what those refugees experienced who proceeded us, or those fleeing oppressive countries, yet it felt very similar to us. Uprooting home, comfort, and family to go to a new land without a job, knowing anyone, or what it would entail; we wondered what it would ultimately hold for us. Yet, there appeared to be no choice. And yes, we were indeed refugees too, gays escaping an oppressive environment.

I had been to San Francisco once, but my partner had not. When we arrived within 100 miles of our final destination, we could sense it as being 'home'.

The couple who graciously hosted us when we arrived, Jerry and Rick, were most kind and generous. We went to find their house on the slope of Twin Peaks, unknown territory to us. Without GPS in those days, we got lost and ended up on the most perilous route up to the top of the Peak! Coming from flat Iowa it was very dramatic. It felt as though we were flying in the air over the city below. We eventually found the house, a beautiful two-story stucco manse with a copper roof and broad dormers. As Jerry was an architect the interior was amazing, and the view across the city beyond breathtaking. They gave us a nice, comfortable bedroom and we learned that the house next door belonged to Art Agnos, the Mayor of San Francisco at the time. We saw a Lincoln Town Car pick up the children to take them to school each morning.

It felt like we were in an oasis, a place of freedom and peace. Being able to quickly get to the Castro, the heart of the 'gay ghetto' was so refreshing and liberating. We could hold hands walking down the sidewalk and no one cared. Our friends back in Iowa warned that we would probably hate the place as San Francisco and the Castro had become a 'dead city'. This was at the height of the AIDS crisis, 1989, and certainly many men were dying, but in no way was it a 'dead city'. Instead, there was an exuberance of care and compassion everywhere, although the local gay paper, *The Bay Area Reporter*, had page after page of dozens of obituaries each week, for weeks on end. It was indeed very sad.

When we drove into San Francisco, and even before meeting Jerry and Rick, we scouted out a bank to deposit the checks we carried with us from Iowa, our lone savings. We found a Bank of America at the corner of Van Ness and Market, parked, and went inside. When a bank representative called me to his desk, I settled in to open an account while my partner sat in the reception area. While filling out the paperwork I noticed the banker had on his desk a framed photo of himself and a man standing closely together. He saw me looking at it and told me that it was his 'lover', a common term then. I was amazed to see something so open in the workplace.

While I completed the paperwork, I felt more comfortable telling him that we had just arrived in town. He asked about my partner, and I pointed him out sitting in the reception area. He insisted I bring him to the desk. We felt so welcomed and the openly gay atmosphere was such a shock coming from Des Moines; yet it was quickly feeling very good. Being ourselves while no longer hiding was extremely refreshing. At the end of our conversation the banker commented he was amazed by our story of coming to San Francisco; and wondered why we would first come to a bank. He said most gay men would immediately go to a gay bar. I guess we were more concerned over the safety of the checks.

Anyway, we made a new friend and were most appreciative to have his assistance while beginning new lives in a place of freedom.

Jerry and Rick did everything to make their home feel like our home in every way. We felt safe, secure, and in such beautiful and comfortable surroundings. Yet, we knew we had to find our own home soon, although they were welcoming of us staying for as long as we wanted. Each of them, Jerry an architect turned realtor, and Rick, a dental assistant took turns touring us around their favorite places in the area.

I had been researching San Francisco apartment rental rates through the newspapers in the Des Moines main library, so I was not that taken aback by the expense. We anticipated paying a great deal more than Des Moines. We also had to find work. I had resumes sent out before we left and had appointments for interviews. Times were good so finding work did not seem difficult. I had hoped for a bit of a break before jumping into something.

Interviews kept coming my way and I found myself getting many offers, always with the request to start as soon as possible.

Firms were actively seeking people, and my experience was right in that sweet spot for most, even though I was new to California. Each interviewer asked me about my awareness of the cost of living, and if I expected to weather the change in expense over the long term.

Just three weeks after our arrival I took a job at HKIT Architects, primarily because I felt very comfortable with those I met, the type of work they were doing; and the firm felt 'right' with the culture I wanted. They specifically hired me for my experience in affordable and senior housing, a big part of their work, and my CADD, 'Computer Added Design and Drawing', skills.

One of the first things I did to celebrate was to go to Tiffany's and buy two silver key rings with my initials engraved, that I still use today.

Concurrent with that event we luckily found an apartment, a pleasant, contemporary place not far from Jerry and Rick, on Clayton Street. It had one bedroom, a large balcony, a Lucy and Desi style 1950s kitchen with pink appliances, and a killer view to the East of the entire city and beyond.

My colleague at work was a man named Linton, and we hit it off immediately. An openly gay man, he empathically told me that he expected me to be 'out' in the office. After hearing my story of how I arrived he said that I was in my 'Promised Land'- San Francisco. There was no need to hide. I listened and greatly appreciated his advice.

In one of those *Tales of the City* moments, and if you have not read this series about San Francisco in the 1970s by the author Armistead Maupin, you should, Linton invited us to dinner at his home in the Castro.

Linton had several housemates, and his place was quite large. He invited them to join us at dinner, and low and behold who walks down the hall but the banker we had met when we set up our bank accounts. He and his partner were a couple of Linton's housemates! We all smiled and shared the connections and comfort of our new home. It was certainly headed in a wonderful direction. We no longer were feeling like fleeing refugees.

My partner soon after found a position in a local public library as the events of the incident in Des Moines did not seem to matter.

The lawsuit carried on back in Iowa and we finally settled out of court. In the aftermath we felt strongly that we never wanted to return.

I am forever grateful to Jerry and Rick for opening their home to us in a time of need, total strangers, and for their warm hospitality in allowing us to get our foothold in a new place.

The experience of having to suddenly leave our home and virtually run to escape did leave an everlasting impression; and made me consider the experiences of those around the world whose fear in fleeing far outweighed our own.

It also made me contemplate the immigrant experience that for generations has endured by the generosity of their own in finding new homes to prosper and live in peace.

CHAPTER 10

The world at my doorstep

At age ten not too many kids can say that the world came to them, but in my case it did. New York hosted the World's Fair in 1964 and 1965 and it was quite the production. It brought a level of excitement and anticipation that for a couple of years beforehand was building with profound hype. I got to watch every bit of it being built at Flushing Meadows in Queens on 646 acres of open land.

Flushing Meadows, otherwise known as Corona Park, is a strange place. Back in the early part of the twentieth century it was the dumping grounds for New York City with a vast acreage of waste, garbage, and filth. F Scott Fitzgerald wrote about it in *The Great Gatsby* and referred to it as the 'Valley of Ashes'. Supposedly, as described in the book, there was an advertising sign for an eye doctor, 'Dr. Eckleburg'. As a road through there went from Great Neck to Manhattan my mother, who lived in Great Neck ('West Egg' in the book) at the time, attested to this place being a dumping ground, and that a sign advertising an optometrist existed there when she was a child in the 1920s.

Flushing Meadows was also a crossroads of sorts, and wide-open space, indeed very rare in New York City. It had been selected and developed for the previous New York World's Fair in 1939-40, just before the onslaught of WWII. My parents and relatives remembered that Fair well, and the many good times they spent there.

In the later 1950s and early 1960s Robert Moses, a city public official and urban planner, decided to create another World's Fair on that same spot.

There was a rift with the International Exposition Committee in Paris, the Bureau of International Expositions (BIE), that ended with the NY World's Fair not qualifying for that designation. Because of it, Canada, Australia, France, and England would not participate. The primary reasons for the rejection were that the BIE charter regulations only allow for an Exposition to be open for six months and that exhibitors are not charged rental fees, both of which this Fair violated.

Yet, since commerce and the growing arena of technology began to take on a bigger role than foreign country participation, the Fair went on regardless of BIE designation.

Nonetheless there were one hundred and forty pavilions and eighty countries represented, along with twenty-four states and forty-five leading US corporations.

Years of planning and excitement went into creating the Fair, and as a child it seemed that the entire world was coming to introduce themselves to me. I started a scrap book to include new articles and pictures of the construction and completed buildings. Three highways passed the edges of the Fair site, the Grand Central Parkway and the Whitestone and Van Wyck Expressways. Additionally, the Long Island Expressway ran right through the site, dividing it in two parts. The Grand Central Parkway did the same for a smaller portion. That meant that all during the construction I could watch the progress of the steel skeletons rising into the air.

Concurrent to creating the Fair it was decided to build a new baseball stadium adjacent to it, Shea Stadium, including a new baseball team called 'the Mets'. That only added to my excitement since Yankee Stadium was so far away in the Bronx that I rarely got there.

All of this would be easily accessible from my neighborhood by a newly improved subway, the Number 7 line with new subway cars and increased efficiency to handle the impending crowds.

The official World's Fair colors of turquoise and orange began to appear everywhere. It was indicative of 'mid-century' design trends.

The theme of the Fair was 'Peace Through Understanding', a noteworthy one under the turbulent times of the Vietnam War, and of national turbulence yet to follow. President Kennedy had just been assassinated the year before the Fair opened. The intent of The Fair was to express a renewed optimism through exposing fairgoers to various nations and cultures, new technology, and prediction of the bright future which included the space age.

The buildup of the Fair's opening, in April of 1964, kept mounting as the day approached. News stories were constant, and millions of visitors were anticipated. For a ten-year-old kid just a few miles away from the Fairgrounds this was quite a bit of excitement. The number of countries exhibiting, as well as industrial leaders, kept growing steadily. The Fair was separated into specific areas, international exhibits, exhibits of the US states, Technology, Science, and Industry (especially the automobile), and entertainment with amusements.

Macy's Herald Square department store had a large-scale

model of the Fair and curiosity seekers came to walk around the perimeter and hear about the various things one would see and do during a visit. My mother and I visited it often and learned about it before opening day.

When that day finally arrived, April 22, 1964, there was great fanfare. The Fair would be open until October 18, 1964; and reopen again in 1965 from April 21 until the final closing date on October 17, 1965. Admission cost was two dollars for adults and a dollar for children under twelve. My parents purchased season tickets for both years so that we had unlimited entry. We went frequently, and I'd speculate somewhere between one to two hundred times during the duration of the Fair, seeing every exhibit at least once, most multiple times. We had some favorites: Pepsi Cola's *It's a Small World*, Bell Telephone, Ford, General Motors, Illinois with an animated Abraham Lincoln, General Electric, IBM, Japan, Thailand, and several others.

There were also pavilions representing religions including the Vatican, Mormons, and Christian Scientist.

I do not recall the date of my first visit, yet I know it was shortly after the Fair officially opened. I do, however, remember exactly what I first saw. Taking the Number 7 subway to the Fair's entry gates was a half an hour ride from my home, with one transfer at Queens Plaza. The new subway cars were sparkling clean and super-efficient. There was a new station constructed for the Fair and Shea Stadium between them. You walked from the station across a long and nondescript concrete bridge over the Long Island Railroad yards until arriving at the entrance gates. After giving a ticket to an attendant you walked down a broad concrete ramp to ground level. The entirety of

The Fair sprawled out before you like a wonderland. No sign of it originally being a garbage dump existed. It was all new and manicured.

The first pavilion I saw, and quite prominent at first glance, was the American Express pavilion with a giant metal tree out front; and one million dollars of money from around the world hanging from it.

Inside the grounds was a myriad of amazing sites, pavilions arranged in a very classically organized manner of street planning and layout, interspersed with fountains, water features, pools, statuary, and green spaces with lawns and gardens.

The symbol of the Fair at its center was the 'Unisphere', a huge stainless-steel globe of the earth tipped on its side as if in orbit, with the continents and their topography well defined. It's approximately twelve stories high and still stands today, fifty years later. At night little twinkling lights shone where major cities of the world exist. A giant pool of water with high, splashing waterspouts rung the perimeter. It was a popular spot for taking a photo.

The Fair was a tremendous educational opportunity for a kid my age. Although the critics of the time said that the architecture was substandard, especially in relation to the Art Deco extravaganza of the 1939 New York World's Fair that preceded it, there was still enough to delight and engage my architectural senses. Probably the most notable was the IBM pavilion, a giant egg sitting on top of a tabletop held up by a forest of tree-like columns, with a 'people wall' that lifted fairgoers from the forest through the table and into the egg! Not exactly Miesian architecture, but still an amazing wonder, nonetheless. In the mid-century modernity of the day, it was futuristic, open, expressive, and clean in detail and freedom of form. Kodak similarly created a moonscape roof that could be walked upon. Many international buildings were eclectic and reflective of the respective culture with embellishments of decoration on simple steel frame buildings.

Very few buildings were intended to be permanent, most built as temporary structures to be subsequently demolished at The Fair's end.

Famed architects of the time were involved. Philip Johnson designed the open-air New York State Pavilion, that I found rather uninteresting and dull. It was a huge colored glass tented structure, a 'circus tent', housing a terrazzo map of New York State on the floor along with three towers, one of which you could ride an elevator to the top and look out over The Fair. Eero Saarinen designed my favorite IBM building, and Charles and Ray Eames did the exhibit, a multi-media show within the egg-shaped theater. George Nelson, a lesser known 'starchitect' designed the Chrysler, US Federal and Ireland Pavilions. Walt Disney, although not an architect, had his creative hand in many of the exhibits as I will describe later.

Some Pavilions were truly wacky. For example, there was the House of Good Taste, an array of houses to exhibit 'good taste' in a variety of styles. Best of all was the Formica Pavilion, a house entirely made of Formica, including all the interior furnishings down to the dinner plates. It was given as a prize at the end of the Fair.

One could walk for many miles within a day. Some days it was so crowded that hordes of people were everywhere and getting into exhibits meant extremely long lines. Other days fewer people attended, and you had the entire fairgrounds to yourself, quiet and peaceful. Both were exciting and engaging in their own way.

I think my mother enjoyed the Fair as much as I did because we went so many times, and my dad would join when he could. We had innumerable experiences and met many people along the way. And we tried different foods and cuisines, especially from the international exhibitors. My favorite was the smallest restaurant at the Fair; it literally was a tiny building with no more than six tables representing Luxembourg. Once when eating at Denmark's pavilion we struck up a conversation with a sole diner next to us, a delightful middle-aged woman. She wanted to know if my mother was Danish, fair skinned and blond; but my mother just said she was of Baltic origin, without identifying Lithuania, which I guess sufficed to draw a conclusion of similarity. Another time we ate at the Korean Pavilion with my mother's cousin, Helen, and it seemed very exotic. The servers wore traditional Korean garb. There were many meals at other pavilions that followed.

Another favorite place to eat was the Wisconsin Pavilion with Tad's Steak House, a chain which still survives in San Francisco today. It was a hearty steak dinner with a large baked potato for a dollar and forty-nine cents. The pavilion also had an exhibit of the world's largest cheese. At the time I had no idea that someday I would end up living in Wisconsin. The pavilion was designed with a quasi-Frank Lloyd Wright modernism. A favorite watering hole of ours was the Lowenbrau Beer Pavilion, only second to Schaefer Brewing. At Lowenbrau buxomly 'Fräuleins' delivered large glass steins of beer, carrying several at a time. It was root beer for me, all in an outdoor German beer garden setting. I later read than many of the 'Fräuleins' were brought specifically from Bavaria to be the servers, and many from aristocratic homes. Years later another Bavarian '*Fräulein*' would be my German language teacher in High School, Baroness Herta von Schmaedel. My German roots were never far.

At each visit exploring The Fair was totally fun and exciting. There always seemed to be something new, especially since the exhibits tended to have a variety of programs and changing shows. My mother allowed me to roam the Fair alone for specific time frames with an agreement to meet up at a specified time and place. It gave me great freedom to discover on my own, and we always met up on time. I felt perfectly safe as I was riding the New York subways by myself at that point, since age nine. Going to Manhattan to shop, or to my music lesson in Hollis, Queens, a three-train transfer of nearly forty minutes, did not seem odd, unusual, or outlandish as I saw many kids my age doing the same, especially to get to school.

I will admit the religious pavilions confused me as they were all purporting their own version of faith and doctrine, somewhat differing from my Roman Catholic schooling and upbringing. Yet, with a Protestant father I knew differences existed. Of course, the Vatican was the most familiar to me, with the Pieta statue brought from Rome. There was a Protestant and Orthodox Pavilion that was a compilation of several denominations that I found interesting. The strangest to me were the Mormons. I could not comprehend what Joseph Smith and his enlightenment derived from a visiting spirit in upper New York State was all about, and I was not about to ask a priest or nun back at St. Patrick's about it, or my parents for that matter. I found it hard to justify and just ignored it in lieu of trying to figure it out.

The other oddity to me was the Christian Science Pavilion. The people there were the friendliest of any religious pavilion, and really enjoyed that kids, including my cousins and I, liked visiting it. It was a very welcoming environment and the exhibit there was quite striking. There was a large table with a bowl and an inset that had a shiny stone at the base of the inset. A person stood nearby encouraging visitors to pick up the stone. When you reached in the stone was not there, just the image of one, like a hologram. I'm not sure what it was intended to portray, and they never explained it, other than it had something to do with the mystery of 'science'.

The Ford and GM pavilions were imposing and enormous. Both had exhibit rides that were fun. Ford had a conveyor of new cars where you hopped into one on the 'Magic Skyway', and the car whisked you through a glass tube on the exterior of the building, and then through an exhibit within. GM had 'Futurama' which was a conveyor of grouped seats that took you by exhibits of a future world, from new and innovative cities to living under water or on another planet. When exiting the ride, they gave you a pin to wear that stated, 'I Have Seen the Future'. They also exhibited the cars they produced in foreign countries. This was a time when no one owned a car for more than two to three years.

The New York City Pavilion, a leftover building from the 1939 Fair, had a wonderful scale model of New York City with every building on it. It is the world's largest architectural model and still exists at the Queens Museum of Art in the same location. It is built to a scale of 1:1200 and occupies nearly 9,400 square feet of space. The claim is that every building in each of the five New York City boroughs is included, whether one story or one hundred. The Empire State Building is approximately twelve inches tall on it. During the Fair a group, up to four, would get into a 'car' mimicking a helicopter that moved around the model as if flying over the City, with a voice description in the background. The car circumvented the entire model. All of this was done indoors in a giant open room, and apparently the model was maintained and updated up through the 1990s. I recall how people with special sponge like shoes would walk over the model to make changes.

There were some multiple exhibits too. The Brass Rail restaurants had cloud like balloon structures that projected high in the air, looked like marshmallows piled on top of each other, and were interspersed around the fairgrounds. Also, 'pods' existed in several places that resembled little spherical white rooms faced with glass and a door, a modern-day phone booth. Within each was a bench where you could go in and make a phone call to anyone, anywhere. But the technological innovation was that it was a 'speaker phone' so for the first time everyone on the bench could be in the conversation at once! It was amazing at the time. The people you called were usually intrigued that everyone could participate on one line.

Along with that, Bell Telephone had a large 'floating' contemporary building on large pilasters with a fascinating series of exhibits that began with a conveyor ride that moved you past a series of telephone technology displays while sitting in a comfortable chair with high sides so you could not see anyone else. After the ride there were more exhibits, and the most fascinating was one where you went with a companion to speak on the 'visual phone'. You were placed in one room while your companion was placed in another. On a shelf in front of you was a TV screen. When the call was placed you could see and hear your companion in the other room while he or she could see and hear you. At the time it was very revolutionary. Phones throughout The Fair introduced push button technology, no longer a circular dialer.

People-moving conveyors were a big thing at the Fair. It kept people from standing and holding up those behind, yet also provided comfort from not walking long distances while instead enjoying the exhibit. Evolving technology was a definite feature of the Fair and Walt Disney was at the forefront of it. He created some of the most imaginative exhibits on display, many including 'animatronics', a form of robotics. The first was a life size figure of Abraham Lincoln for the Illinois Pavilion. Built as a fully completed human audio-animatronic figure it looked exactly as Lincoln did in the 1860s. A visitor to the Pavilion went into a large auditorium where the stage curtain opened to show Lincoln sitting before you in a chair on stage. Suddenly he stood and began to speak while looking around the room. His movements appeared authentic, and he gave a speech, the Gettysburg Address, to the audience. It was somewhat eerie in the realness of it.

Disney did many other animatronic exhibits, probably the most well-known was *It's a Small World*, for Pepsi Cola. A highly popular pavilion you were taken by boat through a series of linked buildings housing several child-like dolls in native costumes from around the world who sang in various languages while also moving and dancing. The exhibit was later moved to Disney World in Orlando after the Fair closed and another companion exists in Anaheim, California at Disneyland. It is truly a 'feel good' experience giving one hope that the world is indeed a good place where we all can co-exist, get along and appreciate each other... 'It's a world of laughter, a world of cheer...', as was the theme song.

The other well-known Disney animatronic exhibit was for General Electric, the 'Carousel of Progress'. An audience sat in a revolving theater that moved and stopped at intervals. At each stop there was a stage set of a period of the twentieth century within the home of a typical American family of the time. It went from the early part of the twentieth century to modern day while showcasing electrical and technological developments from each era. The theme song, 'There's a Great Big Beautiful Tomorrow' began and ended each sequence. This exhibit also moved to the Disney theme park after the Fair ended.

DuPont had an exhibit called the 'Wonderful World of Chemistry' with a magic show, and Johnson Wax had an interesting Pavilion raised off the ground within a futuristic large open canopy. An auditorium within it showed a movie that was quite dynamic and exciting. There was a mammoth projection screen that enveloped you. The large and realistic scenes in the movie compelled the participants to move and shift in the seats in unison with the movement of the scenes, for example a car race around a track where everyone in the audience shifted to the twists and turns of the race.

Coca Cola had a Pavilion with various scenes from places around the world that one wandered through as if you were there. One was a depiction of a woman with a Coke while sitting near the Taj Mahal in India. At the Traveler's Insurance's Pavilion, you walked in timed sequence from exhibit to exhibit and saw scenes through the history of mankind, called the 'The Ascent of Man'. Seeing everything from Prehistoric time to the Black Plague, to more modern times, you traveled the centuries with an audio that gave you a story behind each scene. The Festival of Gas exhibited the amazing qualities of the fuel source, and you could radiate a dime into a plastic keepsake.

The international pavilions were the most interesting to me because it saturated me with places I longed to know about and hoped to visit one day, from Spain, Japan, Austria, The Philippines, Sweden, Africa which was one exhibit with several countries represented, Sudan, Israel, Jordan, Morocco, Greece, Malaysia, as a sampling. The Belgian Village was perhaps my favorite, although they charged extra admission for entry. It was an actual recreation of an historic village, and due to delays didn't open in time for Fair's first few weeks. The famous Belgian, aka 'Bel-Gem', Waffles were a special part of the visit, a large waffle topped with whipped cream and strawberries. The city of Berlin, although divided at the time, was also represented in a small pavilion.

The Swiss Skyride was an open-air gondola ride, comparable to many amusement parks, that took you across the length of the Fairgrounds, also for an additional admission price.

The US state pavilions were a mish mash of styles and sizes, from New Jersey to Montana to a quasi 'Bourbon Street' for Louisiana. Some were more commercial enterprises than others. Other than Lincoln at the Illinois Pavilion nothing stood out as memorable for me. Florida had a pavilion with the scent of oranges in the Amusement area that included a walkway over the water, mimicking the islands of the Keys.

The Better Living Pavilion had 'Elsie the Cow', a real cow that just stared at the fairgoers. How she got in and out of the pavilion was a mystery, or if she just stayed there. Equitable

Life Insurance had a larger-than-life digital screen showing the growing US population in numbers. General Cigar had a giant puff of smoke shot into the sky. The Electric Power and Light exhibit had a powerful ray of light emitted upward after dark. Westinghouse had a time capsule they placed in the ground at the end of the Fair. People could sign their names in a guest book placed in the capsule along with various items from the era. It was buried next to a capsule from the 1939-40 World's Fair, both made to be opened in five thousand years.

In one of the lakes flanking the Fair, in the Amusement area, there was a place to ride in a newly invented 'automobile', the 'Amphicar'. First manufactured in the early part of the 1960s they were produced in West Germany and production didn't last for long. It was a car that also could glide in the water like a boat. It had propellors at the rear that activated when it hit the surface of the water. People were stunned to see these cars driving directly into the lake and yet moving steadily across the water without sinking. They often had convertible tops to enjoy the ride more. Years later a neighbor of ours in Connecticut owned a white one they called the 'Polywog'. I got to paint the license number and name on the side of it.

There were a lot of souvenirs to purchase throughout the fairgrounds, and much more free stuff handed out everywhere, including brochures, pins, and memorabilia. Each exhibit had a gift shop, although somewhat less in the corporate exhibits.

Just walking around was enjoyable and especially watching the people attending. At the end of every evening, before The Fair closed for the day, the largest fountain, known as the 'Pool of Industry', had a sound and light show with fireworks.

At the end of the second year, 1965, The Fair had

approximately fifty-one million visitors. It's best to put that in perspective by knowing that most major cities, for example Mexico City and New York, have around eight million, so a lot of people visited this World's Fair.

The final closing of the Fair was sad and not without issues. In the last days of the Fair people trampled the green spaces while also pulling out plants and flowers to take home with them. Exhibits began to be dismantled and after the admission gates closed for good the buildings began to be demolished. In my scrapbook I had newspaper images of the scrap metal and remains of the buildings I knew so well.

A small number of buildings did survive. The New York City and New York State pavilions were a couple that have lasted past The Fair's closure. The fairgrounds were returned to a public park after The Fair closed, yet it became underutilized and unkept over time. My boyhood friends from Astoria and I would often take the subway out to play baseball there as they had several playing fields as part of the newly created park. Whenever we walked to the baseball diamond of choice, I would look at the open barren areas recalling where each pavilion once stood. Shea Stadium remained, and I continued going to innumerable ball games there over the following years, up until 1968 when we moved to Connecticut. The subsequent year the Mets won the World's Series which I missed and lamented over, having been such a loyal fan.

When at Shea Stadium I'd always eat knishes, a potato filled dumpling. They were delicious! After night games my friends and I walked together from the subway station in Astoria and then would run to our respective houses when we split apart to be safe and avoid any street gangs.

After the Fair closed a new excitement built over the creating of a new Fair, Expo 67 in Montreal. Missing our days at The New York World's Fair my mother was determined that we would go to Expo 67. Macy's had a scale model of it, just like before, and that's where we got all the information needed to plan a visit.

We went in the summer of 1967 and that Fair was indeed a sanctioned Exposition. The exhibits were just as elaborate as New York's, some even more so. France and Great Britain exhibited, as did the Soviet Union and Cuba, quite the thing for Americans to see during the Cold War. The Soviet Pavilion was a stone's throw across a river from the US Pavilion, a geodesic dome designed by Buckminster Fuller. The Soviets draped their windows on the side facing the US Pavilion so no one could see it from their pavilion.

Another noteworthy exhibit was Habitat 67 designed by the Architect, Moshe Safdie. An apartment building of pods made from prefabricate components it was interesting, yet I found it lacking in comfort and privacy. Windows and patios often looked at another apartment's windows or patios. The geometric form, however, was certainly inventive. The French Canadians were not very welcoming of non-French speaking Americans, and we had some very funny experiences when language became a barrier. This was before I studied French in High School some years later. In one deli where we attempted to buy lunch the proprietor refused to acknowledge understanding what we meant by a 'sandwich'.

There was a US policy that Americans returning from Expo 67 were not allowed to bring into the US any Soviet or Cuban products or souvenirs, especially Cuban cigars. Border patrol was ruthless about it at the time, yet we had nothing to declare upon our return by car.

There's no doubt that the New York World's Fair had an enormous impact on my youth and my desire to learn about the world. It was one of the most influential events of my early life and set in place my desire to see and experience all I could in the years hence.

CHAPTER 11

North/South/East/West

Americans are a nomadic people. Unlike other parts of the world where people stay in their birthplace community for generations Americans tend to move often. This might be due to the upward mobility aspirations of life in the United States; yet relocating just seems to be a part of the American mindset.

I've had the distinction of living in four geographic regions of this country, the Northeast, the South, the Midwest, and the West. All very different and unique in their own way, each one of these places contributed to my growth, maturity, and identity as a person. My experiences from each are interesting to compare, and perhaps even confirm some stereotypes. I should clarify that I have never lived in a truly rural area; perhaps Connecticut being the closest, however, it is more suburban in character in its proximity to New York City.

New York City, where I was born, and lived until age thirteen, is both sophisticated and gritty. I was exposed broadly to the world, and it is where I learned survival skills, independence, and caution. It is a place that boldly evolves and grows, and a place that can either absorb and stimy you or catapult you forward. Anyone can easily get lost, stagnate; or thrive. In my youth I knew about the problem of drugs, the Mafia, and crime. Yet I had exceptional parents who transparently taught me to understand it, and how to steer clear of it. All of this is layered with a societal pecking order and a distinct economic hierarchy, perhaps none higher in the world.

The density of New York, especially in Manhattan, is overwhelming. Growing up there it didn't seem unusual to me. In the other boroughs the density diminishes, yet it is an enormous city with millions of people packed into small areas.

Moving to Fairfield County, Connecticut in 1968 at age thirteen was an entirely different world, sophisticated 'country' life. The land of gentlemen farmers and bucolic living it is far more economically uniform and socially isolated. It is not diverse with mainly residential towns of white, Christian people. I knew of only one Jewish family, and they lived in the next town. There were no Hispanic or African Americans. It was primarily made up of people in higher income levels in the areas of commerce, finance, and a smattering of accomplished artists. I learned to conform, excel, and appreciate the natural surroundings. I left it for college at age eighteen in 1972 and returned regularly until 1980 when I moved to the Midwest.

What was most notable about New Fairfield, where we lived, was the total lack of awareness of world events, especially those occurring in the pivotal year, 1968. Assassinations, Vietnam, riots, the Soviets invading Prague. It just seemed like it was 'elsewhere' and didn't much impact the tranquility of the place, or the general concern of the residents.

Living in the South, New Orleans, during my college years from 1972 to 1977 was uniquely different an experience for me, and most foreign. It taught me further independence and how to adapt to varied situations unaccustomed to me. The culture also made a 'gentleman' out of me, for Southern grace and cultural adherence to norms was important; yes, even in decadent New Orleans. It is a place, however, where the social hierarchy is also extreme. Rich and poor predominate in a checkerboarded city layout. A middle class does exist but pushed way out to the outskirts of town in places like Metairie, New Orleans East, and pockets across Lake Pontchartrain and the Mississippi River. I termed the rich natives here, the 'Brahman' class. You would be hard pressed to meet or socialize with any, much less see the inside of their auspicious clubs. Penetrating their stratified lives is harder than in New York.

There was a period from 1977 until 1980, when I was twenty-two to twenty-five years old, when I returned to live in New York City, first in the Upper East Side of Manhattan and then Queens as a working adult. It was my wish to return to New York and live there as an adult, and since my parents were still in Connecticut it made sense to do it then.

I was married in Connecticut in 1978 while living in New York and spending time in each place. In 1980 we moved to the Midwest, Madison, Wisconsin, for my wife to pursue a doctoral degree in psychology. The Midwest turned out to be an entirely different place than I expected, and much different from any prior experience I had to that point. I gained endurance and stamina for one thing, for the weather alone. I also learned about developing 'backbone', integrity, and something about 'veneer'. In veneer I mean that things aren't as they always seem once you dig deeper into them. It is good to scratch beyond the surface of any experience to find the underlying source and not just accept it for what it seems.

I lived in Madison until 1986 when I moved to Des Moines, Iowa and lived there until 1989. My New York friends made fun of me for being like a character from the TV show *Green*

Acres moving from the comforts of New York to the wilds of the Midwest. Madison was a strange place, mainly for its blend of politics, government, and education with the University of Wisconsin such a big part of it.

In 1989 I moved to another geographic destination, San Francisco in the West! When I arrived, the high-tech industry boom made it seem like the second Gold Rush had arrived. The amount of opportunity was amazing. And unlike New York, the East Coast, and the South you did not need a family name and societal connections to prosper. It was a wide-open world for everyone. Most often people have recently arrived from other places, and finding true natives is rare. It is also an open and welcoming place, at least in the Bay Area. I learned to thrive, to take former talents and make them flourish. It made me entrepreneurial. Perhaps age and maturity helped that along as I was thirty-four years old when I arrived. What I found was a place where people created their own families, lacked judgement, and cared about each other and the environment.

So, let me now dive deeper into each of these specific geographic regions and give you examples of each.

The East

New York being one of the world's largest cities, the US financial capital, the home of the United Nations, and a world-renowned cultural hub is considered by many to be the apex of the country. Some, especially New Yorkers, see it as the capital of the world. It is dynamic, fast paced and has a definite inescapable energy. Millions of people have come to New York over the centuries as immigrants. Consecutive waves of newcomers gave the city its vibrancy. Whether through Ellis Island, or not, nearly everyone is from somewhere else, yet the longer your family stays the stronger the foothold in society. If you ever want to get an impression of the immigrant experience, go to the Tenement Museum on the lower East Side as it is very revealing of that life.

The early years of my youth were a unique blend of city life and going frequently, at least once a week for years, to my cousins' home in Great Neck, a town in Nassau County, Long Island, where my mother grew up. The house and property were originally owned by my grandparents. Going from one place to the other is like day and night. Astoria with its hard edges, densely packed buildings and paved surfaces is so vastly different from Great Neck with its stately lawns and broadly spaced properties and estates. I would describe Great Neck to my Astoria friends, and they thought I made it up. They could not imagine such a place existed. Many had never been out of the neighborhood.

Although most of my time in New York was during my childhood and youth I will dwell now on my life as an adult in New York in the late 1970s and the influences it had on me then.

It is interesting how many well-known people or celebrities you can see on any given day in New York City, walking down the street like anyone else. Rarely are they bothered or approached by others. It is so common for New Yorkers to see a well-known person that it is usually just ignored. The celebrities might wear sunglasses or a hat as disguise, but it really doesn't matter. They are just other New Yorkers. Those folks have some peace to lead the same lives as everyone else. During the time I lived in Manhattan, between 1977 and 1978, I saw Andy Warhol (often with a young man in tow), David and Julie Nixon Eisenhower (on East 86th Street near their home), David Frost (standing outside the Plaza Hotel), and Bella Abzug (a local politician of the day who greeted and shook my hand when coming out of a subway station), plus others. At the architectural firm where I worked on West 57th St. there was a man who was an actor in Andy Warhol's movies, yet never bragged and rarely discussed it.

The city is full of distinctive neighborhoods and an array of everything anyone could ever want or need. While living there I discovered entire districts devoted to specific products- the garment district, the potted plant district, the diamond district, along with the better known financial and warehouse districts.

My wife and I had experienced the diamond district first-hand as consumers as that is where we acquired her engagement ring. Studying up on diamonds we did our best to learn what one should know before going to a district like that, especially when being offered discounted merchandise. We studied and read the specifics on clarity and color; and decided to test our knowledge in Macy's jewelry department before heading to the diamond district. Unfortunately, we failed miserably as we carefully examined diamond rings, noting the differences in quality and slight imperfections, only to find out they were all artificial diamonds, zirconia. Nonetheless we headed confidently to the diamond district. The district is one street with diamond merchandizers, just off Fifth Avenue in the East 40s, primarily owned and operated by Orthodox Jews. We walked into one discount center and were accosted by dozens of diamond dealers screaming and hawking at us to come to their counter. We found one vendor we felt somewhat comfortable dealing with and found a beautiful diamond ring right away. It fit perfectly on her finger, so we felt it was good. The vendor insisted we have it appraised and called a courier to walk us down the block to an appraiser, a relative perhaps. He appraised the diamond above purchase price. We bought the ring, and it turned out to be a New York experience not to be missed. The ring turned out to be a very good value.

A friend of mine at work who was about the same age and level of experience, Ray, became a very good friend. We spent many a lunch hour doing fun things together. One day we decided to go look at a new condo building recently built off Park Avenue, on East 57th, 'The Galleria'. At fifty-four stories high it was the height of luxury. Stewart Mott, the head of General Motors, purchased the top floors where he created vegetable gardens as an education spot for school kids. Ray and I decided to make an appointment to look at condos under the guise of being two out-of-town businessmen who needed a place in 'The City', a type of pied-a-terre. It was the only way we'd get to see the inside. One lunch break, in our finest suits, we walked there and waited in the plush marketing office for our appointed time. Running a bit late the marketing agent, a woman, came along with a very distinguished looking, yet somewhat high strung, man who left in a hurry after expressing his appreciation. She seemed totally out of sorts and fixated on him, uncharacteristic of the New York anonymity I described earlier. After gaining her composure she greeted us and said, 'Do you know who that was?' We did not. She informed us it was Prince Vittorio Emanuele of Italy, interested in one of the penthouses. Then she exclaimed, 'He could be YOUR neighbor!' We saw a couple of condos, acted like two guys interested in a condo, and left with a brochure never to return.

There was one remarkable clothing store on East 57th Street, an Italian designer named Fiorucci, that was a must stop for an occasional lunch break. It had high energy, loud throbbing music, and they would hand you an espresso in a cup and saucer the minute you walked through the door. It was fun to browse, and people watch in lieu of buying anything. Retail in the late 1970s was at the cutting edge of chic, and especially shock value. Henri Bendel, a luxury purveyor of women's clothing, started to have extremely controversial window displays with sadomasochistic elements, including some naked manikins. It did compel everyone to walk by and look. Fifth Avenue was the place to shop, from B. Altman & Co. on 34th St. up to Saks Fifth Avenue, Best & Co., Lord & Taylor, Bonwit Teller, Tiffany's, and Bergdorf Goodman in the 50s. So many great stores existed in this stretch of Fifth Avenue. I especially liked going into Steuben Glassware to see their magnificent crystal artwork pieces on display. Cartier Jewelers felt like a hushed tomb of ornate detail within an exquisite townhouse. Many of these places are long gone, yet Tiffany's, Bergdorf and Cartier still exist.

In the 1960s I had an interesting exchange with a salesperson at Tiffany's. Going there to buy a tie tack I asked if they had anything in silver, as I preferred that to gold. The salesperson looked shocked at such a question, perhaps assuming I was too young to know better. I was told quite empathically that Tiffany's does not sell silver jewelry and never would, as it was inferior. It was suggested I go somewhere else, perhaps Georg Jensen, a Danish silversmith and jeweler down the street. I did go elsewhere and found something, but ironically not many years later Tiffany did indeed sell silver jewelry.

Along the storied street of retail, Fifth Avenue, stands two remarkable non-retail edifices. First and foremost is the New York Public Library between East 40th and 42nd Streets. A Beaux Arts monolith of stone, marble, and carved statuary it is truly a tribute to civic design set back from the street in a park like setting. Second to it is St. Patrick's Cathedral located a few blocks north of the library, and on the opposite side of Fifth Avenue. It stands in contrast to the library as a stunning Gothic building of stone that is far lighter and lacier, with spires jutting prominently high above the street. Across the street from it is the beautifully planned and designed Rockefeller Center complex.

I was discouraged from wearing 'blue jeans' growing up as my mother did not find them appropriate for a young man. So up until my college days I primarily wore khakis, chinos, and other types of dressier pants, and uniforms to school. Designer jeans came on the scene in the late 1970s, and Calvin Klein was one of the first to offer them. I decided to buy a pair and headed off to Saks Fifth Avenue, one of the first places to make them available. What I did not realize is that those early designer jeans were fitted by a store tailor. Fortunately, I was twenty-two years old and in-shape, so the jeans fit my physique like a glove. The tailor was very pleased with the fit while commenting that they were not meant for everyone, as he tactlessly pointed to an overweight older man exiting the fitting room after trying on a pair. Afterwards, at the elevators, there were five men standing closely and gossiping. What was so striking was that each wore a massive fur coat, of different fur on each. These coats resembled the racoon coats of the 1920s, but in the 1970s these fur coats were the rage again and far better quality. It was humorous as all you could see was fur with heads sticking out, yet that was similarly the fashion of the day.

Exploring Manhattan, and seeking out free activities, was effortless. There was always something to do, and I enjoyed doing it alone as well as with friends. One day I saw a notice that the old Commodore Hotel on East 42nd Street, next to Grand Central Station, was closed to be renovated. This was Donald Trump's launch into Manhattan real estate as he was brokering the deal. The furnishings went on sale, and anyone could buy pieces. Out of curiosity for an unusual outing, I went. I got there on a very early Saturday morning when it had just opened, and I was the only person there besides the sales staff. You could wander anywhere in the hotel as all the furniture remained in the rooms. It was a little creepy and reminiscent of the book and movie, *The Shining*. Eventually I got to the Presidential Suite which was a large hodgepodge of rooms. It was quite amazing to see, even though a bit on the seedy side by that point. I did not end up buying anything, but it was a good day out, nonetheless.

Donald Trump also came to own The Plaza Hotel at Fifth Avenue and 59th Street. A fixture of society and elegance for decades, it had its ups and downs, including during Trump's ownership. The grand lobby was always impressive to walk through, as was High Tea in the Palm Court. On my wedding night before heading for a honeymoon in Paris I stayed in a corner suite with a round turreted sitting area and several walk-in closets intended for trunks in the days those were commonly used for travel. I had eaten several times in the

Edwardian Room, a posh dark wood dining room, that included a band for dancing during dinner. During the 1960s the Edwardian Room was transformed and 'updated' to become the 'Green Tulip', a terrible abomination in which I once had a burger, but fortunately later returned to its original grandeur. Unfortunately, the Edwardian Room no longer exists as the Plaza has been bastardized again, now with a food court in the basement!

Another New York hotel that I truly loved was The Pierre on Fifth Avenue and E. 61st Street, just slightly north of The Plaza. Staying on the thirty-second floor the view to the Upper East Side and Central Park is simply breathtaking. It was so spectacular that I ordered room service for dinner just so I could sit by one of the huge windows and gaze out at the view while I ate. The elevator attendants wore white gloves, and guests got a real key for the room, no card, as they maintained an 'Old World' style ambiance. There were just four guest rooms on each of the upper floors, and some of the floors below were for permanent residents. I stayed there at a particularly interesting time as the United Nations was in session and many dignitaries stayed there. One day during my stay it was also opening night at the Metropolitan Opera. I couldn't have even begun to imagine the magnitude of the jewels worn by some of the permanent residents taking the elevator as they headed out to that event.

The 1970s were a volatile time in New York. It was edging bankruptcy and quickly deteriorating, although it did not seem so bad at the time. Large corporations and the middle class were fleeing to the suburbs of New Jersey, Westchester, and Connecticut. Manhattan, known as 'the city' to anyone from another borough, was getting gritty and dangerous. Real estate prices dropped significantly, and Times Square became unsafe while resembling a giant emporium for sex. The Mafia was strong amplifying the crime. When I worked on East 40th, Bryant Park was across the street and a drug infested jungle. I observed many drug transactions by office workers as I'd walk through the park on a lunch break. The most bizarre thing I experienced was seeing an apparently homeless middle-aged woman sitting outside a not yet open café on Central Park South early one morning shoving a large roll of money into her vagina, one leg up on the café's table. Trust me, I cannot imagine or make these things up.

In the late 1970s, and before Rudy Giuliani cleaned up the city, the entire Theater District was particularly seedy. I recall my wife and I leaving a theater performance and running to the subway station to avoid being mugged. When we passed close to a trash heap at the curb a cardboard box began to rustle and move erratically. It frightened us and we jumped away, only to realize a homeless person was under the cardboard. You never knew what to expect. Giuliani eventually did clean up the area and some said it looked like Disneyland, very antiseptic and too clean, lamenting the loss of the grittiness. Finding my first apartment in Manhattan when I graduated from college in 1977 was an accomplishment unto itself. Apartments were in high demand and hard to find. It necessitated going through a realtor, and it typically meant paying twelve percent of a year's rent in commission. Apartment seekers waited in line late on Saturday night for the *New York Times* to first come out to check the apartment listings. It was very competitive.

I looked at several over a couple of weekends with my parents along as I did not have a credit rating and they would have to co-sign a lease. They were aghast at the hovels we looked at in many rundown buildings, for what I was willing to pay. One place had an enormous gap at the top of the entry door, and the apartment was filthy. Quite a few people were giving the place a serious look and a very young woman, my age or so, nabbed it right away. My mother just raised her eyebrow in disbelief. Many of the apartments I looked at had a 'tub in kitchen', a bathtub, that was quite common in 'flat' type apartments. Many had been tenements in years gone by.

Finally, I came across a nice studio apartment on East 82nd Street and we literally had to run to the real estate office to secure it. It was a cozy little place in a five-story walk-up yet very convenient and in a nice neighborhood. I later learned that my Great-Grandparents, the Bruttings, had lived on the same block, the German area of Yorkville. The floor was sloped, and it had a tiny kitchen, but it sufficed for my needs.

A year or so later when my wife-to-be and I were searching out another apartment the conditions in finding a place hadn't changed much. We saw apartments without a window in the bedroom, and others equally sub-standard. One on Park Avenue amazed us with its quality and elegance until we were leaving and realized we had not seen a bathroom. When going back we found the toilet was in a two-step up closet in the kitchen, the kitchen sink being the only sink, and that ubiquitous 'tub in kitchen' covered by a piece of plywood creating a kitchen counter. It taught us not to get too enamored too quickly. One evening during that time of searching I stopped by a small, insignificant family run real estate office with a charming Jewish couple sitting behind desks with piles of clutter. The woman took my hand and advised me to go look in

Queens where I would have, 'a chance of finding a decent apartment for my new bride', which I did, and it worked. We found a lovely place in Forest Hills.

I have a good friend who I had met during college while vacationing in Ft. Lauderdale, Mary Ruth. She moved concurrent to mine in Manhattan and we had many fabulous times and adventures together. Her furnished apartment, a 'co-op', was at the corner of Fifth Avenue and 8th Street. It was fabulous, with lots of charm and character. She was renting from the couple who owned it. The doorman, who was also the elevator operator, always seemed suspicious of me. Whenever I came to visit, he had a multitude of questions for me; what work I did, how did I know Mary, and on and on. It seemed like he was hired as a watchdog for Mary. I always went prepared for an interrogation. I found out decades later that the apartment was owned by the actors, Jessica Tandy and Hugh Cronin.

Another friend, Bob, was someone I met at the firm where I first worked. He was a lot of fun and we did many things together after work. I remember fondly that we saw the cult movie classic *Saturday Night Fever* together when it first premiered at the Playboy Theater across from the Plaza hotel. His parents had a penthouse in the East 60s with this phenomenal wrap around patio. They also had a second home in the town where my parents lived in Connecticut, New Fairfield, so I was able to see him there too. He told me a truly funny story about his grandfather who lived in a very posh East End Avenue co-op high-rise. His grandfather became increasingly interested in doing fun things later in life, so he took to rolling toilet paper from his patio down the side of the co-op building. The doorman had to come up and tell him to not do that, but he continued the activity anyway. Every time I heard the story it made me roar with laughter imagining it.

There was an annual event in Central Park, at the Sheep Meadow, a giant open-air field, where The New York Philharmonic gave free concerts during the summer. My all-time favorite was when they did the *1812 Overture* by Tchaikovsky. Sitting on a blanket at dusk with a vast number of strangers doing the same, surrounded by nature, tall buildings flanking the park, the music just resonates in a pure and beautiful way. It is powerful. At the most dramatic part of the Overture church bells chime wildly with canons firing in the distance, as well as fireworks raining down over the crowd. It's always wild with enthusiasm, and the crowd roars with delight. First started by the Boston Pops in the early 1970s it is not to be missed should you ever hear of a planned performance.

One evening I attended a performance of the Count Basie Orchestra at the Brooklyn Academy of Music anticipating some great jazz. It turned out to be far livelier than I expected as the audience stood on their seats swaying, yelling, and clapping with the music. It was quite a loud and very raucous event, and my hearing was impaired for some days thereafter.

Probably one of the most memorable performances I saw was the opera, *Tosca*, at the Metropolitan Opera around 1979. Having box seats afforded a fantastic view and it was one of those wonderful glittering evenings characterized by the twinkling crystal chandeliers lifting-up to the ceiling. The opera began in full force and a very rotund, imposing man came out on the stage about to sing. The audience went wild, standing and applauding vigorously. Admittedly naive I had no idea what the hype was about but immediately learned it was Luciano Pavarotti in the lead role. His voice was unmistakably incredible.

It was also the time of Studio 54, the infamous disco, and partying late into the night. One could throw away lots of money in a night out.

My apartment building on the Upper East Side was owned by 'Iran Importing' which turned out to be the government of Iran before the revolution. As that revolution unfolded in 1978, I left my office one early evening and when turning the corner from West 57th onto 6th Ave. there was a huge brigade of white-hooded protestors, shoulder to shoulder, building to building, by the hundreds, coming toward me. I immediately went in the other direction recognizing their protesting the revolution.

There were also the 'Blue People', or Process People, some sort of quasi-religious groupies/cult who only wore blue. They commonly chased anyone down the street until you engaged and talked with them while demanding a donation. They would nag and follow people for blocks. Whenever one spotted one of the 'Blue People' in the distance, you turned and walked away quickly.

Sometime in 1978 or '79 I attended the *Rocky Horror Picture Show* at a Greenwich Village theater, at midnight, where they celebrated the 1,000+ performance with live actors on stage performing in front of the movie. Props from scenes in the movie were used by the audience. Getting spray gunned with water and rice thrown at you was to be expected, as I did.

It was also a time of some frightful circumstances. 'Son of Sam' was terrorizing the city. A mass murderer he was randomly killing couples out on the town. Many died and the panic level got so intense that women dyed their hair blond so not to be one of the dark-haired women that he typically sought after to kill. Many just didn't go out. David Berkowitz, the killer, was eventually apprehended but it left a deep hole in the psyche of many New Yorkers. Berkowitz admitted to belonging to a Satanic cult and that only added to the weirdness of it all.

Living through two major power outages, 'blackouts', in New York, one in 1965 and another in 1977, when the city went entirely dark was surreal. The one in 1965 was regional and darkened the entire Northeast and part of Canada. The outages lasted for many hours, and the one in 1977 over a day. The nun who taught us at St. Patrick's School told us we should pray intently because the Russians could have taken us during the outage of November 1965. In 1977 people helped each other as much as possible to survive it as it was in the heat of summer, sharing items such as candles and handing out food if needed.

While living in Forest Hills, Queens in the late 1970s there was a major public transit strike. Everything came to a halt, and quite a mess ensued as millions of people could not get to work. The only way to get into Manhattan was to walk or go by car, but it was mandatory to have at least four people in the car. The first day I walked to work in midtown Manhattan, across the Queensboro 59th Street Bridge, just over nine miles. I ended up doing that twice; yet always hitching a ride back. The first time I walked across the Bridge I witnessed the most incredible thing, a woman walking in stiletto heels across the grating of the walkway, being every so careful not to have her heel fall into a hole! After the couple of times of walking, I took to waiting on Queens Boulevard for a ride as cars coming from Long Island would stop to pick up anyone just to get into the city. Private limousines were often the ones stopping the most. One ride I caught was packed with nearly eight people squeezed in tightly and a yappy dog sitting on the driver's lap. Another ride back home I was picked up by a Filipino family with a woman who was nine months pregnant. I hoped we would get across the Bridge without her going into labor; or giving birth. We did.

After a few days of hitching rides, we decided to ride out the strike with our family in Connecticut. Commuter trains were running from some of the outer suburbs, and it took less time, even though an hour away. I was even interviewed by the *New York Times* for a news article on my escape to the country. So, I traveled the commuter train back and forth for a couple of weeks until the transit strike ended, and we could move home again.

I also experienced several major blizzards, one in February 1978 was spectacular and paralyzed the entire city for a couple of days. Looking out of my apartment window on East 82nd Street I saw people cross country skiing down the middle of the street.

Something truly remarkable happened at Christmas time in the B. Altman department store on Fifth Avenue and 34th Street. On the first floor they had a large collection of both costume and high-end fine jewelry, as did many department stores. Having received my first holiday bonus of my career I decided to buy my fiancé a set of genuine sapphire earrings for Christmas; quite an expensive purchase for me at the time. At that time after paying my rent and expenses I usually had fifteen dollars spending money per month, approximately sixty dollars in today's value, so not a lot. I often sought out freebies for entertainment. I found the earrings in B. Altman's fine jewelry case and while purchasing them a well-dressed businessman came up to the counter near me, obviously inebriated. He said to the clerk he wanted to buy everything from one part of the counter to his far reach on the other end, approximately eight feet in counter length of high-end jewelry! Diamond bracelets, rings, brooches, earrings, and an array of very high-quality jeweled items. The clerk asked if he was sure about it, as it amounted to a hefty sum of money, and rather offered to show him individual pieces, to which he declined. He insisted it all be boxed up so he could take it with him. Handing his credit card to the clerk as she glanced at me, she gasped, and went off. She came back with a manager. The purchase had been approved and they began removing the items from the case. The clerk looked at me and said, 'Wow, I wonder what he did to his wife or mistress?' while handing me my small shopping bag with the sapphire earrings I bought. That's the type of thing that happens in New York.

Christmas in New York was a wonderland. All the stores had elaborate displays in the windows. The Rockefeller Center Christmas Tree was magical, every year. It was a fun place to wander around and take in the beauty of the season, and I watched it evolve over the twenty-plus years I lived there, seemingly becoming more elaborate with each passing holiday season.

And I contributed my own unique New York Christmas holiday story! It involved a Christmas tree.

In 1978 my wife and I lived in an apartment in Forest Hills, Queens. As it was our first Christmas after marrying, I thought it would be special to have a pine Christmas tree. I made it my quest to find one and surprise her. During lunch one day I walked down West 57th Street to 10th Avenue where people were selling cut trees on the sidewalk. I saw a batch that appealed to me and the family selling them looked needy, so I thought it a good place to purchase a tree. I searched among them and found a fabulous full pine tree, nine feet tall. I hadn't thought about getting a tree that large, but it's the first Christmas in a new apartment, so why not? I bought it.

As a child our family friend, Vince, would bring cut Christmas trees in the back of a truck to our house and line them up on the sidewalk for my mother and me to select one. It was his gift to us. I remembered the fresh smell of those trees in our house and longed for it again.

I carefully carried the one I bought on 10th Avenue back to the office and bundled and tied it up tightly, as best I could. Then it occurred to me that I had to find a way to bring it home! It was a considerable distance, thirteen miles, which I totally overlooked in my enthusiasm to get a tree. Our car was in Connecticut, and I doubted any taxi would transport it. Facing my dilemma our Marketing Director came by to admire the tree and I told her my problem. She gave me a suggestion to take it on the subway. Indicating that she occasionally carted large items, including works of art, on the subway, she gave me the low down on how to do it without being noticed by subway staff. It meant being quick and efficient, and totally under cover.

I decided to stay late at the office, into the evening, so that the commute crowd would be over; and left around nine in the evening. Arriving at the station I checked to see where the token booth attendant might be, and saw I had a clear run for it. Having my subway token handy I quickly tossed into the turnstile as I tucked the tree under my arm as best I could and walked rapidly down the subway stairs. Arriving on the platform I was greatly relieved that no one noticed. There were more people on the platform than I expected at that time of day, but it was the holiday season, so people were more than usual out and about. The first train pulled in and it was packed full of riders! I panicked. And then the harsh realization came upon me that it was a night when all the theaters were performing, and the museums and stores were open late too. That meant the crowds were still heavy, late into the evening. Not a good thing and poor planning on my part.

The second and third train rumbled in, and out, fully packed. I finally made up my mind to get on the next train regardless of the number of people on board. Certain enough it was crowded, so I took the tree like a catapult and shoved it between the riders and got on the train standing the tree upright. People on the train were stunned and some comments began coming my way. I expected that as New Yorkers there would be an infuriated outcry, or worse. Yet, after some grumbled mumbling nothing happened.

We pulled into the next station and when the doors opened a person on the platform shouted, 'OH MY GOSH, THERE'S A TREE ON THE TRAIN'. She could not get in. After everyone got used to the fact I was there and not doing anything more than standing with my tree a jovial atmosphere developed. By time the train was in the tunnel under the East River the passengers were singing Christmas carols in unison. It was simply amazing, and such a New York experience.

When I knew my stop was coming, I prepared myself to launch out with the tree when the doors opened. Fortunately, some passengers had exited by then, so it wasn't as crowded. We arrived, the doors opened, and I positioned myself to grab the tree and bolt out when I discovered the top of the tree was stuck in the ceiling air conditioning vent! I tugged and tugged some more, and it would not budge! In panic I did everything to yank it out before the doors shut. It would not release from the vent. A couple of people noticed me struggling and started helping me tug on it. Another passenger positioned himself in the doors so they wouldn't close. Finally, after a communal tug it dislodged sending some pine needles on the floor. I jumped off the train with the tree while thanking everyone. As I sighed relief, I saw people waving as the train pulled out.

I then walked the tree several blocks to the apartment. The doorman was totally amazed and complimented me on getting such a nice tree. I beamed when I finally got to my apartment. Luckily, the apartment had more than eight-foot-high ceilings, although I had not even thought of that in my enthusiasm to get a real pine tree. My wife thought I was crazy; but liked the tree!

One major observation I've made about New Yorkers was that their mindset changed after the horrific events of 9/11. Before then they were generally smug, arrogant, impersonal, kept to themselves, and not all that friendly or willing to meet new people.

When I moved to Manhattan this became very clear when I settled into my first apartment and another resident saw me bringing in furniture, abruptly said 'hello', and I never saw him again. In another example the man in the apartment below me, who I never met, died and no one knew it for over five days. I only found out because the police, at the request of his family who asked them to check on him, came to my apartment late one evening to use my window to get down the fire escape to break into his place. He had drunk himself to death. I realized soon after moving to Manhattan that with all the millions of people around me that I never once spoke to a person after I left work until I returned the next day, passing hundreds on my daily walk there and back. After 9/11, when I visited, people were friendly and outgoing. I was surprised when a couple spoke to me, a perfect stranger, while we waited for a light to change at a street corner. It was a refreshing difference from former times.

Living and growing up in New York City, and living there later in my adult working life, was indeed inspiring. It gave me a sense of culture, sophistication, adventure, and worldliness. All qualities I cherish today. I also witnessed the harsh side of life. Not unlike someone who grew up in Paris, London, or Tokyo the allure of a major urban center of commerce and culture has its benefits, as well as some disadvantages too. The downside being crime, extreme density and potential loss of identity should one not apply oneself.

I will not talk much of my time in Connecticut and there will be pieces and recollections about that elsewhere. Just think of it as picture postcard beautiful. Rolling hills and forests, lakes, windy roads, and the splendor of nature. So different from the steel and concrete mass of New York's profuse urbanity. We had a view from our house in Connecticut that looked out thirty miles over hilly, wooded countryside. Watching the seasons change had a particular allure. I will say that Christmas in New England is especially wonderful. Imagine putting yourself into a Currier and Ives scene. Snow, homesteads, roaring fireplaces, eggnog, candles in windows, wreaths, and church bells.

One of my favorite winter activities that I came to routinely enjoy in Connecticut was ice skating. I owned a few pairs of skates and enjoyed going to a rink, but more so out on a pond and skating an afternoon away. It's so refreshing and exhilarating. Sometimes a pond would be difficult as it might be lumpy and bumpy with uneven ice, and you had to be particularly aware of soft, melting areas which could be dangerous.

There is one thing I do want to describe at this point, an event that happened in the 1970s. It was the anniversary of the birth of the composer, Charles Ives, who was from Danbury, the adjoining town to where I lived. A large concert was planned in celebration of his birth, and Leonard Bernstein was the conductor. The state fairgrounds were jammed with concert-goers and Bernstein made a dramatic entrance by arriving in a helicopter. The concert of fabulous, all outdoors, and Ives' music penetrated the surrounding hillside.

Connecticut is a thriving hub of artists and creative people. My best friend from High School, Paul, and his family used to take me to Tanglewood for outdoor concerts in the Massachusetts Berkshire hills. It was always a pleasurable outing for the day. Once Leonard Bernstein was conducting there as well, and there was a special tent specifically for VIP guests. Paul and I wandered around the grounds and unexpectedly saw his father standing in the tent with a glass of champagne talking with Bernstein! We were totally stunned how he got in the tent, yet Paul's father looked very aristocratic and was always impeccably dressed. He was originally from Macedonia. We later asked how he got in, and he said he just walked in, while looking quite distinguished no one blinked an eye. At another concert we attended at Tanglewood the audience was totally awestruck when unexpectedly and totally unplanned Aaron Copeland came out on stage to conduct his wonderful piece, 'Appalachian Spring'.

The Berkshires in Massachusetts was an easy one-day pleasure drive from New Fairfield through the bucolic New England hills and historic towns of Northwest Connecticut. Tanglewood was the primary draw, along with Stockbridge and the white clapboard towns nearby. I dated a girl whose family loved coming to this area and often took me along, typically to Tanglewood too. They had a penchant for fine cuisine, and we would often stop on the way back for dinner at this country inn in Litchfield County that resembled an elegant English pub.

Her family also knew some notable families in the area where we lived that had contemporary houses designed by well-known architects, and she got me invites to see them. I appreciated it greatly and the owners often appreciated showing a budding young architect the designs.

Summer theater was popular too, and New Fairfield had Candlewood Theater where performances took place during the summer months. I saw Marlene Dietrich and the Danish concert pianist/comedian, Victor Borge, along with several plays being tested for Broadway. All of this added a certain flair to living in the country, although quite different from New York.

The South

In 1977 I trundled off to New Orleans and learned about living in the South. A woman I knew in New York, a native New Orleanian, said that I really did not live there, I was merely there on a 'sojourn'. Yes, it was during college, and yes, I usually spent holidays and summers elsewhere including back in New York and Connecticut, yet most of the year for five years was spent in New Orleans.

It is a refined and dignified city, with some debauchery, with elements of surprise at every turn. I often said that people are drawn to live there because of some force compelling them to do it. It has flair, in its jazz music, the culture, and the food. It can be both eclectic and stifling at the same time. As in most places a lot of one's experience happens around the circle of people you associate with over time, and in New Orleans groups come in many types and without much welcomed crossover. It has a deep heritage that residents take very seriously.

As an example, and this is true, I once was invited to a Sorority party at a private Garden District home. Although not in a Fraternity myself I nonetheless got invited to some of these events. I went to this party and nearly one hundred, or so, college age kids were in attendance. It was the home of one of the Sorority sisters from a prominent family. I had a good time, met the parents, and left as it was wrapping up. The next week I saw the girl who hosted the event and went to thank her, but she absolutely would not talk with me and turned away. I asked a friend of hers what had happened in that she wouldn't speak with me. Her friend told me she had been admonished by her father who was extremely angry that

I had been invited. It was the first time since the Civil War that a Yankee had been in their home, and he was not pleased! I would have never imagined, but I did remember saying to him that I was from Connecticut. I guess I should be honored for the accomplishment of breaking that barrier.

I have always maintained that New Orleans is a city of two places, the part that tourists visit and the part they do not. The part that they do not see is the more fascinating, and full of surprises. The beauty of some of the off the beaten paths of residential neighborhoods beyond the Garden District can be very enchanting. Often the oak trees tower above and span over the streets in a canopy, azaleas and other flowers blooming beneath. Near the Mississippi River you can often see ships gliding by, above you, as you are most likely standing below sea level behind a levee. In the 1970s walking up to the levee near Audubon Park, Uptown, you could observe many houses, shanty huts, built by squatters on stilts on the river side of the levee. They were not part of the city, nor had any city services. They paid no taxes and got by just fine with the wood plank walkways to the levee from their homes for access, connecting them to civilization.

My days in New Orleans were filled with exploring a new environment and culture. There was something different everywhere I looked. In my freshman year a group of guys decided to go find Cajuns and took me along. None of us had ever seen one. We had heard about them living in the country beyond New Orleans, and that was about it. So, we got in a car and drove out to 'Cajun Country' to find some. The bayous can be a daunting place and have a surreal quality about it, with tall cypress trees and endless water. We did not have a good map, so we just drove randomly seeking out our mission, to find Cajuns. At one point we drove down a remote uneven and roughly paved road and came to a large mound that we could not get the car over without potential damage. Wondering if it was purposely put there to keep people out, we decided to not chance it. We backed up and went a different way. Driving around another road we finally came to the same hump, realizing we were on the other side of it. We began laughing as we backed up and went a different way. Somewhere later in the day we spotted a station wagon that we suspected was full of Cajuns. How did we know that? Who knows, as we surely did not. All mere speculation but shows how crazy this endeavor turned out.

A couple of years later a professor of mine had an annual Easter celebration at his home in Lafayette, the heart of Cajun Country. A few of us decided to go and check it out, not knowing this was a major event for the area. About a mile or so away we found cars parked on both sides of the road. Getting closer to his house we found that all these folks were at the celebration. There were hundreds of people. We parked far out and walked back. There were people everywhere, and barbeques going in several locations, a lot of food and drink. There was a Cajun band, and it was wonderful… and yes, we were then among real Cajuns. It was fun and the atmosphere very congenial, full of energy, and everyone just enjoying themselves. This particular property was large and extended through the swamps, the bayou, too. A wood plank walkway had been constructed so you could walk above the swamp for quite a distance among the cypress trees and that was a real treat and a delight to experience.

Another Professor, Dr. Bernard Lehman, was a history buff and collected a bunch of us architectural students to go out to the Cajun cemeteries on All Saints Day, November 1. The day after Halloween the cemetery tombs where everyone is buried above ground due to the water table, are whitewashed and cleaned. Family members sit in the cemetery after dusk, light candles and tell stories of their departed relatives. It was fascinating to walk around, see it, and listen to the tales being spoken. Supposedly this is when voodoo rituals take place, so we were hoping for some chickens without their heads, blood dripping; but none of that happened. Years later I did witness a voodoo ritual in the French Quarter on Halloween. People in white garments danced and chanted, beating drums, to the direction of a voodoo 'queen' who sat amongst them. At one point she accepted babies who were blessed by rubbing beer on their limbs. All seemed very odd; but taken seriously.

One All Saints Day Ed and I visited St. Louis Cemetery No. 1 just beyond the French Quarter, which is a favored tourist attraction. The infamous Voodoo Queen, Marie Laveau, is buried there and her tomb is the main attraction. Customarily it is presumed that if you strike an 'x' on her tomb with a brick you will be spared curses. This isn't done so much anymore, but on this day Voodoo practitioners were hanging around and leaving coins on the tomb, another custom you see at various graves.

Years later Ed and I visited a good portion of 'Cajun Country', and we had a particularly interesting time at Avery Island where Tabasco Sauce is made. The peppers are grown on the island, and it has been owned by the McIlhenny family for generations. The minute you exit your car the smell of vinegar permeates the air. There's a small museum and shop and they give out a taste of tabasco flavored ice cream, which is quite tasty.

We also stayed in some classic, historic Plantation Houses along the way, and at my favorite, 'Madewood'. It was Ed's birthday, so the staff served him a special breakfast in the impressive main dining room, the two of us feeling dwarfed by the scale of it. We had also stayed on the property of Oak Alley and that evening when all the visitors were gone, we sat on the verandah in rocking chairs looking out to the alley of oaks. The last time I had been there, decades before, the last inhabitant, an elderly woman, had just died. These houses are behemoths to maintain, but of architectural value, although some of my friends from the south despise that I even go to see them for what they represent.

I also experienced a couple of powerful hurricanes while in Louisiana. They are not for the faint of heart, and the wind is inconceivable. During the first one the University had read-ied buses to take us to Houston if it was predicted to be too dangerous to stay. A couple of us guys ran down to the local supermarket and literally the shelves were bare; everyone was hoarding what they could get. We grabbed some of the last cans of food and got in line to check out, right behind Tulane's President Herbert Longenecker holding a bag of charcoal. Several of us huddled together and slept in one room as the wind blew violently at night. We were on the 10th floor of a high-rise dormitory and had put masking tape across the windows with mattresses up against them. The previous after-noon the water began rising and as I walked from one campus building to another the water was up to my waist and the current ripped open the vinyl raincoat I was wearing.

During the announcement of another approaching hurricane a friend and I unwisely thought it would be interesting to drive to Grand Isle to watch the waves coming in from the Gulf. It was a very bad decision. We did see the surging waves hit the shoreline and thought it best we high tail it out of there only to find the water already rising all around us. Heading back on the only road out of town we lost sight of the road in front of us as it was covered over in water. We just slowly drove on based on the location of the utility poles; truly frightening and extremely dangerous. As we should have known better, the water can rise extremely fast, and the surge possibly several feet high. Coming into another town everyone was sandbagging, and eventually the National Guard came and escorted us to higher ground. That was a very regrettable excursion, never to be repeated.

Many folks with houses on the Gulf, and nearby, just anticipate rebuilding every few years when a hurricane blows through, and often do.

Another fun thing we would do is take up an offer to fly to the beach from a fellow classmate who was a pilot. Tulane had a flying club and owned a small 1950s Piper Cub plane. Three of us would occasionally get invited to fly with the pilot to Dauphin Island in Alabama for the day. The plane was as rickety as one could imagine, and he often did stunts which added to the allure of going with him. Being young these things obviously did not phase us much. Landing on Dauphin Island was challenging since the airfield was very short and unpaved. It was not unusual for an attempted arrival to take two or three times to come to a complete and safe landing. During one excursion when the weather suddenly turned bad, we hand to land in Mobile and wait out the storm. Yet, a day at the white pristine sand, and often quiet, beach in Alabama was very nice.

Since New Orleans was close to other Southern cities, such as Atlanta and Houston, we occasionally visited them for a weekend. In the 1970s those two cities were prospering and had much more in the way of new, contemporary architecture being constructed. John Portman, the architect, was launching great strides in recreating downtown Atlanta, and the oil industry was generating tremendous wealth and new construction in Houston. In later years I would visit Natchez, Charleston, and Savannah, yet those places take on the antiquated charm and character not unlike New Orleans; and are not necessarily progressive places.

On one trip to Atlanta six of us drove together in one car. Somewhere in Alabama at the border with Georgia we got lost, heaven knows how. Ending up in a dead end of stockyards the driver decided to go into an office to ask directions. Two of the car's occupants started shouting, 'NO!' 'Do not go in there!' When the driver turned to ask why, one of them said that if anyone came out and thought that they were Jewish, which they were, it would be dangerous. I just sat there flabbergasted, yet I saw the fear on their faces. It seemed a bit surreal to me, but they were from a nearby area in Georgia. They obviously knew what they were taking about based on their outward anxiety. It was apparent that prejudice reigned beyond being black in these parts. We drove on and found a gas station to ask directions. Nothing more was ever said about that incident.

In Atlanta we saw the new Portman designed buildings, went to Stone Mountain, and to Great America, an enormous amusement park. Another strange thing about that trip was staying with relatives of one of my friends. They gave me a bedroom used by one of the sons who was off on a trip. I got myself settled and suddenly noticed a tank in the corner of the room, a tank with two very large snakes! I hate snakes but just took it in stride and looked away. It was free accommodations so I shouldn't complain. However, when I woke up the next morning, I did peer over to the tank to find the snakes missing. I didn't question it, packed my bag, and left the room, as we were leaving that day anyway.

While in the South I had the pleasure of attending a large Thanksgiving gathering. A friend from my high school in Connecticut, Paula Davis, had moved to Alabama with her family after her father died. Our families had been very close for years, and Paula with her mother and brother relocated there as that was where Paula's mother originally had family and had grown up. Inviting me for Thanksgiving I gladly accepted the opportunity and flew to Columbus, Georgia across from Phenix City, Alabama where they lived. Those two places are interesting in themselves as they fall right between the Eastern and Central time zones. Since most people in Phenix City work across the river in Columbus they use the Eastern time zone, although technically they live in the Central one.

I spent a very pleasant few days with the Davis family and on Thanksgiving Day we went to a relative who was having dinner there. That family lived in rural Alabama, about one hour away from Phenix City. The property was vast and beyond the house not much else to see but openness and trees. The house had just been built, designed, and constructed by the Davis's relative. He was eager to show an architecture student what he had done. It frankly was rather ordinary; very much a typical ranch house, but I offered him praise, nonetheless. One thing I distinctly recall that stood out was a section of tree trunk, about eight inches around, used as a post for a counter. It had been painted a bright red color with a high gloss finish; and was very conspicuous in its distinctiveness.

There were approximately forty people for Thanksgiving dinner, including a couple of soldiers brought from a nearby military base who did not have anywhere else to go for the holiday. It was a tradition for families in the area to bring soldiers into their homes for Thanksgiving. I thought that the hospitality of taking in strangers, including me, for the holiday was very heartwarming. What struck me, and something I had not experienced before, was that all the men were in the living room or on the front porch and all the women were in the kitchen. There was this absolute barrier that neither sex crossed. However, at one point before dinner one of the women came out to get me. I had no idea what was up, but I followed her into the female inner sanctum of the kitchen. She placed a large jar on top of a counter and said, 'Open this, please'. Rather perplexed I went to open the jar. Upon twisting, with all my strength, I realized that all activity in the kitchen had stopped and approximately twenty women were intently staring at me. I felt very uncomfortable. The jar lid popped, and I twisted it with great relief, and the activity started up again. It was then suggested I return to the Living Room, which I did.

Later, I asked Paula what that was all about. She said that they were testing me, my manhood and my strength in performing a simple task. It wasn't customary for a college guy to travel that far, and especially there, and they were very curious about how manly I was, or just some nerd from the city. She said I succeeded in proving my masculinity and value.

It was indeed particularly unusual for a college guy to fly to another part of the south to see a woman friend when it was purely platonic. That was totally out of their way of thinking. In their view there had to be some level of amorous relationship should any guy travel that far. Anyway, the dinner was delicious, filling, and quite delightful, and sitting with forty people at one long table for Thanksgiving was not to be forgotten. I sincerely appreciated the opportunity to experience it. Plus, I gained some new knowledge of the South.

The South is indeed a unique place with its own set of rules and standards. If anything, the South gave me a patina of grace and charm added to my character. It takes a bit of getting used to for a Northerner from the East, like myself, but once you become accustomed to the ways it can be quite delightful too; yet there is still an underbelly of arrogance and discrimination that simply does not go away.

The Midwest

Moving to the Midwest in 1980 was quite the change for me. The heartland of America, the 'breadbasket'. Flat, along with some rolling hills, it has endless acres of farmland with cities sprinkled and nestled in between as it stretches for miles into the horizon. From any large city or town, it is not a far distance to be in rural farmland. The weather is challenging as it goes from bitter freezing winter cold to extreme heat in summer. There is hardly any Spring or Fall and there are lines on the map where the weather gets progressively worse as one goes north at any point. People are fiercely independent, strong willed and determined.

I will explain in another chapter how I ended up there; but suffice it to say that escaping New York and the East Coast for new horizons, while also avoiding the South, was a big part of it.

Arriving in Madison, Wisconsin was truly a unique place in the Midwest consciousness. Liberal and very forward thinking it is a place primarily of politics, being the capital of Wisconsin, and a university town. There was also the Oscar Mayer Meat Co. and American Family Insurance as prime commercial enterprises. Spend any football season there and you will quickly realize what is a priority, in ways like the South. After living in Madison for six years, and then in Des Moines, Iowa for three, I recognized that Milwaukee or Chicago would have been better places for me to settle. The others were just too small and provincial.

The Midwest has endless fields of grain, corn, and other produce. One only needs to stand in northwest Iowa to realize that the only thing one can see is the horizon many miles away, and perhaps a grain silo. It is a land crisscrossed by a checkboard of carefully parceled acreage and roads, some of the most dangerous thoroughfares anywhere. There are many accidents at road intersections because of speeding and the monotony of the long distances through nothingness. In some areas there is hilly terrain, especially in parts of Ohio, Indiana, Illinois, Wisconsin, Minnesota, and slivers of Eastern Iowa, yet the states are primarily pancake flat. The Great Lakes are amazing as they are large bodies of water seeming to appear as great seas between the various states flanking them while being unable to see the land at the other side.

What I imagined of the Midwest before I arrived was a place that is wholesome, hard-working, and consumed with being of the earth. Those traits are mainly true, and there's little variation from place to place; excepting the pockets of ethnic groups that have specific traditions. And there are several pockets of those, some clamoring for tourism through their culture quaintness. In Wisconsin there's New Glarus, a Swiss colony with traditional textiles, Mt. Horeb, a Norwegian populace, with its garden trolls and mustard, and in Mineral Point the English, mainly Cornish inhabitants, primarily involved with mining. Milwaukee is known for its Polish community and lots of breweries. Iowa has a large Amish community in the Amanas, and German in origin. These places are worth visiting, especially for the uniqueness and the variety of ethnic cuisine.

Wisconsin is also the home of Frank Lloyd Wright, and his legacy is everywhere. The town of Spring Green, just thirty miles west of Madison, was his home and where his architecture school existed during the summer. Spring Green is indeed bucolic and interesting to visit. There was a Wright designed restaurant there, on a river, and you can even visit his gravesite, all tranquil, quiet places in the Midwest landscape.

There are many Wright buildings- houses, churches, and other edifices in Madison in his customary 'prairie style'. Examining one closely it is easy to see the poor detailing and why they inevitably leak. Cutting glass to snuggly fit against a jagged boulder with little sealant to bind them tightly together is not the best for waterproofing. I saw this clearly in his Madison Unitarian Church. A neighbor of ours traded the house behind us for a Frank Lloyd Wright house just a couple of blocks from the State Capitol and regretted it forever, for the maintenance alone.

Wright was infamous in Madison for his bold, self-important nature. He apparently lacked for money. I heard stories of him walking into hardware stores or lumber yards and just taking what he wanted without paying. A neighbor across the street from my house, a kindly older man, knew Wright as he was his car mechanic. He told me that often Wright refused to pay his bills, and the last time Wright had a repair my neighbor refused to give him back his car! In Wisconsin you will hear many stories of Mr. Wright from those who lived during his time there.

There was one incident that happened during my travels through the Midwest that stands out above all others. I drove several times back and forth between New York and Wisconsin, getting ready for a move. During one trip, driving a very unreliable Chevy Vega, the car caught fire on a major interstate somewhere in Ohio while heading back to New York. I pulled over on the road shoulder and thought of pulling the luggage out of the trunk, but the smoke got so intense that I couldn't. I tried waving down a tuck and one did eventually pull over. I thought at least a trucker might have a fire extinguisher or the wherewithal to know what to do. Lifting the hood, the truck driver put out the fire and I was greatly relieved fearing the car might explode. He examined the engine compartment further and fortunately could not detect any noticeable damage. He then asked when I might have been to a gas station, and remarkably I had just been to one at the previous exit. He then asked if I had the oil refilled; and the answer was, 'yes'. He told me that the attendant had poured some of the oil over the engine and it was burning off causing the fire and smoke. Only a small remnant remained. He opinioned that it was alright to travel but also offered to follow me for a hundred miles to be sure everything was OK. It was so kind of him, and I sincerely appreciated it. I even offered him some compensation, but he would not take it. At about the one hundred mile mark he blew his horn, passed, and waved with a thumbs up.

Several miles later the car started acting up again, bucking and banging loudly, in a very rural part of Pennsylvania. Arriving at an exit I went to a gas station, and there was no one around. I went inside to see if there was a mechanic, but it was eerily deserted. I stood at the counter and yelled out. Someone then opened a door and I saw a group of men playing cards in the back room. One of them was a mechanic and came out with me to check the car. As I am not mechanically inclined, I had no idea what the problem was, or where to look. Checking under the hood he removed a very dirty round piece of an auto part, put it is his mouth and blew through it and put it back in place. I was shocked that he would put that filthy piece of mechanics in his mouth. Looking at me he said, 'All good' and shut the hood. Asking where I was going, I responded to New York City. He just smiled and pointed outward saying, 'well, just go two hundred and fifty miles that way and you'll be to the George Washington Bridge'. I did make it back without further problems.

I had another interesting encounter while driving in rural Iowa when I got a flat tire. Stopping in a very small town I went into the bar to make a phone call telling my wife that I was going to be detained, and then went to change the tire. While changing it every patron in the bar came out to stand

and watch me, a city guy in khakis and polo shirt, change the tire. It was hilarious as I became the entertainment for the day.

Arriving in 1980 the Midwest had just come through a very serious depression with the value of farmland. During the 1970s the value of an acre of land shot sky high and farmers, some owning farms for generations, leveraged the increase taking loans. When suddenly the inflated land price plummeted, farmers owed far more than the land's value. Many lost their property to corporations, or others they had borrowed large sums. It takes approximately eighty acres to operate a typical farm and when land prices fall by two thirds for each acre, the loss is tremendous.

There were towns throughout the Midwest that became virtual ghost towns. Once thriving places from the turn of the twentieth century with schools, movie theaters, bars, railroad stations and a variety of commerce; all that remained were the bars. Most else was simply boarded up, including the schools. In 1985 one community in Northwest Iowa gave free land to anyone who agreed to build a house worth at least thirteen thousand dollars and live there.

That farmland disaster didn't have a measurable impact on Madison.

Madison, an isthmus, is a bitter, cold place in winter, especially living between two major lakes, Mendota and Monona. There were weeks in January, and into February, when it did not go above freezing and often below zero for days on end. I remember times when the wind chill factor got down to negative sixty degrees. And there's lots of snow. I would often awake to my neighbor shoveling her sidewalk at 6am as it was a city ordinance to remove the sidewalk snow by a certain time. I had a one-hundred-foot-long driveway to shovel too. There were times when I could not see over the snow piles on either side of the driveway, plus the portion between my house and the next where I had to walk the snow out as there was nowhere to throw it. There was always one day in the Fall when the temperature changed, and you realized that winter arrived.

Madison is indeed a beautiful, pristine city, well planned with radiating streets centered on Capitol Square. I owned a house built in the 1860s on the narrowest part of the isthmus. Having an old house that was constructed long ago, without plumbing, central heating system or electric, adapting it over time had its challenges. Although not a large house, one story with two bedrooms and a bath, it satisfied the need and was quite charming. When it was built there was an outhouse that I found on an old map, a good distance back on the property. I could not even imagine going and using it in winter. The foundation of the house was sandstone and amazingly the wood studs were constructed of chestnut. I might be an architect, but my construction skills leave something to be desired. I have little patience and want things done in little time. Yet I did try my hand at several projects, including flashing areas of the roof, and foundation patching too. Although it went well, it took way too much time.

The basement was a place onto itself, dark and creepy, yet it had a lot of space. We eventually installed a washer/dryer there. There was an amazingly large hand-hewn beam that spanned the mid-section of the house, clearly exposed in the basement. Over several months I noticed it began cracking in the middle. The cracks got larger and at one point I could almost see through it. I immediately bought a couple of 'lally' columns to brace it, fearing something was wrong. I invited a Structural Engineer friend over to look at it and to give me his impression of what occurred. He smiled and reassured me it was nothing to worry over. He said that the beam had dried out and strengthened as the house had been newly insulated and sealed, and it was a good thing. The beam stopped cracking.

One evening a woman came to our door and introduced herself as someone visiting from New Mexico who lived in the house as a girl in the 1940s. She asked to see the house since it had been renovated and I invited her in to look around. Having a pleasant discussion with her about the house and its history she mentioned that her mother slept in the living room, she in the larger bedroom and her brother in the smaller one; yet had no recollection where her father slept. One disconcerting thing was her noting that there was never a step down into the kitchen from the main part of the house!

Another visitor unexpectedly rang the doorbell one day. A well-dressed gentleman, probably in his fifties, was standing there, late afternoon, and handed me a bottle of scotch and a *New York Times* and said, 'Welcome to the neighborhood'. I was stunned. He said he heard we moved in and that we were from New York City where he was from too. His name was Peter Draz and he was head Librarian at the State Historical Society; and had worked for Time-Life in New York. He became a good friend; and lived down the end of our street. I soon got to know other neighbors and they were a wonderful mix of folks from varied backgrounds.

I became heavily involved in politics in my time living in Madison. It's hard to avoid there. Coming from the East Coast I was a Republican, but what is known as a 'Rockefeller

Republican' that in no way resembles the party today. It did not lean to the radical right or influenced by religious groups. It was more moderate and fiscally conservative. Madison definitely 'leans' left, unlike most of the Midwest.

The house I owned was in a downtown urban area, just a few blocks of the Capitol Square. Every weekend there is a Farmers' Market that circles the Square with amazing, fresh produce and hand made products. The neighborhood where I lived was one of the oldest with a combination of college students and older residents who had been there for years. I was one of the early 'urban homesteaders' leading to gentrification. There were others, including one of the oldest African American communities led by a dynamic woman named Lucille Miller.

I fortunately found work in an architectural firm, HSR Associates, soon after moving, so that worked out. My wife was attending the University of Wisconsin to obtain her doctoral degree in psychology. We settled into the area comfortably and I felt heartened by a newly found environment, and a much more manageable scale than New York. New York becomes overwhelming at times with the multitude of options and offerings in culture and entertainment. We had attended many theater performances as there was a program that gave low-cost tickets to teachers, a job my wife held when we lived there. That was wonderful yet we yearned for a less frenetic place to live, even with fewer options.

Our sometime escape was to go to Chicago which was an easy day trip. That was a wonderful excursion for a big city fix. Seeing other parts of the Midwest interested me and I got to visit places such a South Bend, Indiana where I encountered a tornado. Kansas City was where I made occasional shopping trips to a beautiful shopping district there called Country Club Plaza. I saw Springfield, Illinois where I had enough time to explore some of the fascinating Lincoln sites before catching a plane. I also saw the beauty of Galena, Illinois where nearly all the buildings there are from the nineteenth century and are on the National Register of Historic Places; and Dubuque, Iowa, an incredible place caught in time, the 1950s, and nothing has changed or ever will.

The Quad Cities of Iowa and Illinois are depressing at best, economically challenged. Once staying in a hotel in Davenport I called the front desk to ask about using the pool, as it was advertised, and was told they had not filled it in twenty years. Minneapolis, however, is completely different; a fascinating, thriving, and progressive city with a lot of great architecture, but super cold temperatures in the winter. Because of the weather they had enclosed sky bridges linking the city blocks, just like Des Moines, Iowa.

My first trip to the Midwest I stayed at the Ritz Carlton in Chicago. On the 'Magnificent Mile', aka Michigan Avenue, the lobby is many stories above the street and the view from the hotel was amazing. The next morning, on a very quiet Sunday, I called the valet to get the car, the broken-down Vega I mentioned earlier. Standing and waiting for the car I heard it rumble around the corner and I knew that the valet would have a lot to tell others about it later, especially at a place like the Ritz. The irony did humor me.

While living in Madison we soon joined the local neighborhood association as neighborhoods are very powerful entities there. We were a part of what was known as the Fourth District Neighborhood that made up a large part of the downtown. We were bordered on one side by a very powerful group called the Tenney-Lapham Neighborhood Association.

What we found was our chunk of the neighborhood was often overlooked and disregarded, the 'second sister' to everything that went on; so, a few of us decided to create our own Association and break away from the Fourth District. Our neighborhood needed an identity and appropriate representation. At a meeting of the Fourth District Neighborhood Association, we announced the break, spoke of our borders, and created quite the kerfuffle. The powerbrokers of the Fourth District, including a very well-known attorney and the City Alderperson for the District, were indignant that we would make such a move.

We named ourselves The Old Market Place Neighborhood with precisely laid out borders carved from the Fourth District, and one edge of it somewhat in conflict with Tenney-Lapham who also was a bit indignant over the creation. Our neighborhood was based on the character of an historic building in the center of our boundaries, a prairie style building constructed as a city Market Place building in the early 1900s. It had fallen into disrepair. We created an image, an identity, and formulated a plan for giving ourselves some clout in City affairs and government, and no longer overlooked. Approximately fifteen very energetic people of varied ages and backgrounds were involved in the formation, all with similar outlook and intent, creating a cohesive neighborhood.

This is when I learned about the power of the press and media. Immediately upon our formation, not a common event in Madison, we were contacted by the local press and TV. Several articles and news items ran about our founding and existence. We became established. Setting up a steering committee, with Lucille Miller included, we created bylaws, and then a monthly newsletter to foster communication. Membership grew and unlike other Associations we made it totally inclusive, including commercial enterprises, churches, and anyone within our borders willing to join. The local Lutheran Church offered us a place to meet, at no cost. They became members as well as the local AME Church that Lucille belonged to and encouraged her pastor to join with us. It was awesome to see the vibrance and energy of so many smart people with various talents coming together.

After we got fully organized with a good foothold, we went to City Council meetings, spoke, got involved and made our voice known. We gained respect and our membership kept growing. We were doing radio broadcasts, including my favorite where I and a neighbor went on a morning talk show at a breakfast restaurant and spoke about living in the neighborhood, being neighbors, the character of an older neighborhood and living in older houses.

Every year there was a major event hosted by developers in the outskirts, 'The Parade of Homes', highlighting new houses being constructed. We had a different event concurrent with it downtown called 'The Alternate Parade of Homes'. Neighbors opened their homes for public viewing, and for a fee you could go from house to house to see what older houses offered. I also developed a walking tour with that event that people could take, and many did, often surprised by what the neighborhood had to offer. It was work, yet enormous fun. It built community among us, and we all benefited.

I was elected the first President and held that position for the first years of the Association's existence. Becoming more established I was invited on local TV talk shows discussing a variety of neighborhood events. One time I spoke about how the popular Farmers Market on Capitol Square got moved to the Old Market Place Neighborhood, just blocks away and at our invitation, for one weekend, to assist when it typically was unable to operate as a major annual Art Fair occurred then. After browsing the Art Fair people poured into our neighborhood to attend the Farmers Market. It further put the neighborhood on the map and made us identifiable.

We also decided to have a major fundraiser and hold a Festival, revolving around a plea for the city to restore and renovate the Old Market Building sitting dismally abandoned. It was a herculean event for our small group and took incredible effort and time to pull it off.

We really didn't know what we were doing but a core group of us worked darn hard to figure it out. Some creative ideas for activities percolated up and we decided to have an auction as well, as part of the fundraiser. We were registered as a legitimate non-profit, so we had the basis to do it legally. For the auction we enlisted neighbors to contribute 'treasures' they were no longer attached to and the outpouring of items was astonishing. One couple who had traveled the world for work gave amazing handmade items from Africa and Asia. Quite unexpectedly a prominent, well-known couple who lived in a large stone historic mansion gave several items. The Harmons, Dolly and Gordon, were socially well-connected people who really did not have much to do with the Association. Dolly was known as 'Dolly Madison' as she wrote items for the local paper under that pen name.

The days before the event there was a lot of preparation. We had procured our permits, insurance, and placed posters strategically all around the city, as well as advertising as much as we could on a limited budget. Word of mouth was beneficial, and residents told their friends and relatives in other neighborhoods about it. We even got some media press around it.

The morning of the festival the core group of volunteers got up early and decorated the street. It took place on a little used street in front of the Old Market Building while we completely closed it off to vehicles for the event. We wanted all the visitors to fully appreciate being up close to the historic Old Market Place Building, where on the opening day in the early 1900s the city served a free lunch to hundreds. We hoped to build a similar hype.

It worked as hundreds came to the festival.

At one point in the afternoon a crowd was milling on the length of the street enjoying the day, partaking in activities, eating food from vendors, and listening to music we provided. It was fun and jovial, and we had activities for kids to enjoy too. The weather is always a chance, but the day was sunny, warm, and beautiful. The weather gods came through for us.

The committee decided that I should be the auctioneer. I was neither qualified, nor knew anything about it. I got up on a loading dock and just started doing what I thought an auctioneer does! We sold every item, at times for rock bottom prices, but it all sold. It was our prime revenue for the fundraiser, so it was important. It was later reported in our newsletter that I got into the role so well that someone said I could have 'auctioned off the Brooklyn Bridge and sold it to that crowd'.

At the end of the day the exhausted group of volunteers

tallied up the amount we had made… and it turned out to be less than a dollar in profit. We laughed, but nonetheless we figured it was a success because of the exposure we gave to the Old Market Building and our neighborhood. We were now on Madison's map, including within the real estate community.

I wrote thank you notes to everyone who donated an item for the auction, and the other contributors. One afternoon I got a phone call from Dolly Harmon. She said that she was so impressed and pleased by my note she had to remark on it. Dolly told me that it was the first time anyone had thanked her for a donation. I was surprised. People, she said, just expect it of them and rarely show gratitude. That taught me the value of thanking people, a simple gesture. The Harmons became active members of the Association, gave ice cream socials on their lawn for it, and helped in many ways, including giving us access to other prominent people.

The Harmons became friends and were a delightful, enjoyable couple.

Politics in Madison, as in most places, was a minefield and I got totally immersed into it with the Association, attending Council meetings, talking with politicians, and learning the ins and outs of a very complex political climate. Madison is very liberal and left wing, often called 'The Berkeley of the Midwest'. Yet there is also a strong and powerful conservative presence frequently at odds, and often controlling policy through clout and influence. I fell right in the middle of it.

There was another well-known family in our midst and had lived in the neighborhood for generations. They owned a big moving and storage business and had little to do with neighbors or the neighborhood association. A phone call came one day, and it was the patriarch of that family who lived in a very nice house a block away from my house. I had never seen or met him, but he called because he was impressed with a commentary opinion that I gave at a city council meeting that he had watched on television. I was advocating for a neighborhood baseball diamond to be refurbished for kids to use in a nearby park, so he wanted to thank me. Soon after his name along with other family members were added to our membership list.

Then I really became embroiled in politics; and learned a valuable lesson from it. My wife and I were Republicans, East Coast types as I had mentioned, like our parents and grandparents before us. This did not sit too well in liberal Democratic Madison. We kept low with our affiliation, and everything held its own in preventing conflict, until…

The Harmons were staunchly Republican and had a bevy of powerful Republican friends, including the distinguished lawyer I mentioned earlier who lived in the adjacent neighborhood. He found us and the neighborhood amusing at best. The Harmons invited my wife and me to all the Republican events and fundraisers as their personal guests. We were a young, up and coming couple, just what an older bunch of Republicans needed and wanted, new blood with some vigor. Gordon decided to run for City Council, and I balanced my affiliation with him and our predominantly liberal Democratic base in the neighborhood and the association. That balance unraveled when I did what I thought was a seemingly innocuous thing. Gordon asked that I be a part of a group to be photographed for his campaign literature. His campaign slogan was 'Stop the PacMan', for his opponent who thrived on PAC donations. The photo was merely Gordon talking with us, a small group gathered near the Capitol, but my neighbors saw it as my endorsing him, and the association backing him. In retrospect I should have known better and not agreed to do it. The irate phone calls that followed were unnerving. Some of my closest neighbors and friends were furious. It eventually passed, and Gordon did not win.

Then astonishingly I received a phone call from the head of the Wisconsin Republican Party nominating committee. They wanted to know if I would be interested in running for the State Senate. I could not believe it. A complete nobody and they want me to run for a major State office with no real political experience. It showed how desperate they were, and I turned it down. Flattered, yet a crazy idea that I would even have a remote chance of winning. No one knew of me outside the confines of our small neighborhood, much less a whole state!

There was some opportunistic crime in our neighborhood too. The most chilling happened to a very kind, friendly older German woman who lived in a larger house across the street. She had this beautiful array of handmade wood furniture that looked as though it came directly from the Black Forest. She also revealed one day that she had a good friend in Iowa, an artist. He would always stop to see her when he visited Madison. If she wasn't at home, he did a sketch and would leave it near the front door. She took out a multitude of the sketches to show us one day. The artist was Grant Wood.

One night there was a piercing scream from her house. She was awakened during the night by an intruder; and saw a flashlight beam in the hallway out of the corner of her eye. Frightened she waited until there wasn't any sounds; then got up walking in the dark slowly and evenly according to her recollection of it. After reaching the bathroom she saw the door slightly ajar in a way she never left it. Opening it slowly she reached into the dark to turn on the light and instead touched the face of the intruder. Panicked she screamed as loud as possible and he fled, through the bathroom window where he had entered. That event put everyone on edge, yet nothing was taken, and thank goodness she was not harmed.

There was a large open lot directly across the street from my house. It was a nice greenspace to look at with a large heritage tree in the center of it. In Madison's history our street, North and South Franklin, had been a canal linking the two lakes since it was at the shortest point, and the lowest. There is no knowing how long that lot had been open, if not always.

A developer came along, purchased the lot, and proposed a condo building. Totally out of scale and character with the neighborhood it was a sham and created a furious outcry. The neighborhood association went on the defensive and fought it vigorously. Yet the neighborhood voice wasn't always consistent. There were many meetings at my house and a strategy developed. We invited the developer and his wife to attend a meeting and discuss our concerns. They did come but the wife was adamant that we did not understand 'progress' and was unable to listen. They didn't understand that most of us were just seeking responsible development.

When they proposed cutting down the tree one of my neighbors went ballistic and made it her personal mission to stop it. One morning as I went out on my front porch, she and her young daughter were chained to the tree yelling to me that the tree would not come down. She said it was a 'neighborhood landmark'. All along she took the position that the property should remain as a 'public park' to benefit the neighborhood. That sounded nice, however, neither we nor the city owned the land. It was in private hands, and they had every right to develop it, unless she was willing to purchase it or come up with the funds, which she was not. A bit of socialist Madison at work. The bulldozers arrived and she was arrested.

The developers prevailed and the building was built, cheaply and poorly designed. I got myself wrapped into a personal vendetta with the developer. I had learned that he was a slum landlord and I made it my mission to reveal him for what he was. The apartment buildings that he owned and rented were full of building violations, including safety, so I alerted the city. It was clear he was just an irresponsible landlord out to make a buck. This obviously irritated him; and he called me at work one day to threaten me. He called me 'despicable' and guaranteed to sue and ruin me. He told me quite clearly that he was a godsend owning these old, dilapidated buildings and I, like everyone, should appreciate it.

That started a whole series of threats and craziness. My neighbors came to my defense, and his attorney was the powerful guy I had mentioned a couple of times in this story. Madison can be a small town. That attorney, who knew me, came to meet me, and tried to reason some middle ground while saying it can all go away if I only apologized, which I would not do. We finally came to a compromise, and it went away after a lot of grief. I did learn if you are going to battle, be prepared for the consequences. Poetic justice came when the developer's wife divorced him, and he had to move into the condo he just built. We saw him daily in the shame of his downfall and watched his Cadillac bottom out on the driveway pavement as it was graded incorrectly.

I received a call from a large Lutheran congregation nearby and they wanted to know if I would be interested being on their Board for a new entity they started, Bethel Outreach. As in many parts of the country in the 1980s the state mental hospitals were closing, and the resident population were pushed out on the streets. This had a profound impact on Madison when our own local hospital closed. Many became homeless, several acting in strange ways. One woman stood on a corner of Capitol Square reading aloud the daily stock market report, and subsequently singing Judy Collins 'Send in the Clowns'. The entire scene was gut wrenching.

Bethel Outreach was set up as a non-profit to help house some of these residents who were now indigent, by creating group homes. They planned to open their first house in our neighborhood and admirably, even though I was not a member of the congregation, wanted a neighborhood representative. I agreed and it was the first of many boards I came to sit on, learning all about *Roberts Rules of Order*, etc., although I did have some exposure from the neighborhood association. It was a wonderful group and I enjoyed so much serving on the board.

I got to know the residents well. The house was well run, with a live-in caretaker. One of the residents, Arnold, wasn't much older than me, and called one day as he wanted to talk. He emphasized that it was important. I agreed to take him to lunch. He had a serious speech impediment and was difficult to understand. Most people ignored him. Over lunch he astonishingly told me of his idea, a plan, to reimagine the neglected spaces in Madison, especially abandoned railroad areas. I sat there totally flabbergasted as it made perfect sense; and was a tremendously thoughtful urban planning scheme. His ending plea was that he wanted me to help spread his message and advocate for him and the idea. I did, and went to several local politicians, but it gained no traction. Arnold ended up writing a book and I have a cherished photo of him handing me a copy to thank me for helping, and for understanding him.

At the same time my own prejudice and liberalism was tested. Another group intending to open a 'club for the mentally ill' put in an offer to purchase a multi-family house on my street. They first sought planning approval from the city and that's how we heard about it. The concern I and others had was how it would function and operate, and details around safety issues. Little was being revealed which made it more disconcerting. Our neighborhood association met with the group sponsoring it and I kept thinking I had to keep an open mind. I remembered my experience in Forest Hills with the fight over the opening of a group home there. These folks were obviously novices and had no experience at running this type of 'club'. At one point I asked what we could expect to see for any impacts in the neighborhood. The answer I got was to expect that some of the club members might come to our front yards and urinate. That was enough for me and the other neighbors. It was defeated, never happened and the proposal disappeared.

Bethel Outreach was a success; and I was happy to be a part of it. It wasn't always smooth sailing, but it did help a very desperate situation.

Our monthly neighborhood meetings were lively and enjoyable as well as intensely packed with solving neighborhood issues. We grew and became a cohesive force.

One late night, around 3am there was a loud pounding on my front door. I went to see who was there while asking through the door; but no one would identify themselves. I went to a window to see if anyone was on the porch, but there was no one. Almost immediately the phone rang, and I picked it up right away. A voice on the other end said, 'I hope you realize your days are numbered' and hung up. It scared the daylights out of me knowing that someone had been at my door, and apparently was close enough to call before cell phones. A couple of days later I got a greeting card in the mail. Inside it stated that I would be killed, along with the President of the United States, so 'be prepared'. It had no return address, signature, or identification.

I called the police; and they came over to investigate. I told them of the recent visit, phone call, etc. They joked that they wouldn't alert the President just yet, but it was a criminal offense to threaten his life regardless. We talked a bit, and they were concerned enough to have a plainclothes officer shadow me for a few days, including to an upcoming neighborhood meeting. Having your life threatened is alarming, trust me. At every corner and every turn any move can put you on edge. Especially when you know someone knows where you live and is bold enough to come by in the middle of the night. Having a plainclothes police presence helped. This all occurred before the incident over Ken Eaton's murder that I wrote about in a previous chapter.

Nothing happened until the evening of the neighborhood association meeting. I could sense this was when the police seemed most concerned, yet they did not let on. The meeting started and there was a crowd of about forty people, perhaps more. Two plainclothes officers were in the room at the sides, observing. At one point I noticed a man I had never seen before toward the back of the room acting oddly, and they detected him too. He constantly fidgeted and grimaced. Being the President I had the floor and conducted the meeting while he kept staring at me intently. After the meeting when everyone started to get up and socialize, I saw the two police officers ask him to go outside, and he did.

Several minutes later they came in to talk with me privately. He was indeed the man who threatened me; and was known by them as being somewhat mentally unstable. They had encountered him from other places. He lived in the neighborhood and told them that he saw me as a threat, a person out to gentrify the neighborhood and get rid of people like him. The police told him it was completely the opposite and he seemed relieved to hear it, leaving, and I never heard another word or ever saw him again; although I was very grateful to the Madison police for getting it resolved.

Life in Madison certainly had its challenges, aside from the weather. I learned that politics was not my game and I have tried to avoid it at all costs, but as you will read later sometimes unsuccessfully too.

During my time involved with the neighborhood association I was also tasked with being placed on a city committee to develop design guidelines for the neighborhood. A grant had been given and a task force developed. Surveying the history of the neighborhood and its structures was the first step. It was quite an interesting undertaking, and those guidelines can still be found online today.

In my professional career I was given the task of redefining the zoning of a particular city owned parcel within the neighborhood. And what was part of that task was to define 'the family'. Now there's something I never expected to have to define, but I did. The family I surmised had to be broad and reflective of the community, more than just mother, father, and children. To my amazement it was approved and became a part of the zoning for that area.

Sometime around 1984 I was invited to a Polish wedding in Milwaukee. I never imagined it to be a two-day affair over a weekend, but I was encouraged to get a hotel room for the night. I did, and soon found out why. The couple getting married were only acquaintances from the neighborhood in Madison, yet they found it necessary to invite me. They were both originally from Milwaukee and were attending the University. After a Catholic Church high mass matrimonial service there was a bit of downtime before the reception. The reception was huge, around four hundred people. These were average, middle-class folks but this wedding was a spectacle. There was so much food, mainly Polish, and drinks that it seemed like five hundred could have attended and be sufficiently fed. It went on until the wee hours of the morning with the band playing continuously with intermittent breaks, a Polish polka band. The next morning the partying continued until late afternoon. I had been to Greek and Italian weddings in New York, but this surpassed any of those by far.

My living in Madison wasn't all politics and neighborhood organizing. It was also driving out into the open heartland with a picnic, finding a field, putting a blanket down and smelling the fresh summer air while eating a scrumptious lunch made from the Farmer's Market produce.

It was also the neighborhood parties where my neighbors

gathered and enjoyed being together, all ages and backgrounds. I once had a Mardi Gras party just after moving in and invited some of the older neighbors on our street. There was wide suspicion about who I was, a newcomer when they had lived there fifty years or more. I learned there was a bit of a telephone exchange with each other confirming it was OK to attend, and they did, and it was a blast.

There was a time when I was preparing for a holiday party and making spiked eggnog from scratch. Unfortunately, I found I did not have a large enough bowl or tub, so ended up using the large kitchen sink, after cleaning it thoroughly. Just when I was pouring in the liquor an older neighbor, very prim and proper, came to the kitchen door and could see me pouring the liquor in the sink through the door's window. A bit surprised I let her in and explained. She sat quietly while I poured in the rest of the bottle and then took a hand mixer to mix it all together. After a bit she calmly said, 'aren't you afraid that the drain plunger is going to come undone.' I never thought of that, and fortunately it didn't.

Also, I had an outdoor party on the front lawn and porch where dozens of people gathered, played music, ate, and drank and laughed all afternoon. Folks just stopped by and came and went. A neighbor who lived in the neighborhood for decades invited and brought a woman who had moved away, Mrs. Brady, who was delighted to attend as her family had built my house back in the 1860s. She grew up in the house next door that her family also owned. She appeared to love every minute of being there. I watched her sitting on the porch and smiling broadly with pride, and that made me ever so happy. She experienced seeing her family's home take on a renewed life.

My absolute favorite party of all time, however, was at our friends' Gary and Michelle just a couple houses down. Young, in their twenties, they had invited some of the neighbors from the street to have food and drink and spend a pleasant evening in their home. A woman who was in her seventies decided to bring a ukulele and we spent a couple of hours singing old songs as she played along. It was one of those magical moments with neighbors that one can never forget.

And one last thing about my time in Madison. It was one time that I had a dog, a beagle named 'Pumpkin'. A rescue dog, a puppy, from the pound she was full of energy and was a typical hound dog in every way. I used to take her out to run across a giant field a block away from our house and her ears would flap in the wind. It was humorous to watch her run. She could be a bit of a problem too! One time in the dead of winter I was trying to put on her leash with it attached to the door frame to go out and do her 'business' and she ran off down the driveway in the freezing weather. I must have been quite the sight chasing her down the street across the ice and snow in my pajamas and bare feet yelling, 'Pumpkin', come back here!'. She eventually stopped and knew she did wrong, as much as when she accidentally knocked over the Christmas tree one year. Then she sat upright in the corner with big eyes trying to convince us that she had no idea what happened.

I am so glad and proud to see that the neighborhood is still identified as the Old Market Place Neighborhood. Being part of creating a neighborhood identity was most rewarding; and seeing some of the images today it has come far from what it was in 1980, including the Old Market Building now renovated too.

In 1986 I moved to Des Moines, Iowa and crossed the Mississippi to live for the first time. An entirely different Midwest experience from Madison, yet not unlike other Midwest cities. It is a larger and more commercially diverse city than Madison, and somewhat more in search of an identity.

This was my first time living as a gay man, albeit closeted, with a partner and raising his two children.

As mentioned before as characteristic of these places, farms are in close proximity. The first time my parents visited from their retirement home in Florida they were taken aback by the remoteness of central Iowa. Taking them to a nice restaurant in the rural town of Pella, a quaint Dutch cultural town where Pella windows are made, was quite the experience. Several miles outside of Des Moines, they became completely silent and at the restaurant, which they did enjoy, confessed to being a bit thrown off by there being no streetlights along the rural roads. It was 'pitch dark' as they said to me in a surprised and quiet tone.

There are skyscrapers in downtown Des Moines and one owned by the Ruan Transport Corporation. It was made of 'corten' steel that weathers to a patina of reddish bronze with streaks. The skybridges essentially eliminates any street level pedestrian traffic as all retail and storefronts are at the second floor. One time walking across one of the bridges near the Ruan Building I overheard a couple looking at it and remarking 'Isn't it a shame that they put all that money into a big building, and it rusted'. I guess not many know the intent of 'corten', as it's supposed to look like that.

Driving through rural Iowa is somewhat monotonous. Once I left work and was driving to another city when I stopped for dinner in a very small rural town. The only restaurant was a supper club, and it was a Friday night. I walked in with a suit, black overcoat and black fedora hat and the entire restaurant, full of patrons, went silent and turned to look at me. When I asked the waiter about it, she told me that my look was quite startling to them. Not only was I a stranger but my clothes were very out of character from what they are accustomed to men wearing, jeans and plaid work shirts. There was another time when I spoke to a high school class about my time in the Soviet Union. It was a rural town called Oskaloosa. The students were perfectly silent, yet very polite and asked appropriate, thoughtful questions. One student later approached the teacher and commented that he had never seen a man wearing a suit before. This part of the country was quite different from my roots in New York City and startling to me as well.

I did get to experience being on a farm for a short time, in Northwest Iowa where literally you can be in a house and not see another house anywhere, just farmland into the horizon. While there I was offered the task of driving a tractor. It was for 'discing' the land which I had never heard of before. But I had a great time doing it. The tractor was very high tech with an air-conditioned cab, stereo, and a computer. The only issue was that the farmer was laughing and shaking his head after I did several rows as they were not very straight! But how exciting to be driving a tractor across the open plains... this guy from New York City!

Going to a big Midwest State Fair is worth the effort. The one in Wisconsin, outside Milwaukee, is incredible. Cream puffs are the thing to eat, and you will find each State Fair has a specialty food item. There is a lot to see and do, music, the

Midway amusements, and hordes of people. The Iowa State Fair in Des Moines is an equally big event. Nearly everyone takes time off from work for it; or go in the evening and weekends. Tenderloin sandwiches are the big food item at that Fair. There are, of course, contests for food, produce, and animals. Iowa has the largest pig contest, and they are huge. These events are in the summer and my only other exposure to a State Fair was the Connecticut State Fair in Danbury that no longer exists. The Connecticut State Fair could not compare in scale to the Midwest Fairs.

As I relayed in a previous chapter being gay in Des Moines, especially as a professional, meant going underground and being quiet about it. There was a liberal element that existed there, yet also a more pronounced and dangerous underbelly of homophobic hatred.

It was an extraordinary eyeopener for me to witness how gay people, at that time, lived in the Midwest. As an example, there was a café in a remote rural area that on weekend evenings turned into a clandestine gay bar, a speakeasy of sorts. It was only known within the gay community, and I went once with my partner and a female friend. I had to wonder if anyone passing by would be curious about the cars outside the café when supposedly it was closed. Yet it was a thriving place for gay people to meet in relative seclusion, and some drove over an hour or more one way to go to it.

While living in Des Moines the Minneapolis Gay Men's Choir came to perform. The network of gay friends sent out a plea to help house them to cut their costs, and we offered to take and host two of them as we had two spare bedrooms. They arrived at our home, and they were gracious, polite, and absolutely perfect houseguests; respectful and very appreciative. One of them, a hairdresser, was flamboyant and quite amusing, and did not hide who he was, or cared to disguise himself. He asked me to take him shopping one day as he needed bronzer; and had never been in Des Moines. I took him on a mini tour of the city, and we got his bronzer at Younker's, the local department store. Walking around the retail area he saw a high-end gift shop and wanted to look around, so we went in. With his overt mannerisms he looked at some of the higher end pieces, prepared to purchase and to bring things home. A saleswoman saw us and when she noticed his effeminate demeanor she was very taken aback and appalled. She immediately told us to leave as she did not want us in the store. Flustered he was more than happy to get out and I was extremely embarrassed by her homophobic behavior toward us. Her prejudice was apparent, and stupidly she missed making a very good sale that day because of it.

Later that day I went in the concert hall during their rehearsal and listened to their voices while I stood in the lobby. They were incredible, so beautiful and serene in their singing. I was so moved, and a memory that will last forever.

While living in Des Moines some employees of Greyhound moved there from the San Francisco Bay Area. Greyhound moved their headquarters to Des Moines in the late 1980s and many people with seniority were compelled to follow the company to not lose benefits they worked years to acquire. It was a very difficult move for most, and the culture shock enormous.

Some of these employees were gay men who had lived comfortably in the San Francisco area for years; and created a network of friends that now unraveled. A couple of these men moved into our neighborhood. We came to know of them through our gay professional network. One was a drag queen. It was interesting as he was a very quiet, shy and withdrawn person. I would watch him walk past our home going to the store looking forlorn and downtrodden. However, whenever he put on his drag outfit, he took on a whole different personality. He was vibrant, personable, and very, very fun and humorous. After living in our area and settled into life there he was encouraged to do a drag show for those of us in the gay community which took place in our neighborhood community center. It was wonderful, hilarious, and so fun; plus, very refreshing an event for all of us who were so closeted. Another time, at a party, I saw him sitting in drag wearing a fox fur around his neck. The host's son, a boy about seven years old, walked up to him and looked at him with curiosity. It became apparent the boy was staring at the fox. The man just looked down at him and said matter of fact, 'Oh, don't mind that. I caught it under the sink this morning'. Everyone laughed, including the boy.

In 1988 I had the opportunity to participate in the Iowa Presidential Political Caucus. Again, I catapulted myself into politics. The Caucus is one of the first of any Presidential election events and Iowans take it very seriously. It is an alternative system to a Primary. Although I knew about the Caucus never having been exposed directly to it, I wasn't sure what to expect. It is a fascinating grassroots movement where every voter's personal opinion has a voice. It starts at a basic neighborhood level and grows more comprehensive as it moves to city, county, and state levels. It culminates in the State Party Convention, one for the Democrats and one for Republicans. Starting with the complete slate of competitors for the Presidency it comes down to who will be chosen at the State Convention level, incorporating all the previous opinions to reach that decision. That person very well could be the ultimate candidate of the party, and often is the person chosen at this Caucus.

1988 was a pivotal time in US elections. It was a time when the Christian Conservative Movement, with people the likes of Pat Robertson, became powerful voices with large contributions to the party, primarily the Republican Party. In my opinion, a sad time and transition in US history. The tenets of separation of Church and State began to morph together, and the separation diminished. Human rights in this country were on the line and very much in jeopardy.

The Caucus starts off in a neighborhood gathering of a few houses, often held in a living room or a garage. Approximately ten to fifteen households will be represented, generally by one household member at this first stage, but it varies in number. Participants sit around and talk openly and candidly about the candidates and the platform, and the reasons they would support a particular person. I attended in my neighborhood and found it fascinating. The participants were involved and thoughtful. Debate on the candidates ensues until the group develops consensus on one. As a Republican at the time, I was backing Pierre DuPont, a moderate.

At each step of the Caucus one participant is elected by the group to go on to the next level to be the representative of the candidate selected. I was elected to go on to the next meeting. This continued, each time at a higher level, city, county, and so forth, to culminate in the State Party Convention where representatives from around the state attend to select the final candidate. I found myself elected at each level to go on to the next step as a representative. It was interesting and stimulating to listen to the perspectives and ideas; and seeing how the consensus system worked. It was quite congenial at the lower stages; and becomes more competitive higher up.

I was eventually elected to be a county representative, a delegate, to the State Convention. This is an important political event where the final selection is made on one candidate to back. This sets the tone to potentially influence other states to follow, New Hampshire's Primary comes next. I prepared myself for the several days of Convention soon to follow.

A gay businessman in Des Moines who was quite well-known through owning a media company reached out to me. He was a Republican. He spoke with me at length to prepare me for what was to come at the Convention, including coaching me in hope of developing some language for gay rights in the platform. While encouraging me to be tough and firm, I became somewhat unsure what I was getting myself into as he told me the right wing and religious advocates would be very powerful and strong.

I received the proposed party platform and read every page, and it gave me pause as well as concern. It was exceedingly conservative, right wing, and had very little room for any allowances for minorities or equal rights. In my opinion in bordered on a fascist document. It made me furious and strengthened my need to stand by my values and not waiver. That while being a closeted professional at the time and very much under the radar not wanting to be detected. And this was certainly not a friendly place to be 'out'.

Meanwhile, I also participated on the other side of the fence with Democratic friends. I was invited to several events with the Democrats, one memorable one at a Unitarian Church where Mrs. Jesse Jackson came to talk with a group of gay voters about the election, and her husband's run for the office. She was warm, embracing, and very gracious, and clear about Jesse and his advocacy of gay rights. It was astonishing to hear that message in that day and age, in Iowa. At the end of her talk a discussion followed ending with a prolonged standing ovation of applause.

When it was announced that Michael Dukakis was the front runner and inevitable Presidential candidate for the Democrat Party, he came to Des Moines on a short campaign stop. He was to arrive in the middle of the night and speak briefly at the airport. Since my partner was a Democrat, we decided to take the two kids to see Dukakis. It was very exciting for them as they had never seen a Presidential candidate before. We got them in the car in complete darkness and headed out to the airport where hundreds of people waited for his arrival. Dukakis got out of his plane and gave his short campaign speech and off he went. We went home to bed.

I was invited to a breakfast gathering for the State represent- atives held on a farm in a barn just outside Des Moines. I really looked forward to having a farm breakfast in the Midwest. They set up long farm tables and had family style platters of food- eggs, sausage, pancakes, potatoes, toast, and homemade jams, that were passed around. Unfortunately, it was neither tasty nor good. The breakfast turned out to be a big disappointment and not like I had imaged, crushing another preconceived notion about Midwest life.

The days of the State Convention were full of activities.

Parts of the platform were up for debate with incorporation of any revisions. I got on the roster to state my views on one, specifically 'family rights'. With my knowledge from Madison of broadly defining the family while working on re-zoning I developed up a very precise scheme to change the wording to be more inclusive in the platform beyond a husband, wife, and children. The platform definition was very clear and staunchly rigid and conservative. I went into the committee meeting well prepared and gave my pitch. I spoke about the validity of non-traditional 'families' mentioning such things as extended, multigenerational and blended 'families', seniors who live together for support and several other likely living situations. I purposely did not mention gay people as that automatically would destroy my case. The head of the committee, a very prim and proper suburban type woman, would not look at me, and when I finished, she spoke directly to the dozen or so others in the room saying, 'We know what this is about. Let us just approve the wording as written and move on'. There was no discussion, and unlike with others I was not thanked for speaking.

It was unanimously approved, unchanged, and I was crestfallen.

The entire platform remained intact as originally written and I was furious. All the talk and committee work were meaningless. The final day of the Convention when the candidate would be chosen came next.

I woke up the day of the Convention, put on my best suit and tie and took out all my tucked away gay rights advocacy buttons to wear. I wore them up and down the lapels of my suit jacket. We had assigned seats in the Convention Center and wore lanyards with our names and county identified. Committed to a task, I went to do what I was sent to do by my constituency, to represent the candidate we discussed and chose, in this case George H W Bush. However, I was not going to hide any longer.

Seated in the vast auditorium I was placed between delegates from other parts of Iowa, a staid looking Insurance Executive and a well-dressed woman who appeared to be in her seventies. She told me she was a housewife. I shared pleasant conversation with both throughout our entire time in the long duration of the Convention. The tone of the gathering was ultra conservative with religious overtones, specifically Christian ones. At one point during a break the woman next to me looked at my lapels and asked about the buttons as she had not seen them before. I was courteous yet direct telling her that they advocated for gay rights. She immediately demurred and just simply said, 'oh' in a hushed voice, and looked away.

The Insurance Executive overheard and asked why I'd advocate for that. I clearly stated because I am gay, and as such face discrimination. There was a bit of silence as he seemed caught off guard but went on to say, 'you know, I never met a gay person before, and you seem quite intelligent, reasonable and nice'. I told him I appreciated the compliment, and that most gay people have those attributes. Then the woman looked back at me and said that she was also pleased to have met a gay person, just a bit surprised. Let's just say that I was pleasantly amazed as I expected one of them to scream or to pull out a bull horn to alert the crowd of my presence and the need to extract me immediately. That did not happen. By time we parted they each shook my hand and told me that they were pleased to have met me, in each their own way. There did not seem to be any animosity or distaste. I felt that single event, in itself, made my participation in the entire Caucus worth it.

George H W Bush went on to win the Presidency and defeated Michael Dukakis. And the right-wing conservatives and Christian Conservative Movement went on to gain power and influence in American politics for years to come. It had begun in the Reagan years but gained momentum and traction under Bush's administration.

The big things to do in Dubuque, Iowa are to ride the only escalator in town, in the Julien Hotel, or a rickety funicular up a steep hillside. I was in Dubuque during a very historic time in LGBTQ+ Midwest history. It is a very conservative, Catholic city and gays were not generally welcomed. In the late 1980s there was a gay pride parade where the participants were pelted with eggs, rocks, and slurs from unfriendly people on the street. Learning that happened the next year the Midwest gay community came together to support them, and when they had their gay pride parade thousands of LGBTQ+ people showed up from all over the Midwest for it. In the morning busloads of gay people arrived from Minneapolis and Chicago to support the Dubuque effort. Participating gay people could have equaled or outnumbered the residents of Dubuque. It was amazing and very moving to witness it. The parade was a mass of gay people marching through the streets and none of the naysayers came to bother anyone. It made a definite impact, and even added to the local economy with the money spent that day. At one point I sat in a park watching it unfold and a very old woman, looking somewhat cranky, maneuvered through the crowd as though full of distain, said nothing, and went her way.

My time in the Midwest was coming to an end. I learned a lot from living there and gained experience in what makes up the supposed backbone of America, the 'Heartland'. I learned perseverance and stamina, and that hiding one's identity is not healthy, honest, or true to oneself, or to humanity. As much as we want to conform it can also be detrimental. My time there, approximately a decade, seemed too long. I was ready to move on, and as noted in an earlier chapter it took a friend's tragic death to cause that to happen.

The West

Driving across the Southwest from Iowa to California and arriving out of an Arctic freeze was like a breadth of fresh air. California holds an allure for so many. Talk to Europeans and they think of sun and surfing immediately. While growing up in Astoria my good friend Robert Dempsey would play Beach Boy records constantly. The California lifestyle was an obsession. When I arrived in 1989 to live in California it was during a high-tech boom and to me felt like the second Gold Rush. Money began flowing everywhere, and opportunity seemed endless.

Settling into a California life was easy, and very different from the Midwest, or South, or even the Northeast for that matter. It is free, open, accepting, easygoing, inclusive, diversified and very relaxed compared to my past experiences in American living. Natives were few and far between and people came from many other places. It was a new place without the binding ties of history that creates a hierarchy of society. Name and status aren't that important. There are seemingly no pretentions.

For several months I'd walk to the Castro, the free and open place for gays and it was absolutely refreshing to be myself without hiding, or concern. At the time a true ghetto.

What I have found most interesting about California is that many people eschew their own families, who most often live elsewhere, and create their own new 'families' locally. It is quite delightful, especially for someone like me who doesn't have many family members.

I, too, have created my own family, and 'adopted' by another. At my first office there was a woman I interviewed for a job, Nila; and I immediately liked her. Vivacious, interesting, talented, and ever so witty. I felt an immediate bond with her and had her hired. She worked with me, and we had a great time working together. There were times she would get frustrated with me, and she let me know it. There was a low partition between us, and we would toss crumpled paper over the wall at each other when we were annoyed with the other person. It was all in fun. Nila was also a prolific artist, a painter of exceptional gallery represented landscapes. She and I would go for fun outings and lunches, laughing, and enjoyed being together. One place we'd go to in the Mission District, called the Slo-Club, was a restaurant and bar. We went because good-looking men hung out there and Nila was looking for dates. I went along for the critique. She eventually, and much to my pleasing, married a man in my office and had a wonderful relationship with him.

Nila introduced me to her family, her mother, Marilyn, and husband, Marv, and they took me in as part of their 'family' spending nearly every holiday celebrating and enjoying being together. It was lovely and I so appreciated being a part of a caring group of people I only knew for a short time. Unfortunately, tragedy struck as Marilyn developed Parkinson's, and then Nila had a brain tumor and cancer and could no longer paint. Then Nila's husband, Tom, developed dementia and eventually died. It just seemed so unfair and untimely, yet we endured together. Without going into details one of the worst days of my life was driving Marilyn early one morning, before dawn, to die as the quality of her life had diminished drastically while no longer being able to walk or speak. She was a caring woman of incredible intelligence, wit, and dignity. When we said our goodbye before she flew off to an assisted death in another country, I gave her a hug and kiss while she sat in her wheelchair. I told her we'd meet again, and she broadly smiled back to me. That truly moved me. I read it to mean that it was OK, reassuring me of her decision, in that she was ready to leave this earth. Regardless of circumstance these folks will always be my 'family'.

Soon after settling in California, I realized it was not wise continuing to be a Republican. I'd be one of very few Republicans; and secondly, I was disillusioned where the party had gone during the past years. It was no longer a party I would want to associate myself. The political climate in San Francisco hit home when I went to vote in my first Primary. Voting was held in a garage of someone's home. When I arrived, there was a line of several dozen people, for the Democrat side, and no one for the Republican side. As I walked up to the Republican table to register there was an outcry of boos and hissing from those waiting in line. This was not friendly territory. I became a Democrat thereafter which I remain today, and proud of it. It saddens me what has become of the Republican party.

October 17, 1989, just eight months after arriving in California, we had a massive earthquake, the Loma Prieta. I had never experienced an earthquake before it, and this was not a good one for a practice run. I had been at a construction site in the East Bay and had just driven across the Bay Bridge when it hit. I sat at a stop light in the Panhandle of the City after deciding not to go back to the office but rather head home since it was already five in the afternoon. And fortuitously a good decision as the area around my office was severely impacted. I probably would have been on the sidewalk when glass came raining down into the street.

Waiting at the stop light my car started rocking back and forth vigorously and I thought I had engine problems, but the car in front of me was doing the same thing. Then twigs and branches started coming down from the trees overhead. I honestly had no idea what was happening. Once the traffic started again it became clear what had occurred. Driving up into Masonic Avenue in the Haight district there were brick chimneys that had collapsed into the street. People were outside everywhere, and it was rather chaotic. I could hear fire engine sirens coming from every direction. With the realization of what had happened I headed to my apartment while holding my breath and hoping it was still there, and it was. Virtually nothing had moved, as fortunately the building was built on solid bedrock, the best of places to be in an earthquake. That evening I walked around some because we literally had no information. There was a person sitting on a porch with a battery-operated TV and a crowd. That was the first time the locals saw the extent of destruction that the rest of the country had already seen in news reports. I called my parents in Florida and they were greatly relieved as they were seeing images of the collapse of the Bay Bridge and major highways along with widespread devastation, hearing that hundreds of people might be dead. Sitting on my apartment balcony that night in darkness, as we had no power, a woman returned home to her place nearby and I heard her scream profusely for several minutes after opening her door. It was chilling.

The next morning, I returned to work and walked up to the fifth-floor office as the elevator was not operational. What astonishes me to this day is that I did not even realize the ceiling of the lobby had collapsed, and I walked across it. That's the psychological trauma of denial and disbelief one experiences in a major catastrophe. I sat at my desk and worked ignoring the fact that there were large gaping cracks in the walls and all the ceiling lights had fallen. The controller arrived to gather up the books and wanted to know what I was doing. When I said I was working he looked in total disbelief and told me to leave the building immediately as it was being 'red-tagged' as it was deemed unsafe, as was every building on the street. I did not know about aftershocks and the risk I was in staying there, an unreinforced masonry building. This was all new to me.

The next day I returned, but now the entire street was barricaded and closed with glass and debris everywhere. I sat at the corner Eppler's Bakery across from the block and got a coffee and cried for half an hour. I wondered if my California dream had ended. But ultimately it did not. The office moved to a new location and thrived there for a decade after until moving across the Bay. The days after the earthquake I walked around and photographed many of the damaged and destroyed buildings.

It is an event I will never forget, and I was lucky to make it through unscathed.

The two children I helped raise eventually came to live in California after getting settled. It was a big change for them from Des Moines, yet they seemed to enjoy it immensely. It was a wide-open place of newness and adventure.

Introducing the girl, Sarah, to private schools in San Francisco did not go well. She found them too stuffy, and elitist, so we enrolled her in public school. At first the San Francisco Unified School District, SFUSD, assigned her to a middle school, many miles away, and in a not so desirable part of the city. I learned quickly about the big differences in schools in San Francisco, a most unfortunate thing. I even wrote a letter and questioned the inconsistent education from school to school to a politician, Angela Alioto, and got no response. Finally, after going down to the SFUSD offices her school was changed to one where she lived. It was apparent one had to advocate for what one wanted; or lose out. Seeing this with a Vietnamese mother months later trying to navigate the system and an application for high school with limited English proficiency drove home how some are lost. Now, many applications come in a variety of languages.

I was totally incensed when she brought home a form from school to be signed by the parents. There was to be a diversity class taught and the parents could opt out their student because it did discuss subjects such as drug addiction, pedophilia, incest, alcoholism, and homosexuality. I was aghast that homosexuality would be lopped in such a group of negative images. I expressed my outrage only to be told that it was not directly a SFUSD mandate, but a statewide mandate. I still could not tolerate the inclusion so wrote a multitude of letters. Not much changed it.

But my outrage got to a San Francisco councilperson who called me to his office. I went and he encouraged me to run for the School Board. He said he would back me and that it would be a beneficial to have a gay man with children in the school system on the Board. I was done with politics from my previous encounters, and politely declined saying that my professional life took up too much time for me to do the job properly. He scoffed and said doing the job didn't matter, just sitting there was all that counted. I could not believe what I heard and furthermore was repulsed by the suggestion. I left the meeting and he never spoke with me again.

Shortly after that I was appointed to the SFUSD ad hoc Finance Committee where I sat for approximately three years with some very intelligent people trying to figure out and correct the debacle of the fiscal problems in the district. I did learn that simply throwing money at a problem, or problems, doesn't necessarily solve them. I was appointed to act as the liaison to the gay community, which I did to the best of my ability. Discouragingly, and after developing some very good strategies, the committee was disbanded, and nothing came of it after a change in Superintendents.

When applying for high school for Sarah another issue arose. I brought the paperwork down to the SFUSD offices and they would not accept it from me. Why? Simply because I was not the legal parent. OK, I get that, but as a gay man unable to marry my partner and make us a 'family' other than through adoption, when she already had legitimate parents, there was no option. Besides I was acting completely as an accepted 'parent'.

Again, I submitted a determined complaint. It apparently was noticed as one day while I was at the office, I was told that the Superintendent of Schools was waiting for me in the reception area, totally unscheduled. I took him into the conference room, and he profusely apologized for the treatment I received at the SFUSD office and allowed me to sign the papers for the girl's application. The political tide for gay parents was changing.

What I found was that even in San Francisco things at that time were not always perfect or respectful, or honored, for gay families.

I've had the opportunity of sitting on two juries while living in California and learned a great deal about the jury system. The first trial was a malpractice suit and planned to be a couple of weeks in duration. A multitude of doctors and professionals testified for a woman with cancer who was dying. It was intriguing to watch the process of a Stanford professor put a dollar value on her remaining life should she live. She was a stockbroker, and it was far less than I imagined. But they calculated things such as her husband's loss in her not cooking meals. The day she was to testify we were informed she had died overnight, and the trial was abruptly ended. I believe most of the jurors left in disbelief. The lawyers asked to talk with each of us, but I declined. It was too depressing.

The second trial was a criminal charge against a woman, mentally handicapped, who had threatened the lives of her mother's conservators as they would not give her money. The threats came by telephone and constituted a crime. I was surprised as when that happened to me in Madison, and then in Des Moines, that was not specifically mentioned, although laws may be different. The trial went on for approximately a week and I thought very well done on both sides, prosecution and defense. Twelve of us jurors were then placed in the deliberation room, and we spent nearly two days hashing it out. They elected me foreman, a job I never did before.

At the end of the second day, it seemed unanimous to give a guilty verdict. Except for one lone holdout, an older Italian woman from the North Beach neighborhood of San Francisco. As foreman I prodded her about her reasoning and justification when the facts seemed clear. She just kept repeating that in her conscience she could not convict the woman as a criminal. It really irritated every juror because there was a clear basis in the law. Not everyone necessarily agreed with it, but we had to abide by the letter of the law as stated. I tried a tact to try and have the woman see another rationalization. I gave an example. I asked her what she would do if I would slap her in the face, expecting she would say she'd call the police and have me arrested for assault. Similar to the woman's threat to the conservator who reported it to the authorities. In responding to my question, the woman looked at me and said that she would just slap me right back. Everyone laughed. It ended up a hung jury. Afterwards I saw the woman in the corridor and approached her. I requested she forgive me for the question I asked her and wanted her to know that it was only to have her see the situation differently. I let her know that I would never actually slap her. She gave me a big hug and said she knew that, and all was forgiven.

In October 2008 Ed, someone I met in 1997, and I were legally married as it was allowed by California law, just before the passing of State Proposition 8 that passed successfully banning same-sex marriage. I got into a tussle with the Catholic

Church over it and it was unbelievably sad and humorous. The Church forcefully campaigned to end same-sex marriage, and I took issue with it based on the country's fundamental separation of Church and State. Amazingly I was surprised that they paid any attention to my message, but I got into a furious email exchange with the Council of Bishops. Within minutes of my sending a message I would get a personal response. In the end it did no good other than quell my disgust. Regardless, our marriage remained legal and valid.

Before the Proposition 8 ballot measure in November 2008 there were many legal same-sex marriages in California. They were such a joy to attend and to see the deep love within the community, and beyond.

Ed and I were married in a ceremony in Piedmont, near our home, and we decided to keep it very low key. We had been a couple for ten years at that point, living most of that time together. Deciding on the date we chose a Thursday evening figuring few people would attend on that day, to make it simple. We invited fifty people and low and behold everyone did accept; and attended. It was beautiful and we were so honored. It did lead to getting a caterer, music, photographer, and flowers. Many of our neighbors attended which really was so nice, and many asked to bring their children, even more special. A dear friend of ours, Cliff Hamilton, a gay man in his late 80s at the time came to celebrate with us. It was the first same-sex wedding he ever attended and certainly a big thing for him to witness. That made it extra heartwarming.

I had known a Presbyterian Minister for many years, a lesbian, and asked if she would officiate at the ceremony, and she did. We went through the required pre-marriage counseling with her. The day was magnificent, and Ed and I shared our joy in the moment. A couple of people even shed tears. We decided not to do everything traditionally, for example, we had no wedding cake but since it was Fall, we had pumpkin bread pudding, and our guests loved it.

Two things happened during the event that stood out, and most touching too. Both were indicative of California and the people who live there. Piedmont is a progressive place yet also a staid, highly respectable community. While taking wedding photos outdoors a well-dressed man in a conservative suit walked by with his dog. Seeing two grooms he stopped in his tracks, hesitated for a minute, smiled, and said, 'Well, I guess congratulations are in order!' It was wonderful and meant so much from a stranger. Then when we were packing some gifts into our car the custodian of the community hall where we were married approached us, and in taking each of our hands he said in broken English, 'I wish you both a very long, happy life together'. It was truly unforgettably moving.

Unfortunately, some time thereafter the Minister who married us was put on trial by the Presbyterian Church for performing ours and several other same-sex marriages. We went to the trial to testify on her behalf. Neither of us are Presbyterian but thought it important to support her. We had never witnessed any Church or religious trial before, and it is not much different than any court trial. She was admonished for her actions, yet one of the jurors approached us privately and apologized for the Church's stand regarding our marriage. We also met a Methodist minister from Maryland who came to see the proceedings as she was sure she'd face similarly in her domination.

Let's hope time will change and heal these ills. I am no theologian, and I respect peoples' beliefs, yet I do believe that we should remember that these 'books of law' were written in former times, primarily by men. And perhaps men who saw women as 'property' in a marriage situation.

So much of this has led to my skepticism over organized religion, although in my experience I can attest to the enormous and very important work done by the Franciscan Friars and The Sisters of Mercy. That will be discussed in other chapters.

For many years Ed and I attended the San Francisco International LGBTQ+ Film Festival in June, a fabulous event. It is held over eleven days and is a constant barrage of films about gay, LGBTQ+, people. We would sometimes attend fifty to sixty films during it, many experimental or independent films. This was accompanied by other events and parties. Held in the grand 1920s Castro Theater it is truly a fun Festival to attend and the energy is amazing. People wait on lines for hours for some of the movies being shown, many being premiered and shown for the first time. We often remarked that people sit in the same seat every year, and it becomes their 'seat'. Because of it you know the people around you well, but you never meet the people on the other side of the theater. As with season ticket holders to the opera, ballet, symphony, or theater performances you develop a camaraderie that often leads to long term friendships.

I have met so many intriguing and interesting people in California. There is an endless array of talent and ingenuity. Many are trailblazers. Being immersed in the hi-tech world innovation is everywhere, and growth of thought and creativity surpasses so much else I have witnessed elsewhere.

California is full of surprises and beauty. There is natural beauty everywhere one looks in the variety of geography, from desert to alpine mountains. It is amazing and unsurpassed, unlike anywhere else in the United States. The shear magnificence is inescapable, and very inspiring. The economy is the seventh largest in the world. It could easily be an independent nation, and a very well-adjusted thriving one. Californians are aware, conscientious and are concerned about the environment and take it seriously. It is progressive and respectful. Yes, there are pockets of conservativism, and socio-economic problems, but overall California flourishes in free thinking, opportunity, and liberalism.

Although not as prevalent and strong as in East Coast cities, and New Orleans for that matter, there is a social and class hierarchy in San Francisco and Los Angeles although they are different. Los Angeles is more entertainment and status focused. Coming from a pioneer family does hold some status in California, although not much, except for a club you can join, The Society of California Pioneers. And yes, there are several elite social clubs in San Francisco including the Pacific Union Club, aka the 'PU', the University Club, Bohemian Club and the Olympic Club where membership is select and dues expensive. I've visited all of them as a guest at one time or another and they are nice, yet a bit stodgy and somewhat pretentious. There is a hierarchy among the clubs as well, and a new club for techies and creative types emerged a few years ago, called The Battery.

There are so many magical places in San Francisco. The hidden stairways that lead up into interesting hilly neighborhoods, the vistas from promontories, and the quaint and off the beaten trail cottages and homes that tourists never experience.

One of my friends, Vince, lived in the Glen Park section of the city in an ever so cute little cottage sequestered behind a fence and garden that when you are there you feel as though you were in another world beyond a city.

One of the most splendid things one can do in the Bay Area is to get out on the Bay. It is calming and refreshing, and equally invigorating. With a couple who are good friends, and accomplished sailors, I got to sail a boat under the Bay Bridge on my own, a very thrilling and memorable thing for me. The open water and the surrounding flanking hills are gorgeous. On that excursion we came close to tankers too and it makes you realize how insignificant a small sailboat is in comparison. One place that is special, and an oasis away from the city, is Angel Island. It is not only protected open land but the vistas to the city are magnificent. It has a history too, once being the West Coast immigration point, the Ellis Island, primarily for Asians immigrating, particularly Chinese people. There's a museum and exhibits that tell the story. My father was stationed there during WWII, and he absolutely hated it. He spoke strongly about being 'stuck out there', isolated, and needing to look at San Francisco while unable to go to it. He said it felt like being on Alcatraz, in prison.

Now living in Oakland, a city in similar geographic area to San Francisco, the landscape is somewhat different. More diversified and certainly a city where there are great advantages and problems. There is the upscale hilly areas and the disadvantaged flat lands. It was tough for me to cross the Bay Bridge and leave San Francisco, my haven for so many years. I often quipped that someone would need to take me kicking and screaming across that Bridge, but you know, it was fine in the end.

Living in a cohesive neighborhood in the lower hills has been nice and its quasi-suburban atmosphere seems a departure from the big city. Every Halloween there are hundreds, yes literally, of costumed children who 'trick or treat' in the neighborhood. It is wonderful to see, as it is very safe and secure. They come from outlying areas and that's OK. Vans drive up packed full of kids who run from house to house, get back in the van and go a bit further and do it again. On occasion you will recognize the same costumed kid a second or even a third time, and that's OK too. Recently, we've taken to wait in the driveway for them as we have seen little kids struggling to come up the twenty steps to the front door.

The most fun on a Halloween was being underprepared for the hoards to arrive. Suddenly running out of candy I decided to run quickly to the store to get more. I had to drive slowly to be careful of kids darting suddenly into the street running from place to place. While I was gone Ed decided to give out money instead. With cell phones and text messages our address suddenly moved up exponentially in popularity when the money came out! By time I got back with more candy there was a barrage of kids waiting to get to the front door!

One thing is evident from my living in and experiencing different regional areas of the United States. I have learned to understand a different perspective from my own, and it has challenged me to see that culturally people do live and think in a variety of ways. Our country is vast, inhabited by people extracted from many backgrounds and places from around the globe giving it distinct flavor, traditions, and viewpoints. It is ever evolving, and that adds to the excitement and beauty of being here whether you live North/South/East or West.

CHAPTER 12

Roots

In 1991 Pam Am Airlines, one of the world's premier carriers, collapsed as a business and went defunct. I had traveled on many of their stellar 747 planes, often with names such as 'Star of the Sea'. They were luxurious, comfortable trips unlike what air travel became years later. The flight attendants were multi-lingual, professional and always accommodating. When I was a child in the early 1960s one of my neighbors in Astoria was a Pan Am flight attendant and she regaled me with stories of trips to Egypt and other exotic places that I could only dream over.

When the airline went out of business, I still had a lot of airline miles entitling me to a free trip somewhere. Fearful I might loss them it turned out not to be the case. Other airlines bought the Pan Am routes and I was able to use my saved mile allocation on Delta Airlines. The total accumulated miles could get me to two places on the purchased routes, either Kenya or India. I thought it best to use them up quickly. I booked a flight to Nairobi but later cancelled it due to political unrest in Kenya at that time. I switched the ticket to New Delhi, India instead. Since the flight had a change of planes in Frankfurt, I decided to extend my trip and stay a week in Germany first.

I will explain my trip to India in another chapter. I will specifically address here my time in Germany, for that portion turned into a search for my 'roots'. My father's family originated in Germany, and I knew little about it, other than I went supplied with a list of names, dates and places by father's aunt, Aunt Betty, had recorded over the years. The places were in a specific part of Bavaria, and I searched it out on maps beforehand. The internet wasn't available then, so it wasn't easy to locate the specifics on smaller, lesser-known locations. I brought with me maps, lots of maps. I also spoke with a man at my office who was from Germany and told him of my dilemma in finding information, and he was helpful. When I commented that I supposed many of the places had been destroyed in the wars he corrected me by telling me that the destruction was primarily in the cities, and not so much the villages and smaller towns that mostly stayed intact.

I had a layover and plane change in Cincinnati and finally made it to Frankfurt only to discover that I made it, but my luggage did not. For those of you who have ever experienced being at the luggage conveyor and all of it has come off the plane and yours has not, you know that sinking feeling. The conveyor goes round and round and no one is there any longer, and the luggage is no longer coming. A sense of doom emerges. I walked to the Delta baggage counter and explained the situation. The woman was quite pleasant and said they would put a tracer on it, and I needed to give her the address where I was staying. She did find that the bag was placed on the wrong plane in Cincinnati; but wouldn't say much more. I had no reservations to stay in Germany and intended to drive and find a hotel, not knowing exactly where I'd be at the end of the day. When I told her that she looked at me like I had lost my mind. I sensed that my cavalier approach to 'winging it' in another county without proper preparation was very 'un-German'. I was indeed anxious, and she gave me a phone number and told me to get some sausage and beer, relax, and call when I had a location.

I got my rental car and headed east on the A3 Autobahn from Frankfurt into totally unfamiliar territory. All I had were the names, places, and maps to where I might find out something about my father's maternal family, the Rodamers. The countryside was beautiful as I drove the highway and getting close to where I thought I should be I exited and began to look for a place to stay. There were several houses posting signs with rooms for let, but I wanted something more private. I happened upon a small inn with a butcher, a *Metzgerei*, downstairs. The inn had eight rooms in an upstairs area. The owners ran the butcher shop and the inn, and the wife was most engaging although spoke no English. We managed with my limited German.

I asked to use the telephone to call the airport with my location. I conveyed the details of the name of the inn and the town. Going to my room to settle in I took out a large map of Germany to locate exactly where I was at that location. Much to my surprise, and dismay, the index revealed that the name of the town, Aschbach, was the same as several towns across Germany! Germany was originally a conglomeration of small principalities before being unified in the mid-1800s and the name of this town was common in several, as would be 'Main Street' in cities across the USA. I fretted over how the baggage would ever get to me and how they would know where I was exactly. Every time a truck would go by the inn, I would jump up to see if it was my luggage arriving, but each time, no. I gathered I would have to call the next day to alert them.

My great-grandfather, Andreas Rodamer, was born in a tiny rural hamlet called Oberrimbach in 1865 according to the records I had from my Aunt Betty, his daughter. I had located a town by that name on a map of Bavaria, so I figured that was the place. I did know from relatives that he was indeed Bavarian.

My first day out I decided to find the town which appeared to be approximately six miles or so away from the inn. Without GPS, which didn't exist at the time, I just drove into the countryside in the general direction. I had a habit of checking for my family name, Brutting, in phone books all around the USA as it is quite rare, so I did likewise in Bavaria for the Rodamer name. In a phone book containing the town of Burghaslach I did find some people with the last name, Rodamer; and it was a town not that far from Oberrimbach, my destination.

Driving through Burghaslach I found a road appearing to head west toward Oberrimbach, so I took it. Going through some rural countryside, quite lovely, the road came to an unexpected dead end, in a field with domesticated beehives! I sat there laughing to myself because there I was in the middle of Germany, and the middle of nowhere, having no idea where I was going.

Turning around in the field I returned to Burghaslach and to a different road, at least knowing I had to head west according to the map. These backcountry roads were not shown on the map as it is in such a remote area. Driving a bit further I passed a road rally in progress. Everyone waved to alert me as I wasn't supposed to be on that road during the rally, but recognizing I was a foreigner they let me through after I told them where I was headed. I then saw a sign for Oberrimbach. I took a photo of myself at the sign as I knew no relative had been to this place since my great-grandfather left there around 1880.

The town was charming and very small, primarily agriculturally based with some of the houses having barns attached; yet all very neat and clean. I walked around enjoying the fact that this was part of my 'roots', my heritage. I discovered an old church, quite simple and statuesque out in a field, and found that it was built in the fourteenth century. According to the records I had it was where my great-grandfather was baptized. That church was no longer used and there was another newer Lutheran Church nearby. It happened to be a Sunday, so I stood at the back of the church during the end of a service. As everyone departed, I waited for the minister and introduced myself. He seemed disinterested in my family's origin in the town. I had some photos of my great grandparents and showed him, and he just shrugged, so I moved on.

I tried to imagine what life would have been like there in the mid-1800s, so remote and off any beaten trail. I wondered if any of the houses were where my great-grandfather and his family had lived. I found the town did have one inn and restaurant and I decided to eat lunch there. I introduced myself to the waitstaff and the owner came out to sit with me. He spoke some English and between my German and his English we had a pleasant conversation while I had a delicious German meal. He was fascinated by my story and took it all in, quite graciously. As I showed him the photos and historic records I had, he kept shaking his head, saying, 'Amazing'. '*Sehr Interessant*' in German. He ran into the inn and came back with a book for me. Wanting me to have it as a gift from him, I was most appreciative. It was a bible from one of the rooms.

I thanked the innkeeper, shook his hand, and drove around the outskirts of town, primarily rural farmland, and fields. Returning to the inn where I was staying, I expected to find my bag waiting for me from the airport, but no bag. It was very frustrating, and I wondered about the duplication of town names across Germany and thought they might be driving it from place to place trying to find me. That evening there was a knock at my door and the woman who owned the inn asked me to come downstairs. A man residing in another building nearby was from California and she wanted him to meet me. He was staying there while working locally. We greeted each other and said some quick pleasantries, but there really was not much to say, however, the sentiment of bringing us together was nice, nonetheless.

The next day I decided to go to the location noted in my information about the place where my great-grandfather was confirmed into the Lutheran faith, a place called Münchsteinach. Finding it on the map I saw that it could not be more than ten miles, or even less, south of Oberrimbach so I headed back there. Finding a road heading south out of Oberrimbach I drove through the most incredibly beauty landscape and forest; pristine, lush, and green. There were marker signs for wild boar. Until then I hadn't known how much protected forest and greenspace existed in Germany. This area was the Steigerwald, a protected land, and I thought it was simply amazing.

Arriving at Münchsteinach I found a town larger than Oberrimbach, also with a lot of aged 'Old World' character. Finding the church, which wasn't hard with a large steeple looming overhead, I learned that it was attached to a large monastery, in a decidedly Germanic architectural style. Walking around the interior of the Church it appeared to be centuries old. Then I discovered a plaque on the wall listing the past head ministers, and the respective dates of their service. The name of the minister listed in my family records was on the plaque during the years my great-grandfather would have been confirmed into his faith. Proof that I had found the right place and I had indeed discovered my 'roots'. I then contemplated the difficult trip from Oberrimbach in that day to get there, especially since his confirmation was in the winter.

Heading back to the inn where I was staying, I first walked around the town and then back to my room. Anxiously, I inquired about my bag. Nothing had been delivered. It was extremely frustrating as I had intended to leave the next day and drive on further to do some touring, and in just a few more days fly to India. I needed that bag!

I planned to call the airport the next morning and tell them I was going on to another location. I practiced my German for the conversation and what to say if the person at the airport might not speak English. The next morning, I went down for breakfast with the intention of calling the airport first. The innkeeper smiled broadly when I got to the reception desk and pointed behind it… there was my bag! I was so relieved and thanked her profusely. She said it had arrived during the night.

Going into the breakfast room I felt a refreshed energy in being on the trip, and a weight of worry lifted from me. There were a group of older German women sitting nearby eating breakfast. I could hear them criticizing the innkeeper's poor choices, in their opinion, of the decorating of the room, pointing to things, and laughing; being very rude. The innkeeper must had heard it because when they were about to leave, she looked directly at them and said in German while pointing to me, 'look, I have a distinguished, international traveler with style, at my inn, and he's about to fly to India!' It was her badge of credibility and I nearly applauded. She wasn't going to let these old 'cranks' get away with their sour attitude and condescending manner.

I thanked the innkeeper, paid my bill, and loaded my car to drive on. I had heard the butcher, her husband, cutting up meat and preparing the store that was directly below my room as a new week had started.

Looking at the map I decided to drive to Bamberg. I felt I had completed my task of finding my roots, or what was available to me at that point. The drive, knowing my suitcase was safely in the trunk, was pleasant and easygoing. I put on a German radio station and sang with the tunes.

Bamberg is a larger town in Northern Bavaria, the Franconia region. Extremely charming with lots of character and historic buildings, the absolute prize is the highly Baroque City Hall spanning over the Regnitz River. There are fresco type paintings all over the sides of the building, and some are three dimensional. There are-half timber buildings everywhere you look. The city is known for a unique very dark beer, *Rauchbier*, or Smoke Beer in English, that tastes like smoke and has a very high alcohol content. Bamberg was heavily damaged in World War II and subsequently had an American military presence.

I am not certain what drew me to that place, yet I ended up there and loved it. Finding a hotel, I settled in and went to tour the sights, really delighted with such a find. Every street and alley had something interesting to see and take in as a visitor.

I decided to stay three nights as I felt I had hit the jackpot of interesting places to see.

I did know that I came to this part of Bavaria to see a very well-known and famous Rococo pilgrimage church in the countryside, Viersehnheiligen; several miles north of Bamberg. It sits prominently on a hilltop overlooking the valleys below it, in the Main River area. I had studied it extensively in architectural school and my professor, Leo Oppenheimer, went on endlessly about its attributes of being the height of the Baroque-Rococo style. It was constructed in the mid-1700s and designed by an architect named Balthasar Neumann. I went to see it and it is indeed magnificent. A Cathedral type structure the interior is an explosion of fanciful decoration, statues all around it, and not a right angle in sight, all in vibrant bright white and gold. The exterior undulates with stonework, again with no corners. I was very glad I came to see it. It is a place where supposedly fourteen 'Holy Helpers', or apparitions, appeared in a field. A farmer in the 1400s had seen an apparition of a child there, and then other apparitions, who pledged to help eradicate the black plague and death in the area if he and others built a church on the site, which they did, followed by healing miracles; becoming an important Roman Catholic religious site for pilgrims to come to this day.

I also visited another important religious site nearby, Kloser Banz, an old abbey with an equally impressive church, also out in the countryside. Both Kloster Banz and Viersehnheiligen flank a small village called Staffelstein. I drove into that town with its quaint and very beautiful half-timbered downtown area of shops, cafes, and civic buildings. It had a charm that I wanted to take home with me, and never intended to share with anyone else as a place I had discovered and wanted to remain that way, undiscovered.

Later while walking casually around the central part of Bamberg across old streets and cobblestones I looked up at a sign outside a café and stopped suddenly to be certain I saw it correctly. It said 'Brütting Brau'. There was my last name! On a sign!!! I knew very little about my father's father side, the 'Brüttings', yet I did know that they were probably from this area, not that distant from where my Rodamer side originated. I knew that originally there had been an *umlaut*, or double dot, above the 'u' in my name before it was Anglicized in America.

I immediately went into the café to ask about the sign, and they told me it is a local brewery, and they sell their beer. Buying several bottles, I brought them back to the hotel. I removed the labels as best I could to bring them home as I could not take the bottles with me. I tried each of the beers; they were all very tasty and quite good.

That evening I went to a local tavern, or gastropub, for a bite to eat. I found a seat at the bar among several people already there eating and drinking. An older gentleman was next to me, and we started up a conversation. When he saw me struggle with my German conversational skills he immediately went to English, that he knew quite well. He was delightful and told me that he had been a seaman and had traveled the world. He told me of many adventures over the years and it was fascinating to listen to him. We laughed, told stories of our lives, and I shared a second beer with him to continue our chat. I mentioned why I was in Germany, my quest for family roots, and my astonishment seeing the 'Brütting Brau' sign in Bamberg. He told me that was the premier 'county beer' in those parts.

He went on to tell me that the brewery and family are in the nearby town of Staffelstein, the town I had just visited that day! He strongly encouraged me to go and introduce myself to the family; but warned me that the elderly matriarch was a nasty, mean person, without qualifying why he thought that. Saying our goodbyes, he wished me well on my adventure and asked me one favor. Handing me a card with his name and address he asked if I would send him a postcard of the Golden Gate when I returned home to San Francisco as he had been there many years ago and thought it was so beautiful. I told him I gladly would, and I did when I got home.

The next day I headed back to Staffelstein.

For me this was like finding the 'Holy Grail' of my family's roots. I had always wondered about the Brütting family origin, my namesake, but knew little to nothing about it. The name is very rare in the United States and only about 50 people have it as a surname, some more in Germany, especially in this region, but not many. I have read that there are more Americans with heritage from this area than Germans living there today. Immigration during the 1800s was widespread and it makes one wonder why some stayed, and most did not. This is not a heavily touristed area for foreigners to visit. Germans, and perhaps Czechs. who are nearby, are more likely to come here, yet it is a hidden gem full of historic towns, many dating back to the Middle Ages.

Arriving in Staffelstein I slowly drove around looking for any signs of the brewery or the Brütting name. Finally, I happened upon a large commercial building, quite close to the town center with large windows and insignias, like crests, of lions with words beneath. I parked and saw the name Brütting Brau.

That was it, the brewery. Ironically, I had passed it the day before not even noticing, but I did recall seeing the insignia that appeared, at a glance, to be British. I simply ignored it. Attached to the brewery is a stately traditional inn and restaurant, a *Gasthaus*, named the Grüner Baum, or 'Green Tree' in English. It has three floors and makes a prominent presence on the street. The street is the Bambergerstrasse 'Bamberger Road' inevitably the original road connecting it to Bamberg before the highway was built.

Walking around I saw a stone tower, the Stadtturm, near a flowing stream. It had a Visitors Bureau, so I went inside and introduced myself. I found that my limited German and their limited English, plus sign language, did the trick with communicating. People are very patient and friendly, especially with my attempt to speak the native language. The woman at the Visitors Bureau counter took out a map and showed me where the Brütting house is located, right behind the brewery.

It was an easy walk to the house, and I immediately made my way there, a sizeable and newly constructed house in a traditional design. I approached the door and saw there were two doorbells, one for a Dr. Brütting and another next to it, so I rang the first one for Dr. Brütting. I held my breathe in an anticipation of what I'd say, but no one came to the door. I rang the bell again, and nothing, so I rang the next doorbell, and nothing there either. Very disappointed I walked on and decided to walk around town. The center of Staffelstein is utterly charming and one feels as though you have stepped back in time. Looking in shops and restaurants along the narrow, windy streets makes for an interesting stroll around town.

I then decided to drive back to Kloser Banz as I had not been able to get into the church the day before, and this time it was open. Another Baroque masterpiece, not quite as elaborate or expressive as Viersehnheiligen, it nonetheless holds its own in design quality. The countryside of the Main River Valley around it is spectacular. You can see across to Viersehnheiligen from there and to the rolling hills beside the massive, impressive Staffelberg, the principal mountain, or '*berg*', that looms over the countryside. The name Staffelberg literally means 'staggered stone' in English.

Leaving Kloster Banz I decided to make one final attempt at the Brütting residence. Parked out front I was about to get out of the car when a Mercedes drove into the driveway to the left of the house. I got out and walked up the driveway. A man was getting out of the car, a distinguished looking older gentleman, very well dressed, and he seemed annoyed by my presence on his property. He yelled out to me in German and wanted to know who I was and what I wanted. A woman of similar age also exited the car, equally elegantly dressed. I explained, at a distance, that my name was Brütting and I was from the United States. He calmed hearing my explanation, but still was not all that welcoming. I took out my passport and walked up to him to show him my name. He seemed surprised and astonished. The woman then came close to look as well, smiled, and extended her hand to greet me. They introduced themselves as Josef and Elisabeth, and yes, they were indeed the Brüttings. Being invited inside I felt my heart pounding as it truly seemed that I had found my lost family, my roots. I sat in their living room as we traded conversation in both German and English, which Elisabeth knew quite well. She called it 'Kitchen English', what the simple people in the kitchen would speak. My German, frankly, was not much better, certainly not *Hoch Deutsch*, or proper German.

They had just arrived back from a Spa holiday, and frankly it was amazing that the timing worked out the way it did.

Sharing family information with each other they were simply amazed. Elisabeth only knew one person in the United States, a cousin who had married an American and now lives in the South. Both were quite charming and personable once the barrier of my mysterious appearance was put aside. Their house was very comfortable and had a wonderful view of the Staffelberg. Josef told me that the house was indeed recently built and that it was designed with a roof to mimic the shape of the Staffelberg behind it. He was an economist, with a PhD in Economics, and did own and operate the brewery and the Grüner Baum Inn, both enterprises the family had owned for generations. The brewery was founded in the mid-1800s and very prolific in the area. Before the new house was built the family had resided within the Grüner Baum. They also explained to me that there was a separate apartment in the new house, hence the second doorbell, that was made for Josef's mother, Babette, who was recently deceased. I thought she might have been the 'mean woman' the man had referenced at the tavern the night before.

They told me they had two daughters, both living in the Munich area, and about my age. One, Gabrielle, was a medical doctor and her sister, Christine, a teacher. Christine was married and had children. They seemed to be a close-knit family.

Our enthusiasm over meeting each other grew exponentially, and the discussion became lively and friendlier. I told them of my travels, my search for family roots, and that I was headed to India. Before our conversation ended Elisabeth disappeared and came back with a box. It was a gift of six Brütting Brau beer glasses with the insignia. I was honored even though I would cart them around India. It was a very important gift, and I would not refuse it. At the time it was such a precious gift to me I didn't even think of packaging them to send back home before heading on.

This meeting led to many years of close family association, and they hence referred to me as 'family'. I was elated and honored. We have no idea if we are truly blood relations, yet it seems irrelevant now. We share the name and have 'adopted' each other. Josef had vague recollection of hearing of a relative emigrating to America in the 1800s and that may have been my great-grandfather, Johann Brütting.

Elisabeth and I continued to share letters nearly weekly over several years. I learned that she had always wanted to visit the United States and somewhat did so vicariously through my correspondence and things I sent over time. We shared many gifts and every year I would send her a calendar for the next year with scenes of California, or the U.S.A., that she could hang in the kitchen. Subsequently her daughters told me that she would diligently study every image on those calendars.

Elisabeth's family were bakers, the Nagel family, and owned a leading bakery in the small city of Forchheim, approximately thirty miles to the south of Staffelstein. Her family must have known Josef's for many years as Elisabeth showed me a photo taken when she and Josef were children siting on the lawn together. Elisabeth was also an excellent baker and made delicious pies, cakes, and tortes. Every year I would get a box of handmade chocolates and homemade treats for the holidays.

I returned to my hotel in Bamberg quite proud and happy with myself; in finding 'my family'. I was elated. The biggest surprise, however, was to learn that the Brüttings were Roman Catholic, and not Lutheran as I had always been led to believe. My grandmother, Ollie Rodamer Brutting, would have never let that be known as she was staunchly Lutheran, although not practicing, and not pleased that both her sons married Catholic women. Keeping the fact suppressed that the Brüttings were Catholic seemed likely as I had no exposure or knowledge of them in the U.S., or otherwise.

Subsequently, on other trips, I had opportunities to visit Staffelstein, staying at their house and at the Grüner Baum, and as well met their daughters and families and became close with them too. They are all delightful, wonderful people, including Josef and Elisabeth's three grandchildren who I greatly admire. During one of my visits Elisabeth invited another Brütting, a relative in Staffelstein, to come meet me, but the woman refused saying she was not interested in meeting a Brütting from the U.S. Elisabeth was annoyed by it.

Staffelstein holds some other surprises other than its charm. There is a large porcelain factory there, Kaiser Porzellan, and it has an amazing shop that I was told frequented by many American military families over the years. There are also wood-working shops where you can purchase hand carved wood objects and sculptures.

Over time both Josef and Elisabeth discussed their living through World War II. Both had parents, the fathers, who were imprisoned by the Nazis for a period for non-conformance. Elisabeth's father was incarcerated for refusing to hang the Nazi flag from the bakery that was prominently located in the town square of Forchheim. Josef, who served in the German Air Force had been captured and was a POW in England for a period. He told me that the British were very kind to him during this time there. His brother, Ambrose, had been wounded. Josef, the usually mild mannered and relatively quiet man would heighten his voice when speaking of the craziness of Hitler and his insane 'Thousand Year Reich'. Elisabeth spoke of the difficulties during wartime and the hardship with hardly any bread or food. They were elated when the Americans finally arrived and took the town. The Grüner Baum became their headquarters and she described how the servicemen would play the piano and some danced on it too. As the war ended Josef's parents were told he was killed; and were shocked when he appeared a year later from England.

Josef, by the way, was an accomplished classical pianist in his own right and I would love to hear him play music in such a skillful way. One of our typical outings when visiting Staffelstein was hiking to the top of the Staffelberg to see the incredible countryside and view. It is breathtaking and you can easily see both Kloster Banz and Viersehnheiligen, like tiny miniature buildings nestled in the landscape.

In 2000 Staffelstein celebrated the 1200th anniversary of its founding. I was there and an amazing several days of festival, a parade, and merrymaking. It had a homemade rural country edge that was very endearing. On the main day of celebration, the parade was followed by the town creating the longest beer table to be placed in the *Guinness Book of Records*. The continuous table wound through nearly every street and people sat on either side, drinking beer! Bands played and it was very festive. People came from many places around the area to join in the celebration.

The other important milestone for Staffelstein was becoming a '*Bad*' or spa location with natural springs, a very important designation as it is now called Bad Staffelstein and has an enormous spa complex for visitors to relax and rejuvenate.

Brütting Brau brewery ceased operations in the 1990s after over a hundred years of exceptional beermaking in the traditional German style. Contrary to what was happening in the United States with the proliferation of microbreweries in Germany they were either closing or being absorbed by the larger German breweries, Lowenbrau, and St. Pauli Girl. The Brüttings sold the brewery and the land and amazingly a U.S. brewing company came to buy the lauter tuns and copper kettle equipment, which is expensive and hard to come by these days, as well as the older equipment is quite cherished. Much to my surprise Elisabeth wrote that an American Brew Master had come to get the equipment and to ship to the U.S., and she sent photos of it being removed from the building for shipping. The equipment ended up in California at the Anderson Valley Brewery, in Boonville, so nearby my own home as though it was destined; and to draw us Brüttings closer. I visited there after a new brewhouse was built and the equipment installed. I took great pride in seeing the large Brütting Brau signs displayed within the building.

Both Josef and Elisabeth have passed-away, and it greatly saddens me after having such a long and warm connection. They were wonderful people, and I will never forget them or how kind they were to me, my 'family', my roots. I am now close to their offspring which is something I detected Elisabeth wanted to happen. I have great memories and will continue returning to Staffelstein as I consider it 'home'.

The family also suffered a tragedy, a sudden death, in recent years, and I flew there to be with them during a difficult time. They are such an impressive, inspirational family in many ways. I saw firsthand their resilience, but mostly the care, warmth and love they exhibited to support each other. Having seen so many dysfunctional families in my life, and especially when tragedy hits, my observations of this family were very heartwarming. They are very close knit and wonderful to be around under any circumstance. The three children, siblings, of the generation beyond me are amazing adults.

After that first time in Staffelstein I left Bamberg, and before returning to Frankfurt Airport to fly off to India, I stayed overnight at Schloss Weißenstein in Pommersfelden, not far from Bamberg. The Schloss, or palace, is a massive Baroque residence built in the early 1700s. It is also an inn, and you can stay in the elaborate outbuildings converted to a luxury hotel which is most pleasant for a stay. The Schloss itself is now a museum, although in private hands, and you can visit at arranged times. Elisabeth told me that General Patton used it as his headquarters after the War for some time.

I headed back to Frankfurt quite pleased that I had accomplished my task of discovering my roots. Never expecting all that much it turned out very rewarding, and I met some incredibly wonderful people who became life-long 'family' along the way.

CHAPTER 13

The dawn of Aquarius, aka The Internet

The Internet was undoubtedly the most life changing invention of my lifetime. Like the invention of the automobile, elevator and steel fabrication of my grandparents' era, the internet was a defining moment of my generation.

Cyberspace hit the world like a meteorite.

Before 1995 there was little exposure to the internet, and it is amazing what it has done for humanity in such a short time. I couldn't have imagined how it would transform our lives.

I had encountered computers from my teenage years, as my father was involved in computer technology from the 1960s onward. He was with a company in Connecticut named Alpex Computers in the 1970s that designed and built computerized cash registers. Computers were fascinating to him, and he knew how to build them from scratch. I must admit I got bored with computer conversation during dinner, but I did admire his wherewithal in embracing the technology.

I started working directly with computers around the early 1980s. We were moving from using typewriters to hybrid, word processors, where you could work through a television screen using a keyboard and printer.

In the early 1980s I was also introduced to using CADD, computer added design, for my architectural work. The firm I worked for had a contract with the State of Wisconsin and they insisted that all the work be done on CADD as they believed it more efficient and cost effective. No one had much knowledge of it then, and the equipment was large, cumbersome, and expensive. When the firm balked over having to use it the State offered to train me on their equipment, so I went to a state office building several days a week for training.

I did all the State work on CADD, enjoyed it, and became proficient at it. The floor plates of the state office buildings were large and unwieldy, and this really helped to avoid producing large hand drawings. Knowing CADD helped me get my job in San Francisco, as it was a newer qualification developing quickly.

During my career one of my client's representatives was a retired IBM executive. He said when he worked with computers in the 1950s IBM estimated that there would be an ultimate need for four computers in the world, mainframes for governments. Boy, was that shortsighted!

I remembered when I was studying at Tulane the computer gurus of the time carried around these punch cards that looked like alien text. Stacks of them customarily wrapped in rubber bands.

My other exposure to computers in the 1970s was when I had a summer job during college with a Silicon Valley company with a branch in Connecticut, National Semiconductor. They hired me as they were building an addition to their facility and capitalized on my architectural schooling to be their on-site representative. It was both fun and educational. What amused me about working there was they played background 'Musak' throughout the facility with only songs about California. I performed hands-on work hooking up nitrogen lines in the new laboratories, and similar small construction tasks. Another part of my job was drafting the semiconductor components. They also gave me special access to the 'Gold Room', a highly monitored and regulated room where few could enter because it was filled with gold, used for coating the semiconductors. It was my job to go in at the end of the day a brush up any of the microscopic gold filings that happened to fall on the floor or the counters.

One day I made a fatal mistake, one of two during that summer. I was walking through the construction area, and I moved a pipe out of the way so that no one would trip on it. Immediately the plumbers walked off the job. I had no idea what happened but was called into the main office and reprimanded for it. I was emphatically told not to ever touch any piping, electrical, or other construction materials that were not assigned to me since only Union card construction workers could do that. I was aghast. They walked off the job because I moved the pipe.

Then another day I was cleaning up a new lab after installing some nitrogen lines and accidentally backed into a counter. A box fell on the floor and when I picked it up it was full of round discs, computer chips, and they were now broken in snapped shards. I believe the damage came to about forty-five thousand dollars in hardware; but I was thankfully absolved. It never happened again.

During one of my last days on the job, before heading back for school, the laboratory addition was nearly complete, and I was working in a lab when an alarm went off. People started rushing frantically down the corridor and when I looked up from my task, I saw a man completely engulfed in flames while running. The sight was terrifying. With the screwdriver I had in my hand I ran too, out the exit door. Outside everyone was standing around watching an ambulance arrive. I did not see the man who had been burned again and I was sent home, like everyone, after learning that a bottle of a flammable gas had fallen and exploded in a room where the man was at the time.

It had been a very interesting computer related summer job!

My first exposure to the internet came around 1995 when my partner had access through a city government he worked for at the time. It was all 'dial up' and slow, but I was enthralled by it. To think that I could put in any subject and get all types of information as if it was an Encyclopedia was utterly awe-inspiring. I remember one of the first searches I did was of Luxembourg, a random choice, and took a comprehensive tour of the country 'virtually', in photos, plans, maps and other documents. Although in its infancy, with little in the way of web pages, it was nonetheless a game changer in our lives.

After I started working at HKIT Architects, in 1990 one of the Principals, Bob Tucker, brought in this machine, a box, called the 'Apple' or 'Mac', by Macintosh. It had a little screen and a keyboard connection, and something called a 'mouse'. We were all rather intrigued by it, and Bob really enjoyed touting the joys of using it. Not long after an 'Apple' appeared on all our desks, one by one. It became the method to word process, write letters, do spreadsheets along with producing other documents.

Even though I had CADD skills the firm did not take advantage of it and over the next couple of years CADD did get slowly implemented into all our work. One of our Administrative Assistants was very resistant to the new computer technology and would not give up her typewriter until we very gently coaxed her into it, and eventually won her over. I was very resistant, at first, to introduce the Internet into the office since I worried over cyber security, but as the boss Bob prevailed. Gradually, I came to write more reports and eventually all my documents on the computer, and over time we upgraded to better equipment. We were hooked in the computer world, then software contracts, and printers! Once into it, there is no turning back.

At home I decided to buy a computer with an enormously big, bulky CPU, 'tower', as I wanted the capacity to do CADD work at home. It stood nearly four feet tall. The internet expanded as rapidly new web sites surged and blossomed into everything imaginable.

I recall a lot of complaining when the FAX machine was introduced into the office. Suddenly everything coming through it was 'URGENT' and needed immediate response. It really was not necessarily urgent, but that was the materialized expectation with the new technology.

Then came email! Oh yes, everyone got an email address! How exciting. Now you could have virtual correspondence with other people who also had an email address. Software companies and those with names with Microsoft, Oracle and others were becoming mega businesses. Floppy drives and other advances emerged and before long architects were hardly drawing any longer. Our drafting equipment, T squares, Triangles, etc., became obsolete.

Some people even had two or three email addresses, just like having two or three phone numbers, for various reasons. There were free email services, like Hotmail and Yahoo, while others charged a fee, and the San Francisco Bay Area became the center of the high-tech universe. The Peninsula evolved as a mega complex of offices for the development and creation of new computer inventions. Innovation was all around, and the money flowed as no one escaped the grasp of technology.

Then there were computer video games, and I readily admit to having enjoyed some. Everything from 'Tetris' to 'Candy Crush' flourished as entertainment. My all-time favorite is a video game called 'Titanic'. You search for clues to solve a mystery on board the ship and be saved; or if not, you drown. It's timed to the actual days the ship sailed, and a virtual clock keeps time. The prime objective is to recover a copy of *The Rubaiyat* of Omar Khayyam and get it off the ship before it sinks. You encounter passengers and crew during the voyage, and you can speak with them, and they answer in real voices, all stock questions, and answers, of course. There are shady characters on board the ship and you must avoid them. The video is so authentic that it is difficult not to get immersed into it as though it's real. The first time I played the game it got to a point where the ship is sinking, and I ran to find a lifeboat. I met a woman on deck, a passenger, and she alerted me that all the lifeboats were gone. I felt a traumatized emotion at that point as the ship kept sinking, and finally submerged, me with it. The reality was an astonishing sensation.

Social Media then got a foothold, web sites for chatting, connecting, and extolling any bit of information you cared to share, including photos, or 'pics', as new lingo developed with it. Facebook became popular, and I for one have never joined and never will. I have professed to be the last person on earth to join Facebook, and only if forced.

Ed and I met on a web site, in 1997, called gay.com, a place for gay people to connect with 'chat rooms'. That was back in the day when your domain server had to be listed and I saw that Ed was in Benicia, with a Benicia 'domain', where a friend of mine lived. We started chatting and the rest is history. If it wasn't for the internet our paths may never have crossed. That web site included people from around the world, and it was fascinating what developed from it. Those of us in the Bay Area created a monthly coffee get-together where we would meet in a different coffee shop, in person. Many of us became friends. We also became friends with a man in Italy who turned out to be a priest. He learned English by chatting on the web site. When in Rome one year he surprised us. He had quietly found out from others the day we were arriving and the hotel where we stayed. He sat there for hours awaiting our arrival, and we were indeed surprised. He gave us a glorious tour of Rome, from the Vatican to the Catacombs, taking us places the public were not admitted. He was a Catholic historian and full of incredible in-depth information. He even corrected the tour guide in the Catacombs on a fact she got wrong. None of this would have happened without the internet.

Years ago, I had a beautiful lamp with a hand painted glass shade and a pressed bronze base that belonged to my paternal great-grandmother. It was passed down to me by my grandmother. It sat on my bedroom desk for years and I did all my homework with it on. During an unfortunate cleaning the extremely fragile shade was destroyed as it broke into a hundred pieces. Remarkably, thanks to the internet, I found the exact same lamp and shade forty years later, from a seller in Ohio, and immediately purchased it. It now sits in my den and reminds me of my grandmother every time it is lit.

Indeed, a lot of good has come from the computer age. Data collection is one reality. The ability to connect across miles is another. Getting information is now instantaneous.

When the firm gave me my first cell phone, a flip phone, around 1995 I looked at it and wondered why? The partners thought it beneficial to have good connectivity to the office when I was out at construction sites. I was the first in the firm to get one. It did prove of value for quick calls to resolve issues. Now we have the 'smart phone', and I wonder what is next? I recall my stepdaughter, Sarah, getting a pager about the time I got my cell phone and could not imagine why anyone wanted to be connected that way, with such a quick need to get in touch. However, it had a purpose for her generation that I did not understand.

Now when I ride our public transportation system, BART, everyone's face is buried in their phone. We have disconnected while connecting. The days when you sat in a train and looked around, observed people, perhaps even smiled no longer exists.

We are now programmed like Pavlov dogs. How many times have you heard a cell phone ring and the owner jump immediately to get it? We can now identify the caller through our online contact directory. Land line telephones are obsolete.

Although I like and embrace technology, I wonder if we have gone too far and how much further into automation we will fall. The future is arriving at record speed. It concerns me to see so many be entrapped by cyberspace and no longer fully engaged in the real world around them. Computers and the internet are indeed marvelous inventions transforming our lives, yet we should maintain them as tools in lieu of an escapism and crutch.

When I was in Los Angeles earlier in 2020, I had a hot dog at Pink's, a well-known hot dog stand, and when walking back to my car a box on wheels came rolling right by me on the sidewalk. It was a delivery box, artificial intelligence, taking something to someone. It stopped at the intersection for the stop light, and when the light changed it crossed the street.

Evolution is amazing, and the world is indeed ever evolving.

CHAPTER 14

Not just any tomb - Lenin's tomb

Tulane University, where I attended college, has a Junior Year Abroad program which at that time was to England for architecture students. I was neither invited to participate, nor did it interest me. I did not see the value of studying in England. I was much more adventurous.

Around my second year of school a group of my college buddies got the idea to circumvent the globe by ship and study in Australia. That seemed exciting. We booked on a ship called the Australis, the Chandris line. It was 1974 and six of us signed up. Our plan was to sail to Sydney, attend school there for a semester, and return on the ship continuing in the other direction to complete our round the world excursion. We had not consulted our parents, Tulane, or a school in Australia. We were just going. The bubble burst when we finally came to find that being in the southern hemisphere the school year was opposite ours, so our sojourn would take two years, not one. End of story. The bookings were cancelled, and it was never mentioned again.

Tulane, in conjunction with the local American Institute of Architects, also had a traveling fellowship, The John W. Lawrence Fellowship, awarded each year to one student based on a proposal submitted. I decided to apply, and my proposal was to go to the Soviet Union to study architecture.

I applied in early 1976.

We were in midst of the Cold War, and it would be akin to a student going to North Korea today. The idea of going to the Soviet Union on your own would be as easy as a trip to the moon. It was almost unheard of, and nearly impossible. It just was not done, and the Soviets did not allow it. Only tour groups through the Communist State Tourist Agency, INTOURIST, were allowed entry under their restrictive guidelines. I was nonetheless determined and not deterred.

I spend days meticulously putting together my Fellowship application with my planned itinerary, and the general scope and explanation of the trip. One requirement was to include a budget. The funds available would not cover the trip so I included an offer to put in my own money to cover the cost. I submitted the application with great enthusiasm, and it went dormant for some time until the selection committee met to review proposals.

One day while in class the Dean came to the door and called me out of the room. That raised curiosity with everyone, including the professor, as that rarely happened unless something drastic had occurred. It crossed my mind that perhaps someone died. He took me into a vacant room next to the classroom, extended his hand congratulating me saying that I've been awarded the Fellowship. The committee was most impressed with my proposal, groundbreaking, and they wished me well. Then he patted me on the shoulder and said, 'indeed, good luck!'. It felt exciting and daunting at the same time, yet I was elated.

I went back to the classroom with a huge grin and a few of my friends who knew I had applied assumed that my proposal was accepted. After class I was just beside myself with anticipation... I was going to the Soviet Union! Excitedly I went back to my place and called my parents to tell them, although I had not told them I applied. There was utter silence on the other end of the phone. I tried to get a response, but nothing, just silence. Then my father said, 'congratulations' in a hushed tone. I knew they were not thrilled with the whole thing, yet usually supportive of my wild ideas, in time. My mother's parents had fled Lithuania, most likely to escape the never ended Russian occupations. The Russians were never thought of positively in my family, and always considered the enemy. No doubt they thought I was unreasonably placing myself in the hands of the enemy; and jeopardizing myself.

That was fundamental, a very good question.

My application explained my reasoning for the trip. At that time there was little in the western world, especially the US, known of Russian architecture. Random photos in some books, generally written in Russian and usually from the 1920s, were the only things available. I found very little when I scoured libraries and looked for resources. There was one good book, *The Design of Cities* by Edmund Bacon, first published in 1967, that included a great explanation of the urban planning of Leningrad. That became a prime resource for me, and it included a small map. I was able to piece together a sketchy history of the development of Russian architecture, including its influences from Byzantium, plus how the iconic onion domes were developed- to shed snow easily. Even though it was a notable world architecture, that was the extent of what we had available.

I put together a basic itinerary that traced Russian architectural history from ancient to modern times; and intended to visit and study in these key places. My hope was to stay in student dormitories that might be available to me; and lessen the expense. Travel to the Soviet Union at that time was costly. The flight alone was pricey and once there you are at the mercy of INTOURIST and the authorities with overall expenditures.

Hence my saga began...

My determination far outweighed reality. After some searching and questioning of travel agents, I landed on one in New Orleans with Thomas Cook & Co. He had experience with travel to my intended destination as he was at one time with the embassy in Finland and knew the ins and outs, the intricacies, of getting into, and out of, the Soviet Union. At our first meeting he had maps of Saudi Arabia out on his desk as a client wanted to do a driving trip there. He raised his eyebrows and gave me that look of impossibility, yet he wanted to accomplish the trip for them. When I explained what I wanted to do he just folded his hands on the desk and said, 'Hmmm'. Admitting there were many hurdles he was willing to take it on.

Originally, it was proposed to spend my time in Moscow and Leningrad, formerly and now St. Petersburg, but I knew to get the full depth of Russian architecture I had to travel farther afield, making the trip even more difficult. There was some sort of regulation that foreigners were not allowed to spend more than three days in any city at a time. That complicated it, a lot. The travel agent was creatively trying to develop some plan where possibly my suitcases could move to various hotels after three-day stints, or even travel back and forth from Moscow to Leningrad every three days, which seemed ludicrous. We considered all options to circumvent these obstacles.

At one point as I did everything to push my point with the travel agent he just sat back and said to me, 'now look, if you truly believe you're going to just settle in over there and comfortably write and sketch in Gorky Park like it's the Tuileries in Paris, that isn't going to happen!'. Reality settled in as I heard his words. I felt a slight chill recognizing the relinquishing of freedom and choice to a communist state. I was a kid from Connecticut with a Republican family during the U.S. bicentennial wanting to jaunt off to an enemy country that was staunchly communist with an 'Iron Curtain' between us. I remained determined.

I spent time writing to Universities in the Soviet Union trying to find a place to stay in a dormitory as a 'visiting student'. The response was always, *'HET!'*, or 'NO!'. It was not possible. Discussing it with the travel agent he patiently told me that I had no choice but stay in INTOURIST sanctioned hotels. When I saw the prices I balked, yet there were no options. These were hotels for foreigners only, and Russians were not allowed in them. He reinforced that one does not go there and 'mingle'. I was getting a dose of Soviet reality.

It was apparent I needed an itinerary fixed through INTOURIST, and I couldn't work around it. I wanted to include the cities of Kiev, Volgograd, and Tbilisi in Soviet Georgia. The only way to communicate with INTOURIST was by wire transfer, and it took days and costly. Each request came back rejected. I got frustrated. After the third or fourth round INTOURIST was becoming impatient with me and sent me their itinerary with a take it or leave it note attached. It had places I never heard of, but the worst part was that most of my time would be spent traveling on trains. It seemed like they set me up to just travel continually by rail, with overnight excursions, and see little in between. I rejected it.

We got into a stalemate. I was flustered and the travel agent continued being patient with me, in almost a fatherly way.

Running out of time I came up with a specific route and sent it to INTOURIST through the agent by wire. Waiting with trepidation it came back accepted. I would not travel on trains, rather by air, on Aeroflot, the official Soviet airline with the worst record for air safety. At least I wasn't wasting precious time on trains. In the meantime, I kept my parents uninformed of all the planning, other than I was going. I also had to go back to the Dean to advise him of the change from my original proposal, that in turn had to be reviewed and again approved by the committee. He told me that he was not surprised and anticipated it, and the committee approval came in little time.

I would visit Leningrad, Volgograd (formerly Stalingrad), Tbilisi, Sochi, Kiev, and Moscow. It followed a route that some of the foreign tour groups followed. Fortunately for me it also allowed me to effectively trace Russian architectural history as well, perhaps not in the exact sequence of its development.

The next step was to acquire a visa. The travel agent helped me with it, and it was extensive. I was attempting to do something quite unique, travel as an individual. Somehow, I had to 'blend in', rather than stand out as an individual, and he was very intuitive and creative as to what INTOURIST might consider. They did, yet the visa was not immediately issued.

My travel agent did everything seemingly possible to assist in my quest, including using past contacts and knowledge. I believe he became intrigued by the depth of my earnestness in making this trip possible.

After reaching my first milestone success, one fine morning I woke up and realized another important necessity, in that I had to learn Russian! I had to learn it quickly. Not only is it a very different language it has its own alphabet, Cyrillic. I got an available course, books, and tapes, and mastered the Cyrillic alphabet in little time. Then I mastered some Russian phrases and basic conversation. I am fortunate in that I can learn languages without much difficulty. What I found in mastering the alphabet is that once you know the letters, they can correlate well to English in words that are familiar. As an example, the word, Restaurant, in Russian is *Pectopah*. P is like our R, C is S and H is our N... so phonetically *Restoran*, Restaurant. It isn't always like that, but I discovered many similarities through figuring out the alphabet nuances.

I immersed myself in finding every available resource to accomplish my mission. Maps were hard to come by, and books on the subject, as noted before, were rare. I searched far and wide for everything I could, and I did find some basic information. What I did not know, unfortunately, was that a professor in Slavic studies was at that time looking into the history of Russian architecture too; and traveling there as well. There was, however, a Tulane student who had visited the Soviet Union. Friends linked me up with him, which was helpful, and after my return I spoke with another student intending to travel there as well. Word of mouth without the assistance of guidebooks and/or maps was very helpful.

There were no guidebooks, so information was scarce for an independent traveler. It wasn't like traveling to other European countries where you went down to the bookstore and got what you needed. I had to paste things together, especially maps, from resources I came to find in old books.

Back in Connecticut, I went to Yale University several times to scour their archives and they were most generous giving me admittance to libraries. I think they may have felt sorry for me, yet I uncovered some vital things I needed from those visits too. Pouring over old volumes I found resources, most written in Russian. As I was not all that proficient in reading Russian, I did my best, with a Russian-English dictionary in hand. What I did learn was that Russian architecture was influenced primarily by foreign styles and architects who worked there, and that there were distinct historic periods. Some periods were purely Russian stylistically and indigenous there alone. Many of the early influences came from ancient Byzantium moving through the regions of Turkey, Armenia, and Georgia and eventually north to Moscow and beyond. The shallow dome of Byzantine architecture became tent shaped in the Caucasus region and then eventually the ubiquitous and often elaborate onion shape in the north.

The local newspapers in Connecticut learned of my impending trip and began announcing and reporting on it. My parents were quite proud that I received the Fellowship yet remained mute on the purpose. In the coming days I learned the depth of concern in other people I knew.

Something totally unexpected transpired and to this day I do not know what to make of it. One afternoon in Connecticut the doorbell rang and there were two men in suits looking very serious-minded at the door. They showed me identification that they were from the US State Department. That made me uneasy, and you can imagine my parents' reaction seeing them. They asked to speak with me and allowed my parents to listen, as they thought it beneficial. They had come to warn me of some of the problems and issues I might encounter with my trip, especially in the way I was attempting to do it. I was amazed they even knew I was going.

They offered the following advice. First, that I should not be surprised if I were to land in the Soviet Union and be turned away immediately, not allowed to enter the country. They said that is not unusual in circumstances like mine. Second, while in the Soviet Union should I be stopped by the authorities I should not go with them, anywhere. They informed me that it was not uncommon to have them take a person to a security protected location and claim they found you there, and immediately arrest you for espionage. They said if detained I should hold my ground and insist on contacting an American agency immediately, including the US Embassy in Sweden. Handing me some contact information they finally told me that should anything happen the U.S. most likely will not be in a position to help, rescue or protect me. I would be on my own. I could see my parents grimace at that point, and very little conversation took place about it thereafter.

I intended to photograph as much as possible to record the trip. My father bought me an expensive Canon camera and a variety of lens, from wide angle to telephoto, for the trip and I purchased dozens of rolls of film to bring along, primarily slide film. With x-ray machines at airports at that time you had to be careful with film being over-exposed, so I purchased several lead bags to store the film. I would be going through many airports, including within the Soviet Union, so it was important.

There were very strict guidelines as to what you could not photograph. There was no photography allowed of airports, military facilities, factories, churches, and from an airplane over cities or the countryside. Like anywhere it was proper to ask a person to photograph them before doing it.

I waited a very long time for my visa to arrive and nothing came, month after month. In frustration I kept calling my travel agent who did everything he could to find out what had happened; but came back with nothing. Panic set in when I was one week away from leaving and had everything in order; but no visa. I anxiously waited for the daily mail delivery, and when we reached four days before my departure I catapulted into action. Contacting the travel agent, he still had not heard anything or could find out anything about it. He said it wouldn't be surprising that they pushed it aside or tore up the application; be prepared for defeat.

There was a Soviet delegation in New York associated with the United Nations. There was no Embassy or Consulate as the U.S. had no official ties with the Soviets. The travel agent suggested that is probably where they would issue a visa to a U.S. citizen; so being in Connecticut my father and I drove to Manhattan and went for a visit. It was not exactly a warm reception and I pleaded to find out what they might know about my application. They had us wait a very long time while supposedly searching it out. Sitting for what must have been two or three hours a man then came out and handed me a document, my visa! I was astonished and elated. He simply conveyed that it was placed inside someone's desk drawer. With the visa in hand, I realized that had not I been so close in proximity to New York I would have never seen the visa in time to leave.

The visa itself was intriguing with my photo, of course, my name in Cyrillic, and a detailed list of where I was to be, when, and the exact times. It appeared that there was no deviating from the established INTOURIST issued itinerary.

Packed and ready to go I was Best Man at a wedding the day before my departure. This is when I found out what people thought of my adventure. Solemnly nearly everyone at the wedding came to me, hugged me, or held my hand, and asked me to be careful. It felt as though I was in imminent danger. People were seemingly saying 'goodbye' as if they did not expect to see me again. A couple of them literally said, 'don't let them brainwash you over there'. It became very clear that in their view I was going into the hands of the enemy.

I left on my adventure on August 1, 1976.

Being twenty-two years old I had been to Canada many times, but only abroad one other time for a trip I made to Europe by myself three years previous. I had visited all Western European countries. I had heard that the further one goes East beyond East Germany the more austere things become behind the Iron Curtain. I was headed deep into it.

My parents drove me to JFK airport in New York and we said goodbye. They did not express any concern or acted upset, just take care.

I was supposed to fly through Warsaw but that was changed last minute to my flying and changing planes in Frankfurt and then Helsinki before landing in Leningrad.

The flights were smooth except I did have a long layover in Frankfurt which wasn't awful as it broke up the trip. Flying over Finland was a delight to look down on all the green and lush islands, eventually arriving in a very contemporary, wood paneled airport in Helsinki. Boarding the plane to Leningrad, on Finnair, was a bit more disconcerting, yet full of anticipation. I observed a considerable degree of reduced service from the flight attendants on this short flight as they appeared quite surly, compared to the other flights I had taken. At one point a flight attendant looked irritated, left the cabin, and quickly closed the curtain behind her, as if to say, 'don't bother me!'. Flying into the Soviet Union airspace I did my best to see what I could out the window, but it was foggy and overcast with not much to see. I chortled to myself that the Soviets probably arranged it that way. What was out there remained mysterious.

Landing in Leningrad I disembarked, gathered my luggage, and then went to the border patrol and customs area. There were armed uniformed guards everywhere. I moved quickly through the que and kept thinking of the State Department comment about the possibility of being rejected and sent back. That did not happen. My bags were checked as there was huge black market in items such as blue jeans which people tried to bring in for making large sums. I kept myself very clean from any such activity. The amount of money being brought in is also carefully checked and recorded, as there was a black market in foreign currency too. It is again checked when you leave, requiring everyone to keep all receipts for whatever is purchased. It's a signal if you are leaving with far more than when you arrived having changed the Russian *rubles* back to dollars as it was illegal to take *rubles* out of the county. I have never kept such a detailed record of my spending as I did that time.

Finally, I found myself out of the airport and into the Soviet Union. It did feel somewhat like I imagined landing on the moon. Everything was different and unfamiliar. There were few automobiles, and a military presence was apparent. The clothing people wore was outdated and drab, plain, without any style. I felt the sense of emptiness. A man met me, speaking impeccable English, to take me to my hotel. During the drive he went on incessantly about the quality of Russian ice cream.

Getting to the hotel I settled in comfortably. It was new and contemporary with a distinctive Scandinavian aesthetic. It soon came apparent that only foreigners were staying there. I had an amazing view from an upper floor over the Neva River, with the ship, Aurora, in the foreground and the city beyond. Every day the Aurora shot a canon. I really couldn't complain about the accommodations, except I was paying way beyond what any Soviet would pay in other Leningrad hotels. It was annoying as INTOURIST required me to prepurchase all of my meals which would be taken only at the hotel. That too was outlandishly expensive. However, I soon found that restaurants were far and few between, so it was convenient. The hotel restaurants may have been the best choice, although I would have preferred more interaction in public places.

INTOURIST also assigned me a 'guide', named Larisa. A delightful, young woman who was only available for questions and advice. At times I felt she was hovering just to keep an eye on me. We would check in occasionally, she more on me. I was not sure about the logistics that my travel agent arranged through INTOURIST or any unique nuances in my visa, but once there I had few restrictions. I felt very comfortable just roaming and moving about at will. It was possible to deviate from the itinerary to go to outlying areas, but only with a car and driver and INTOURIST approval.

Once there I did not have any sense of fear or uneasiness.

Two things stood out about every hotel where I stayed. First, on every floor there was an older woman stationed at every elevator bank who sat at a desk, typically with a scowl, who never spoke, nary a greeting. In a ledger in front of her she would carefully record whenever I left and when I returned. The Russian name for these gatekeepers was 'dezhurnaya'. It soon became apparent that Soviets worked many menial jobs, keeping everyone in the communist state employed. This created a huge bureaucracy of inefficiency. As an example, should you go into a store you would first be met with a person to select your purchase, then another to pay for the purchase, and lastly another to pick up the purchase; all at different locations within the store. The other thing that stood out was the foreign hotels had a store within them, called the 'Beryoozka' or little birch tree in English, that only accepted foreign currency. They typically carried a variety of goods, especially luxury goods such as furs and other high-priced items, unavailable to the average Soviet citizen who was not allowed in them.

Anyone who visited the Soviet Union knows this dynamic well. The shameful and rather sad part of the Beryoozka stores was that at nearly every hotel where I stayed Russians would hover and linger nearby and literally beg me to go in and to buy them needed goods, primarily toothbrushes, toothpaste, and especially razor blades for shaving. They were difficult commodities to find in local stores, yet readily available in the hotel stores for foreigners. I never partook in this exchange, as much as I wanted, due to keeping a lower tolerance on risk. You never quite knew who these people were, possibly the authorities out to entrap.

I recognized two distinct differences about the Soviet Union from the United States. In the Soviet Union there were far fewer vehicles on the streets, and basic goods were very hard to get. Stores were generally sparse with available items, and when something became available lines would form immediately buying it out. People would buy two, three, four or more of an item, just to keep it on hand, or give it to a neighbor, as it might not be available again for some time. This applied to everything from socks to lamps.

I'm not certain what happened to the 'three-day' rule about staying in any one city, but I spent several days wandering throughout Leningrad freely and openly. It is a beautiful, classically designed city founded by Peter the Great in the early 1700s, moving the capital from Moscow, to become the 'Eyes on Europe' to rival any other capital. It was also a flat forbidding land, mainly mud, with extremely cold temperatures, mosquitos, and a very harsh inhospitable environment. The Russian aristocracy disliked it but went along to please the Czar, yet, returning to Moscow whenever possible. It's often referred to as the 'Venice of the North' due to its many canals.

My first impression was the scale, especially in height. There are no tall buildings and like Paris, it is regulated. The spire of St. Peter and Paul Cathedral, where the Czars and Czarinas are buried, on an island in the Neva River stands above everything. The city plan is uniform and formal, resembling Paris or Washington DC with straight processional streets. The buildings are primarily in a classical style, most being designed by Italian architects brought here to create the new city. It soon became clear to me that you could recognize which architect designed a building by the color. Each architect used a unique color, of yellow, blue, or other pastel.

Nevsky Prospekt is the main boulevard of the city, the equivalent of the Champs D'Elysee in Paris, or any other major city's 'main street'. It is the heart and soul of Leningrad. There were commercial buildings, offices, apartments, and churches. St. Kazan Cathedral stands prominently there. At that time, it was The Museum of Atheism. What stood out was how the buildings were grimy and dreary, looking rundown and unkept. There was a large food store in an extravagantly elegant building, still standing today, founded in the Czarist era, called 'Gastronom No. 1'. Amongst all the splendor of chandeliers and gilt décor, albeit somewhat dusty, there was very little in the way of food to purchase. It was sad.

I wandered the city in every direction with great enthusiasm snapping photos everywhere. I found former mansions of the aristocracy, now being used for other purposes. The size and scale of these aristocratic houses was impressive. The Czar's Winter Palace is a seemingly endless stretch of building along the length of the Neva River. Catherine the Great had added a large addition for her private art collection, now part of the Hermitage Museum housed in the Winter Palace. St. Isaac's Cathedral is a replica of St. Paul's in London, exhibiting a borrowed copy of foreign architecture. What I found particularly interesting was the use of stucco by the Italian architects who worked here. Stucco is not the best material in such a harsh climate, and it cracks constantly. All over Leningrad there was scaffolding repairing and repainting stucco facades.

There were many churches I saw either abandoned or in disrepair and scarcely attended. I visited as many as possible.

When open and functioning, there were always just a few older women wearing babushkas present, looking tired and weary. Occasionally I saw these women walk the outside perimeter of the church kissing the walls as they walked around it before they entered. Religion was scorned and not commonly practiced.

Since it was forbidden to photograph in churches, I used high speed film and while holding my camera at my side I would discreetly photograph as best I could, even hiding behind a large column to snap a photo quickly. It was a haphazard attempt, but it sufficed under the circumstances.

Returning to my hotel one afternoon I found something a bit disconcerting in my room. I often wondered if the room was bugged. I thought that was senseless to think anyone would care to know what I was doing; but I was still careful even though I had nothing to hide. Being extremely meticulous with how I arrange, fold, and place things I can always detect if anything has been moved from how I placed it. That afternoon it was evident someone, besides housekeeping, had been in my room and went through all my clothes and other items, including my suitcase. I casually mentioned this at breakfast to other Americans staying there and they told me it happens a lot, so not to be surprised.

There was a total lack of news from the West. If it didn't happen in the Soviet Union or satellite countries, you just never heard about it. That became frustrating and the absence of free speech and available press or media was alarming to me. Soon I learned that the only method of learning news from the outside was to find someone in the hotel who just arrived from the West. One day I heard someone mention that thousands of Americans were dying of a strange disease in the United States.

I eventually learned it to be the first outbreak of Legionnaire's Disease and the number of deaths, although alarming, was nowhere near what I had originally heard. Snippets of news came in a variety of ways.

One afternoon I decided to walk into the classically designed Astoria Hotel near St. Isaac's Cathedral. It was beautiful inside and finding a café there I decided to try it out. I ordered caviar and vodka. Caviar was something I wasn't that accustomed to, but there it was undoubtedly the very best I have ever eaten, even to this day. It had the consistency of butter, smooth and delicious; not at all fishy. With a glass of vodka, it was heavenly.

Being young I could maintain long hours of exploring, usually up and out by 6am and back by 10pm while only returning in between for meals. I never felt limited or hampered in my exploring. Fortunately, I was there in summer, and daylight existed for nearly twenty-four hours.

The black market offered many opportunities, but I steered clear of it. I stood out as a foreigner by my clothing and many people approached me to talk, some wanting to make 'a deal'. I usually did OK with my Russian; and many spoke German too. So, between my 'broken' and limited Russian and German I got though many conversations. And it is amazing how sign language can fill in the gaps.

Anyone who approached me to talk would only do so outside, never in a building, café, or a very busy public place. Public parks were usually the place they felt most comfortable. Once people felt away from possible surveillance, or being overheard, the conversations were candid and honest. Most had an insatiable interest about the West and learning about the United States, and my life. They generally would not talk about politics as they said we cannot change it, so why waste our time with the subject. Most were frank that they neither hated Americans, nor necessarily thought of us as their enemy. I was often told that in their view our leadership had ideological differences, but they themselves were more complacent of the animosity between us. It was so different than I expected. Meeting people of all ages and backgrounds most parted by considering me a 'friend'.

In an early evening I had what was my most interesting encounter during a walk. A couple of young men, about my age, approached me and wanted to talk. We conversed for a bit, and they asked if I'd like to accompany them for a drink, and I agreed. They both told me they had been in the military, and one spoke English relatively well. To keep the other man involved in conversation we primarily spoke Russian, but occasionally the one reverted to English to clarify some point he wanted to make to me. We walked to a large ship, resembling a schooner, moored on the Neva River, not far from the Admiralty. There was a gangway onto the ship and an armed uniformed guard at the base of the gangway. When the guard saw me with them an argument ensued as we tried to board. It was obvious he did not want me to board the ship. The two men were quite adamant and held their ground until the guard finally, and very reluctantly, acquiesced to allowing me to board. I did not know the issue or concern and they did not explain. I also didn't know the purpose or function of the ship. The man who spoke English told me not to use my camera; or take it out of my camera bag for any reason.

We boarded the ship and there were a few tables with chairs on the deck with only a couple of other people there.

It appeared to be a café or bar but when I inquired the men didn't care to give me any answers. It felt very bizarre. A person came to the table, and they ordered drinks and appetizers, *zakuski*, for us. We had a very pleasant time, and the evening air was delightful. We shared stories of our families, music, pastime activities, school, and some about our hope for the future. After an hour or so it didn't seem like there was much difference between us.

We had a couple of drinks each, and they asked if I would like to walk along the beach near the Fortress. I agreed. We walked for quite a distance, chatting as we went along. They suddenly stopped when no one else was around or in sight. The one who spoke English asked to compare our shoes. He pointed to the sole on mine comparing it to theirs and mine was obviously more substantial. That was followed by him asking if he could buy my shoes, taking out a bundle of *rubles*. I told him I really needed them for my trip, and he seemed annoyed. He then wanted to know if he could buy my belt and pants, while inquiring how many pairs of blue jeans I had brought with me. I was confounded as to what was he expecting, perhaps intending we trade clothes as part of his 'deal' right there. I again refused, telling him I just had a couple pairs of jeans, and couldn't sell them. He got more annoyed with me. His friend seemed frustrated and equally annoyed by the impasse. Finally, the English-speaking guy looked at me, said, 'goodbye', and walked off with his friend. I had to wonder if it was truly a 'black market' deal, or a set up.

The struggles the city has faced over the centuries is most exemplified by the great 900-day siege of Leningrad during WWII. The Nazis endlessly bombed and held the city captive while countless people starved or died, by the thousands. The impact was still felt during the time I was there. Older men proudly wore their war medals, every day, with enormous pride. I went to visit the famous cemetery of mass graves, of those who died during that time. It was an extremely moving experience as there are large mounds, each with a plaque of the year bodies were placed there. Silence is required while visiting and classical music is played in the background from speakers in the trees. It can put a chill up anyone's back, but important to remember the severity and magnitude of the event.

One day while out walking I saw what appeared to be a military-supply store, like our Army-Navy stores in the United States, but far larger. I walked in and there was a brisk business going on, although the place looked as dreary as any other with bad lighting, old fixtures, and dusty wooden cabinets. There was military gear of one type or another and I focused on finding Red Army belt buckles as they were extremely popular back in the States at that time. I finally located some and a counter person came to help me. She became somewhat suspicious when she found my Russian to be somewhat sketchy with an indeterminable accent, plus looked at how I was dressed. I pointed and asked to buy some of the buckles, taking out *rubles*. She looked sternly at me, forcefully chided me while saying it was not possible. Calling over a couple of uniformed men they promptly escorted me out of the store.

I picked a nice sunny day to take a hydrofoil out to Petrovordets, the summer palace of the Czars located several miles outside the city. The ride was smooth and fast, and I was delighted to find a good café counter on board for a snack. The palace is magnificent and the fountains cascading down from it and out to the Bay of Finland are particularly noteworthy. In gilt and gold, the fountain's statues are whimsical and impressive while the cascading fountains are feed by gravity with a high spout at the bottom. The palace itself was bombed and destroyed during WWII but lovingly restored. As people heard it would be a possible target for the Nazis bombing this building, they took great strides in removing all the furniture and placing it in the woods and other structures. Much of it was saved through this valiant effort, but the building was obliterated. I took photos of photo prints I found of the place after it was destroyed, and it is quite amazing that they were able to bring it back to its former glory. Side by side the images of the bombed remains and the reconstructed structure are quite extraordinary. I spent a considerable part of the day exploring the palace and grounds and I would certainly suggest that it rivals Versailles, which was the intent when it was built.

When my days in Leningrad were over, I left for the airport to catch an Aeroflot plane to Volgograd, formerly known as Stalingrad. Aeroflot is an experience onto itself with rickety planes and a horrible track record of accidents and crashes. I humorously speculated that INTOURIST devised this plan for me to fly in hope that I might expire somewhere along the way and leave them alone. The engines are noisy, and it seemed they had difficulty keeping the plane from bouncing and shifting vigorously. Comfort is an anomaly on an Aeroflot plane, nor do they seem to care. Some planes have exits through the tail, different than anything I'd seen before.

In comparison to Leningrad, Volgograd, further south and east and on the Volga River, is an entirely different place. The city was founded in the 1500s and known as Tsaritsyn. Little if anything remains of that time, and subsequent eras. I went there specifically to see how a city was re-built after WWII. Stalingrad, as it was known then, was completely obliterated in the war and some of the worst fighting occurred there. In the Russian history books this place has the reputation as having changed the course of the war. They were able to stop the Germans there, forcing them into retreat. The Battle of Stalingrad lasting nearly seven months in 1942-1943 left an indelible mark on this city.

The only thing left from before the war is an old flour mill that is the focal monument of the victory. There is also a statue commemorating the Battle on a hillside that I will describe later. The old red brick mill, although a bombed-out shell, is considered an important historic structure. There were plans to reinforce it and have a series of walkways with exhibits to visit it and tout its significance. It may have a lot of symbolic meaning, but it is essentially an old brick building without much character.

The rebuilt city, to Soviet standards using their three-five-and thirty-year plans, is dismal at best. Stark, bland, and lifeless there is little to say of what was created there. I was amazed at the shoddy, cheaply detailed construction, especially in the long, boring lengths of apartment blocks. There's little vegetation and few places for social gathering, interaction, recreation, or play areas. The housing complexes are block upon block of mid-rise housing, feeling like baren wastelands. Constructed in a way to house everyone quickly it was evident the buildings were also not being maintained.

Commercial buildings in the downtown area were somewhat better, but still stark and lacking character. There was a beautifully designed promenade and series of pedestrian platforms leading down to the Volga River which had places to gather, and boat launches for commercial vessels.

My hotel was on a major square downtown and looked over a park along with a war memorial. Every day a troop of young girls in red uniforms, white blouses, red bandanas around their neck, and red ribbons if they had pig tails, would visit the monument walking in a goosestep in unison. It was also common to see wedding parties come here to leave flowers as a commemorative gesture to those who died so the couple could marry. That was a common practice everywhere I visited.

My hotel room was comfortable, but very much a product of the late 1940s. Not much had been refurbished since then. It had high ceilings, basic ornamental details, yet it was bland and felt like a transient hotel. It was where I first encountered the amazing complexity of Russian windows. There are two sets of windows with a big air gap between them and smaller panes within the larger window that can open separately, near the top, for ventilation.

Going to the hotel dining room felt like something out of a Fellini movie. Waiters stood around looking bored with typically few patrons present. I cannot say the service was cordial. Most people sat alone, usually smoking, at a table with their respective country's flag.

If people treated me with curiosity in Leningrad, people in Volgograd would stop in their tracks and stare as I passed. It became apparent that Westerners didn't customarily travel to this place. I smiled and even gave a friendly wave at times, always met and returned with a cold stare. People never seemed to smile. I had some conversations, but not nearly as many as I had in Leningrad. People just did not want to interact, cautiously suspicious of my presence.

One day I went out to visit Volgograd's other famous landmark memorializing WWII outside the city, the Mamaev Kurgan hillside with the unfathomably enormous statue of Mother Russia, 285 feet high, completed in 1967 and called *The Motherland Calls*. The statue holds a sword extended outward toward Berlin encouraging the Russians to fight on to victory. The sword extends out eighty-eight feet, or similar to an eight-story building extending horizontally outward. There is a shawl at the back that is an equally amazing cantilever. It is one of the largest statues in the world, the largest of a woman, and well worth seeing. People standing at the base look like tiny specks from a distance. This is the site where some of the fiercest fighting occurred during the Battle of Stalingrad.

The statue is part of a hillside complex that is vast with a series of platforms, stairs, fountains, and other herculean sized statues in a processional walk to the top of the hill topped by *The Motherland Calls*. Overwhelming is an understatement.

There is a Pantheon at the complex with an eternal flame and a constant watch by military officers. Names of the dead from WWII line the walls.

The magnitude of this event in Volgograd's history and psyche is undeniable. From an architectural standpoint the entire complex is simply phenomenal and a most appropriate tribute.

My days in Volgograd were illuminating as I recognized the rebuilding effort in a city after it was destroyed, and the Soviet vision to house everyone soon after; yet the reality is a dismal, dreary place without much soul. Architecturally plain and unremarkable it says something about the need to provide without much concern of aesthetic; or uplifting the human spirit.

I have little recollection of the Soviet airports which leads me to believe they were unimaginative. I flew to Tbilisi, the capital of Soviet Georgia, over the Caucasus Mountain range. I was pinned to the window the entire time as the jagged snow peaked mountains beneath me were beautiful to behold. The terrain seemed forbidding and appeared to be a distinct geographic border from the Russian territories.

Georgia is an interesting place and quite exotic, in some ways more Middle Eastern and Turkish in flavor than Russian. Located next to Armenia, Azerbaijan, and Eastern Turkey it also is a close neighbor of Iran. Although Georgia is on the Black Sea, the capital, Tbilisi is far inland. It has distinctive architecture influenced by Byzantium and its neighbors to the south and east. I found something else unexpectedly distinctive too, they have their own language and alphabet! As there were no guidebooks and with this unknown to me, it became immediately concerning. The alphabet appeared to be a cross between Cyrillic and Arabic and unlike anything I've ever seen before. Fortunately, most Georgians spoke Russian, so that was good, except most of the street signs were in the Georgian alphabet. I often had to write out the characters of a street on a piece of paper to find my way since maps were scare and not reliable.

Josef Stalin, the wretched dictator of the Soviet Union for decades, was Georgian and because of it they benefited from a level of freedom and independence unknown in the other Soviet republics and satellite nations. The people seemed to be happier, more outgoing, with darker, olive colored skin, protective of their identity and culture. There wasn't as pronounced a military presence as in Leningrad or Volgograd. The other surprising thing was the amount of available produce, fruit, and vegetables, all fresh and widely available.

My hotel was a contemporary high-rise structure, relatively new, and comfortable. Tbilisi is very hilly, and the hotel stood high on one of the hills overlooking the city and I had a wonderful view outward. The landscape was obviously drier than the two previous places I visited, and it appeared to be more Mediterranean than northern European.

I really had my work cut out for me in this city as I knew so little about it; and wanted to learn as much as possible. The city was founded in the fifth century and for years had been ruled under the Persians, Russians as well as independent at various times. It is in a geographically significant and strategic spot between the Soviet Union from Turkey.

What I did know is that Russian architecture was greatly influenced by Byzantium in ancient Turkey and that influence came through Georgia and Armenia as a stepping-stone north. One of the distinctive architectural features of this region is the tent shaped roofs on religious buildings of an earlier era, usually accompanied by domes flanking it. As these elements moved to the north into Russian architectural styles, they morphed into the ubiquitous onion shaped domes so familiar to us. As I wandered about it became apparent that there was also a strong Art Nouveau influence, and some unembellished contemporary Soviet structures intermingled in the fabric of the city.

A major river, Mtkvari, meanders through the central part of the city, often with high palisade cliffs at its edges. There are amazing old decorative wooden houses that appear to hang off the cliffs and are quite distinctive. They have elaborate balconies and seem like something out of the Arabian Nights, 'One Thousand and One Nights', book of Middle Eastern tales. I saw beautiful wooden houses and buildings, unpainted with an amazing patina, thoroughly the Soviet Union, most often in the outskirts of the cities. Intricate carved wooden details typically surround the windows, doorways, and eaves.

Elsewhere in Tbilisi there is also an ancient fortress that exemplifies an earlier time of military prominence.

The hilliness of the city is a defining factor in its urban layout, and it does not feel as packed and dense as Leningrad or Volgograd. Fortunately for my young age I was able to forge the hillsides and wander neighborhoods for hours, photographing everything. As you get further up into the hills it seemed that the neighborhoods were more neglected. Getting goods and services up there was a bit of a challenge.

There was a lot to explore, and I took advantage every day of seeing a new part of the city. It was a feast for the eyes as every street had something new and different, a quilt of interesting architecture and topography. People were very friendly and curious; older people sitting on benches would smile or wave. I found it a delightful change from the coldness of Volgograd's residents. Walking down one residential lane I encountered a small group of children playing badminton. When they saw me, they stopped and stared with inquisitiveness. I smiled and they came running up to me, pointing to my camera bag. I took out my camera and they got excited, and without prompting they got in formation for a photograph. The pose was so perfect and their expressions totally captivating. I snapped a couple of photos and took out packets of chewing gum I had brought with me. They were thrilled and a couple of them ran into a nearby house. Soon after a woman came back with them, probably their mother, but none of them could communicate with me. The woman smiled broadly and greeted me warmly, and with sign language asked that I wait. She ran back into the house and came back with small gift for me. I was so taken, and extremely appreciative. It was a small wooden animal. She removed the head and showed me it was a salt and pepper shaker. She pressed it back into my hands and smiled again. I departed and the kids waved vigorously, yelling something that I surmised was in Georgian. I waved back. It was one of those moments that becomes forever ingrained, and I have never forgotten the warmth and friendship of that moment. These people were not my enemy, or afraid of me, nor me of them.

One night I ate at a sit-down style restaurant, not a café or hotel dining room, perhaps the first of my trip. I enjoyed a feast of Georgian food. I randomly pointed to menu items, doing my best with the Russian translation and my Russian dictionary. It was very uniquely different from the Russian meals I had been eating, and more lamb, figs and other fruits cooked into the dishes. But the absolute highlight was the bread. I have never tasted such delicious bread in my life, and unfortunately, I cannot tell you what it was. I just know it made an impression.

I had been keeping a daily diary, but kept it under wraps as best I could, even using coded words to make it indecipherable should it be looked at or confiscated. To the best of my knowledge no one ever looked at it. I wanted to capture the moments that made the trip, and my architectural observations, memorable; yet I had to be careful not to be too overtly critical.

Getting up one morning I found myself incredibly ill. I wondered if it was a virus, food poisoning, or something worse. The headache and fever were intense, and I suffered from nausea and severe diarrhea; something you do not want to have happen that far away from home, and alone. I called my contact, Larisa, who as I remember it told me to just rest. That wasn't very comforting. I decided to go down into the lobby and dining room that afternoon in search of Americans as I knew some were in the hotel. I found an older American couple from California eating lunch. I explained the problem and the woman went to her room and brought back some prescription medication, primarily for diarrhea. Not wise to do, but I took it from her as I was feeling terribly sick, and not yet prepared to get medical attention. It worked because by the next morning either my body's natural immunities, or the medication, brought me back to normal, or both; and I was very relieved.

I skipped breakfast and had some toast and tea and went out for the day. Inquiring at the hotel desk about getting to another part of the city they recommended I take public transportation and told me where to get a bus. After waiting a very long time a van holding about twelve people pulled up at the bus stop. It was old, worn, and dirty. I had been told that you customarily do not get on if there are no seats available, and since it was full, I waved it on; but the driver signaled me in. When I stepped in a bunch of faces stared at me and I wondered what to do, prepared to stand and hold on to the back of a seat. Suddenly a person in back pulled out a wood plank; and placed it between the two opposite seats across the aisle. A man pointed to sit on the plank, which I did. There I sat on a wooden board in the aisle and the ride was less than comfortable, especially with the shifting and weaving through narrow streets; yet I made it to my destination.

My days in Tbilisi were both interesting and fun, with one final unexpected event that made it all the better. As I had accomplished what I wanted in terms of architectural exploration; and discovering the examples of how Byzantium had moved through this region to influence Russian architecture many years later, I decided to just wander. While walking down a street I encountered a group of men sitting in a walled courtyard by a large building, an older building of some character and beauty. They smiled at me and called me over. We conversed in Russian and they invited me to see the building's interior. To my amazement it was an active, practicing Jewish Synagogue. This was a time in Soviet history when Jews were, yet again, being suppressed and persecuted; many trying to leave for Israel, if they could. Finding a Synagogue in such open splendor and in pristine condition was incredible. The men were obviously proud, and certainly aware of their freedom of religious expression. I was asked to place a handkerchief on my head before they would let me into the sanctuary. They lit the entire room, and it was just beautiful with chandeliers and sconces shimmering on the surfaces of the walls. Well kept, and ornate it stood as a gem of architectural magnificence. I took some photos and thought that this had to be a highlight of my trip.

Leaving Tbilisi was difficult for me as I enjoyed it so much. I wondered what lies ahead in my travels.

Years later, this country would be befallen with considerable strife, and I am certain some on the splendor destroyed in conflict. The ravages of war are indeed sad.

I took a short plane trip to my next destination, Sochi, a resort city on the Black Sea. What amazed me on this flight was the attendants gave the passengers a bowl of fruit that was passed around from passenger to passenger. The fruit was extremely fresh and delicious, and obviously a product of Georgia, delivered with pride.

So, why would I visit Sochi? Resorts and holiday locations are integrally important in Soviet life, especially warm weather ones. This was, along with parts of the Crimea in the Ukraine, the largest and most popular one in the Soviet Union, and within the Russian federation. It was founded in the mid-1800s for the Russian elite and was further popularized by Josef Stalin in the 1930s. The various Communist committees gave workers time off to visit places like this, most often at a 'Sanatorium' for health and mental revitalization, rest, and spa treatments. Most of the constructed city is relatively new and resembles any resort type city in the West. It very well could be the Miami Beach of the Soviet Union, although hilly and with a mountain range nearby.

I was really smitten with Sochi as it has a mild climate and very unlike a place one imagines of the Soviet Union. It is indeed a place to escape to rejuvenate among the palm trees, sand, and lush vegetation. The beach stretches for miles and is extremely well used. There are well designated public and private beaches, and the private ones are secured; generally belonging to the many hotels that line the waterfront. My hotel had a tongue twister of a Russian word for a name that I had to repeat over and over to get down to be understandable for taxis and asking directions, '*Zhemchuzhina*', or in English, the 'Pearl'.

Crowds of people in bathing suits line the beachfront and there are small food stands along with areas where men play chess at large tables, in their bathing suits, with a crowd of people watching. The Russians embrace chess in a big way and it's very evident here.

The other thing that impressed me was that there was a no smoking policy in Sochi to promote good health. That applied everywhere, including indoors, outdoors and on the street. I had never heard of this in any other place, and I was very taken with the progressiveness of it.

Sochi had a large circus building, much like any sports arena. In the Soviet Union nearly every major city and resort has a prominent building, typically round, just for the circus. The circus is a cultural icon for the Russians, akin to the ballet or the symphony.

It is a city where the word 'Tovarishch' or 'Comrade' lives strong. Everyone seems in a good mood and celebrating life to the fullest in a holiday atmosphere. People stroll the streets and parks and unlike the gloominess of Volgograd there is a sense of happiness and joy here. Many people engaged and smiled as I would pass, yet there were still many who stood near the hotel discreetly asking for me to shop in the store for them. I always reluctantly said I could not, and none seemed surprised or taken aback, just resigned.

The contemporary buildings were quite nice, simply designed and streamlined; usually white or bright in color reflecting the light. I visited a few of the Sanitoriums, and they tended to be designed more in a classical style with embellished columns and pediments, and classically proportioned windows and openings. The Sanitorium do have a medical, institutional aesthetic in the interior décor, but the dining rooms tend to be lavish and quite beautiful, generally with great views out to the landscape or hills, or the water.

One day right after lunch I decided to take a swim in the Black Sea. Getting into my bathing suit I went to the private beach outside the hotel, without much sand but rather small black rocks, generally with a white crystal-like fissure within them. They are quite beautiful, and the beach looked black at this location. There was no one at the beach and I had it all to myself, quite a luxury compared to the overcrowded public ones. I enjoy swimming a great deal and had many opportunities during my life in pools and in the ocean, both in New York and Florida, and I can swim quite well. The sea was relatively calm, and I swam way out when suddenly my entire body cramped up. I could not move and began dunking beneath the water. I was horrified and scared. I remembered that the beach did not have a lifeguard, so I was basically out there alone and weakening. While struggling I remembered that the rule is not to panic as fighting it only makes it worse. So, with all my might and wits about me I stayed focused and tried my best to get myself back to shore. Exhausted, I did make it to a point where I could stand and walk, and I made it to the beach where I collapsed, gagging from the water I took in. After composing myself I went right back to my room and decided that it was not wise to swim alone, especially in a foreign country. It also made me wonder if there is some truth about getting cramps when swimming right after eating, as I had done that day. I had heard that as a child and believed it to be a myth.

I spent my days wandering the city and beachfront with my camera and got some great photos of life in Sochi during that era. Walking in the hills was an absolute pleasure. The semi-tropical vegetation shrouded everything and now and then a beautiful *dacha*, or holiday home, would appear. I enjoyed the panoramas and vistas and liked that the city was not that dense or tightly constrained. The pulse was primary pedestrian oriented, and everyone was outside walking and strolling, which was wonderful.

Sochi became the site of the Winter Olympics in 2014 and probably more than ever that event put it on the map, like Lillehammer and other smaller, out of way places around the world that became Olympic venues. I left this bit of paradise realizing the vastness of the Soviet Union, the diversity of architecture and culture, yet also knowing I was only seeing a fragment of its totality.

My next stop was Kiev, the capital of the Ukraine which is the 'bread-basket' of the Soviet Union. An ancient city on hilly terrain it holds a vast array of fascinating and significant historic buildings. For centuries it was a religious center with monasteries that were powerful and influential. It is a sprawling city of new and old. There is also a unique architecture that is traditionally Ukrainian in design. There were several styles over centuries. One unique and distinctive feature are the domes of the churches and religious buildings. They are helmet shaped as opposed to the tent or onion shaped as seen on Byzantine or Russian churches.

My hotel was older and on a major street overlooking a park and large square. I settled in and found a few Australians staying there. At least they spoke English, and some had recent news of the outside world. Again, there were various flags of nations on the dining room tables and I often ate alone at the one with the US flag. I wondered what would happen if I defected over to an Australian or other country's table, and the real purpose of it anyway. But I did not want to test the scrutiny, because nearly all the staff knows where everyone is from.

There is a lot of territory to cover in Kiev. I tried to map it out historically and I found the depth of old architecture to be very rich, some stretching back to the year 800. The embellishment and detail of design is reminiscent of Ukrainian Easter eggs, very elaborate and carved sharply in geometric shapes. The massive churches were most impressive, and some of the catacombs were mostly creepy. There was a lot of walking, and what I was pleased to discover is much of the city is laced with a network of beautiful parks and outdoors spaces. The riverfront of the Dnieper River is gorgeous, with high cliffs and beaches well used by the residents.

I discovered a preservation effort to protect Ukrainian history and its buildings and that pleased me a great deal. I also found that Ukrainians are rather nationalistic, and do not in any way consider themselves 'Russian'. Seemingly, at least at the time, comfortable under the Soviet umbrella I sensed that communism was comfortable to them. Everyone had a job, and everyone had a place to live, and health care.

One day I did speak with two American women at the hotel who had a specific purpose for being in Kiev. One of them had relatives who were Jewish and lived there during WWII. They had been massacred at a place called Babi Yar, outside the city. She came to see the place and pay her respects. They rented a car and driver arranged through the hotel and INTOURIST that took them out to the location. She said it was very moving for her to be there, and her friend was wonderful moral support in seeing the place where her family had been exterminated. I had never heard of it, but now the name of that place sticks permanently in my mind, especially after coming home and reading that over 30,000 people had been killed there.

Centuries of buildings exist in Kiev and seeing them is quite the feat, especially without maps or a lot of information. I did what I could to find out important pieces of architectural information; and did a lot of inquiring along with as much reading of plaques and other identification pieces using my Russian dictionary as was possible. What I found was exploring on my own and just plain wandering led to a lot of good and valuable notes, and photos.

There are two significant religious places to visit, one was St. Sophia's Cathedral that dates through several periods of history. The other was the Pechersk Lavra complex that can take a full day of exploring alone. These buildings are quite striking and well preserved. The gold domes glisten in their prominence. They appeared to be considered far more sacred that any religious structures I encountered in Leningrad, or anywhere other than the Synagogue in Tbilisi.

There are some fascinating Art Nouveau and large Soviet era structures too. One building that blew me away in its enormity, and perhaps garishness, was the blood red University building in a classical style. Enormous in scale the red color is extremely off putting.

Leaving Kiev left me with the impression of a Soviet republic that conformed with Communist rule; yet had an edge of independence to it as well. It had a feel distinctly different from the Russian parts of the Soviet Union I visited, and more inviting, complex, and uplifting.

Boarding my plane for Moscow, *Moskva* in Russian, my final destination, put me on edge as I knew it would be an overwhelming part of my visit, and it was indeed. I was introduced quickly to Soviet control when the plane landed at a different airport than scheduled, without notification, or explanation; and I only found out when I entered the terminal building totally disoriented with my plan to get to my hotel.

The ride into the city was impressive, the buildings and cityscape most memorable. In a size and scale to any major world city it obviously is a capital, with a strong presence on the landscape. The seven Stalinist 'Wedding Cake' skyscrapers stood proudly out from the rest of the city. The Moskva River meanders prominently through its center, and past the Kremlin. The Kremlin was recognizable by the immense imposing red brick walls encompassing a vast acreage. I was amazed by its dominating the center of the cityscape.

My hotel, the Rossiya, was at the time the largest hotel in Europe. Nearly three thousand rooms with four lobbies on the four compass locations. I was on the West side facing the river. My room was on the top floor, the twelfth, with a magnificent view of the river and city beyond. The ships and boats traversing the river made it fascinating to peer out. It made for some very spectacular photos, both day and night. The hotel was very contemporary and just a stone's throw from Red Square and the Kremlin, so very convenient.

The lobby was one of the most fascinating places to linger. Foreign visitors from so many countries, and it was the first time I ever saw Mongolians in tradition garb. It also had the best store, a 'Beryoozka', for foreigners to purchase items made in the Soviet Union. I had been told by several people to wait to buy things there. I did get some wonderful architectural pieces, handmade wooden buildings, and even small bronzes of Kremlin structures. A lacquer box I purchased became a prize possession, and an American woman I met who knew about them helped me select one of the best. I bought several books, and a Russian fur hat, the type with the flaps that come down and tie under your chin.

As soon as I had settled into my room I headed up to Red Square. It just was mind boggling in size and you literally could not see the entirety in a glance. The walls and buildings of the Kremlin are on one side, GUM department store that goes for what seems a mile on the opposite, and a very imposing red colored building at one end, The State Historical Museum, with St. Basil's Cathedral with its incredible onion domes on the other. People seemed like ants walking across the cobble-stoned open space heading in a multitude of directions. I was quite impressed with it, and it felt like I had fallen into 'Oz'.

During my time in Moscow, I was able to get inside St. Basil's Cathedral, perhaps Russia's best-known building, which is built in a traditional and authentic Russian architectural style. Built in the 1500s by Ivan the Terrible this Orthodox edifice emulates the height of Russian culture. It is claimed by some to resemble both Asian and European influences. Once inside I was interested in the beautifully painted surfaces, like stencils on frescoes, but the spaces themselves were surprisingly small, dank, cramped, low and oppressive as opposed to high and uplifting. I expected there would be volumes of open space, as in cathedrals, but it was just the opposite.

Further into Red Square, next to the Kremlin wall, stands the very large and looming red stone edifice of Lenin's Tomb.

Guards stand continuously at the entry doors. It was possible to visit and view Lenin's embalmed body, but there are alternate days for Russians and foreigners. In all Soviet buildings that you can visit, museums, libraries, etc., foreigners get preferential entry before Russians. This seemed odd to me, but some told me that the Soviets believe that we are guests of their country, with limited time, so foreigners should have easy access to sites of interest.

The designated day for foreigners I waited in line to see the tomb, and Lenin. The line was about a mile long. Each day a similar line snakes along the length of the Kremlin wall with visitors waiting to get in, either Russians or foreigners. The main attraction, morbidly so, is to see the actual body of Lenin in a glass sarcophagus in the center of the building. Going through the entry doors and past the guards there is an air of mystery, and total silence as you reach the place where Lenin lies in State, supposedly forever. I have to say it was interesting to see him, but somewhat creepy too. To think of this person who died decades ago just lying there and stared at by hundreds of thousands of people passing by him was the height of totalitarian dictatorship worship.

If you look closely at the imposing Kremlin Wall in the general vicinity of Lenin's tomb you will notice plaques in the Wall. These are places where important communist leaders and politicians, and other prominent figures, are buried. It is a great honor to be buried in the Wall.

Then, there's GUM department store, right across the Square, an elaborate labyrinth of stalls on several levels selling 'stuff'. Some vendors had socks, others had shoes, some blankets, and on and on. All of it looked old, tired and none of it was orderly, just randomly thrown into bins to scour. Generally, there was no color selection on items, or any indication of having a choice. The funniest thing I encountered was a crowd gathering to watch the launch of a new television. With fanfare the TV was rolled out, looking like a 1950 vintage American television, and the salesperson turned it on with pomp and great pride, only to have it start smoking from the back and needing to immediately roll it away.

As I wandered beyond Red Square it was readily apparent that Moscow was the poster child of the Soviet Union, the epitome of its strength and will to become the star jewel in the crown. It had some of the best design of all the eras I had encountered anywhere else. Broad streets, beautifully constructed iconic buildings and what seemed like, on the veneer anyway, a superior lifestyle that would shine outwardly to the world expressing Soviet ingenuity.

There were modern, well-designed skyscrapers of housing, cinemas, retail, and even restaurants along the broad boulevards. The city had a cosmopolitan texture to it and people rushed around like New Yorkers do. There were more vehicles and traffic than I had seen elsewhere. One standout of the Soviet vision was New Arbat Avenue, not far from the Kremlin. There are striking contemporary high-rise apartment buildings, designed with style that embrace Scandinavian influences, angled to the street as opposed to straight on, giving the street some added breadth and interest. The ground floor pedestrian areas are mixed with businesses, but also retail, theaters, and restaurants. I had not seen anything like this anywhere else I had visited.

There was one large restaurant on the New Arbat Avenue that

caught my eye. Since it was so limited with opportunities to eat outside the hotels, I decided to try it out. I was seated with other Russians at a large table as I imagine that sitting alone is frowned upon, or I assumed. It was one of the first times I encountered permission to mingle with citizens. My fellow diners, however, were not very open to conversation. I noticed that the crowded room was primarily full of people who had come in groups, and they were very vocal and animated. It appeared to be a place people came for celebrations. At one point during my meal a large group at a table nearby broke out in song. The whole restaurant stopped and listened. I do not remember what I ate as it was not that memorable, but I do remember I enjoyed the exuberant atmosphere of the place.

Days of exploring led me to some fascinating buildings, like the early Communist era buildings that were intended to be cities within a city, a prototype in living. You could reside and work, buy food and goods, get day care and health care all within one structure, and never leave. Perhaps that seemed appropriate where the winters are brutal, and while I was there the cold weather was extremely forbidding. Being outdoors was not always pleasant.

The subway system, the Metro, was very impressive, and I rode it extensively. The stations were elaborate and designed in fanciful ways, some elegant and embellished with statuary and stone details. Others were plain, yet still striking in design and aesthetics. Most had very prominent, noteworthy light fixtures, either sconces or chandeliers. I was told by some residents that the stations were designed to be uplifting to the workers and residents. Trains were clean and ran on time, and many of the stations were considerably deep underground with escalators that moved rapidly into the depths of the subway system.

I spent a full day wandering around the inside of the Kremlin grounds and it was fascinating. Getting in seems rather ominous. The grounds are extensive and well maintained, and the compound has many buildings. The buildings were from both the Czarist and Communist eras, and since it is the seat of government armed guards are omnipresent. I found it easy to move about at will and several of the historical buildings, especially the churches are open for viewing. The buildings were forbiddingly large and out of human scale. Each church had a specific purpose in Czarist times, whether it be for a baptism, coronation, or a specific holy day like Easter. They were very impressive and cover several styles with onion domes everywhere you look. There was a huge bell, with a section broken out, that I presumed was rung when Napoleon attacked on the city, much larger than our Liberty bell. There was a museum where I saw many of the famed Faberge eggs, which were incredibly intricate and amazing in small detail. One had a train that could only be seen through a microscope.

There was a lot of activity, pedestrians moving about in every direction, both political workers and tourists. I took many photographs and found myself mesmerized by the extent of the entire complex. I did walk into one of the official government buildings and was promptly chided and escorted out.

Moscow has a fascinating complex of windy streets behind the GUM department store known as the Kitay Gorod district, one of the oldest sections of the city. The architecture is a variety of historic styles. Some of the area was in relatively pristine condition, however most in need of renovation with deferred upkeep. In this area and elsewhere I began to make a significant architectural discovery. As I had seen in Kiev, and elsewhere, there was an abundance of Art Nouveau structures in Moscow. I photographed them and it amazed me the extent of use of this style. After the Revolution of 1917 there was an extensive free-thinking movement that fostered a huge outpouring of creativity, that very well brought the Art Nouveau movement to the Soviet Union. The Constructivist artists and other 'avant-garde' groups flourished in the new communist environment but later were squelched in the 1930s by Stalin. Many of the creative types left and fled to Western Europe and the United States.

The other older neighborhood of distinctive architectural character is located off one end of Red Square, Gorky Street, now known as Tverskaya Street. There is a variety of interesting and noteworthy classic buildings. It is the Champs Elysees, or main boulevard, of Moscow and has been for decades.

One afternoon while lunching at the hotel they brought me a complimentary glass of chilled vodka, probably since I had eaten so many meals there already. That is a big thing in Russia and typically the men swallow it down right away. I don't drink that much but felt compelled to do as the Russians do and downed it. It was powerfully strong. The waiter was apparently impressed because he immediately filled a second glass for me! It would be rude not to appreciate a gift, so I downed the second one too. I was blitzed.

That afternoon I took one of my random, exploratory walks and came across an amazing surprise. Outside an older building there was a plaque in Russian that noted it was the Museum of Architecture. What a discovery, and I was elated. I walked in, no one was present, and I wandered the various floors all alone. It was a treasure trove of drawings, models, illustrative designs, etc. I felt like I hit the jackpot of my trip, even in my somewhat inebriated stupor, which fortunately by that time was wearing off.

I immediately took out my camera and began photographing everything is sight. Designs from the pre-Stalinist era right up to present time were on display, plus some historic documents and models too. What was most interesting were the plans and layouts for communist apartments. None of it was available in the West. I left and never encountered one person during my entire visit to this museum.

The Stalinist 'wedding cake' skyscrapers are hard to miss in scale, size and height, and I made it my mission to see some and to enter them as best as possible. I recall they were very elaborate and beautifully decorated inside, with large rooms and areas for sitting and dining, although finding out the purpose sometimes was difficult. Primarily built after World War II they have a distinctive presence on the city skyline. There are hundreds of rooms and hundreds of thousands of square feet in each building. They are generally built in a Russian Baroque style leading to the 'wedding cake' name, tiered and stepped back as they rise to tall heights. A couple were hotels, not intended for foreigners, and not accessible, although I was able to sneak in and photograph the Hotel Ukraine. Another was the enormous Moscow State University, a place I tried to infiltrate to learn and stay while arranging my trip, so I was most curious about it.

Since the Russians are so inclined to participate in and watch sports, I sought out sports arenas and venues on another excursion around the city. Generally, I used the Metro to access the locations and it gave me an extended opportunity to see a variety of station designs. There were some magnificent stadiums right within the central city. Most of these buildings were very well kept and the price of admission seemed extremely reasonable, if not free in some cases.

My days in Moscow were full of things to do and see and the city is large enough that I could spread out in every direction. People tended to keep to themselves, and I did not have as much interaction as I had in other cities I had visited. I'd typically return to my hotel for dinner and then wander out in the evening again, camera bag always in tow. At night I would sit by the window in my room and peer out at the sparkling lights of the city's buildings and along the river. During a few nights, at about two or three am, the phone in my room would ring. When I would answer someone in a very quick agitated voice would loudly talk in Russian, and I couldn't understand any of it. This went on for several days and I would say little except, 'hello', listen and hang up. I never figured it out, but it was annoyingly persistent.

One clear day I was walking down a series of streets after coming out of the Metro and saw a fascinating building, so I started photographing it. While standing in the street two uniformed soldiers with rifles on their shoulders hurriedly approached me. One of them grabbed hold of my arm while the other grabbed my camera. Immediately the warning of the US State Department folks rang strong in my memory. They spoke firmly and sternly to me in Russian and I just stood still. I only caught bits of their words, and I knew it was trouble. The guard with my camera looked at it discernibly and I fully expected he would pull out the film and expose it which was a common practice. I decided to act innocent and just grumbled some Russian words together acting stupid and unknowing. My groveling must have worked because the guard shoved my camera back in my hand and signaled me to get lost. The other continued to have a firm grip on me and even began shaking me. After the one guard said something to the other, he let me go, and I promptly walked away rather shaken. I was able to find out about the building later, it was unmarked, and turned out to be KGB headquarters.

I realized in a short time that the systems for nearly every function in the Soviet Union really did not work. Things were not efficient and there was a lot of waste and complexity to everything. Nothing seemed simple and the work force was vast and complicated beyond necessity to keep everyone employed. Many workers I encountered seemed bored, but at least had work. It appeared that no one had incentive. It also became evident that things were not maintained. Whatever objects existed were rarely treated with care and typically fell apart and wasted away, everything from appliances to buildings. The exceptions were the things the Soviets hoped to profile and have wide exposure to the world. The Kremlin and surrounding areas being one of them. The only true maintenance I saw in Moscow were very elderly women with babushkas sweeping the streets with brooms made of twigs.

I had heard about the Exhibition of Achievements of the National Economy (VDNKh) and decided to check it out. A Metro ride away from Red Square it was a trade show exhibit of Soviet achievements, and a quasi-recreation park on vast acreage. It reminded me of a World's Fair with pavilion buildings, gardens, and fountains. The place is impressive and still exists today. Started in the 1930s this park has had a continual run of showcasing Soviet economic strength and inventiveness. Each pavilion had a theme or represented one of the Soviet republics with their respective achievements on display. One building held the Soviet achievements in space, which at that time the USA was in a race and in stiff competition with them. I had a tremendous education wandering around and taking it in. What was interesting as well was the number of visitors present. The Russians love and cherish their parks, and this place seemed to draw them in numbers, perhaps uplifting their lives as well. Outside the park, near the Metro station, vendors were set up selling wares and flowers on the sidewalk. Flowers are a big and important treat to the Russians and vendors exist in many places, generally manned by older women.

An excellent book, that helped me understand the Russian Soviet way of life as a must read, was Hendrick Smith's, *The Russians*, first published in 1975. I found this the best resource for Westerners like myself to understand the psyche and functioning of that country, as he captures and describes it so accurately and well.

While in Moscow the temperatures plummeted, and I felt bone chilling cold. I had warmer clothing with me, but nothing seemed to keep me warm enough. During this time, and toward the end of my trip I caught a cold, and it really hampered my last days of getting around.

My last day in the Soviet Union I sat in my hotel room and reflected on the trip. I felt it was a success. Although I was unable to visit some of the smaller historic cities, I believed I got a highlight of architecture from a variety of periods, and enough to create a strategy for pulling together my findings, primarily through photography. I had many film rolls and looked forward to getting it developed back home.

I will note that one thing I learned to do in foreign hotels was to check out the fire exits, as it was apparent few fire codes existed. Unfortunately, at the Rossiya I could find no exit stairs. They may have existed, but I never found any indication of any, so that was somewhat disconcerting. I was too intimidated to inquire about it. The reality of it set in when just a year later the hotel had a horrendous fire when dozens of people were killed, primarily Eastern Europeans from the communist satellite countries. That sent a chill up my back imagining the chaos that probably ensued in trying to escape. It was noted in the press that many had jumped from the windows to their deaths. The hotel no longer exists.

I got to the main airport, Sheremetyevo, to fly home via Copenhagen. There was a long line of people waiting to go through customs and the security checkpoints. I had all my documents, purchases, and receipts handy and ready for inspection, including a complete accounting of my expenditures so they could verify what I brought in coincided with what was remaining. It is important to mention again that you could not take Russian *rubles* out of the Soviet Union, yet I stuck some in the bottom of my sock in my shoe as a souvenir. During the accounting of my expenditures, I said I used that amount for ice cream and vendors, so I had no receipts.

While waiting in line there was this delightful older woman behind me, Russian, but living in San Francisco. We started a conversation as the line took forever to move forward. I remember vividly that her name was Nina Tarasov. She had been born in Czarist Russia and during the Revolution she was one of the 'Old Believers' who fled with her family and settled in San Francisco. They maintained the religious Orthodoxy that believed the Czar was god. She told me how during the Revolution many of them, along with her family, went first to Siberia, then China, then Brazil and finally to the U.S. The moves were political and due to discrimination and persecution of their religious beliefs in each of the places, hence they had to move to consecutive places. It was fascinating to listen to her life story.

Getting close to the check point she pulled something out of her bag to show me. She was extraordinarily proud to have visited a very elderly teacher of hers who was still living, and the teacher gave her a gift of a beautifully gilded icon. I was struck horrified at that moment, as much as I appreciated her sharing it with me, and the story; however, it was strictly forbidden to take antiques, historic items, and especially religious icons out of the country. Not only would the item be confiscated, but the person holding it charged with a crime; and perhaps anyone knowing about it too. She seemed innocent about it as I strongly encouraged her to put it back in her bag immediately. I did not want to be implicated for having seen it and not mentioning it. I remained mute and just went innocently through the process. I was cleared into the airport. I did try to separate myself far from Nina, regretfully, and never saw if they searched and took the icon. I had hoped not.

The other important thing that occurred was that they took my visa away. They also did not stamp my passport, as when I entered the country. This was apparently by some agreement between the USA and the Soviet Union so that it became undetectable that you had ever been there, and to protect a person while using the passport later in other countries without it noting that you had been in the Soviet Union. I forever regret not making a copy of the visa before I left home, yet as you might recall I was just glad to get it in the hours before I left the U.S.

I also was given a card, and I do not remember if it was in the Soviet Union or the U.S. that I was required to carry for one year after my visit. It was a health card relaying that I had visited Leningrad. It seemed bizarre without any passport record, yet I had to always carry an official 'health card' identifying I had been there. What it meant was that I had visited a place with a notorious disease, called 'Leningrad Sickness'. There was a parasite in the water system in Leningrad that impacted foreigners. Apparently, the residents of Leningrad were supposedly immune to it, but if you got it then it was inevitable that you would be very sick, perhaps for up to five years thereafter. I carried the card diligently and fortunately never had contracted the illness. I was careful to only drink bottled water my entire time away, but one never knows the true source of the water you drink in a foreign country, even from a bottle.

When we landed in Copenhagen I was astonished as the entire plane burst into spontaneous applause. It was if everyone felt freed of having been behind the Iron Curtain. I have never experienced a reaction like that when landing at an airport.

I was somewhat miserable on the plane back. It was in the days when you could fly with few people on board and stretch out on four or five seats. While over the ocean the flight attendants assigned one section for folks to do that, and I slept sprawled out for a couple of hours.

While on board and eating a meal, I met an American woman who had also been in the Soviet Union for some time. I had previously met her at my hotel, in the lobby, at one point and she was young and vibrant, but did not seem eager to engage. Seeing her on the plane again she seemed much more open for discussion. She told me that she was Jewish and had been there on a special mission, to help Jews trying to emigrate to Israel. From what she told me once it was known by the authorities that a Russian Jewish person intended to emigrate you became a citizen non gratis, meaning you probably lost you job and even your apartment and had to fend on your own. Plus, it could take months, if not longer, to gain the appropriate authorization and paperwork to leave. It sounded horrifying. She told me she had brought in wrist watches to give to families, as on the black market they could sell them and hopefully live for many months off the proceeds to survive. The other thing she did was to get letters from each family she visited to account for the troubles they had under Soviet rule, as a testimony to their plight so that it could be better known in the West. She had folded and stuffed those letters in her bra to get them out of the Soviet Union, and she succeeded under tremendous risk.

She also told me that she had wanted to become more friendly at the hotel, and even considered inviting me to a couple of the houses she visited for me to experience Soviet life. As she knew of my purpose in being there she decided not to tell me about her mission or to invite me to go with her in case she was apprehended, and I might be implicated too. The entire story left me speechless, and all I could do was wish her well with the information she gathered when back in the U.S.

My parents met me at JFK airport in New York with obvious

relief. They seemed more at ease than when they took me to the airport, and I tried to regale them with stories of my trip on the drive back to Connecticut. The only communication we had during my entire time away were my postcards to them. It was unreliable for me to get mail.

It took me several days to reacclimate to life back in the U.S.A. The many days of hotel life and dining were thankfully behind me. I felt a sense of accomplishment. It seemed evident I had done something quite remarkable.

It wasn't too long after that I returned to New Orleans and back to Tulane for my final fifth year and thesis work. That in turn was stressful. Everyone was curious about my trip, and I spent days talking about it, answering the same questions many times. I felt a bit drained but once I got all my film developed into slides, I was delighted with the results of what I had brought back with me. I had not only photographed a vast amount of Russian-Soviet architecture but also captured the Communist Soviet world at that point in time.

As I prepared for my thesis and continued my studies, I progressively became ill. Sometime about a month after my return I began passing out in class, and it was worrisome. I tried to fend it off but there was a strong pain throughout my abdomen, at times unbearable. Some of my friends became concerned. Visiting the Tulane Health Care Clinic, the doctor suggested I go through several tests. I went to a local clinic adjacent to a hospital where they did Upper and Lower GI x-ray tests to determine what the issue might be causing my pain.

Of course, I took out my health card that I carried related to 'Leningrad Sickness' and they ruled it out immediately as I had none of the typical symptoms.

With one of the tests administered I had to take barium sulfide. I returned home after the test, felt slightly distressed and decided to rest. The phone rang and a nurse informed me that they had forgotten to tell me that I needed to flush the barium from my body and to get a laxative immediately and take it. Thank goodness they caught that. When the results of the tests came back, they found nothing. It was extremely frustrating as the pain persisted.

It took approximately two to three months when unexpectedly the pain began to subside. Over the days I kept feeling better and my overall strength improved. During one of the visits to the doctor he suggested that perhaps I had severe adverse psychological trauma from the cultural reaction and shock from my trip. It surprised me that they were not coming up with anything else. Nonetheless the pain went away and that's all that mattered.

Part of my Fellowship agreement was that I was to give a presentation to the University on my trip and findings. On top of my thesis this became a gargantuan task, but one I embraced as I was so pleased with what I had done. I toiled with a media savvy friend and put together a very complex sound and light show for the presentation. It involved two slide projectors coordinated with a musical score of Russian classical music.

My trip was gaining some notoriety, and the Tulane press and local *Times Picayune* newspaper interviewed me about it. The Tulane reporter was impressed with my command of the Russian dialect from my pronunciation of names and terms. They asked to take a photo of me in front of one of my slide images, so I selected St. Basil in Red Square.

When the *Times Picayune* news article was published, I was

somewhat taken aback. I quickly learned to be careful of the press as they will sensationalize as much as possible to enhance a report. In bold headlines the article stated, 'Connecticut Yankee Comes Home a Raging Patriot'. Is that really what they got from interviewing me? The article highlighted some of the downsides of what I encountered, like being caught photographing the KGB headquarters and being 'roughed up', words I didn't use. I later learned that the article was read in some New Orleans elementary schools by teachers who believed that young people should learn of the perils of Communism. It seemed we had our own propaganda.

My presentation to the University was held in the Kendall Cram Room of the Student Center. There was an announcement in the newspaper a week beforehand. When I arrived, I was stunned as the room was packed, standing room only. Except for class presentations I had never spoken publicly to a large crowd. I was a nervous wreck; but went forward. A couple of my friends stood in the back of the room to prompt me if I was talking too fast or too slow. That relieved some of my nervousness. The show went well. Everyone saw what amounted to hundreds of images of the Soviet Union, a totally unique experience for Americans. Afterwards some of the people who spoke with me were Russian emigres and thanked me for what I had done. To my surprise my travel agent, and several others from Cook's Travel attended too. He smiled broadly to shake my hand afterwards.

What I had learned in my adventure of 1976 was that even though the Soviet Union was powerful and a world leader, life behind the Iron Curtain was somewhat dysfunctional and we really had no reason for the extreme concern and hyper level of threat purported in the West. Also, that most Russians did not hate us and were not our enemy. The last thing I learned was the enormous treasure trove of architectural styles that remained mostly unknown to us.

In 2013 I had the opportunity to revisit Leningrad, now St. Petersburg again. I went with my husband, Ed, and we entered through Estonia which was an effort onto itself. This time there had been a six-page visa application to complete, and I purposely did not mention having been in the Russia before to avoid undue questions and concern about what I was doing there thirty-seven years before then. I also listed my marital status as divorced, which was true, without mentioning my marriage to Ed, which could have been an issue.

During that trip I was unfortunately dismayed how little had changed. I had expected the country to have been uplifted by the fall of the Soviet Union, but the streets and buildings were still drab and unkept, and other than more traffic and more young people attending church very little, if anything, had changed.

Ed and I took a canal boat ride around the city, a truly great way to experience it. I pointed out places to him that I had visited decades ago, and I even spotted the hotel where I stayed which was remade into a commercial building for Samsung.

At one point our hotel safe broke and I called to have it repaired. It was like the old Soviet days as three very official looking people came and stood and examined the situation. One had a clip board and wrote down details. A task that should have taken one repair person took on an operation of major proportion by several. The woman sitting at the elevator no longer existed, and foreigners were not made to stay in specific hotels, but the old systems remained intact.

Just a couple years ago I found the exact *Times Picayune* photograph they had taken of me for their newspaper article on sale on eBay, the online retailer. The *Times Picayune* went defunct and a company bought all of the paper's archived photos. The caption on the photo read, 'THOMAS BRUTTING, TULANE STUDENT IN FRONT OF ST. BASIL, MOSCOW, 1876'. I laughed to myself and contacted the company. They specifically sell 'historic archive' photography. I told them that I'm the person in the photo and that they were wrong, the year was 1976. I got a terse response that they do not make mistakes and the year is accurate. So, I purchased the photo for ten dollars.

CHAPTER 15

Summer Daze

Summer is my favorite time of year. I am lucky in that my birthday is in July so unlike so many other children I was never in school on my birthday. Summer birthdays are the best.

As a child my summers were full of travel and exploration. Often my parents took a road trip, and we'd generally tour New England staying in roadside cabins, most often ending up in Maine where my father's uncle had an incredible place on the ocean in a small town called Friendship. We'd most often spend many days there with my father's aunt making lobster dinners and going out into the acres of blueberries to pick and eat them fresh. There were approximately seventy acres to roam around with a small island and a cabin just off the rugged shoreline. The air was fresh and the days full of exploring the coastline.

When my great-uncle died in Maine, sometime in the mid-1960s my parents, my father's brother, and I drove in the cold of November up for the funeral. I will never forget going into the large house with lots of people, primarily relatives and some neighbors all dressed in black, and my great-aunt separated in a parlor accepting to see people in specific order by family. Afterwards my father contemplated buying the property as he knew his aunt wouldn't stay there but figured the price would be too high. It was tragic when he learned that she practically gave it away for nothing, and I believe he always regretted not at least asking her about it. Anyway, that ended those summers on the Maine coast.

When not off on a driving trip I was usually sent to a relatives' house to spend time. You'll read later how I once went on a long sojourn with my grandmother to a place near Albany, New York where she spent her summers. There were many summers where I would shuffle from one relative to another at a variety of locations. I always enjoyed it.

One of the usual places I spent a great deal of time was in Great Neck, Long Island, in my grandparents' house where my uncle, aunt and cousins lived after my grandmother passed away, and my grandfather moved to a smaller place elsewhere in town. That was one of my favorite places to stay and I had a great relationship with my cousins who were like siblings to me. I was somewhat jealous in that they had summer programs at their school where my inner-city school essentially closed and had nothing available. Since there was a lot of property, we were able to play and have a great time. There was a cabin at a far end of the property where we commonly ended up playing. My aunt liked making pies so we would often be sent to the orchard to pick peaches, apples, and other fruit for her pie making.

One of my favorite places on that property was at a far remote end of it in a grove of pine trees. I would sit on the pine needles under the trees, and it was so quiet and serene. I always felt secure and isolated from the world there.

We were very creative kids and did not need a whole lot of things to entertain us. We concocted games, put on plays, and lots of 'pretend' things, for example running an office where we each had a position. We'd come up with a company name, logo, and a business venture outlook. Once we created an airline, my one cousin aptly named, 'Jefferson Airplane'. We'd set up desks, man the telephones, type letters, and pretend we were running the office.

Another thing we did to pass time was to play this crazy word game called Mad Libs, available to buy in stores. It was a booklet of stories where you had to fill in missing words that were random choices for an adjective, noun, person's name, etc., and it made for a wacky story when read aloud. We would laugh ourselves silly.

When not playing around the property we would go to the Merchant Marine Academy nearby in Kings Point, only a stone-throw away. My uncle had a position there, so we were most welcome, any time. I particularly loved the large outdoor pool, and we did a lot of swimming with the cadets. I recall the cadets all had dark blue swim trunks as part of their 'uniform'. The property was on the former Walter P. Chrysler estate with the mansion still standing quite stately in the middle of the Academy property. When I was very young, four or five, my mother bought an Admiral's outfit, with a long winter coat and hat that made me look very official, especially at the Academy. The officers enjoyed when I wore it there; and saluted me.

My cousins and I would sit on a bed and watch our favorite TV programs, one called 'Shenanigans', and another called 'Chiller Theater'. 'Chiller Theater' had horror movies and we would huddle together and be petrified watching them. During the showing of the *Monster of Piedras Blancas* I went quickly to the bathroom to brush my teeth. When I returned, I was holding my toothbrush and the open toothpaste in my hand right when the monster walked in with a severed head hanging from his hand. I clenched the tube of toothpaste so hard that the paste shot up and hit the ceiling. My cousins laughed hysterically until we realized we had better get it cleaned up before anyone saw it… and we did.

Typically, at least once during the summer, my Great Neck cousins would come and stay at my house in Astoria. We would go bowling, to the movies, or anywhere to get in some air conditioning. In New York City the summers got sweltering hot, so being inside a chilled space was always a welcome opportunity.

When I was about eight or nine years old my parents decided to send me to a summer camp, a CYO day camp in outer Queens. That lasted two days as I absolutely hated it and asked not to go there. The kids were so rowdy, rude and misbehaved that it drove me crazy as it was the antithesis of how I was raised. Every activity turned into a nightmare of who would scream at who, act out, or beat someone up. When I explained it to my parents, that ended that.

When not off on a trip to visit someone, I would run down to the local Boys and Girls Club in Astoria where I'd play pool or swim in the indoor swimming pool. I learned to swim in the pool, took lessons, and came to love swimming. It was a great diversion from just staying at home.

My father's brother and his wife, who also lived in Astoria near us, had a summer house in Hopewell Junction in upstate New York. I'd spend time there with my four cousins and often their cousins too, so all typically a tribe of kids of various ages. There was a pond on an adjacent property where we were allowed to swim. You had to jump over a stone wall, and I once unexpectedly landed on top of a king snake. Thoroughly shocked I took off running like a maniac down a road near the pond. Although nonvenomous I hate snakes and wasn't going to stand around looking at it.

We'd ride bicycles down the country roads, and I enjoyed the many walking trails through the woods. Once while riding a bike too rapidly down a steep country road, I hit a patch of gravel and spun into a ravine. Landing on my hands and face a man near a house saw it from a hill above and came running. I was bleeding some, although not badly, but a piece of gravel jammed up into the knuckle of my finger. He took me, along with my cousins who were biking too, to his house where he carefully removed the gravel chunk and bandaged me up. I was very grateful. People were generally helpful in that way.

Another time we went on our bikes down some unexplored country roads and discovered a tiny old country church. It appeared to be abandoned and had thickets and vines covering it. Next to the church was a very old graveyard, from Revolutionary War times, with headstones crumbling and lots of overgrowth. Looking over the headstones I came across one totally covered in weeds when I noticed something sitting on top of it, totally grown over. I moved the weeds and found a tiny bible, no bigger than the palm of my hand just sitting there. I was amazed, and looking inside found it was very old, from the 1800s. It was a bit tattered and worn with a leather cover, but generally in good shape with a strong binding. I wondered how it lasted in the elements, and for how long had it been there. The headstone was barely legible, someone who had died in the 1700s. I still have that bible and keep it safe as undoubtedly it would not have lasted there forever. It is a total mystery how it got there, and why it was kept in open exposure to the elements.

Going on long hikes through the woods was another favorite pastime. The Appalachian Trail ran through my uncle's property although I was never exactly sure which trail it was as I walked the woods. Another pastime was playing cards and I believe I played more 'gin rummy' games in those days than anyone could imagine.

My older cousin, Kevin, loved to go fishing and would wake me at the ungodly hour of 5 o'clock or so to go with him up to the reservoir to fish. I absolutely despised fishing and found it boring. My grandfather had once tried to entice me into it on Long Island, but never got very far. As my cousin prodded me so much to join him, I would reluctantly go, so he didn't need to go alone. During one excursion, that became quite a point of discussion, he taught me fly fishing. I could not stand it, and at one point when I cast the line I just let go of the pole and it went right into the water. The pole was not retrievable. My cousin was not amused, but I got out of going fishing again.

My uncle had a station wagon and all of us kids would pile in the back for the trip from New York City out to the country. There was always a lot of laughing and teasing, but all good fun. My aunt's father, Mr. Hughes, a quiet Irish gentleman often would be staying there too, or my grandmother.

It was a big, old house that my uncle carefully renovated over time with many bedrooms, so everyone had a comfortable place to stay. I often bunked with one of my male cousins. There was also a large attic that had additional beds and a large open space for a pool table and play area when it rained. The kitchen was large and had two round tables that accommodated everyone for meals. My aunt also created a 'Chinese Room' with red walls and a black ceiling with Chinese antiques in it, that we rarely ever entered.

My uncle and family eventually moved there permanently selling their city house, as many families including my own began to leave New York City for outlying areas in the late 1960s and early 1970s. We had already moved before them, to Connecticut in 1968. Unfortunately, their house burned to the ground in the late-1970s after it was completely renovated. The fire trucks couldn't get over a private bridge over a stream on the property to reach the house, so it was a total loss. Being home from college my father took me there after the fire and I was amazed how nothing was left. The only recognizable object in the charred debris was a crumpled piece of metal that had been the refrigerator. Sadly, some dogs died in the fire, although Kevin who was the only one there, napping, was able to escape.

Returning from a few of my sojourns during the summer my music teacher looked at me and called me 'the galivanting boy'. He had that down perfectly.

After moving to Connecticut as a teenager the emphasis of my summers changed.

Shifting gears, I was thirteen and no longer the kid that would be shuffled around to relatives and various places to stay for weeks on end. It did not seem to matter to me as I quickly made new friends nearby. Additionally, a couple of my New York City friends came to stay with us for visits.

One of those friends, Robert Dempsey, was a very good friend of mine for years through elementary school. I knew he and his brothers well and they were a close-knit Irish family that met tragedy when their mother, at a very young age, had a severe stroke and was incapable of doing much thereafter. A vibrant and very engaging person, it was sad to see. The sons rallied around her and made her life as comfortable as possible, even though she couldn't walk well, or talk. The last time I saw her, in my twenties, she lit up and smiled, pointing down the street to where I had lived and in a slurred, muted voice said, 'boy'. She recognized me.

Robert came to Connecticut, and we played badminton and he met my new friends and we had fun. It was a different world than exploring the paved, concrete alleyways of New York as in Connecticut we had open land and forests to roam, and we did. Further down the road from where we lived was a stately old-abandoned house on a hill. It had a strong presence as you drove by and it looked out on to the reservoir across the road. We decided to hike up there and check it out.

The front door was unlocked, and we walked in. It was one of the creepiest places I have ever been. The rooms were musty and worn, peeling paint and in complete disarray. It was obvious it had been abandoned for some time.

The house was a conglomeration of styles, apparently built and added on over time. The oldest was a typical New England salt box, with subsequent additions that culminated in a large Georgian style structure at the front, giving it the prominence from the street. It had a portico with slender square wood columns extending up two stories, and a multi-fan window in the attic gable facing outward toward the reservoir.

Wandering through the rooms we sensed there had been a type of coziness to the place, yet it was also difficult to decipher the layout of rooms. There was a front hall and a stair, and we wandered up to check out bedrooms and then up to the attic where there was a line of bookshelves with some books remaining. The entire place smelled musty and was also drafty, although that did not matter much with the summer air.

Walking back to the ground floor we found a stair to the basement, dark and dank, and decided not to go there. The property was overgrown with a couple of out buildings, and I also have a distinct recollection of a broken-down gazebo in back.

Out in front of the house there were high stone retaining walls on a steep hill that created a flat area of lawn. In the center was a cloverleaf fountain, then filled with debris and leaves. We spoke about how this house must have been quite distinctive and interesting in the day.

When we left the latch of the front door fell out into my hand and I kept it as a souvenir.

Later that summer, and after Robert had left, I learned about the house. It was the home of Bruce Rogers, an internationally known American graphic designer and typographer, one of the greatest book designers of the twentieth century. The house had been called 'October House'. Our little New Fairfield Library history section had a couple of books about him and the house, and several news articles that I read. The Librarian at the time, Mrs. Fairchild, knew the house well and had a fondness for it; and I believe was happy to learn of my interest in it. Rogers had died over ten years before, in 1957, and I presumed the house had been abandoned since then. I also heard from Mrs. Fairchild that Rogers had fallen off a board into the fountain while cleaning it out; and died subsequently of pneumonia.

October House remained in my sights for a long time after, and I even found floor plans, and did a design project at the University making it into an art center. Unfortunately, no one ever took up the mission to save the house and it was eventually demolished.

Many years later a man I know in San Francisco, Charles Martin, began working at a printing establishment called Arion Press that design, create, and bind books in the honored craft style of Bruce Rogers. Charles had me talk to the owner of the company who was amazed that I had been in Bruce Rogers' house and wanted to know all about it. He contemplated doing a book of my experience and having me do sketches of my recollections of the rooms since I was an architect, but the endeavor never came to fruition. Nonetheless, I will always remember October House fondly, as even in shambles it left an indelible impression of history to an honored man.

At age sixteen my summer adventures expanded as I was able to drive. One place I gravitated too frequently was Newport, Rhode Island, an easy day trip from my home. I had the route down like the back of my hand and was often accompanied by friends. I loved the atmosphere of Newport, on the ocean and full of history, both colonial and the Gilded Age of American history. Summers there were easygoing, fun, and interesting. It was before Newport became a huge tourist attraction.

After spending so much time there I joined the Preservation Society of Newport County. It was a group organized to preserve Newport's heritage, and in particular the Gilded Age mansions, several of which remained unused after WWII. They put out a monthly newsletter, a booklet, and I was bemused when a couple of issues included one of its prominent members, Claus von Bulow, who was accused of attempting to kill his wife, 'Sunny'. She remained in a comma for several years, and the movie, *Reversal of Fortune* tells the story of that event.

Newport to me had a particular air of true Americana. It was a seaside port town and had a rich history spanning before the Revolution, with historic architecture in its downtown to match. The physical landscape was breathtaking and any drive around the perimeter of the peninsula is more than spectacular with the views and vistas. A walk along Cliff Walk even more so, with the fresh sent of ocean air. There always seemed to be something to do in Newport, including its noteworthy festivals. I even enjoyed it in the winter when it seemed particularly quiet.

A symbolic item that comes from Newport is the image of a pineapple, as the symbol of hospitality. Pineapples were rare and exotic in Colonial Newport and presenting them to guests a great honor. My bedposts as a child had miniature pineapples, and I have seen the symbol used again and again in wood-work across this country. Newport has it in various decorative features in and on many buildings, and pieces of furniture.

In 1970 I got the notion to travel to see another of my father's aunts and uncles who had retired to Hollywood, Florida; yes, in August! Hollywood is between Ft. Lauderdale and Miami. I was sixteen years old and discussed it with my parents as I intended to pay for the trip on my own. They seemed OK if my great-aunt and great-uncle agreed, so I called them; and they did.

I booked a flight on the Northeast Airlines, 'Yellow Bird'; that flew between New York and Florida in those days. The 'Yellow Bird' airplanes were very identifiable by their bright yellow color as they flew in the sky over New York. It would be my first airplane flight and I was going it alone. I packed my things, and my parents drove me to the airport and off I went.

There were probably no more than fifteen or twenty people on the plane and when the 'Stewardesses', as they were called then, learned it was my first flight they thoroughly indulged me. Of course, I was dressed in a suit and tie as was customary in airline travel at that time.

The flight was wonderful, and I gained an immediate appreciation of flying, that would last a lifetime; at least until it got overcrowded with people who no longer cared how they dressed to travel, or how they acted at the airport, or in flight.

Landing smoothly in Ft. Lauderdale my Great-Aunt Betty and Great-Uncle Charlie were standing on the tarmac waiting to get me. I saw them out the window as the plane pulled in near the Ft. Lauderdale airport. Passengers used the movable stairs brought to the plane to exit.

I intended to spend two weeks and ended up extending it to three since we had so much fun together. We played cards, I listened to their stories of bygone days, my great-uncle's time on the New York Central railroad when they lived in White Plains, N.Y., and met many of their friends. There were many retirees and clubs with membership from the state you were from originally. Most amusing was how the older folks gravitated to me and I got lots of attention. They had two close friends, a couple, and the wife was Native American, a striking, beautiful woman with jet-black hair. They were very kind to me, and she took me under her wing telling me wonderful stories about her background and life. I enjoyed these folks immensely.

We took a lot of road trips around Florida going to Key West and the Everglades, Miami, and Palm Beach. I toured the old Florida mansion, Vizcaya, in Coconut Grove and really enjoyed seeing such a splendid piece of 1920s architecture, and gardens.

Flying home the flight was very bumpy as we hit extreme turbulence. An older woman sitting across the aisle was terrified and asked if she could sit next to me. I agreed and she immediately came over and grabbed my hand and squeezed it for over an hour, completely terrorized. I felt badly for her and kept trying to calm her down, but to no avail.

Generally, my summers were full of time with friends. One of my best friends, Joe, came from a well-established, old Connecticut family, 'Yankees', having lived there for generations. He and I spent a lot of time together hiking the woods and exploring. We would also play badminton and board games. My mother always fretted as he would ride his bicycle down the narrow, winding roads to get to our house, yet he always appreciated and refused to have her drive him, in the days when we could not yet drive.

His family was very religious and extremely kind, wonderful people. Often, he would eat a meal at my house, or me at his, as it felt like we were one family. Joe and I planned on attending a movie, as we frequently did, and I suggested we go to *The Godfather* which had just come out in theaters. His mother was not pleased with the selection as she had read the book and thought it inappropriate for teenagers. Nonetheless she let us go, violence, sex, and all.

Several years later Joe visited me when I lived in New Orleans for college. We spent a week together and had a great time, including riding bicycles through Audubon Park and other parts of the city. At one point I took him down Bourbon Street and with the honky-tonk, bars and strip joints he looked at me and said, 'I guess this is good for me' as he'd never been exposed to so much debauchery before then. But, hey, it is New Orleans!

Another good friend, Paul, and I also spent a lot of time together. Paul knew Joe well as their families lived close to each other. Paul's aunt had a swimming pool where we would often swim in the heat of the summer. I very much appreciated the access to be able to swim as I greatly enjoyed it.

Dan Johnson was another very good friend, and his father was an artist and the prolific Western painter, Harvey W. Johnson. Mr. Johnson resembled Teddy Roosevelt and had an equally big personality. Both he and his wife were very gracious always welcoming Dan's friends openly into their home. Their house was deep in the woods and a treasure trove of Western memorabilia that formed the base of Mr. Johnson's realistic art. He used Dan and his brothers as subjects in his paintings, dressing them either in cowboy garb, or in Indian clothes. We were allowed to use the art studio to sit and talk, and I have the fondest memories of how fun it was to just be in such a creative space with all these wonderful artifacts.

It was a small clique and Dan knew Joe and Paul as well. Dan's family subsequently moved to the Southwest as did Joe's, to Arizona. It was a big deal for Joe's family to leave the family homestead after so many generations.

Connecticut at that time was a mix of 'Yankees', families who had been there for generations, and newcomers like us. The 'Yankees' kept to themselves, and all knew each other well; some of those families having had their property deeded to them by the King of England before the Revolution.

My ex-wife and former in-laws lived among some 'Yankee' families in the northern part of New Fairfield where those families had vast acreage. One friend of theirs, Mary Merritt, was the widow of Walter Gordon Merritt, a prominent Wall Street

Attorney who argued many well-known labor cases, including that of his family's company in the Danbury hatting industry. It was said that Merritt Parkway in Connecticut was named after his family. He amassed over a thousand acres of beautiful land, 'Great Hollow', he hoped would be preserved. His wife, Mary, was younger than he and he died in the late 1960s. She was the daughter of immigrants and was his second wife, and known to my good friend's mother, who attended school with her. It was a very small town, in many ways, and everyone knew someone you knew.

We visited Mary Merritt once at her home, a bucolic New England home that rambled and looked like something out of England. There was a long procession of apple trees leading to the house and she was most gracious and hospitable. She described the legacy of her husband, and her interest in decorating, including pointing out the vibrant colors and fabrics she had brought into the house. She mentioned the maintenance of the apple trees and how much effort it took to care for them. I offered to care for one to help her, and my former mother-in-law intervened knowing I would not have a clue what to do with it. She was right. In any case, it was an enjoyable visit.

Our house in New Fairfield sat high on a hill with a phenomenal view. It was incredible to watch the seasons change the vegetation year-round and frankly sitting in the living room with two large picture windows was mesmerizing. My parents had lots of parties and often had neighbors over for drinks, so especially in the summer the house was always an active place.

After I came of driving age, I also started dating, so my

evenings were filled quickly. My dating ramped up exponentially in summer as there weren't school nights and homework to worry over.

The dates typically entailed a movie and a pizza afterwards. One evening I returned home after dark and as I pulled into the driveway, I noticed what looked like a lot of sparkle on the pavement, so I stopped and looked before driving up to the garage. It turned out to be broken glass strewn everywhere. I left the car parked at the end of the driveway and went into the house. I woke my parents and asked my father what had happened, but he had no idea. We walked around and finally found a large rock in one of the bedrooms, above the driveway. Someone threw the rock through the window, but my parents had not heard it. There was glass in the bedroom too.

A band of teenagers had become notorious in town as going around pulling pranks and doing deeds like what was done at our house. My father went down to Town Hall the next day and talked with the First Selectman. He was mortified. The next night we noticed a car parked, lights out, in an unusual place near our property with someone apparently sitting in the driver's seat. My father went out to check and surprisingly it was the First Selectman. He was determined to find the kids, and believe it or not, he eventually did. Not on that night but a subsequent one. We were amazed that he took it upon himself, yet he was so irritated by the activity happening in our small town.

Sometimes we would take a drive to the Pennsylvania Dutch area where the Amish held events and festivals. These country fairs were interesting and fun, simple. My favorite was taking home a Shoo-Fly Pie!

My summers all through my childhood and thereafter were wonderful. I have so many fond memories of those fun days. As I got older in my later high school years, and college, I did work too, but there was always the fun, laid back sense of summer warmth. There was nothing better.

CHAPTER 16

Annus Horribilis... more than one

The story within the chapter entitled, 'Unprecedented Times' could easily be placed here, but it deserved a place by itself for its unfathomable magnitude of impact on everyone's lives. Yet, other significant dreadful times existed specifically in my life too.

There are periods in life, often beyond our control, when things go very bad. Queen Elizabeth used the phrase *'Annus Horribilis'* in 1992 when so much in the monarchy was going in a very bad way. The phrase is Latin for 'Horrible Year'. It was first used by the Anglicans to describe the problems of imposed dogma by the Roman Catholic Church in the late 1800s.

A popular term used by Americans to describe coping with a crisis is, 'to weather a storm'. As with *'Annus Horribilis'* it is an acknowledgement of difficult times; and making it through whatever pain and suffering it involved.

As a youth my mother would sometimes impart her wisdom by telling me that, 'life will have many disappointments'. At that time in my life I did not recognize, experience, or care to contemplate disappointments; yet she was right. Indeed, in getting older, and with more time to know what life can bestow upon us, I did have many disappointments.

I have learned that no matter how much pain one had in life those around us may have had more, and you may not know it. People generally keep their pain to themselves. Yet, if someone recognizes your suffering, they are likely to share their pain too, most often to comfort. I have had this happen a couple of times and it amazed me what people carry on their shoulders, hidden away. Perhaps, the old saying 'misery loves company' is true.

I took a course in college that I very much appreciated, called 'Divergent Forces'. Geared to building and development issues the professor, a well-known and respected architect, led the class through a series of case studies showing how some things work against us, no matter how much we try to maintain control or manage a situation. The unexplainable, the unexpected and the unbelievable things that can and do occur. The course's premise was to teach how to sustain yourself during the ensuing struggles that can hamper progress by having a person prevail and overcome the situation through strategic thinking.

Another phrase I've used often in describing the unexpected trials in life is 'Ontogeny Recapitulate Phylogeny', the 'biogenetic law'. It is such a great phrase and always throws people off track when I say it, yet most are also anxious to know more about its meaning. It has to do with evolution and growth; and it's interesting that recently it is considered mythology. That leads me to wonder if the science of the tragic times in our lives is a form of fabled lesson.

The nuns in Catholic school used to tell us students that we would have our 'crosses to bear'. It sounded rather ominous, but OK, perhaps doom and gloom is possible; yet I have faced several trials in my past that play out both the nuns' warning, as well as my mother's destiny of disappointments.

Facing being gay was difficult, but when I found acceptance

within myself, I also found strength. I learned not to worry much about what others thought. When I was young society taught us being gay was wrong, bad, and inherently evil. When I felt some uncertainty about my orientation, I sought out books to help me understand my feelings, yet little to none were available. It was a difficult road to travel, and it took me nearly thirty years living life as a 'straight' man to dispel the myth. Fortunately, times have changed considerably since that time.

The divorce from my ex-wife was perhaps the low point of my life. It was extremely difficult and went in a way I never wanted. Once it took off there was no stopping the path, or the pain. I learned some harsh lessons in the two and half years of going through it, essentially a custody case within the divorce, and I never wish similarly on anyone. Seeing some of the foibles of the legal system, the law, and the court system was maddening at best.

My intent, hope and desire were to remain integral in my son's life; and remaining in cooperative and friendly terms with my wife, but that did not happen due to several factors. In the 1980s, there was a common curve ball that could ruin any parent, particularly fathers, from having a relationship with a child, and that ball was thrown right in my face. Unfounded accusations were brought against me of being an unfit parent, and while entirely untrue, it started a firestorm of disastrous events. In retrospect I should have handled the 'divergent forces' differently. The justice system, especially for the boy, failed miserably.

Witnessing an alcoholic attorney, a police officer who lied under oath, a string of made-up occurrences and scenarios, plus learning that anyone could hire any number of high priced 'expert witnesses' to say anything you needed to be said, was downright unconscionable, but it happened and probably still happens today.

So many friends rallied around me, and I was amazed at the outpouring of support from people I least expected, and who had no real reason other than kindness and care. My good friend, Jack, offered me his house whenever I needed a place to stay during the hearings. A friend who was a closeted gay man in government service even offered to risk coming 'out' to testify in my behalf, as he had seen me together with my son several times and had firsthand knowledge of the relationship between us. The former wife of the man I went on to live with after my separation drove for many miles to testify about my parenting skills. A social worker in family practice she testified that she would allow me to help raise her children, as I was doing at that time. Another time a co-worker and his wife offered to get court ordered approval to supervise time with me and my son so we could be together. That didn't happen but the expression of support by many was heartfelt.

The expense and number of psychologists and social workers involved was mind boggling. There was a time, late in the divorce process, when I was staying with a friend, a minister, after a particularly trying and truly discouraging day. While driving in the cold winter of sub-freezing Wisconsin weather I just wanted to just stop the car, lie down in the snow, and die. I felt completely paralyzed and numbed. Yet, I made it through, and my friend offered me needed solace.

During the several-day divorce hearing the courtroom had cleared for a recess and it was only me and my father who remained there. I broke down and starting crying, stress and tension rising full level inside me, and having my parents listen to everything being said, it just got overwhelming. My father immediately came over and gave me a big hug and held me. It was a cherished moment I will never forget, and I am forever grateful for his love, and that of both my parents for their complete support through it.

It took family, friends, endurance, stamina, and lots of feeling horrible about what was out of my control to reach a conclusion.

At one point I left the courtroom to use the men's room and a man with his young daughter were standing outside the courtroom doors. He asked if he could enter so his daughter could watch a court case. I admired him for wanting her to witness the legal system but advised him that it was probably not the case to have her witness. It was such a robbery of justice that I really thought she should not be exposed to the downside of the law.

I was not the victim in this situation, but rather my son. It was a severe loss that has lasted since then. I know how parents must feel when a child is removed from one's life, either through a legal means, or death. Considerable mourning and sorrow ensue. It is certainly complex and complicated yet for the courts to restrict and prevent legitimate parental rights and even grandparent rights, which happened too, is purely unconscionable.

Sometime later the court contacted me and relayed that they learned my ex-wife had completely removed my parental rights in another state where she had moved. They advised me to pursue a case against her, but I declined as by then it served no purpose, only to further damage an already broken system, and relationship.

There was one very memorable, reassuring moment that I won't forget. It was being at my friend Jack's house at the end of the hearings, and everyone involved, on my side anyway, were there for one of Jack's wonderful chili dinners. There were so many people present and we sat at a long table together. It was such a calm, soothing time in being together.

Jack's mother was also there, and she lamented over the court system to my parents as she could not believe that they were restricted from seeing their grandson; for no just cause.

Yes, this was one of my *'Annus Horribilis'* times, and one that left me forever sad.

Another *'Annus Horribilis'* time was when my father called me in college to say his business had failed, gone bankrupt, and I wondered the fate of my family and my education. Fortunately, that lasted only for a few weeks as he was soon absorbed and taken on by another company. These momentary events do have a lasting impact too.

Cancer has taken another toll on my family, for both my parents, and myself too. We have all suffered the fate of this horrible disease.

My mother was diagnosed with uterine cancer in 1975. I got that call at college, too, and it was upsetting. The prognosis wasn't great, but there was hope, and we hung on to it. She was fifty-six years old and still had a lot of life to live.

I was home from college when she entered Danbury Hospital for surgery. Fortunately, she had excellent care and we had a considerable trust in the doctors. However, treatments were not what they are today. It was determined that a complex, major surgery was necessary to remove all the cancer. The result of that kept her in the hospital recuperating for many weeks thereafter.

One afternoon during a visit I found her suffering in incredible pain. I immediately went to the nurses' station for assistance. I became very impatient and quite annoyed when they didn't rectify the situation in a timely manner. It was clear that being an advocate for someone in the hospital was essential.

She returned home quite weak and unable to do much. I could tell it was taking a toll on my father and I did all I could to support them through a very turbulent family time. She was determined though, and I could tell she was going to do everything possible to recuperate.

There was a woman who lived across the road, and she had noticed a light on in a bedroom we never used. I had decided to move there from my usual bedroom, for merely a change of view. Being true to the nickname we gave her, 'nosy neighbor', she inquired of me if my father had moved into that bedroom, 'because of your mother's illness'. It was one of those times when I nearly lost my composure as it was none of her business. I let her know that I was sleeping there now. Of course, not too long after she tried to marry me off to a niece she had brought from Czechoslovakia. The girl could not speak English, so we conversed in French which drove the neighbor crazy with curiosity. She wanted everything translated into English for her to know what we were discussing. During those already stressful times other unnecessary stressors can occur as well. Best to avoid them whenever possible.

My mother eventually recuperated to full strength; but had to remain on one floor of our house for almost a full year. I do not recall what we did about follow-up medical appointments, other than her doctor probably made house calls, but I do remember how difficult it was for her because she could not walk well after the surgery. I will never forget the day she was first allowed to leave the house. I took her slowly and carefully down the stairs and got her in the car for a drive. She was so pleased to be outdoors again, and I felt the sense of exhilaration in her.

In recovery she lived another thirty-five years. That time, however, was indeed an *Annus Horribilis*.

Not long after that my father was diagnosed with prostate cancer, yet fortunately it appeared they diagnosed it in good time. He went through treatment and after five years of monitoring we celebrated the success of his being cured. It was certainly a relief compared to my mother's ordeal.

Fifteen years later his prostate cancer resurfaced again, this time much more invasive. This was the beginning of yet another *Annus Horribilis*. At that time, he had retired and was living with my mother in Florida. They had a wonderful number of retirement years traveling extensively and making many new friends. Life was good until this second round of cancer hit.

Serving on a medical malpractice case as a juror I had learned during the testimony from Stanford doctors that small cancer cells can live on and reestablish in various parts of the body, even after one is diagnosed as 'cured'. In his case the cancer had survived after all.

I watched him diminish in health over a year and it was alarming and depressing. Both my parents were always active and fit, gave up drinking liquor when he retired, never smoked, ate well and always looked ten years younger than their actual age. But there was no escaping the cancer. He went through extensive radiation treatments, and finally one day while I was living in California, he called with the news that the doctors gave him a month or two to live. The cancer had invaded his liver. He was very steady and matter of fact when he called, and I admired his stoicism.

During his illness I flew countless times between California and Florida to help and support my parents during this dreadful time. My father, who always was a thin man, began to drastically lose weight. He was drinking supplements constantly to maintain some pounds, energy, and vigor. During some visits he slept a great deal which was unusual for him. At one point I surprised myself by asking him if he was afraid to die. He said 'no', he was ready. I felt he must have been in such agony, and it was sad to see him trying his best.

My last visit with him was for his birthday in April 1995 when he turned seventy-six years old. He was literally a bag of bones, skeletal, could hardly keep his pants up, and extremely weak. I believe he weighed less than ninety pounds, and for a man who is five foot ten that isn't much weight. I noticed an acrid odor when he spoke as though his insides were burning up. My mother was determined to be at his side constantly. In November they hoped to celebrate fifty years of marriage, and they wanted to see that day come. In a matter of fact my mother told me that at times my father would become incoherent and just say the word 'fifty' over and over.

I asked him what he would want more than anything for his birthday, and he said a seafood dinner at his favorite restaurant. I immediately agreed. We did exactly that on his birthday, April 2. I ever so carefully got him in the car, and we drove there, then realizing that he could not walk distances that well. We failed, for whatever reason, to have a wheelchair or walker. So, I lifted him in my arms, then had him lean on me and with all my strength I slowly walked him into the restaurant while he dragged his feet on the floor. People stared at us, but I didn't care, and I detected he didn't either.

A waiter assisted and I placed him as comfortably as possible in a chair, with my mother next to him and me across from him. I remember so well his shallow and withdrawn face, cheekbones recessed. He wanted the 'grand seafood platter', and I was more than happy to get it for him. He didn't want any celebratory thing, or even a birthday cake, so we went with his wishes. When the platter arrived, he literally lit up and smiled broadly. I have a photo of him with that platter I will always cherish with his smiling face looking at it. He ate vigorously and seemed to enjoy it so much, and it gave enormous comfort to my mother and me. After the meal he felt he could walk better, so I held on to him and he shuffled out of the restaurant. Back home he immediately went to bed to sleep.

When it came time to leave, I hugged him realizing that most likely that would be the last time I would see him. I seriously doubted he would make it to November to their anniversary. I held the man who stood by me through so much in my life, rarely criticized and always supportive. He sometimes said that I created my own problems, and he was right. Yet, he was a tremendous influence and inevitably someone who everyone loved.

They got hospice for him right afterwards, and those folks were wonderful. They called me periodically to check in and let me know how both were doing. My mother was struggling and a couple of times when he fell, she could not lift him and had to call the fire department to get him up. One August afternoon she called and said that he had fallen in the bathroom, and she had to get the firemen to lift him, yet again. She was determined to do everything to assist and be at his side, but it was getting to be too much. Hospice brought in a hospital bed for him that day and set it up and called me to say that he probably would not be able to get out of it again. I was so saddened and struggled with the situation as I knew my mother really could not handle it much more. Getting my wits about me I became determined to call the next day and insist that we place him in a nursing home for everyone's best interest. I knew that would be a very difficult call with her.

I arrived at work the next morning and planned on calling around nine o'clock, Pacific time, noon by them. At eight-thirty the bookkeeper came and said my mother was on the phone for me. I picked up the receiver and all she said was 'he's gone'. He had died peacefully during the night, and they had just removed his body. She called me back later and said he looked content and at peace. He died just three months before their fiftieth wedding anniversary.

Immediately flying to Florida, I helped her with the details as well as cleaning out his clothes and getting life back to some level of calmness for her. We went to the funeral home as they had bought a 'cremation package' years prior, so everything was taken care of and simple. However, the funeral director took us into a room with caskets and pointed out the various models, 'Woodmont' and 'Cherished Loved One', or whatever they were called; mahogany and lined with padding and lace, etc. as options for us to consider. He then pointed to a cardboard box in the corner with the words 'Head Up' at the top and said that was the standard for our 'package'. So, which did we want for our dearly departed family member? I will never forget that my mother turned and looked at me and I looked at her and simultaneously we pointed to the cardboard box and laughed. How ridiculous to spend thousands of dollars when he is being cremated, and knowing he'd be furious if we spent more money.

He was interred at Grace Cathedral in San Francisco, so we had to make plans for it. I intended to fly his remains back with me, but the ashes were not ready and had to be sent. That troubled me as I wanted him to be with me, but I had no choice. Back home his ashes finally arrived the day before his memorial service. When UPS delivered them to me I had only a half an hour to get them to Grace Cathedral so they could prepare them for the ceremony. I put the urn on the passenger seat and drove quickly through rush hour traffic to get them there in time. The urn would not stay in place, and I had to hold it in my lap. I made it to the church offices with only five minutes to spare before the offices closed. Running into the reception area I put the box on the counter and a man came out to greet me. I told him why I was there and started crying. He asked if I was alright, and I responded, 'I just don't leave my father anywhere' in an upset stern voice. I have no idea what that meant but it added a bit a levity to my stress, as he also smiled and assured me that he would take good care of the ashes.

The memorial service was very nice with a small number of people. My mother refused to come and didn't want to make the trip cross country. I believe it was just too difficult for her. So, this was yet other *'Annus Horribilis'* that passed.

My mother moved to San Francisco the year after my father

died, in 1996. She adapted and thrived in her new home, until the day I got the phone call from her friend, Marguerite, to tell me she talked with my mother, and she seemed incoherent. I called my mother and she said she fell during the night and was alright, however, I asked that she get dressed so I could take her to the doctor to be checked. When I arrived at her apartment, she could not open the door as she had fallen again. I attempted to open the door with my key, but she had the security chain latched. I called building management and they suggested I call 911, emergency response, and I did. They sent both the fire department and an ambulance.

After they cut the chain, we found her on the floor, and they placed her in a gurney to take her to the ambulance. Once secured in the gurney she looked at me and chuckled a bit while saying 'look at what they did to me'. At the emergency room they started doing tests and it took hours. She began to hallucinate and thought she saw birds flying over her. I was concerned and when I mentioned it to the nurse, she only shrugged. A nurse, who's a friend, told me later that it is not unusual for older people to hallucinate in the emergency room, out of fear for nothing else. It would have been nice if somewhere had suggested that when I brought it up.

While not finding any issues from the tests, they finally admitted her to the hospital, and she remained there for five days 'under observation'. A friend familiar with hospital protocol cautioned me about Fridays; it's apparently the day they release as many people as possible during shift changes. Friday arrived and when I walked into the hall outside her room several patients were being rolled off in wheelchairs to the elevator. Then her time came. The doctor entered the room to say she's being discharged. I challenged him based on the fact we had no idea why she had fainted and fallen twice, or how to handle the situation going forward, especially when they had determined that she had been unconscious for 10 hours or more after the first fall. That was only a part of it because after I had returned to her apartment after she was admitted I surveyed her place and it looked like a major disaster occurred. Things were strewn across the floor, all her bedding torn off the bed, chairs upended. It looked like either she had struggled for some time, or there had been an attack of some type. I ruled out the attack as the door was chained when I arrived.

Confronting the doctor did not help matters. My friend had given me all the ammunition and proper terminology to keep her there until they determined something about the state of her health and why she fell, but the doctor angrily scolded me and said she was being discharged and I couldn't stop it.

I took her home and stayed the weekend to observe her. By Sunday I had the alarming realization that she was not the same person as she was very disoriented in her apartment. She could not find basic things and I was afraid to leave her there alone, yet I could not continue staying with her either. I called an acquaintance who was a CEO of an Assisted Living community near her home, one my firm had designed, and explained the situation. He immediately sent someone over to assess her. Let me say that knowing people in the senior living and care arena, or at least having a plan, before an 'event' like that happens, is extremely beneficial. The assessment seemed OK, including her mental capabilities, but during the exam my mother looked at me and said, 'You're putting me away, aren't you?' It just tore me to pieces.

Ed and I had seen signs of concern over a year or more. Her apartment was not being kept as neat and tidy as she always maintained it, as she lived to a high standard of cleanliness. Then she was not eating well, which was also confirmed by her friend who went shopping with her. We started bringing her preprepared dinners and placing them in the refrigerator, which annoyed her as she did not want any help. And she was concerned about compensating us for it, which we refused. Eventually Ed just told her that he got coupons for free preprepared dinners from all the business supplies he purchased, so that quelled her concern. 'White lies' sometimes help in these situations. However, we noticed she only ate bits and pieces of the dinners.

After her assessment the CEO at the Assisted Living community suggested I bring her over for dinner so she could see and experience it, and I did. Returning afterwards, I asked what she thought of it, and she commented, 'they're all old people'. It was hard for me to refute that fact. When speaking with the CEO he suggested we move her into a guest apartment for a week under the guise of 'respite care' to acclimate her, so I could return home and she would be monitored. Fortunately, she agreed. That next day, Monday, I moved her in and got her settled.

She appeared to like being there and said it was, 'like living in a hotel'. They provided meals, cleaning, laundering and all the basic living necessities including medication management. Near the end of the week the CEO spoke with me and said a decision needed to be made whether she would move in permanently or go back to her apartment. In my view staying was the best thing. When I spoke with her about it, she was highly resistant and insisted on returning to her apartment. I had to find the 'Achilles' heel' to change her mind. During a heated discussion about it I said that if she didn't stay there, I would worry endlessly about her and possibly stay awake at night and be unable to effectively work. That changed her mind immediately as she said that she never wanted to be a 'burden'.

She was also very concerned about the cost of living there and we decided to just tell her another 'white lie' because I knew she wouldn't stay if she knew the true cost. I told her I knew the people there and they were giving us a big break on the cost, but not to tell anyone. That allayed her angst over that issue. I had effectively taken over her finances at that point anyway and that settled that problem.

We made plans to permanently move her into an empty apartment of her choosing. She looked at a couple and made her preferred selection. Still reluctant to move from her high-rise apartment Ed and I encouraged her to look to the care and convenience of her new place. We had to downsize so began the process of picking and choosing what to take, or not; and cleaning out a rather large apartment. She lived a practical and spartan lifestyle, so it wasn't terribly difficult. When we included her in making decisions about what to keep, she just shut down and wouldn't respond, so we just alleviated the distress and took her out of the decision-making process all together.

We had some help with moving from a local charity to move the few pieces to her new place, and partly to help give people some paid work. When I went to pick them up on the designated day one guy did not show up, but another had a solution... to have me drive down Market Street in San

Francisco while he yelled out to his indigent friends to see who might want to join us! This made me a bit uncomfortable, but why not? We did find another guy to join us. The items got moved successfully and the three guys helping were marvelous, diligent, and hard working. When the work was done Ed and I took them for sandwiches, sat down and talked with them. All great guys they were just down on their luck. They were so appreciative of the work, and the meal, and I have to say it was very enriching to have met them and hear about their lives.

I spent the next consecutive days emptying out her large apartment. I found some disturbing things during the process. My mother was hording cereal boxes and I found many of them stacked in the pantry. Then I found a pad of paper in her bedside table. Page after page she had written the numbers one through ten. It upset me as I realized she was doing that as her memory was fading, and she most likely knew it. It saddened me greatly to see such a vibrant woman seemingly struggle. Closing out the apartment, which I did every evening after work, was exhausting, but the apartment was soon cleaned, and she was moved.

My mother was extremely frugal, undoubtedly a product of living through The Depression and a World War with rationing. She clipped coupons and never missed a bargain. If a product she bought wasn't up to her standards, like the English muffins that weren't completely pre-cut correctly, she'd call the company and tell customer service about her complaint. She had fastidious standards.

The only thing that perplexed me after her move was that I had not found any of her jewelry. Perhaps she sold it; or gave it away; and I did not know how to ask her about it without upsetting her. Over lunch I casually broached the subject in conversation and got no response. I figured best to drop it. Then when I brought her suitcases to Goodwill to donate, I heard a unusual sound in one of them. When opened it was empty, except a large, zippered side pocket seemed to have something in it. Unzipping the pocket, I found all her jewelry tucked in small boxes. Another lesson learned, check everything.

This began a five-year long multiple *'Annus Horribilis'*. Her care was good, and it removed some of my worries. I saw her, however, gradually withdraw, and diminish, but in her true style she got up early each day, exercised, walked all the corridors, and did whatever she could to enhance her day.

Her memory continued to dwindle, and I tried whatever I could to help her. Along those lines I learned about not correcting those with advancing memory loss as it only upsets the person. I made a daily phone call to her every morning at 7am and Ed and I typically spent every Saturday with her, also having her stay at our home at times to give her a mini vacation as well.

Our home is alarmed during the night and one early morning when she was staying with us Ed heard the early warning chime of someone inside the house opening the front door. He immediately got up and found her standing on the front porch attempting to lock the door behind her, totally unaware of where she was at that moment. She said she was going to breakfast. That was the last time we felt it safe for her to stay with us.

Then while visiting Ed's family in Washington State I got a phone call when we were at restaurant. It was the Assisted Living community informing me that my mother had disappeared, and they were unable to locate her. In total panic I was in the midst of preparing to finalize arrangements to fly home when I got another phone call that they had located her, and she was safely back. With her walker, she casually walked out the door and strolled across two golf courses and ended up in the next city. A couple of Jehovah's Witnesses were walking behind her on the sidewalk and thought she appeared confused, so they spoke with her. Realizing she wasn't sure where she was headed, they took her to a house and the person there saw she had a key ring on her wrist with the community's phone number and called them. Talk about Good Samaritans! Someone from the community, a woman named Reggie, who my mother loved dearly, went out to get her and bring her back. It was a wake-up call that we needed to have her more carefully monitored.

We all tried our best to maintain her independence, but there is a time when that is no longer practical or wise. They moved her to a Memory Care area and when I got back home, we permanently set her up there. We had her tested and she was finally diagnosed with dementia, then shortly thereafter diagnosed with Alzheimer's disease. I was told her memory was like a sponge and nothing could reverse it. At times she called me 'Willie', her brother, and I did not refute or correct her. It was best to just surf the tide and be in 'Dorothy World' as we came to call it.

She enjoyed car rides but soon that diminished too, and all too often she was beginning to fall and being sent to the Emergency Room.

While at a convention in Los Angeles I received a call one late afternoon that she had been taken to the hospital. I arranged to fly back immediately, and this was not the first time I had to arrange to return home suddenly for an incident. Riding in the cab to the airport I received another phone call, from the hospital, informing me that she was being admitted for emergency brain surgery. I was shocked and inquired why while reiterating a few times that she is over ninety years old and having a surgery concerned me. The doctor said they found fluid on her brain during a test and surgery was necessary. I instructed them not to operate until I was back and in the hospital.

The minute that I arrived at LAX I received another phone call from another E.R. doctor informing me that my mother had been admitted to the hospital. I thanked her as I said I had already been informed and was returning to be there. She then went on to say that my mother was admitted for a urinary tract infection. Being totally aghast I asked about the emergency brain surgery, and she had no idea what I was talking about. I told her that I am not a doctor but to the best of my knowledge you do not necessarily admit someone to the hospital for a urinary tract infection, you use antibiotics. This definitely concerned me, and I asked to talk to the head of the E.R. who was not available. I emphasized my mandate about not doing anything until I arrived as I had the legal authority through my mother's medical directives.

When I got to the hospital she was admitted and in a regular hospital room, no longer the E.R. She seemed in good spirits, so I did not mention anything about the surgery so not to alarm her. We waited nearly a week to see a neurosurgeon about the surgery. When the surgeon finally came to see her, he told me that there was no need for surgery as they looked at her records and the fluid had been there for years and contributed to her dementia. Apparently, they could not access her records from the Emergency Room as they were elsewhere in the hospital.

Since her primary doctor was located at that hospital all her records were there, so it didn't make any sense. She was wrongly admitted, and they immediately discharged her. Subsequently a bill for $75,000.00 arrived that I vehemently fought. I also filed a complaint against the hospital.

The head of the hospital called me and in an abrasive tone said, 'well, Mr. Brutting, you sure have a problem, now, don't you?' Sounding unduly sarcastic as well I was not pleased and reversed it by saying that he had the problem, not me. He excused all the charges. I had to ponder how often this happened at hospitals.

I learned two valuable lessons from these experiences. One is that if someone you know goes to the hospital you absolutely need to be an advocate and be there all the time, and secondarily that if a person is sent to the emergency room you may not know which one. It depends on available space that an ambulance can access. A couple of times I ended up calling a variety of hospitals to find out where she was taken, as even the ambulance company wouldn't provide that information.

One day I arrived to visit my mother at the Assisted Living community, and they had taken her to Church. She wasn't a big church goer in those last days, but I was glad they took her. Going over to the church I stood in back during the service and saw her sitting there with her rosary in hand like a little schoolgirl attentively listening to the service. I felt the role reversal of parent to child and that memory sticks vividly in my mind. It was very touching.

There were also times when she became surprisingly lucid and would say things as clear as ever, sometimes calling us on our lack of including her in a conversation.

My mother became mostly child-like, complacent, and calm, and not as some with dementia who become combative and argumentative. She acquired a stuffed rabbit, a floppy thing that had a big bow around its neck, and that became her best friend. She cared for it like a cherished pet, and had it placed on the front of her walker so it could go everywhere with her. We called it 'Bunny'. She petted it and made sure its ears were pointed the right way and pampered it every minute of the day.

She also began sleeping a lot, although they did try to keep her awake with activities. It soon became apparent that she needed a higher level of care, Skilled Nursing. Due to the cost, I checked on Board and Care residences and found it to be a nightmare of places. They are usually in private houses they do afford more of a 'home-like' environment with fewer residents. Most of the conditions I saw, however, were deplorable. That is not to say that good ones don't exist, they do. I just saw a minimal number in my searching before I gave up. I also checked on nearby nursing homes and that wasn't much better, sometimes with three to four people to a room.

A nun with the Sisters of Mercy called me to talk with me about her care, as she was part of the same system as the Assisted Living my mother was in, and her Skilled Nursing Facility was close to my home. There was a placement available in that Skilled Nursing unit, and I agreed to move her there. I moved my mother from San Francisco to Oakland, essentially with two suitcases of clothes and personal items. The care there was incredibly supportive, and the nuns were so focused on providing a quality of life with dignity; and enabling people to live satisfactory lives regardless of limitations. I felt so comfortable leaving my mother in their care and visited frequently. I visited at least three times a week and usually fed her in the dining room as she could no longer eat on her own; or communicate. I held her hand after dinner for at least a half an hour as we watched some television.

Ed would often join me in the visits. The dining room table where she sat had four residents including her, and it was interesting to say the least. We would sit on either side of my mother and the woman to the other side of Ed always thought he was her husband. She would smile at him. and he played along with it, yet occasionally she cried, and Ed consoled her. There were times when she would spit out her dentures into her dinner plate. After a few times nothing surprised us. Next to me was a nasty woman everyone called 'Grandma'. She would throw food, fling her fork at others and just be ornery. Plus, much to my chagrin she took a liking to me and would smile engagingly. That was fine, but in the next moment I felt her hand rubbing my inner thigh under the table. I would immediately stop her, move her hand, and she would get angry and upset. Some dinners were like a circus, but we just rolled with it. The fourth woman was a very dignified woman who could not speak, younger than the rest, and seemed to have had a stroke or brain injury. She was always well dressed and wore nice jewelry. We would greet her from across the table and she would always smile back.

There were still good times as well, and the most wonderful, cherished memory I will keep in my heart of her time living there is on my mother's last Mother's Day in 2010. It became apparent she was losing all ability to focus, and her health was further declining. That Mother's Day they gave us a private dining room for the three of us to be by ourselves, next to a fireplace with linens and candles, crystal glassware and even wine. The meal was wonderful and while feeding my mother I knew she was happy being with us. I just could sense a joy within her. I am forever grateful for such a memorable time in her last days.

The months wore on and toward the Fall she began to refuse to eat. Anything you would place in her mouth she would just drop out. Ed tried ice cream and water just to have her have some sustenance, but she refused to open her mouth. One night, around three in the morning, I got a phone call that they believed she was in her last hours. We quickly dressed and went to her bedside where she passed away. While holding her hand as she struggled to breathe, I told her, 'it's OK to go', all would be alright. They had her on morphine at that point.

A nun was with us and comforted us. We deeply appreciated it. Her memorial service at Grace Cathedral in San Francisco was attended by close friends, and she was placed next to my dad in eternal rest.

That ended a very difficult period for me although I was appreciative to have had her in my life during those final years. It was 2010, an *'Annus Horribilis'*, which also followed Ed's mother dying earlier that year and his brother just before of cancer. I will write more about that in a later chapter.

I was very fortunate to have had both my parents for who they were, and the encouragement and sacrifices made to give me the best life possible. I learned a lot from them, and they are forever in my heart.

Then came another *'Annus Horribilis'*... 2012

I had noticed that I was getting frequent nosebleeds, for no apparent reason. It continued for a couple of months and when I went for my annual physical the doctor indicated I had dry nostrils and should use Vaseline, which I did, but it did not help. The nosebleeds weren't constant but usually intense.

During this time, I went to New Orleans for board meetings at Tulane University. One day I stopped by St. Louis Cathedral in the French Quarter for a bit of respite, and to pray. I enjoy the quiet and solitude there, and it gave me time to reflect on times I had spent years before at various services there, including being in the wedding party of my friend, Rich McCloskey. While sitting in a pew a nosebleed came on suddenly. I pulled out my handkerchief and it was soon soaked in blood, including some down the front of my shirt. It concerned me and seemed more than just a nosebleed.

Returning home, I visited the doctor again and he suggested I see a specialist which I did right away. The specialist thought it might be wise to take a biopsy and I went in the following week. This was during tax season for Ed, and I did not want to unduly worry him, so I kept my medical appointments to myself. I went back for the results and the specialist informed me I had cancer, a very rare form of nasal cancer. They would need to establish a treatment, but he could not detail any course of action. He did say that everything I was doing in my life would need to cease immediately, and I'd need to concentrate on my treatment. I was in midst of a dental reconstruction and asked if that could continue, and he said absolutely and emphatically 'no'.

I must have been completely startled by the news because the doctor looked at me and asked if I had someone who could be of support. I nodded I did; and left.

Totally shaken I got in my car and started driving down

Geary Blvd. in San Francisco. I found my nerves on edge and pulled off to the side of the road and parked. I called Ed on my cell phone, but he didn't answer so I left a message for him to call me back, not saying the reason. That was followed by my breaking down and crying, feeling exasperated and bewildered, scared. Cancer was something I have always feared because of both my parents having been victims in the past.

I drove back to my office and sat there for about an hour unable to do anything and decided to drive home where I knew Ed was working that day. Going home I told him what was going on, and about the diagnosis. He immediately started doing internet research and it did not look promising with my specific type of cancer.

This was followed by other doctor visits, tests, and examinations. Finally, I was given an appointment to meet with a 'cancer board'. They would outline the treatments proposed. Ed and I went for the board consultation and several doctors participated. The first indication was that I should expect my nose to be removed completely. It would be reconstructed through plastic surgery. There was some indication that the cancer may have entered my lymph nodes and even my brain. They did not immediately know the extent. I was also told that most likely I needed a feeding tube and would go through extensive radiation and chemotherapy lasting several months. They also were going to consult with some other specialists before making definitive decisions, but we needed to act quickly.

The news was devastating.

Meanwhile I had to work, and I decided no one should know other than my closest friends, some family members, and my partners at work.

The medical team decided that I needed to have a follow-up MRI so that was scheduled. When I went the technician told me to keep my head totally still and not move. I did my utmost to comply.

A day or so later Ed called me when I was out at a job site overseeing construction and said a doctor had called and wanted to speak with me immediately. It seemed odd, but nonetheless I called this doctor whose name I never heard of before then. The doctor was a surgeon in Marin County and asked me to come to his office the next day because he believed he found a possibly solution to my treatments, which Ed and I did.

The next day in his office the surgeon explained that the MRI had revealed some startling facts that were very encouraging. First there was no evidence of cancer in the brain or lymph nodes and because I kept my head so still he believed that he had isolated the extent of the cancer. It was a Wednesday and he scheduled me for surgery that Friday morning. I was a bit indignant as I thought my treatment would be near my home in Oakland, and he looked at me directly and said, 'either do it, or not'. So, I agreed.

Thursday evening, before the day of surgery, I stopped at the supermarket to get bread, feeling very frazzled. Standing in line at the checkout counter an adjacent checker called me over, so I proceeded to walk in that direction. The woman in front of me with a full basket of groceries started screaming at me, calling me names, and saying I was not going to get ahead of her. I was so annoyed I walked up to her and put my face right up to hers and said calmly and firmly, and not loud, 'you know something, tomorrow morning I'm going in for cancer surgery and I don't know if I'll live; and thank you for making my last moments so enjoyable.' She pushed me aside and went up to the checker who called me over. Another woman who overheard it came up to me and said very gently, 'Let it go'. She told me that she worked in hospice and saw incredible pain and suffering every day, and these small seemingly petty things in life are not worth getting worked up over. I thanked her so much, she smiled, and winked. I considered her my guardian angel that day, who came down from wherever in that moment of need.

That Friday we drove to the hospital and arrived at 6am for my scheduled time. I was prepped for surgery and Ed waited in the outer waiting room. We were told they did not know how long the surgery would take but that it could be several hours. In the end it took twelve hours. Ed told me that he had been concerned as patients and family members came and went after surgery, and he kept nervously waiting for any word on me. Finally, the surgeon came out to him and said that it looked successful, and showed Ed a three-inch long cyst, a tumor, that he removed from high up inside my nasal passage causing the bleeding. Fortunately, the cancer grew outward and not inward into my head.

I woke up in the recovery room sometime around eight o'clock that evening. I felt like hell and the only thing I could think, after blurting out some profanity, was that I could not believe I was living through this ordeal. The feeling of agony was intense beyond comprehension. Ed came to the bedside and after I became fully conscious, they wheeled me to the car and Ed took me home. That was a mistake and today in retrospect I should have remained in the hospital as that night the bleeding was profuse. Fortunately, they had given instructions in case that happened.

They had packed both nostrils so I could not breathe, except through my mouth. There is no describing how horrible that can be, especially for a prolonged period. One night I got up and while unable to catch my breath I made steaming hot tea to try and relax my mouth and throat. I thought for sure I was not going to make it, probably pass out. I considered calling an ambulance, but the steam did help settle me down.

Many days later I went to have the packing removed from my nostrils which was quite the effort and painful experience onto itself. Ed, who witnessed it, said it looked as though the doctor was pulling pairs of blue jeans from my nose. But I was cured. I had my nose intact, and I felt as though God had given me a second chance, a new life. Without any doubt I was extremely thankful of the surgeon, who literally changed the course of what could have been far worse in treatments. There would be no radiation or chemotherapy.

It was a terrible, horrible, and forever life altering moment.

For now, anyway, that was my last *Annus Horribilis*. I truly hope I won't have more.

CHAPTER 17

What I did for love

Love is a temptress and what we do to satisfy desire can be an adventure onto itself.

I have had three major relationships in my life, a heterosexual marriage that lasted eight years, a gay live-in partner for twelve years, and finally a same-sex marriage of twelve years within a relationship of twenty-two years.

All have been filled with love and affection in different ways.

For a reason that I am not totally certain about I have never been out of a relationship since age sixteen, in one way or another. I do recognize a fundamental basis of my life, undoubtedly learning independence as an only child, in that I am very comfortable being alone and living alone. Yet I also recognize that a relationship adds a level of satisfying richness too.

My current, and I trust my final, relationship with Ed York has been wonderful. We get along splendidly and share so many things together, although we do have our own interests as well. His is cars, and mine is classical music. I find it to be a deeply loving and caring relationship. We seem to be aging well together, growing in new ways and dimensions, as we enter our senior years.

No relationship is perfect, and there will always be bumps. Love, however, endures and the foundation of deep loving care is what endures no matter what.

When I took my vows with my former wife I did so with every intention of it being a love we would share together until we no longer existed on this earth. The curve ball came when my true gay identity, first characterized as being 'bi-sexual', arose and became insurmountable. That emptiness and longing for what was truly my nature was something not fair to either of us, and indeed traumatizing.

In retrospect I suppressed my gay self because in my youth it was considered 'wrong', 'evil', 'unhealthy', 'deviant', and whatever else one could find to call a 'sick, wayward person'. I longed to be a 'better person' and achieve what I could. At that time being gay would not get me there. In the 1960s and 1970s, and certainly before then, homosexuality was considered a mental illness and one could be arrested, incarcerated and/or put in a mental institution for acting on it. Besides, I was physically and mentally attracted to women; yet within me I also found men attractive too, with a more intense longing in desire.

Looking back on my life now I wonder what it would have been like if the world had allowed me to explore being gay in a decent, humane way. What if I had been able, and it was accepted, to date guys in high school, college, or thereafter? What would my world have been like, and what would I have done? Would I have taken the same path? I will never know, so I do not dwell on it much either.

I came down a road followed by many people, both men and women. When my wife, who was a psychologist, and I discussed my homosexuality, and the impacts in our marriage, her comment was that she believed our situation was just the 'tip of the iceberg'.

My wife belonged to Mensa, a social group of intellectuals,

and we once attended their conference in New York City. We were married a couple of years at the time. I knew something wasn't right when at the conference my eyes fixated on a very attractive man wearing a silk bomber jacket with a map of Vietnam on back, and I couldn't look away. I just kept glancing at him and felt these pangs of desire that I could not shrug off. We later saw him on the subway when we were heading home and, again, I felt this intensity of attraction to him. I never made any true eye contact with him; but was afterwards quite concerned why that happened to me. I did not tell my wife. These inner truths surfaced and were hard to disregard.

A societal intent of heterosexual marriage is procreation; yet I was never that interested in having children. I was, however, blessed with three children, nonetheless; a boy born of my heterosexual marriage, and later a boy and girl who were my partner's natural children. I cherished each of them dearly. Each brought immeasurable joy and happiness into my life.

Love isn't always joyous.

The saddest, and most profound, loss I have ever felt was becoming estranged from my own son, then two years old. Perhaps the greater loss was his and, unfortunately, it occurred in the wake of my starting a relationship with a man. For a couple of years, I traveled regularly across two midwestern states to be able to see him. I struggled and anguished for a very long time to maintain a relationship, but it was removed from me. Attempting to reestablish it when he was an adult, it was to no avail. The damage was done, and I have moved on from it. I have kept a box full of all the documented details that I hope one day is in his possession should he care to know more, and that I had not abandoned him.

In mentioning the experience of traveling across two states to see him, I will divert to a story that became a lasting memory of those trips. Visiting a friend's house afforded me a convenient place to stay for me to see my son. During one visit I was there alone as everyone in his household was away. I arrived one night, quite late, and decided to just bunk in the family room that had a sofa bed. During the night I awoke and felt a very strange sensation. I was sleeping near an open screened window as it was summer, and awakening I saw what looked like a face in the window. Putting on my glasses I saw it certainly was a face, a man's face. A person was right there and staring at me, no more than four feet away. Fearfully, I gradually slid off the opposite side of the bed on to the floor. I lingered there for some time and did not move or make a sound. He said and did nothing. There was nothing but silence.

After some time, I slowly looked up over the bed and the face was still there. The man was just staring and not moving. Unnerving as it was, I did not move as I knew this person could easily come through the screen and window at me. He obviously knew I was there and was watching. Many thoughts went through me as to what to do, thinking it best not to scream. I knew there was a phone in the kitchen, and I grappled with the idea of slowly crawling across the floor until I could get there to call the police. Yet I knew the person would probably see me doing that, so I just stayed put for what seemed like an eternity, on a couple of occasions peering over the bed to see if he was still there.

Terrified and frozen I remained scared to move. After a very long period of time, more than half an hour, I looked over the edge of the bed and the face was finally gone. I slowly went to the window, closed, and locked it. While locking it I heard water running, as if it were within the house. I listened for a bit and then it stopped.

Getting back into bed I contemplated calling the police; but decided against it since it wasn't my house and I really didn't know how to explain it, or what I was doing there.

In the morning while thinking about it I became convinced the side of the house with the window must have a ground level that was much lower than the window, and that it would be impossible for to a person to stand and peer inside without standing on something. Although I had not been to that part of the yard but maybe once, I decided to check it out to dismiss the whole thing entirely. I could have dreamt it. Walking to the back of the house, I saw the ground was mounded with a berm where a person could easily stand at that height and look into the window. Then I saw a water spigot close to the window, probably the water I heard running. It seemed likely this person turned it on to alert me that he was still there.

When my friend returned home, I told him about it, and we decided not to call the police. Subsequently the house next door was broken into several days later. There is no telling if the incidents were related.

To this day I have no idea who the man was standing there staring in the window, and why it went on for so long. I also do not know the intent or reason why it happened.

The unknown perils of doing something for the benefit of someone I loved- merely to visit my son.

Not all those trips were as dramatic. Another time I stopped slightly past midnight at a roadside rest stop that had a hill with a picnic table on it. I parked and walked up in the solitude of the night to just sit under the night air and look at the stars and moon. The silence and beauty of the night was unforgettable. I was in the middle of rural Iowa and could see openly in every direction. At that moment I felt the beauty of life, our earth, and the universe beyond. Sometimes love brings solace.

When my grandfather was very ill and dying at home, he looked up at me when I was quite young and consoled me in my sorrow and anguish in seeing him that way by saying, 'don't you worry, Tommy, we will dance again'. When I was a young boy there was always dancing during holiday gatherings. I have never forgotten those words, and I am not sure what he meant other than we would someday have good times in another life.

One night after a visit with my son I had an intensely real dream, one that was so powerful that it has lasted with me. I dreamt I was with my young son and we were in a cafeteria somewhere. We were laughing and I took his hands and we started swaying and dancing together. Just a simple little dance with my arms extended out to him, holding his small hands. The music, which was very vivid, was 'What I did for love' from the musical, *A Chorus Line*. I looked at him at the end of the song and I said, 'someday we will dance again'. I woke up in tears.

I moved twice for love, once to Madison Wisconsin from New York City for my wife to pursue her doctoral degree at the University of Wisconsin. That was the primary, but not the sole, reason as I was also anxious to leave New York as well. I was just not necessarily focused on the Dairy State and bitter winters as a new home. The other time was when I moved to Des Moines, Iowa from Madison, again for love, and again not necessarily for the fields of the 'Corn State'. Both times I had no regrets, but it was dramatic change in both cases.

Lastly, there was a surprise birthday party that changed my life's direction and fostered a new focus of love.

It was my forty-fourth birthday when Ed decided to secretly arrange it for me.

Unfortunately, the surprise was revealed before the event occurred. The circumstances around it were rather strained and complicated, and it caught me between the twilight of one relationship and the commencement of another. The party was, however, a momentous occasion and one I will always cherish. The pendulum of love had swung in new ways.

Shortly after the celebration, and my realization of what life and love meant, I moved into a new apartment. I found the cutest 'Romeo flat', an Edwardian apartment in the Presidio Heights neighborhood in San Francisco, that I adored and had many great memories for the year I lived there. Ed spent every weekend with me, and we had the best time ever. We then decided to move in together finding a bigger Pacific Heights apartment to bring in the new Millennium, the year 2000.

Love brings happiness and tears. It is a human emotion that changes our lives in so many ways. We are blessed by love when it enters our lives, and the mystery of its allure is always with us.

Chapter 18

Ollie

My parents had me in the 1950s when they were older than most parents at the time, in their late thirties. They had been married nine years at that point. Being right after World War II I am certain that they were just getting on their feet, and my dad had started his electronics business. Being frugal I imagine a child did not fit into the immediate picture for them. In retrospect their being older than most of my friends' parents also meant that they were wiser and a bit more mature than many.

The story goes that I was supposed to be twins, as the doctor had explained it to my mother when she was pregnant. Well, that didn't happen. As a cesarean birth I was the first and only child they had. They told me my name, Thomas, comes from the possibility of being a twin, and that the name wasn't common in my family. Perhaps, more so 'Thomas the Doubter' is more appropriate as it my natural characteristic.

Since they were older, and nearly a generation beyond most of the others having children, my grandparents were that much older too. In a matter of fact, I only knew two of my four grandparents. My paternal grandfather had died two years before my birth, supposedly on Wall Street, during the Christmas holidays. When he died of a heart attack he collapsed near the gutter and no one cared to check on him because people assumed he was drunk, or so the story goes.

My maternal grandmother died two months after I was born. I have only one photo of her holding me as an infant. I was her only grandson. My mother told me once that I was, 'born with a bank account because of her'. Apparently the first thing she did when learning I was born was to go to the bank and open a savings account in my name with five hundred dollars.

She was quite worldly. Having immigrated from Lithuania sometime around 1909 she came with two sisters. Those two sisters returned to Lithuania and left her here alone. She was sixteen and was watched after by other Lithuanian immigrant families as was customary for the time. Living in Brooklyn she got work as a domestic for a wealthy woman. I have photos of her with this person. Being quite entrepreneurial, as described by her nephew, she married and became rather well off by becoming a bootlegger during Prohibition. I only found that out through that nephew when he was in his nineties. It made me very proud of her.

She acquired property, in the upscale community of Great Neck on Long Island, and the family lived there for over seventy years. Interestingly the property was only in her name, and not my grandfather's, and she drove very expensive cars while he rode a bicycle. She also traveled, to Europe, I presume by ship, as well as to California, and Mexico in the early days of passenger aviation. She took my mother to Lithuanian friends in Coral Gables, Florida for the winter. I can only presume she kept my grandfather off all titles and ownership in case she was ever arrested for bootlegging, so he would not be implicated. But that's merely speculation.

In all the photographs I have of her she is laughing and apparently very content. She is buried in the same cemetery as

Margaret Brown, 'Mollie Brown' of Titanic fame. Two strong women with interesting histories buried in close-proximity.

My maternal grandfather, Stanley, 'Grandpa' as I called him, was the world to me and my two cousins, Cynthia and Gloria. Upon my grandmother's death he moved out of the family house and into another residence in Great Neck. My uncle, his wife and my cousins moved into the family home where I came to spend a lot of time in my youth.

Grandpa was somewhat of a character, and fiercely independent. He lived simply; yet lived well. He enjoyed gardening, foraging for mushrooms while storing them in large jars, and taking care of his parakeets. Much to the consternation of my mother, he let the parakeets fly around the house at times. He claimed it was good for them to be out of the cage and fly freely. My mother also did not like that he taught me how to play poker, wagering with pennies. He just shrugged it off and continued doing it when she was not around.

He arrived in the United States from Lithuania about the same time as my grandmother, around 1909. I know little of his background or exactly where he was from in the old country. It always amazed me how these people could pack up and leave their parents and family behind for new lives, but they did. His family name was Kasilauskas.

He also came with two sisters, both who married and remained here for the remainder of their lives. I only met one sister, Kate, whose last name was Trepkus, at my grandfather's funeral. She lived in Edison, New Jersey, and I am not sure how much my grandfather saw her over the years. His other sister, Magdeline, lived in Windsor Locks, north of Hartford, Connecticut, and married a Lithuanian tobacco farmer there, with the last name Waicunas. My mother and her brother apparently spent many a summer on the tobacco farm with that family in their youth. I never met her, to my recollection, but knew her daughters, my Aunt Eva and Aunt Helen, including their children, especially Aunt Helen's daughters, Vicki, Leslie and Tina.

I remember my grandfather sitting on the sofa and complaining that the United States was like 'goulash', a place where you just mix all these random people together, and this is what you get. Mostly we all ignored him when he went into one of these rants.

He did cook Sunday dinners too, typically kielbasa with pealed boiled potatoes, and some type of green. We ate the kielbasa with horseradish. It was true Lithuanian cooking, but perhaps not the best.

He died when I was twelve and it was terribly traumatic for me. I loved and cherished him dearly, especially for his quirks and how kind he was to me. He was my first close relative to die. When we got the call to come immediately to the hospital as he had a heart attack I started to cry. We knew that he would probably not survive. My mother was upset enough, but more so by my crying and looked at me and sternly said, 'you DON'T cry!'. I stopped and was unable to express my grief until the day of his funeral when I just totally broke down during the church service.

When we arrived at the hospital, I sat downstairs in the general reception area as children were not allowed upstairs. So, I never had an opportunity to see my grandfather is his last hours. I sat there, alone, for quite some time when my uncle appeared and asked me if I knew 'Grandpa' had died. I told him I did, although I had not until the moment that he told me. I felt tremendous sadness; but I did not cry.

I recall vividly the tears streaming down my face as I received communion at his funeral at St. Aloysius Church in Great Neck, my mother undoubtedly mortified. My father's cousin, Barbara, who you will read about later, said that I came from a family stock of 'stiff upper lip' types and that my mother was the epitome of it. It was back in the days when everyone wore black to a wake and a funeral, without exception, and most went and bought new black clothes for it, so the tone was always somber. There was no such thing as a 'celebration of life' at that time. A matter of fact the day he had died my father's brother and his wife came from their second home in upstate New York and had purchased and wore new black clothes before coming to our house that evening.

Limousines took us out to the cemetery, and he is buried not with my grandmother but elsewhere several hundred yards away. I do not know why. There was a huge reception afterwards and I remember so much food and drink that it was impossible to comprehend the magnitude of it all.

When we cleaned out my grandfather's house my mother was carrying some items out to our car and slipped and fell on the sidewalk and injured her knee. The pain from the injury lasted for years. My uncle insisted that my grandfather's spirit had pushed her. It made me wonder about it as he always said that if the afterlife wasn't good, he'd come back to warn us. Perhaps this was his return?

My paternal grandmother was the last grandparent to survive in my life. Her given name was Margaretha Ulrike Rodamer, Brutting by marriage, and her nickname that everyone used was

'Ollie'. I do not know how that came to be. She was one of nine children from a German immigrant family. Her father came from a small village in southern German, Oberrimbach, in the Steigerwald forest. Having found it and visited I can attest to it being charming and quite small. The place is frankly idyllic, and you'd have to wonder why anyone would leave it. You expect *Little Red Riding Hood* to come out from around a tree at any moment. It is very agrarian, and he was born there in 1864.

His wife on the other hand was from a northern part of Germany, now a part of Poland since the end of World War II, Pomerania. She was from a city named Koslin. The only thing I know about her family is that her sister and husband died on the 'side of the road' while being forced to walk by the Russians from their home to Berlin after the war had ended. They were in their seventies.

Ollie was a product of these people, and this is the family I knew the best while growing up. Her brothers and sisters were a big part of my life. They lived throughout Westchester County in New York, where she was raised, and into New England. Her youngest sister, Adelaide, lived near Augusta, Maine and their brother, Otto, had a seventy-acre homestead on the ocean. They were a close-knit family.

Her husband, my Grandfather Brutting, who as I mentioned earlier died before I was born was another matter. I knew little to nothing about he or his family, except there were uncles and cousins I never met, and would never meet. The story goes that the Bruttings did not find my grandmother suitable enough as her family were 'country people'. For that or whatever other reason my father did not know them either and were always distant. I know that one uncle ran a newspaper in

New Canaan, Connecticut, and that is about all of it. Once my Aunt Betty, another of my grandmother's sisters and a twin to Adelaide, told me she saw my great grandparents, the Bruttings, in church in the Yorkville section of Manhattan, the German section where they all originally settled, and that both were extremely well-dressed, with my great grandmother wearing a very elaborate lace blouse. She saw them but there was no conversation between them.

Every family has secrets and mine came out after several people had died. I learned one, in particular, after both my grandmother and father had passed. My mother said that my grandfather, Ollie's husband, had a mistress, and openly flaunted it to the consternation of all the family. My mother said she and my father once saw him on the street and she asked my father if they would at least go to say 'hello', and he absolutely refused. I also was told that at his funeral the mistress showed up and Aunt Betty told my father to go tell her to leave as she was not welcomed, and he did. All very sad indeed.

My grandmother Ollie was born in September 1891 in Manhattan. In her lifetime, she lived to be ninety-six, she experienced incredible change. Imagine living through the turn of the nineteenth century, the Gilded Age of enormous Fifth Avenue mansions and the times she remembered of swimming in the East River off a beach near Sutton Place. She had lived through World War I, the Depression and World War II. She saw the automobile come into prominence, skyscrapers hit new heights, along with the invention of the elevator, steel construction, and innumerable other inventions of the day, like the light bulb. She was twenty-one when the Titanic sank. So much to live and experience in a long life.

She refused to have a telephone, and disliked talking into the 'contraption', as she called it.

Grandma Ollie saw nearly every bridge built in New York City during her lifetime, except the Brooklyn Bridge that was constructed seven years before she was born. In my childhood I saw the Throgs Neck Bridge built in 1961 when I was seven, and the Verrazano Narrows Bridge built in 1964 when I was ten and I can attest to the fact that it is quite an amazing thing to watch. I saw the Throgs Neck Bridge constructed in near proximity observing it from the Merchant Marine Academy in Kings Point. Bit by bit went into place like synchronized clockwork. Watching these feats of engineering do make an impression on the progress of our world.

Yet, Ollie outlived her peers, and that loneliness was probably the worst part for her. She was once asked by a reporter about the success of her longevity and she said, 'eating onions and garlic'.

I remember her being very gentle and kind, yet stubborn and set in her ways. There was little changing what she thought or did. Every morning she walked down the street to get her newspaper and when she returned to her apartment building, she would walk up the four flights of marble stairs to her apartment to make toast and feed the birds on her kitchen windowsill. She insisted on buttering both sides of the bread as she claimed they wouldn't eat it only buttered on one side.

She kept a newspaper clipping pasted on the wall above her kitchen table of a log cabin in the woods which she said was her ideal home. It was her dream to end her last days in a place like that.

Calling her home 'Old Astoria' she talked of days gone by

in the neighborhood and mentioned frequently how much she enjoyed the local hardware store down the street from her, on Broadway.

She had a hearty laugh and enjoyed good humor. Her childhood was spent first in Manhattan and later in Westchester, primarily Hartsdale, Valhalla, Greenburgh and on property my great grandparents had adjacent to the Rockefeller estate near Tarrytown. She relayed how she and some friends had encountered old man JD Rockefeller while they were roaming on his property, and he caught them. He sternly shooed them away and, according to her story, ran in horror of this mean man who appeared out of nowhere. The story continued that they ran down to the road and a chauffeur-driven car came by and took them home as they were waving their hands for it to stop. The car was owned by Jay Gould. It was somewhat later that my great-grandparents' property was taken by eminent domain to build a new freeway, that avoided touching the much larger Rockefeller estate.

Whether true or not she talked proudly of having kicked Governor Nelson Rockefeller in the shins when he closed a senior center she frequented and enjoyed going to nearly daily. She also spoke of her encounter with a nun she did not like very much at the elementary school my cousins attended in Astoria, Most Precious Blood. She claimed the nun annoyed her so much when going to collect my cousins from school that she grabbed the nun and told her that if she knocked the black habit off her head the nun would be no better or different a person than she. Do not mess with Grandma Ollie. Probably these events would be punishable offenses in today's legal system.

She went on to live nearly most of her adult life in Astoria after marrying my grandfather. We spent many days and nights talking and she was often forthcoming with tidbits from her past. She said that when my grandfather died that she was out in the cold financially since he did not save money or believe in retirement. She took jobs as a seamstress which she enjoyed, and wrapped packages at B. Altman, a well-known Fifth Avenue department store in Manhattan. I always knew her to live in a modest yet comfortable apartment.

At one point after my parents bought their newly built house on Crescent Street in Astoria, she moved in with us. That was before I can remember as I was less than one year old at the time. There was space on the first floor that was intended for an apartment and that is where she lived. My mother told me that my grandmother greatly favored my uncle over my father, his younger brother, and she said Ollie treated him like an 'adopted child'. It greatly annoyed her, and she never understood why it was that way.

What apparently brought the arrangement to an end was when my grandmother took to bringing my cousin, my uncle's child who was slightly older than myself, back to our house and coddling him, walking him outside, while ignoring me. Again, I have no memory of this as I was too young, and it was merely my mother's telling of it. It did, however, come to a head as my grandmother did leave and moved into an apartment close to my uncle and his family, albeit just a few blocks away from us.

Growing older I did become close to my grandmother, and we developed a good relationship, even if she spent more time caring for my cousins. The details of the family dynamic will perhaps never be known. Regardless, I will always remember Ollie fondly.

She had many friends, was socially active, and remained close with all her family, especially her siblings throughout Westchester and New England. We would often take her on trips to visit each of them, as well as friends from the past. I recall on one of these journeys, I was probably around six years old, we visited friends of hers that we did not know that well. I sat politely on the sofa while they all talked. At the end of the visit the man we were visiting asked my mother if I was blind. She looked perplexed, and I recall this exchange vividly. She said, 'no'; but questioned what made him ask. He told her that I sat so upright and still throughout the visit and never once reached for the candy dish on the coffee table in front of me. I was taught that was being polite, and I would only take something if offered, but it totally made him wonder about it.

Ollie was also an artist, an oil painter, as that was her hobby. She had other talents that she did not pursue, as an example she made an incredibly elaborate cruel work bedspread for my parents' wedding gift. It has grapevines and grapes over the entire piece and is intricately stitched. I still have it and nearly everyone who has ever seen it finds it a remarkable piece of artwork. Yet, oil painting was her passion. Expressing an interest in it she took me under her wing to teach me the basics. She taught me about the use and value of turpentine, 'turps' as she called it.

Without any formal training her style was that of Grandma Moses, flat and without perspective or a third dimension. Primarily painting landscapes, flowers, and animals they were very precise and realistic, yet flat. They were interesting works in their own genre, and a painting she did of pansies sits on the shelf above where I write this now. They are colorful, vivid, and precise.

Along the way she came to befriend a neighbor of her sister's, my Aunt Betty, in White Plains. Her name was Joan Howe and a very prolific, accomplished painter. She was the granddaughter of one of the well-known Hudson River School painters, and the daughter of Richard Anderson, a well know illustrator. Joan and her husband, Melvin Howe, owned houses in White Plains, New York; Marathon, Florida; Altamont, New York, and Missouri. They had a yearly rotation where they spent approximately three months at each residence coinciding with the best season at each location.

Joan did beautiful oil paintings, represented, and sold in galleries, and was very well regarded in the Florida Keys where Marathon was located. Generally, she painted local landscapes and still life, and occasion portraits. My grandmother was one of her portrait subjects, and there were several paintings made of her. One was sold to a bank in the Caribbean where it hung in their main banking hall, and I have one smaller one in my home of her painting at an easel. Because of the subject it is particularly special to me and very glad I have it. In the painting she is wearing an apron and my mother did not like it because in her view it made my grandmother look 'fat', and she wasn't.

My grandmother introduced me to Joan and explained my interest in painting. Joan was delighted. I remember Joan as distinguished and always well dressed and well spoken. She obviously had a good education and an artistic pedigree.

On occasion we would drive my grandmother several hours north to upstate New York to the Howe's home in Altamont, near Albany. It was simply amazing to me in that the property was enormous, many acres of fields and open land in a totally bucolic setting with a historic house built a long time ago. It had belonged to Joan's family, the Andersons. On a visit I recall Joan's mother, in a wheelchair, sitting at the front entry door peering out through the screen door to the landscaped gardens and long, curved entry drive with a stone wall running alongside it. There were giant trees that shaded the yard.

One summer my grandmother decided to take me for several weeks up to Altamont. It was a huge treat and I had just turned twelve years old. As the Howes were not there yet we would have at least a couple of weeks for just the two of us together, and I was elated. My parents drove us up and stayed overnight, leaving the next day. That visit was one of the most memorable times for me, and so happy it was with my grandmother, Ollie.

After we settled ourselves in place, she immediately began a vegetable garden. No small task but my grandmother was intent on having fresh vegetables for the summer. She tended that garden like a child, and it did produce lots of fresh vegetables, including rhubarb that I will mention later. What fascinated me was her fondness for all animals too, like the birds back in Astoria. She adopted a snake. It was long, black and would slither up to the kitchen back door where she would leave little bits of meat for it. I was a bit taken aback but accepted that it was her pleasure.

The house to me was something of utter amazement, not only for its age and details, but how it was furnished. The rooms were very large and formally planned. The main parlors had oversized Empire style furniture. I nearly got engulfed in the size of the chairs with high arms. One room had a piano that I loved to play.

It was an antique upright type. There was a beautiful country kitchen and what impressed me most was the artwork, the paintings, throughout the house. Most done by either Joan's father or grandfather they were museum size and huge. They were of rural agrarian landscapes, large open fields, and hay bales. It was overwhelming to take it all in. I was very impressed with the quality and beauty of them. Around the house were also several of Mr. Anderson's illustrations. Again, beautifully executed, and so fine in detail. His work was sometimes displayed on the cover of renowned magazines, such as *Town and Country*.

It was an utter delight for me to be in this house and place, and alone with my grandmother who I could come to bond with her in a major way. We laughed, cooked, and told stories. Our evenings, after dinner, were usually on a porch overlooking the vegetable garden or in front of the large fireplace in one of the front lounge rooms. There were rockers there and we spent hours sharing stories, and I absolutely loved every minute of it. I think she did too. As she told me at one point that 'we both have a gift for the gab'.

There were two staircases in the house, one off the main central hall and one off the front lounge space that went directly to the master bedroom above. I do not have recollection of all the rooms, but I knew I could easily get lost if I wanted to be alone. My bedroom was a small room directly above the main entrance of the house. It was a delightful room with a view out to the front, very much like what Mrs. Anderson saw when she sat in the entry doorway below. Above the bed was an oil painting of a handsome boy, about my age, blond and blue eyes that I came to learn was Joan's brother. He kept watch over me at night while I slept.

Occasionally a possum would hang from its tail from one of the trees in the front yard. It repulsed me to see it hanging there with its glaring eyes staring out at me.

Since the house was very old there were floor creaks and a definite patina of age. It just added to the character. Outside the house there was a formal arbor and flower garden that had become overgrown. There was also a studio, perhaps for painting, in a separate building beyond the garden. Next to the house was a large barn although I do not remember ever going into it.

A relative once asked me what things inspired me to become an architect. My response was that this house with its beautiful, aged, and simple character, along with the huge hand-hewn wood beams in the basement exhibiting clearly the structure holding up the house.

Beyond were fields and fields of open land, some of which they were loaning to a neighbor, the Brenner family, who had a large property next to the Howes, to cultivate for crops. However, there were even more fields beyond that. I really felt so free in that environment and spent so much time just running through the fields. The backdrop was quite spectacular as there was a state park with cliffs as tall as the skyscrapers. Punctured into the cliffs were caves that were made by the Indians many centuries beforehand, and my grandmother called them 'the eyes'.

As a New York City kid visiting and staying here it was pure bliss. All the open space, outdoors, nature, fresh air. They said that during the 1950s when I grew up in New York the pollution was so bad it was equivalent to smoking three packs of cigarettes per day. One can imagine the change in such a pure environment, 'God's country' as my grandmother so aptly called it.

We spent our days active and restfully too, tending to the garden, cooking together, oil painting, and me just wandering and exploring the land while my grandmother took a nap. One day my grandmother looked forcefully and uncharacteristically agitated and bolted out the back door. I watched as she walked with determination into one of the back fields. There was quiet and then she returned. It turned out she heard gunshots and went out to find hunters on the property who she immediately told to leave; needless to say, a dangerous way to do so!

Ollie was also a person who nurtured and shared her knowledge openly. She enjoyed teaching me simple German phrases she had learned as a child, or a song or two, and gave me instruction in such things as the term 'newel post' at the foot of the staircase railing.

As for the vegetable garden things grew very quickly and I did not know my grandmother had such a green thumb. One thing that grew that was unfamiliar to me was rhubarb. These strange-looking, long red-green stalks with large, green leaves that she warned me were poison. As it matured, she decided to make a rhubarb pie. I had never had rhubarb pie and watched her prepare it. It looked putrid and disgusting to me, these mangled stalks cooked down into what appeared to be a stringy mess, which they were not in reality. I turned up my nose and told her I really did not care to ever try it; unusual for me since I did like trying new things being exposed to all the variety of unusual ethnic dishes in Astoria.

She put the pie on a window ledge and went to take a nap. I stared at that pie and it began to call me. While she slept, I took the pie down and tried a tiny little piece. It was delicious! The sugar obviously took off any bitterness from the rhubarb stalk. I took a bigger piece, and another, and then a third. When she awoke and went to check on the pie half of it was eaten. She just stood there with her arms on her hips and began to laugh. She ended up giving me a hug for my 'bravery'.

We had one strange incident during a violent rainstorm when a tornado hit, but it was only about four feet high! We watched it whirl between the barn and the house and it was the most absolute bizarre thing to witness. Twice it hit the side of the barn but did nothing other than sling mud against it, but unfortunately headed to my grandmother's garden where it ripped out several of the plants and tossed them at a distance. She was very upset to go out and review the damage after the storm subsided.

There was a smaller house near the beginning of the driveway at the main road, quite a distance so you could not see it. I think it may have originally been a caretaker's cottage, and it was being rented to two older women who were quite pleasant and fun. One continually talked about her time at the 1930s Chicago World's Fair as though it had happened a month ago. At one point a nephew of one of them came to visit and stay with them; he was perhaps three to five years older than me. We became instant friends as there weren't many opportunities to meet others and we spent a lot of time together in the week or so he stayed with them.

These women also told us that recently the house we were staying in had been broken into a couple of times over the past year, when the Howes were away. It was supposedly teenagers as nothing was taken, just a lot of mischief and some damage. The house had several large round and oblong rugs that were made of cloth and rags woven in rope strands, common in country houses. We were told that whoever broke in took jars of canned jellies and jams, smashed them, and smeared it on the carpets.

Very late one night after I had gone to sleep, I awoke to sounds coming from downstairs and it startled me. The stories of the break-ins came immediately to mind. I presumed it to be around three in the morning. As I listened to footsteps and some rummaging coming from what seemed like the kitchen, I became increasingly alarmed. After sitting up and taking note further I heard the footsteps approach the staircase and slowly start walking up the stairs. I got out of bed and grabbed a large rock that was being used as a doorstop for my bedroom door. Standing at the rear of the stair I had a clear view halfway down the stair as it was open on that end. As the person slowly approached coming up the stairs, I took the rock intending to throw it at this person the minute I saw him or her. A nightlight from the bathroom shone on the person and it turned out to be my grandmother. She had made a cup of tea for herself. In relief I stammered back to bed, only to realize how easily very serious things could occur. Fortunately, I saw her before throwing the rock.

One afternoon I heard a car coming down the driveway and looked out the window. It was a bright Cadillac; I believe a gold color. It was Joan and Melvin Howe arriving for their couple month stay after being in their Missouri home and intending then to head to their Florida one afterwards. I stood at the back door as my grandmother went out to greet them. After they came into the house, I was introduced to them. With them was a small dog, new to them, and I learned they called her

'Tiger Lily Lotus Blossom Howe'. Joan was a tall, blond haired woman and Melvin was very engaging, yet I do not recall much of his physical characteristics.

The dynamic of the house changed after they arrived, and it was lively and active with four people and a dog. Melvin immediately took to working on the property doing various tasks and he often enlisted my help, which I enjoyed. It is interesting as I cannot recall eating any meals together, although we must have done so. Melvin also restored houses and enjoyed tinkering around with construction. He'd drive me out to places to buy reclaimed lumber and supplies in a variety of places, some far and some near. He was so amused when we once pulled into town for lunch and when we walked up to the café door a sign was turned stating it was closed. Melvin teased me that I caused the immediate closure when they saw me coming. I enjoyed his humor, even when it was at my expense.

When my grandmother and Joan sat down to paint on their individual canvases, they included me with my own. I was very honored in that Joan, such an accomplished artist, gave me lessons. It was all very enjoyable, but she often became frustrated with me. When I was unable to mix my colors properly, she would say, 'Is that the color you *really* see?' referencing some object we were painting. It usually was not even close. Joan believed you could only paint things you can see in front of you, a realist. She did not think one could or should create scenes that did not exist from imagination, and to only attempt to do so when you've perfected realism. In the days we painted together I did get better.

What I found fascinating, and I do not know why, was when we would all retire in the evening Melvin would grab a bottle of rum and carry it to their bedroom. I never saw him intoxicated, yet it was an evening ritual to bring the bottle upstairs. Ironically, I never saw any bottle go downstairs.

He often went off to lunch at some nearby club called the 'Kings Club' with friends.

After weeks of being together in splendid bliss my grandmother told me it was time we would have to leave. It somewhat saddened me, but nonetheless the summer was coming to an end. Joan was having some sorority sisters over to the place for a summer retreat and she needed the beds, so that helped move us along.

I will always vividly remember the day we left. I said my goodbyes, and especially to Tiger Lily who had bonded with me. It was the last time I would see Joan and Melvin. A taxi came to take us to the station in Albany and in a typical movie style ending I so recall looking back out the rear window at the house and property as we left. It was a wonderful summer, and Ollie and I had a wonderful time together.

She made deviled eggs that she carried in a shoe box for our trip back and they were delicious. When we arrived in Manhattan the intensity of seeing the city again just overwhelmed me. We got a taxi to return me home and the cab driver was a lunatic, going the wrong way down one-way streets at lightning speed in his attempt to locate the entrance to the Queensboro Bridge. My grandmother just looked at me, winked, and we laughed.

The minute the taxi pulled up in front of my house my mother came running out and welcomed us back. I had been weeks away and it felt strange returning to my usual existence.

It did feel like I had a wonderful adventure, and so much enjoyed being with my grandmother, Ollie.

The last time I saw her was when I had her over to my apartment in Forest Hills for lunch, in 1980 before I moved to Wisconsin. When I returned her home, she would not allow me to come up to her place. I had found over time she was not as resilient as she always had been, like always meeting me at the train station when I came to visit. She began to forget I was coming. Eventually she did not want people in her apartment.

She died in 1988 several years after I saw her last. She was truly my only grandparent for a significant part of my early life. At ninety-six years old Ollie's body eventually gave out. She died in a nursing home.

Sadly, none of us could attend her funeral as I was engrossed in my divorce proceedings. I felt sad for my father for having to miss it as he was at my divorce for support, and Wisconsin was a long way from New York.

Today I look at the oil painting of her that Joan Howe painted many years ago hanging in my house and remember the good times we had together.

And yes, she will always have a place in my heart, regardless of the history surrounding the extended relationships.

CHAPTER 19

Pig's feet, frog legs and oysters

My parents had some peculiar and unique eating habits, in certain things they enjoyed. I have mentioned my love of food and cooking in a previous chapter but this one will focus on the things I remember most from their culinary choices as remembered from my youth.

Eels heavily populated the Long Island Sound, and the very first time I went fishing with my grandfather, an activity I strongly disliked, the first thing I caught was an eel! He helped me pull it out of the water and it was a couple of feet long, or more, and wrapped around his arm as he tried to subdue it. It was utterly disgusting. This big black snake of a thing. Who would ever eat that? But it is a delicacy in some sectors and not only he, but also my parents, loved it. I think it might be an immigrant derivative. I eat many things, but eel is not on the list.

There was a restaurant in Sheepshead Bay, Brooklyn called Lundy's. It's an 'Old World' styled restaurant, dark and clubby, with a look of a Spanish colonial hacienda. It had stucco arches and columns with tile roof and many dining rooms inside it. We would go to Sheepshead Bay to meet the fishing boats when they came back to the docks to buy fresh fish from them, and a stop at Lundy's for lunch was always a part of the excursion. My father always headed to the bar where oysters were served.

He would tell the bar tender to just keep on opening the oysters until he was done, usually at least a couple dozen. He washed it down with a beer. There were these folk tales at that time about only eating oysters on months that end in an 'r', and to never eat them with hard liquor as it would make your throat swell and kill you. My mother ate some, but not nearly as many, and I would get a small bowl of oyster crackers and a soft drink. It became a ritual whenever we came to this place, and I never remember ever actually eating a full meal in the restaurant. On occasion my dad let me try an oyster and I grew quite fond of them, as I am today.

They would also frequent certain restaurants for frog legs which they loved. It looked rather repulsive, so I refrained from even looking at them, or ever trying one.

My mother would also buy pig's feet at the market and make them for herself and my dad, again something I avoided. They looked gross, these little pudgy stubs of flesh and meat with the hard-edged hoof. Never tried one.

Occasionally my mother also bought tripe, the most disgusting thing of all. She would not eat it but would cook it for my father who liked it as a delicacy. I could barely look at it.

Then there were the holiday rituals! For New Year's Eve we always had creamed herring. It was an absolute must, and supposedly it brought good luck. Every New Year's Eve just before midnight the jar of creamed herring came out. It is very much like the absolute 'must do' ritual of the Brazilian women in Rio de Janeiro who dip a toe in water at midnight to please the goddess of the sea for good fortune, *Iemanjá*. I still do it today; and love the stuff. Once when I was in rural Iowa for New Years, I went to the store to buy some and the storeowner looked at me perplexed when I asked for it and said, 'why would you want to buy fish in a jar?'. They obviously didn't have any, nor had ever heard of it.

Easter has another unique ritual. Coloring Easter eggs is not uncommon, and we did it every year. The color dye kits were widely available and at least a dozen hard boiled eggs were made and colored each time. What we did with the eggs afterwards was where it became a bit different. On Easter morning each person would take an egg and try and crack another's egg by holding it firmly in your fist and hitting theirs with yours. It became a game to see whose egg lasted the longest without cracking. Once all the eggs were cracked you then ate it cold with butter and horseradish. This was also accompanied with very hearty dense black bread. I could only attribute this to my Eastern European roots, but hard to know for sure how it came to exist as a tradition.

I am an aficionado of bagels and lox, with all the accoutrements, including good quality cream cheese, sliced onion and tomato, and capers. That along with babka, chopped liver, rye bread, or any other Eastern European-New York Jewish food, except gefilte fish, I am sent right to gourmet heaven. My parents introduced me to all of it.

Lastly, my parents had a fondness for unusual sandwiches. They would make sandwiches of just onions and garlic on buttered bread. The absolute worst was limburger cheese sandwiches. That smelly cheese sent me to the farthest room possible and I could not imagine the appeal. My mother also had a fondness for sardine sandwiches.

My early exposure to these oddities of cuisine never stopped me from exploring new things and certainly trying new dishes, however, some of these forever remain off the list of possible options for me; yet I remember them well in what my parents passed down as part of their own repertoire.

CHAPTER 20

Planes, trains, and automobiles

I have often said that I will go anywhere once, and I will. Just suggest something.

Having visited forty-six of the fifty United States, the four remaining are Idaho, Montana, North and South Dakota. The last four will be easy to check off on a future road trip.

I essentially grew up in a car. During the 1950s and 1960s the automobile was 'king' and my parents used theirs extensively for weekend excursions. Our weekend trips were legendary, often one day drives to the far reaches of New Jersey, Upstate New York, Philadelphia, or Montreal. Yes, each in a day's drive. Highways had been paved far and wide and one could go very far easily, and we took advantage of it. I think they would have attempted Washington DC in a day trip; but rather the time we went we spent a week. Most memorable of that trip was visiting the inside of the White House, during Kennedy's administration.

It is also important to know that once becoming an adult and 'out' as a gay man, I found that travel is very different for the heterosexual vs. homosexual traveler. I have spent at least a third of my life living as a 'straight' man and saw that side of it. When I was living 'straight' discrimination and fear never entered my mind, but as a gay man I consider carefully where to go and the socio-political circumstances of a place. There are still places in the world where a person can be imprisoned or even put to death for being homosexual. So, it tends to make you think about these things. I will say, however, that in all the places I have stayed in a hotel with a man with one bed both in the U.S. and abroad thankfully no one has raised an eyebrow over it.

I have traveled in five continents, each multiple times. Europe has been the most frequented. Each trip has been enlightening and I find travel to be one of the most beneficial ways of educating oneself about the world and various cultures. My travel patterns have changed over time and in my youth, I would rapidly move about with long days of exploring, usually from early morning into the late night seeing as much as I could absorb. Later in life the pace has slowed and become equally enjoyable in that I take my time to spend more quality time in a place and really appreciate what it has to offer, including off the beaten path. I do my best to experience it as a local, not a tourist. Of late I have found the Airbnb online booking service to be the best way for me to experience a place by staying in a home in a residential neighborhood as opposed to hotels, which I have found to have diminished in service and comfort over the years, including the very high end.

Some of the most rewarding Airbnb experiences I have had were staying in a classic Old World style apartment in Vienna; a grand Victorian in Eureka, California; a variety of residential homes in England, a stone cottage in the Peak District, a Georgian manor apartment in Bath, and a contemporary two-story penthouse in central York; a swanky beach house in the exclusive Seadrift area of Stinson Beach, California; a ultra-contemporary house on the ocean in Bodega Bay,

California; high-rise condos in Boston and Philadelphia; and the Maybeck designed house, the 'Guy Chick House', in Oakland, California.

I will not attempt to describe all the places I have visited over fifty years of travel, covering some domestic, but primarily focus on the international as it is the most interesting; and hit the highlights. I have been to places as far reaching as Greenland and Tasmania. Without any doubt everywhere I have been has further enriched my appreciation of the wonderful world we inhabit.

On a note of interest is that there are two countries where I have experienced a distinct smell, an odor, unique to that place that has lasted in memory. It is odd, but when I have been in both Russia and India each has a very distinctive smell that is inescapable. I cannot say it's good or bad, just unique to the place and omnipresent. I had been forewarned of it before visiting India and the minute I arrived I knew exactly what others had told me. What I find interesting is that on occasion, rare occasion, I will be somewhere else and smell one of those distinctive scents and immediately think of one of those places.

Before going on to my international travel let me relay that in my college years I journeyed a great deal by flying across the U.S. For Thanksgiving I usually visited with friends and their families in places such as Fort Lauderdale, Phoenix, Alabama, or even places in the Midwest. During other holidays I would fly between New Orleans and New York at least four times a year, sometimes with college friends joining me to stay with my family in Connecticut. Most flights were typically in solitude, and I very much enjoyed the window seat to look out on the geography of America. At night, the lights would twinkle in cities and towns, and I would do my best to identify the cities that were thirty thousand feet below me.

Returning to New York for Christmas in 1974 I was on an Eastern Airlines flight from New Orleans and experienced the worst flight of my life. After a rather routine trip we were approaching LaGuardia airport during considerable air turbulence. We were advised to be prepared for a bumpy landing, and it turned out to be worse than I could imagine. As the plane descended it tilted back and forth. When we came down on the runway the wing, next to the window where I was seated, tipped, and hit the ground damaging the wing. There was also a loud crashing sound underneath. Within seconds we were back in the air as the plane lifted off the ground.

It was apparent people on board felt a sense of panic; unsure what was happening. There were loud gasps and shrieks. We continued flying in circles around the airport. Strangely what I remember most was looking down on a cemetery we flew over repeatedly thinking it looked ominous to be doing that. The circling went on for some time and the pilot came on and said we were going back in for reentry, and we should brace ourselves as it would be an emergency landing. I undid my tie and opened the top button of my dress shirt. A woman next to me was completely traumatized and began weeping. The landing was hard and abrupt, and we skidded across the runway with lots of tossing about in our seats. I observed they had foamed the runway and there were emergency vehicles everywhere. We then learned the landing gear had also been damaged on the first landing attempt.

There was a lot of heightened chatter as the plane came to a stop and we were informed that we would deplane on the tarmac. As we exited everyone seemed concerned yet relieved. My parents were in the terminal and witnessed the entire event. They were very quiet when I came up to them, carrying a crumpled flower bouquet I had brought for my mother from New Orleans. I had regrettably squeezed too tightly while holding them in my lap during the incident. My father said very little. During WWII he was randomly removed from a military plane about to take off from the Philippines to Hawaii to board a wounded soldier. He watched the plane take off and it blew up within minutes of leaving the ground killing everyone. Because of it he never flew until trying it again in 1986, some forty years later. He did not trust flying or aviation due to that experience so I believe seeing this incident occur was bringing back vivid memories he would rather not remember, while also watching it with his only child on board.

Six months later, another Eastern Airlines flight, Flight 66, from New Orleans to JFK airport in New York crashed killing nearly everyone on board.

Flying was not my only mode of transportation in my college years. There were still many automobile trips after those taken with my parents. I made several car trips with my college friend, Mark, in his classic Mustang between his home in New Jersey and New Orleans. We had fun each time. The Mustang that garnered a lot of attention in the rural south. We had a typical stop at a café in Montgomery, Alabama when the same waitress would serve us each time; and she'd remember us too. We called her 'our gal in Montgomery'. He later got a more efficient Volkswagen standard transmission. I did not do well with standard shift, but my father taught me to drive with it so I could also use Mark's new car. I did very well in first gear on the highway, but I never wanted to exit or do anything where I needed to shift. Mark always cringed when we went through a toll booth as I would not stop, but rather slow down and toss the coins into the basket as I rolled through the booth timing it not to hit the barrier.

A very memorable trip I took in college was with another college friend, Jose, by train, The Sunset Limited, from New Orleans to San Antonio, for a Thanksgiving excursion. We were quite excited about traveling by train. It would only take the better part of a day to get there; yet, doing long distance train travel was a first for both of us.

After boarding the train, we settled into two comfortable seats and watched the landscape of Louisiana and Texas pass us by. It was mesmerizing to view the expanse of geography and the towns we went through with some stops along the way. We played some cards and for dinner went to the dining car which was a treat onto itself. You needed to write down your order on a piece of paper so that the waiter could come by and pick it up. I remember the meal being quite good as we watched the sunset view out the window.

When we arrived in San Antonio, we were sorry to not have gone on further, and vowed to take a longer trip sometime in the future. We had backpacks and planned on staying at the YMCA which would be cheap accommodations. It was night when we arrived and when we walked to the 'Y' it was already past midnight. The doors to the 'Y' were locked and a janitor was mopping the floor in the lobby. Knocking on the doors the janitor came and only spoke Spanish, and fortunately Jose is fluent. It turned out that the YMCA does not rent rooms. We were in an unfortunate situation. Besides that, Jose went on to complain about the Mexican Spanish the man used as it wasn't as proper as his own Cuban Spanish.

Not certain what to do we wandered around some and finally spotted a hotel, The Alden. Appearing rather down we went inside to find it was a transient hotel where folks rented by the week or month, and very spartan. The night clerk did have a room for us, at seven dollars a night, so we were elated to have something. When taking us up to the room in the elevator he coughed profusely as he told us how he had just be diagnosed with tuberculosis. That made us a bit squeamish.

The room was down a dark hallway and it appeared not to have been painted in many years. It was very shabby and even appeared somewhat dirty. The room itself was big with two single beds and linens piled on each, and two tall windows facing the street. The bathroom was down the hall. There was a makeshift closet braced up in the corner. For the price we were not about to complain.

After getting settled I felt somewhat uncomfortable and decided to sleep with my wallet under my pillow. Overall, the room worked well for us and we slept soundly. The next morning, I walked down to the communal bathroom. Some people were already there, quite friendly, and curious about us. I learned that some of them were long term residents, seniors living on meager social security payments. That made me more comfortable with the place.

We spent our days touring and walked around the city. We laughed over the tourist excursion boats as they lumbered down the windy river canal with everyone on board fixated on the surroundings. We dubbed those boats the 'refugee boats' as everyone looked as though they had just arrived in a new world.

The river was sunken so that it had a very strange cave-like atmosphere albeit quite lush with vegetation.

We saw just about every site from the Alamo to the Tower of The Americas built for the Hemisphere World's Fair in 1968.

Our final day we bid farewell to The Alden and headed out for where we were meeting up with another college friend, Don, who's uncle lived there. The plan was we would spend the night there before driving back together to New Orleans.

Don was from a prominent Dallas family and had instructed us to just go to his uncle's house in an outlying area of the city. His uncle and aunt would know we were coming. Jose and I picked up our backpacks and decided to walk it, perhaps a distance of three to four miles, not very far. It gave us an opportunity to see more of the city from pedestrian viewpoint. As we approached the neighborhood with the address in hand, we found the houses became more substantial, and the properties very well-manicured. By time we reached the street where the uncle lived, we were in an area of older mansions. Approaching the house where we would stay Jose became squeamish as it looked very inhospitable to him. He refused to go to the front door, and I just tugged him along.

I rang the doorbell and we waited. After a bit of a wait the door opened, and a man stood there looking at us with a bit of sternness. It turned out to be servant, I believe a butler. I introduced myself and Jose and he let us into the entry hall. The place was definitely grand in scale, and he escorted us into a conservatory room suggesting we make ourselves comfortable while he informed the owners that we had arrived. Jose and I just sat there, quietly, taking in the surroundings and I could tell Jose was quite uncomfortable.

A man and woman entered the room and graciously welcomed us. The uncle was a retired Colonel and his wife stately in appearance. They were formally dressed, and they told us they were preparing for dinner, at home. Sitting together they engaged us in conversation. Asking us about our trip they wanted to know where we had stayed. I froze and Jose practically fell off his chair. Neither of us wanted to admit the reality of where we stayed. I hemmed and hawed a bit and then said I forgot the name of the hotel, perhaps it began with an 'A'. My foil wasn't working. The wife said, 'Oh, that must be the St. Anthony!', one of San Antonio's poshest hotels. The uncle smiled and looked at us and said, 'You boys stayed at a flop house, now, didn't you?' Embarrassingly, I admitted to it. He went on to ask how we had gotten to the house. Again, I was a bit hesitant, and then just admitted we had walked. He smiled again.

After such an uneasy encounter we were saved from further questioning when Don and another friend of ours from school arrived. The air became more cordial and adding these newcomers helped break the ice that had encompassed the room beforehand. We went out to dinner while the Colonel and his wife went into their dining room for their meal, served by other servants we had not seen before.

When we returned to the house, we were informed that Jose and I would be staying in the guest house and Don and our other friend were taken upstairs to their bedrooms. Jose and I followed a servant to the back building and found it to be quite comfortable and accommodating. In a way we were happy not to be in the big house. I was bemused as when I opened a closet door inside were stacked some very fine paintings. I looked at a couple of them closely. Both of us were taking an Art History class and it was apparent these were very high-quality Impressionists works. I closed the closet door and did not open it again out of fear of damaging anything.

After sleeping well, we went into the main house and breakfast was being prepared for us. Don told us to go into the kitchen, and low and behold there was the Colonel at the stove preparing our breakfast. It really surprised me. We all sat at a large table, and he brought us a very nice, large breakfast and sat with us and ate too. He looked at Jose and me and said, 'You know, I greatly admire you boys'. I did not know how to respond, but he went on to tell us how the admiration was for how we made an adventure of our trip, staying in a lesser hotel, and walking all the way to their house while eschewing luxury and comfort to experience life differently. He said his own son would never had done that and he wanted to complement us; and make us breakfast.

We left with good wishes from both he and his wife. The four of us piled into Don's SUV and headed back to New Orleans.

When living in Wisconsin I took a driving trip to Minneapolis which was very interesting. It was known in the 1980s for its progressive city planning and architecture. It had 'sky bridges', or covered overhead walkways linking the blocks together, very much like in Des Moines, expressly for the harsh winters. As US cities go it is worth a visit, including the outlying areas with a multitude of lakes and bucolic landscapes.

Living in Des Moines a couple of years hence my partner and I decided to take our two kids on a road trip to Colorado. I do not even remember why we picked there, but part of the plan was to stop at as many Presidential Libraries as possible, as an educational thing for the kids. I was surprised how many exist in the Midwest, from Hoover to Truman to Eisenhower. Colorado was fantastic with the natural beauty alone. We stayed in Denver and drove up into the Rocky National Park winding our way to Colorado Springs so the kids could see the Air Force Academy and then driving home across Kansas, which the kids found super boring ending up arguing in the back seat. There was one time in Colorado, however, where we had a bit of a frightful experience. Parking and walking up to find a waterfall we descended a hillside at dusk and got lost. There were too many trails and we forgot which one we had taken. We had only been gone a few minutes yet lost our route. Our daughter, Sarah, figured it out and we got back to the car before nightfall. It taught us a lesson to be more careful before wandering off into the wilderness without a real plan.

In any case these driving trips were fun and memorable.

On to my international travels, in 1978 my wife and I spent nine days in Paris for our honeymoon. We spent the days wandering the city and visiting the typical tourist sites. The day we arrived we decided to venture out and act like true Parisians. We found a small café with outdoor seating near our hotel, the Hotel du Louvre, in which we had a balcony looking down the entire length of the Avenue de L'Opera. Our plan was to sit outside and watch the world pass us by as we sipped wine. Not sure what to do, whether to sit down and wait to be served, or go inside and get our drinks, we wrongly decided on the latter. We ordered two white wines, in our best French, and then realized a waiter was serving the outside tables. Looking at my wife I said, in English, 'we should just 'down it' and go'. So instead of sipping we chugged the wine down, much to the shock of the man behind the counter; and we went on to the next café where we sat outside and waited for the waiter to serve us. We missed the mark of being true Parisians, but slowly sipped the second glass while watching the crowds go by us as originally intended.

We took a day excursion by train out to Versailles and not only saw the palace but wandered the extensive grounds seeing both Trianon, and the village where Marie Antoinette had her little working farm for her pleasure. We decided to stay in town for dinner but wanted to check the train schedule beforehand, so we went to the station first. I did not quite understand the timetable, so I approached a very distinguished looking gentleman with a walking stick and asked, in French, about clarifying the schedule. He was very patient with me and at one point I wanted to ask about a later train; but could not remember the French word for 'later'. I turned to ask my wife, she shrugged, and the kindly gentleman said with ample respect toward me, *'Monsieur,* it is *plus tard'.* He understood and spoke English perfectly but graciously had allowed me to plod through my French inquiry. Quite embarrassing yet very touching too. We ate dinner in a wonderful creperie and had this incredible crepe with a soft-boiled egg inside it.

The firm I worked for gave us a wonderful wedding send off with a gift of a bunch of French *francs* to spend so we did so on our last night at Fouquet, eating upstairs and having a feast. It was quite memorable.

Returning to the USA on July 4 we landed where we had taken off, at the iconic TWA building at JFK Airport in New York.

There was a trip to Mexico City that my partner and I took

that was equally enjoyable, and I had never realized the size of that city. One of the largest cities in the world it sprawled on endlessly as the plane landed at the main airport. Having been in several Mexican cities, primarily coastal resorts, I truly appreciated the flavor of this capital city. The diversity of museums and neighborhoods was extremely noteworthy, as well as the regional and traditional Mexican foods. True Mexican cuisine, an ancient one, is unlike anything typically found in the U.S.

We had read about a town that produces pottery on the outskirts of the city and decided to go find it. We got a taxi and went for miles across arid terrain. We finally arrived at a small town with enormous pots and jugs displayed outside every building. This was not the place we wanted, and the taxi driver was giving us a hard time about it. My partner spoke Spanish and was arguing with him, and finally said to return us to Mexico City, as we wouldn't get out and possibly be stranded there. The driver was indignant, yet we assured him we would pay him for a round trip. When we got back the fare came to something comparable to a couple of US dollars in *pesos*. I paid the driver and he shorted me an amount in change, and I began yelling at him. My partner finally pulled me away as it amounted to about ten cents, not worth the bother. We never found the pottery place.

One day we headed off on a bus to Teotihuacan, the ancient ruins of the City of Gods located in the Valley of Mexico. It is an amazing complex of buildings and infrastructure. The pyramids are breathtaking. I climbed both the Pyramids of the Moon and the Sun, and it was awe inspiring.

In 1987 he and I took an impromptu trip to Brazil and Argentina. Rio is a bizarre place, yet geographically one of the most beautiful places I had ever been. The harbor is amazing, yet the city itself is dangerous. There is considerable crime and poverty, and it is the only place where I have eaten a burger, a 'Bob Burger', at a fast-food establishment with armed guards outside. I picked up enough Portuguese for some basic words, but nowhere near able to converse. Going to the top of Sugar Loaf, a sheer mountain cliff, was striking, but the two-tiered tram taking you there is a bit disconcerting in safety standards.

We found voodoo rituals on the Copacabana beach, and everyone ate huge quantities of meat, and smoked.

Rio was the only time I was robbed while on a trip, fortunately it was merely a pair of sunglasses. I was getting on a city bus and the person in front of me was stalling to find his money while boarding. Unbeknownst to me the person behind me was going through my camera bag; and took the glasses. They were working together. I only noticed that the zippers were tampered with when I got off the bus and luckily that person did not get my wallet that was in there too.

At a store where the clerk spoke English she wanted to know where we were from, and I said Iowa. She smiled back and said, 'oh yes, corn!' I was surprised she knew that.

Every day a staff member in our hotel wanted to know if we needed 'foreign exchange'. We did not, but then one day we decided to try it out. We were offered a high rate of exchange but were taken to a hotel room where the exchange occurred, obviously black market.

We took taxis nearly everywhere and wrote down the destination to give to the drivers. I wanted to see the tropical rain forest, so we got a taxi, and I gave him the name 'Tijuca' on it. We drove and finally turned into a shopping mall. Looking totally flustered I turned to my Portuguese dictionary to ask what happened? He pointed to a sign on the center, 'Tijuca'. We all laughed, and we just went back to the hotel.

Buenos Aries is a much more formal and cultured city than the laid-back beaches of Rio. Enjoying the European flavor there is so much to see throughout the city, and we did a lot of walking. Going to the grave of Evita Peron was an event, especially when we saw the enormous accumulation of flowers left at her tomb. We were surrounded by cameramen and the news media as it turned out to be the anniversary of Evita's birth. They thought we were Americans who were 'Peronistas' who had come specifically for the event. No, we just stumbled into it.

One night we went for dinner, steak, of course. The Argentines, like other Europeans, eat very late and often the restaurants do not open until 9pm for dinner. We were amazed how the Argentines stay so svelte and healthy when they smoke like fiends and eat nothing but grilled meats and fried foods, plus eat and stay up late into the night. There wasn't a vegetable to be found anyplace, only the canned variety from what we found. The restaurant was packed with people, mainly natives. When I tried to order the waiter would not agree with what I wanted, a sampler platter. He indicated that there was no possible way I could eat it, but at eighteen dollars I thought it couldn't be that much. Yet he absolutely refused and showed me an option, which I got. A young family of four was seated near us, very well dressed and polite. I was amazed that two very young children were up at 10pm about to eat dinner. The wife wore a fur coat and they all put their coats over a couple of chairs and then proceeded to cover them with napkins.

When their meal arrived at their table it was the platter I had wanted to order, and it was stacked two feet high with a variety of meats, obviously meant for several people. I recognized why the waiter would not let me order it. The family dove into the platter and bones and grease were flying everywhere. I understood why they covered their coats and enjoyed their meal.

One evening we went to a gay bar and found it to be a very weird experience. The bar seemed empty and after getting drinks we stood in the center to the room. Looking around we saw that men were standing at the periphery of the room in the total darkness. No one was standing where it was lit. We met a journalist from Washington DC, and he explained that the '*Portenos*', as residents of Buenos Aires are called, are afraid to be seen in the light for being recognized and exposed as homosexual.

The 'Mothers of the Square' still marched every week with white kerchiefs over their heads from Argentina's 'Dirty War' and we witnessed it one day in front of the Casa Rosada, the main residence of the President. They were representing the 'Disappeared Ones' or family members who for political reasons just disappeared, probably murdered.

All these adventures were a form of education, and seeing the varied cultures made it more so. What fascinates me is revisiting places over a couple decades and seeing change.

Once settled in California we made a trip to London one spring, in March. The weather was ideal and what impressed me most were the amazing flowers in the public parks and especially the multitude of daffodils that seemed to go out to the horizon across the fields behind Hampton Court. Deciding to go to a play, spur of the moment, we searched out something playing one evening. Since London has such a major theater scene getting tickets wasn't exactly easy, but we snagged a couple of a new musical we hadn't heard of before, *Miss Saigon*. It was spectacular, and especially impressive when an actual helicopter landed on the stage. I was also educated on proper British pronunciation when I went into a pub and ordered some 'pasties' which I initially pronounced to sound like a stripper's flimsy garment; and was quickly corrected.

In 1993 I went to India, using airline miles. Except for a couple of guidebooks and some maps that I had not consulted, I was ill prepared for this adventure into an entirely different culture. The flights were long and arduous, but I marveled flying over territory I had never been exposed to before, such as Afghanistan in moonlight. When I landed in New Delhi, very early in the morning before dawn as is customary for international flights, I immediately was confronted with uncertainty and dilemma. Looking for a currency exchange I found indication of one near a makeshift sign, but there was no one there. After most of the passengers had their bags, a man carried out a table and chair and set up a bank under the sign. People immediately lined up, so I got in line. When it came my turn, I signed a couple of traveler's cheques and the man opened the desk drawer where there was cash strewn throughout it, not organized in neat piles by denomination. He grabbed a fistful of cash and put it on the table for me to take, never counting it. I picked it up, bewildered, and presume I appeared relatively shocked. He then reached in the drawer and grabbed more cash and promptly placed it on the table. I took it and walked off quite taken by the entire exchange. When I was able to organize and add it up, I did quite well. At that moment I recognized that systems in India were not quite as I had been accustomed to, and it was rather jarring.

I sat outside the airport on a bench, in the dark, not knowing at all what I was doing or where I was going to go. Nothing seemed organized or clear to me. An older man in a uniform with a rifle over his shoulder came and sat next to me and stared. When I looked over at him, he smiled and had only one tooth. I smiled back, got up, and walked on. I saw what looked like a bus stop and a woman waiting there. She was European and in the same predicament. We decided to stick together and see if we could get into New Delhi. We boarded a bus, without windows, only bars on the openings, that did get us there. We parted and I headed for the Imperial Hotel where I got a room. They charged me full rate for four hours of sleep and a shower, and I ordered a hearty room service breakfast. I searched around and then checked into another hotel, The Marina.

I was not ready for the chaos of an Indian city, between vehicles going every which direction, hordes of people, and animals in the streets, it was mind boggling. People were bathing nude on street corners at water sources, and extreme poverty was quite evident. I spent a few days touring the city and went to the train station to buy a first-class rail pass. It seemed impossible, so I went to a vendor outside who was selling them. Giving him several hundred dollars, he said the pass would be ready in a few hours. Leaving I feared I would never see him again. But when I returned to the stall he was there. He handed me the pass and I had to wonder if it was real or forged. It thankfully was real. Booking travel wasn't easy either and that became nearly a month-long odyssey.

My next stop was Agra to see the Taj Mahal, and frankly that made my entire trip worthwhile. I stayed an entire day to watch the light change off the white marble and it was spectacular. My hotel, a high-rise, lost power that evening and I ate in the dining room in the near dark by candlelight with a German family at the next table. We seemed to be the only two guests at the hotel.

The focus of my trip then moved on to explore Rajasthan, a historically rich area of Northern India. That took me to Jaipur which was very beautiful, and I treated myself by staying at the Rambagh Palace. My room was palatial and what I recall most was the bathroom, which was enormous and completely clad in a red granite- floor, ceiling, and walls. Seeing many of the sights I then headed on to Udaipur, a relatively unvisited city at the time. I stayed five days which was almost unheard of before it became a popular tourist attraction. I found a delightful room in an older hotel, and I had a balcony overlooking a lagoon. It was Diwali, the Festival of Light, and at night it was magical with the flickering lights and sounds of the celebrations.

Train travel was interesting, both good and bad. I found it very hard to navigate. As an example, when I arrived in Udaipur, I decided to make a train reservation for my next location. There were no schedules or timetables, so I simply asked at the ticket desk. I was told the next train out, to anywhere, would be in a month. I was totally taken aback, but soon realized the ticket agent was just waiting to me to give him a monetary tip, '*baksheesh*', to get the information I wanted. He said so. That really irritated me. I gave him money and got the details I needed; a train would be forthcoming in a few days. There were times when I could not find the train car I was assigned to from a list of names posted in the station, as they would occasionally translate my name into Hindi. Some of the trains were pleasant to ride, others not so much.

Train stations are microcosms of entertainment venues onto themselves. It is a great place to people watch and a source of amazement how animated a place it becomes when a train is imminently due to arrive. I did see some disturbing things, too, emulating from India's ever-present caste system. I observed a group of Brahmans who were seated waiting for a train, and one threw a wrapper on the platform and told someone of a lower caste, an untouchable, to pick it up and throw it in the trash.

Then there are the monkeys. They congregate at the train stations, apparently for handouts. They are feisty and mischievous. Large orange strands of marigolds are left on the platform, and they gather them up, play with them, wear them, and in some cases I believe even eat them. Monkeys come in all shapes and sizes and the smaller ones I found to be the most devious.

I met some very interesting people with whom I shared a rail cabin while on route. One was a soldier from Southern India going to the front in Pakistan where there was rising political tension. Another was a businessman who offered me an apple from his garden which I peeled to eat. That offended him and I kindly explained the health concerns. He understood, yet not totally, but we started a discussion on our lives and families. When I asked about his wife, he became very indignant and defensive and said he does not talk about his wife, she's there to serve him. However, he was more than willing to tell me about his children. He then offered to buy me tea at the next stop, and I appreciated the offer. A vendor walked by our window, and he got us two cups. It was good, however, as we were pulling out of the station, I noticed the vendor washing the cups in a public fountain where people were also bathing. One must adjust to different standards, and fortunately I did not get sick.

My favorite cabin mates were a family of five, three generations of travelers. While I attempted to sleep in the upper bunk, I noticed the grandmother sitting upright with her arms folded staring at me, apparently fearing for her family's safety. Every time I opened an eye she was still sternly staring. None of them spoke English so I was uncertain how to get through that I was not a danger.

My final train trip was from Udaipur to New Delhi was nearly twenty-four hours long. It was dusty and my clothes were filthy by time it concluded. I got accustomed to the 'veg.' or 'non-veg' meals that were served on metal trays, brought to the cabin by attendants after ordering. Arriving in the New Delhi train station was utter chaos, as though all of humanity was there, including animals on the platform. I wanted to call The Marina Hotel to book a room and found there were only two telephones in the entire station. One did not work so I waited on a long line at the other and called the hotel only to find that I could hear the person at the hotel desk, but he could not hear me. Frustrated I went outside and got a rickshaw that took me to the hotel. When I went to the desk and asked for a room, I was highly scrutinized, perhaps for my dirty clothing. The desk clerk had to get the manager who came out, looked at me, and said they have no rooms. I knew I was being judged so I reminded them that I had stayed at the hotel previously and tipped quite well. That did not matter. I grabbed my bag and left, refusing to allow the bellboy to assist with my bag.

Infuriated and tired I got out into the street and the same

rickshaw driver was still there waiting, smiling. I turned away and walked to The Imperial Hotel where I spent my first night. I walked up to the desk claiming I had a reservation, which I did not. But I knew that was the only way I would get anywhere. The desk clerk checked the computer and said she did not see any reservation. I sternly informed her to look again as, 'I had called five days before and had made a reservation', which of course I had not. Looking intently at the computer she looked up and said, 'Oh, yes, I do see the reservation'. I got a room for five nights.

I decided to just relax, use the pool, and take my last days in stride. Deciding one evening to forgo the hotel dining room I walked up to Connaught Square where I had seen a Chinese restaurant and went there. I passed the armed guards at the door and had a very nice meal. Leaving and walking back to the hotel a couple of young children approached me, a boy and a girl, and the girl tugged my shirt sleeve and asked, 'Will you please buy us?'. I stood there totally confounded and then when I realized what it was about, it was more than I could handle. They were no more than ten years old, but obviously some came there for that purpose. Completely repulsed I walked away and started back to my hotel when a young man came up and said I have something on my shoe, and offered to clean it off, for money. This had happened once before, so I knew the scam. Someone squirts a substance on your shoe when you're unaware and another young man approaches you to help with it. I told him, no, and he became insistent. I suggested we get the police to discuss it, and he ran off.

After that I did not leave my hotel room for the remainder of my stay. On the third day a note was slipped under the door.

It was from the Hotel Manager telling me that it appeared I was to check out the next day, which I was not. I took the note down to him and loudly told him he was mistaken and to look at my reservation. He looked and then agreed.

I have a habit of securing my hotel room door at night for security and safety, and in this case a closet drawer could be opened to block the door on the inside. During the night someone opened the door and hit the drawer, several times. When I turned the light on, it stopped.

When I first arrived in New Delhi after a long day of walking, I intended to take a short cut to my hotel from where I had toured that day. Walking over a pedestrian bridge I was horrified to see a couple of dead dogs in the pathway. Looking ahead from the top of the bridge I saw what was truly apocalyptic- a vast slum beyond anything imaginable. I did not go on, but rather took a long way back. Planning to leave some clothing and shoes near that slum for someone to use as I was at the end of my trip, I just decided last minute to do nothing. I was utterly frustrated and drained by the entire experience.

My journey to India was mixed full of reactions, both wonderful and some extremely disturbing. What it did, however, was teach me about the diversity of our world and exposed me to an entirely different way of seeing it. Overall, I would not say it was a bad trip, just very enlightening in so many ways. It took me out of my comfort zone. Perhaps if I had planned better before my departure, it wouldn't have been so surprising.

My former partner and I had promised our daughter, Sarah, that should she complete four years of German in High School that we would take her to Germany for her graduation present, which we did. I had contact with a travel agent in Munich and he set everything up for a driving trip that would take us nearly a month going from Berlin to Munich, with stops in Dresden, Weimar, Staffelstein, Bamburg, Heidelberg, Rothenburg ob der Tauber, Schwangau, and Munich. We had a small car and driving on the Autobahn was quite the experience. I drove faster than I ever have in my life watching the speedometer nearly go off the charts. It is important to watch the speed limits approaching cities as it is highly regulated.

It was great fun and some of the Germans we met said we were seeing more of Germany than they ever had. There were those frustrating times too, for example when I drove around Heidelberg for over an hour through narrow streets trying to locate our hotel to no avail, pre -GPS and internet. I finally became so discouraged that I just pulled over in an open parking spot and decided not to move until I had my wits about me again, only to discover I was parked in front of the hotel! Then there was driving through Coburg where I apparently took a wrong turn in town and ended up facing the car into a staircase to a lower street. I was on a 'pedestrian only' zone. And, yes, I did back up. By time we got to Schwangau I think Sarah may have had her fill of German culture because as we were eating dinner a woman came out to sing and entertain. Sarah looked up and said, 'If that woman starts to yodel, I am out of here' immediately followed by the woman starting to yodel! It was an adventure and we saw a lot of Germany. One of the fondest memories I have of that trip was entering the courtyard of the Baroque styled Zwinger in Dresden right after a rainstorm. It was magical and the buildings magnificent as the sun came out to highlight them.

A couple of years later, in 1998, I visited central and northern Italy for nearly a month, traveling by train. It was a splendid trip visiting Rome, Siena, Florence, Bologna, Ravenna, Venice, Mantua, and Milan.

All those places are amazing, and I was particularly impressed with the uniqueness of Ravenna where some of the most spectacular Byzantine and Romanesque buildings exist.

Rome is a city of magnificence and there is far too much to see and take in during a week stay. You do have to be careful of the gypsies. While in the subway station a gypsy woman approached me and grabbed my jacket attempting to get my wallet from my breast pocket. It was the only time I have ever struck anyone, and I yelled loudly. A well-dressed Italian man came up, scolded her, and shooed her away. While on a very crowded subway I could feel something in my pants pocket, and it turned out to be a very young boy working the train to steal and pickpocket from people. He was putting his tiny slender hand in my pocket to see if anything could be lifted. Again, I yelled, and he ran for another car.

I had another experience at the Roman Forum where a group of youths came at me with cardboard that they were going to use to push me to take my camera bag. I had heard about this happening to others, and fortunately the guide I was with stopped them before getting too close to me.

There was a humorous experience taking the train from Rome to Siena, where there would be a change of trains in the town of Chiusi. As with many things in Italy the trains suddenly went on strike. No one knew when trains would run to Siena, so I waited. I saw a group of older women heavily engaged in a heated exchange with a bus driver and I walked over to check it out. They had convinced him to drive them to Siena, and I was welcomed on board. Although not a train I was able to experience seeing some incredible Tuscan landscapes on the roads we took which would not have happened by train. I was lucky with something that seemed at first unfortunate.

I had the most amazing culinary experience in Mantua; one that I will always remember. It was cold and it began snowing. I decided to go find a restaurant and headed across the Cathedral square. No one was around as the snow gently fell on the ancient stone pavement. I noticed a small restaurant nearby and decided to try it out. No one was eating there, and there were approximately ten tables. I was offered a seat and then a menu. Since I was uncertain what to order the owner came out and speaking only in Italian offered to make me a *pasto speciale*. I just put myself in his hands and went with it, not knowing what I would get, or the cost. But I figured what could go wrong, I was in Italy and ready to feast.

I ended up eating a three-hour feast of food and the entire time I was the only patron. They treated me like a king and dish after dish kept coming out for me to savor, and the wine flowed too. It was the first time I had lightly fried squash blossoms and also pumpkin ravioli. It was splendid. The owner was very concerned that I was enjoying it, and I nodded constantly in affirmation. When the bill finally was presented to me, I cringed, and it came to a very small amount; if I remember correctly, less than the equivalent of twenty US dollars.

In Milan I decided to treat myself to some high-end, designer brand men's fashion. I headed to the district with luxury level designer stores and was quite intimidated by it. Every store was posh and very elegant. I noticed a pair of shoes in the window at Palo Zileri, a designer I did not know that well. Trying on a pair they were very comfortable, so I bought them for an incredible sum of money. They fit like a glove, and I wore them for a good ten years thereafter, always commenting that I introduced men's 'square toed' shoes to the US. They became popular here right after I returned and wore them. I then went to Zegna, a line of men's clothing I like a lot. I was immediately greeted when I entered the store and introduced to a salesperson who spoke impeccable English to wait on me. He followed me throughout the store offering suggestions, many of which were way above my comfort price level, yet beautiful pieces of clothing. I spotted an unconstructed sports jacket and tried it on for size. It fit perfectly and priced within my realm of reason, so I purchased it. These two items, plus a couple of other things I bought, cost me a lot at US Customs where I had to pay tax on them. I am not a shopper and usually when traveling abroad I come back with little to nothing, so this was a surprising exception in my usual consumption habits.

Two marvels that I remember well in Milan were seeing DaVinci's Last Supper and climbing to the roof of the Milan Cathedral. Both well worth the effort.

I have visited Venice three times and each time have found it to be a magical and an amazing place of unsurpassed uniqueness. The lack of vehicular traffic alone is impressive.

The real time to experience Venice is after the hordes of tourists leave for the day. It's then that you can have Venice to yourself and savor all it has to offer. I recollect one late afternoon leaving my hotel near St. Mark's Square, at the mouth of the Grand Canal and walking into the Castello neighborhood and beyond, eventually finding the lush green of Giardini Della

Biennale. It was such a calm and restful walk and I saw the citizens of Venice walking by with satchels of groceries for the evening meal. To escape the crowds and experience the richness of Venice is an absolute treat.

Venice is for wandering aimlessly and getting lost in tiny back alleys along canals while listing to the sounds of the city around you.

The other thing not to be missed is to sit at the front of the *Vaporetti No. 1* from St. Mark's to the Railroad Station, the entire length of the Grand Canal, and visually experience the city as it meanders and unfolds around you. Rest assured it isn't easy to get that seat.

During my second visit to Venice, I was eating lunch at a way off location in a tiny café and looked up to see someone I knew from San Francisco eating a meal! As we both glanced over to see each other at the same time we were equally surprised by the encounter, agreeing it is indeed a very small world.

I must admit that my first visit to Venice in 1973 was not so endearing as the canals were filthy and smelled with garbage and floating cabbage heads. That thankfully changed in subsequent visits.

It's also enjoyable to visit the Lido that is essentially a long sand bar with formerly glorious resort hotels of a bygone era.

My last time there my hotel was right across from my favorite church in the city, Santa Maria della Salute, a Baroque wonder. Having breakfast on the terrace and seeing it in the new sunlight with boats on the canal whizzing by is an event. It makes one want to linger and stare for hours.

There is no denying that in loving Venice for all its glory and magnificence it is unique in the world, and I hope one day to spend a month or more there enjoying all it has to offer beyond just being a tourist.

I have stayed in countless hotels, bed and breakfasts, and inns around the world and each has been its own experience. Some make me reminisce with laughter, like the hotel rooms in London and Mendoza, Argentina that were so small you could hardly walk around suitcases, especially the one in Mendoza where one could literally flush the toilet from the bed with your foot. I've been confounded by bidets in Europe, especially the one I first encountered at age nineteen in Paris, when I thought it was a urinal since the bathroom was down the hall. That was an especially interesting stay in that they placed me, an American young man, on the same floor as the representatives from North Vietnam staying there for the Paris Peace Talks. I had to walk by their open room doors and use the same communal bathroom which was unsettling being that close to the 'enemy'.

I have also flown on innumerable flights, some as short as one hundred miles and some as long as a non-stop from San Francisco to Sydney. Once while boarding a domestic flight, I was pulled off the line and asked if I would be willing to do the airline a favor. They would give me a flight coupon if I obliged them. It turned out that they needed someone to hold a box during the flight and hand it to the counter at the arrival destination. I agreed and they handed me a box that was approximately a one-foot cube. It had all sorts of warning labels on it, and it turned out to be human eyeballs in some type of fluid, dry ice, or something. I did it but it was the creepiest flight I ever took, and they assured me that no one would sit next to me, and no one did. I certainly didn't want to explain that to a stranger.

In the 1990s I took a variety of retreats at religious centers, primarily monasteries, both Roman Catholic and Episcopalian. The religious retreat centers tend to be located on old estates that are repurposed, having been donated or purchased for less than they are worth. The settings are often very beautiful, often with historic buildings, primarily former private homes. I stayed in one in Napa, in the hills, and one in Santa Barbara. Both were quite spectacular settings, inspirational, and quiet places to just reflect and rejuvenate.

One of my favorite retreat places is in Vina, California. It is the location of the monks of The Abbey of New Clairvaux. It is a large property in the broad valley north of Sacramento, and near the American River on property formerly owned by Leland Stanford. The monks primarily have orchards and grow walnuts and plums to make prunes. They also have vineyards that produce exceptional wines. The monks are a silent order, so the retreats, too, are silent. I went for a week and it was truly a moving experience in self-examination and peaceful-ness. Some laughed that I would be unable to make it a week without talking, yet I did. Sarah, my stepdaughter, suggested I sit in the car and talk to myself if I got desperate. There is no need for cell phones, or the internet, and you become totally unplugged with the outside world. You can do whatever you want to do, but alone and in silence. I tended to walk the orchards which is a soothing, cathartic experience. The endless rows of straight-lined trees in the orchard are mesmerizing. On occasion, while walking through the orchard, I would pass a monk on a tractor who typically would wave and smile to me. Meals are silent and I learned to engage and appreciate my food while eating absorbed in concentrating on it. You get a tiny one room stone, contemporary building with bath to yourself. It got very chilly at night. After a day or two time stands still. You can participate in the prayer 'rules' that take place seven times a day; one is at 3:30 am. I did that sometimes and it was very enlightening to get up in the middle of the night, walk through darkness to the chapel being beckoned by the bells, and then hearing the chanting of the monks during prayers.

The retreats were just another form of travel and experiencing culture and the world in a different way.

Ed and I decided to visit Australia, where I had been before, but we wanted to also venture into new territory, Tasmania. We flew to Melbourne via Sydney where we spent a few days. It is a magnificent city, yet we found it a bit conservative and stodgy compared to Sydney which we visited at the end of our trip. We explored a lot around Melbourne and enjoyed it immensely, including excursions out of town. We did have one unfortunate, and very infuriating experience, when we walked by the University. Passing one of the classroom buildings someone tossed ink on us from an upper story as we walked on the sidewalk. Ed had it all over him, on his clothes and in his hair. We went to complain, and no one seemed to care. We even filed a police report. It was terribly annoying; and did not leave a very favorable impression.

Tasmania was a netherworld of beauty and unbelievable places. We spent days driving around the entire island, from one end to the other, and back. We stayed in Strahan at the far west side and had a cabin at Cradle Mountain in the interior. The landscapes and animals, all indigenous and only found there, were remarkable. It was fun sitting by a window and having a kangaroo hop on by us. Wandering down trails felt like being in a set from Jurassic Park. We stood on a platform totally removed from civilization looking out at the Southern Ocean, never knowing such a body of water existed. We drove for hours without seeing a human or building anywhere, as it gets very remote. Tasmania has an incredible cheese and wine industry which they do not export. That alone is worth a trip. In Launceston we toured around Tasmania's second largest city, next to Hobart. It had a British aesthetic that was quaint. We took an incredibly scary chair lift across a canyon where I nearly lost the clogs dangling off my feet. At the airport we contacted the car rental company to learn where to leave the car and they said to just leave it at the curb with the keys in the ignition. We were assured it would be safe there.

Sydney is a very cosmopolitan city and we latched on to a restaurant serving Malaysian food and could not get enough of it. We saw many unique neighborhoods and even took a day trip by train out to the Blue Mountains. We did a lot of exploring and walking.

Later that year we took a group trip to China as part of a trade-business exchange. It was fascinating and we were treated like dignitaries the entire trip. We started in Beijing and went to Suzhou, Hangzhou, and Shanghai. One of my reasons for going, besides wanting to see China, was to visit the hutongs in Beijing before they were destroyed by the government. These are typical traditional narrow street neighborhoods with court-yard dwellings. We took a rickshaw through one; and ate a meal with a family in another. The meal was prepared in a kitchen no larger than a small bathroom and the noodles were homemade and ever so good.

We saw all the major sights in each city, from the Great Wall of China outside Beijing to the Pudong of Shanghai where we stayed in a new high-rise hotel, The Eaton. Only open a few days before our arrival the clerk at the desk apologized for placing us on a low floor, the thirty-sixth. Even the view from there of the city was awe inspiring. Shanghai at night felt like a scene from the *Blade Runner* movie, a cult classic. I have never seen so much neon outside of Times Square in New York. We visited factories as well, which were very depressing. The conditions were not good, and they were undoubtedly showing us the best.

We traveled with a group that included several professional black women. It became quite apparent that some Chinese we encountered had never seen black people before, and they stood and stared. In Beijing several circled around the woman in a mob type scene, trying to get a look, some indicating they wanted to touch their hair. The best, though, was on a bus from one city to another when a truck passed us and the driver did a double take when he saw the women sitting in the bus!

It amazed me how many rise-rise apartment buildings were being built, by the hundreds; many unoccupied. In the countryside there were houses with just a bare lightbulb you could see in the window after dark. Ed and I often wandered on our own and our biggest surprise took place in Hangzhou. Walking through a vibrant housing 'estate' within a walled area of apartment buildings we saw so much activity as residents congregated in the evening. Then leaving the grounds we walked along a major thoroughfare. There were commercial storefront windows with sofas in each, and women sitting on them. When we walked by the women would stand and wave. Turned out they were prostitutes plying their wares! Most amusing was the police station at the end of the street, just beyond the storefronts.

China was a very interesting and unique country, one of contrasts; and one I would not mind exploring further sometime in the future.

Having banked some airline miles Ed and I made plans for flying first class to Argentina. We had our own personal pods on the plane, and it was quite luxurious, including getting pajamas and slippers. It was the first time the flight attendant sat down with me before flying, knew my name, Mr. Brutting, and went over the meal menu of the entire flight so I could make selections. Every flight should be so nice.

Argentina was very different from the twenty years before when I visited. Not as many people smoked, beef was not totally the only thing on menus, and fresh vegetables were readily available. The 'Portenos', however, still ate late at night. There had also been an economic crisis, not unusual for the country, and the middle class were in dire trouble. We watched in the late afternoon when businesses and large residential buildings threw trash bags in the street only to have many people descend and look through the bags for anything they could salvage, including food. We watched a woman set up a small business operation outside the window of a restaurant where we were eating and watched her meticulously wrapping small bundles of small blue flowers for sale. She was so thoughtful in her wrap for each batch. Ed and I felt sorry for her and said we'd buy some from her but soon after she sold them and completely depleted them by the time we finished our meal.

My second visit to Evita's grave wasn't as startling as the first-time years ago when I was surrounded by the press and media. This time a cemetery guard stood nearby whistling the theme song from the musical, *Evita*!

Ed has a client who has a beach house in Uruguay and offered it to us. We were thrilled and took him up on the offer to stay there. We booked passage on the 'Buquebus' ferry from Buenos Aires to Montevideo and planned on staying at least a week and renting a car. Ed's client arranged for his Uncle Tono to meet us at the ferry landing to help get us settled. All we had was a photo of Uncle Tono and he had one of us. We found one another and he was the kindest, most hospitable gentleman; ever so welcoming and kind. There was only one issue. He spoke no English and we spoke no Spanish, but we made it work. It is amazing how sign language works just about anywhere.

He got us to the car rental place. No one there spoke English, but they did have our reservation. The friendly clerk helping us did have one vital question and we did not understand him. He explained it to Uncle Tono who in turn just explained it to us, again, in Spanish! It was like a skit from an *I Love Lucy* episode. The clerk decided to call a branch in Buenos Aires where someone spoke English. The clerk at that end said he only wanted to know if we wanted comprehensive insurance for one dollar a day. We laughed, smiled, and nodded to the clerk on our end. Well, of course. Taking off Uncle Tono directed us to the beach-house, which was a good distance north from Montevideo, on the ocean.

It was the most charming, authentic Uruguayan home imaginable. It had so much character and was part of a compound with other family members, all of whom Uncle Tono introduced us to before leaving. There was one last task. He wanted to take us to a grocery store for some food, so we went to a small rural general store and picked up some basics. When going to buy some wine he steered us away from the bottles and pointed to a box. We were very hesitant, but he insisted we buy it. The wine was very good. We parted; but did see him again on a couple of other times during our stay.

We were informed to never leave the car outside the compound. Each time we had to open the gates, but they also had two very ferocious guard dogs on the property. I tried my best to open or close the gate quickly and get back in the car before the dogs arrived. One time I lingered a little too long and the larger of the two dogs, stood up in front of me with his front paws over my shoulders looking at me with his teeth, face to face. I was terrified and did my best to stay calm. I did not want to be bitten. The dog eventually released me and got down and I sighed in relief. After that we decided to keep doggie treats at the house and they then became our best friends, also becoming used to us being there. Every morning we'd open the shutters and there they stood looking in the open window, acknowledging that they knew exactly where the treats were kept. And they always got one each.

Walking the beach by the ocean was incredible. There was no one along a very long stretch of pristine beach and oceanfront. We prepared our own meals and planned daily excursions. We saw a lot of the country, which is not that big. One day we went to historic Colonia, and another to the Punta del Este area, including discovering Jose Ignacio before it became a popular destination for the jet set. Driving through the cattle region we saw real life gauchos on their horses and visited a quirky little town called Rocha, that we really could have missed.

It was such a delightful excursion in such a beautiful country, very different from Argentina. On the last day we drove into the larger town to buy some pasta and vegetables to make for our final meal at the house. Driving there seemed odd because typically there were few cars on the road, but this time there was traffic. We got to a gas station where we intended to fill up for our next day drive to the ferry, which would be long, and the line of cars was over a mile long, so we went on. Something peculiar was happening. In the supermarket I tried to find someone who might speak English to determine what has happening. I finally spotted a well-dressed woman and she spoke only a few words of English. I asked, '*problemo?*' pointing to the parking lot of cars, and she confirmed by shaking her head in affirmation. Then she said, '*gasolina*'. That was all I got from it.

We returned to the house and none of the other family members were home. Few spoke any English anyway. I decided to turn on the radio to get news and Ed laughed at me. All the news is in Spanish; however, we did hear the word '*gasolina*' repeated several times. We were concerned as we needed to fill up with gasoline for our next day drive. In the end we found it was a gasoline strike, but it lasted only several hours and by the next morning the gasoline was flowing again, and all was back to normal.

That last night we prepared the pasta and vegetables and ate around 7pm and readied for bed a couple hours thereafter. We had a long trek back to Buenos Aries the next day and then flying on to Mendoza. At 10pm there was a knock at the door. After a second knock we heard a woman's voice saying 'Eduardo, Tomas, hello?'. I opened the door and one of the cousins from the compound was standing there with a platter of food, a feast. She said it was for our going away, in sign language. We let her in and although we really were not at all hungry, we sat down with her and ate the food to be polite. It was an incredible feast of grilled meats and many other Uruguayan delicacies. We were grateful, emptied the platter and were overly stuffed, and said our goodbyes.

Before leaving South America, we visited Mendoza, which we heard was a wine region that looked like Napa in the 1970s. Those assessments were accurate. Mendoza seemed like a sleepy place but quite nice too. There are public squares everywhere supposedly because there are continual earthquakes, and these squares are used for shelter when they occur. We walked a great deal and took in the beauty of this South American city, and then rented a car to explore the wine districts, mainly interested in the local hero, Malbec. The wineries were very laid back yet also very inviting. We were welcomed everywhere, and there wasn't a big tourist industry. Driving the countryside with the Andes in the backdrop was incredibly picturesque.

We decided to drive up into the Andes too and went a long way up a mountainside road to view Mendoza and the valley from above. It was spectacular except we were taken aback by the amount of garbage on the side of the road.

Back in the valley we searched for a place to eat and saw a small sign for a 'delicatessen', so we decided to try it out. We got to a gate with the sign 'deli' on it, and rang the bell affixed to a pylon. We said we were interested in lunch and the gates swung open. It was a place called 'Almacen Del Sur'. To our surprise it was a very elegant and well-established hacienda type place. There were orchards, gardens and sustainable organic vegetables grown there. We were told we could have a special lunch, a bit pricey, but we went with it and it was well worth it. A multi course meal of freshly made home-made ingredients from the gardens. It took a couple of hours to consume, along with great wine, and we took back some jarred goods, tomatoes asados or roasted tomatoes, which were wonderful.

Back in Mendoza we found a very nice wine sampling business called The Vines; and sat in a courtyard sampling the many varieties. This was a very nice way to wrap up our trip and head back to the States.

On another trip we went to the Baltic countries of Lithuania, Latvia, and Estonia, ending up in Russia. It was a very enlightening trip in that we saw enormous progress in these Baltic countries since their break away from the former Soviet Union. We learned about the 'Baltic Way', a very significant movement where citizens across all three countries linked arms and hands while joined in unison to break away from the Soviet Union, which they did, one by one. We were so impressed by Vilnius and the citizens were open and friendly, the food quite good, and fashion at a height. High end luxury designer brands were flourishing, and the main boulevards of the city resembled Paris with the way people dressed.

I was especially pleased to see Kaunas where my maternal grandmother was born, and my great-grandfather an organist at the main cathedral. Searching for amber on the Baltic Sea beaches was a treat and we ate homemade meals in a couple of private homes. One town we visited near Poland announced in their town newspaper that, 'The Americans Were Coming'. We were welcomed warmly. Riga in Latvia was a treasure trove of Art Nouveau and Art Deco architecture, and Estonia is a very progressive, Scandinavian type place. Each country likes to tease the other for its differences. In Estonia there is no future tense in their language, and the national way to salute someone when having a drink is something comparable to saying 'terrible sex' quickly. We were told the Lithuanians say that the Estonians have 'terrible sex and no future'.

On another trip in Germany, we returned to Frankfurt to fly out the next day and tried to find a hotel. To our chagrin all were booked as there was a trade show underway in the city, unbeknownst to us. We had a rental car and we drove the hinterlands and it was the same story everywhere we went. Locating a small inn in the suburbs I went inside to find it run by a Chinese family. I pleaded with them for a room and the woman shook her head in apology until a younger woman, I presume a daughter came out. It was very difficult, but I was able to communicate with them as they spoke German with a Chinese accent. The young woman indicated they had a basement room under the front steps they reserved for visiting family and she offered to make it up for us. We were forever grateful, and it was quite comfortable.

That rental car was a bit of a problem too. The rental agent convinced us, cunningly, that it would be better than the Mercedes we had reserved, a Chrysler Seabring convertible, a '*konvertier*' or '*cabrio*'. As the weather was nice and we were primarily in countryside settings during that trip we enjoyed having the roof down, however, the mechanics in that car are such that once you turn the car off it does not start up again for fifteen minutes. That becomes quite a dilemma in touring, and we learned it when it first occurred in the small town of Pottenstein where we sat for fifteen minutes staring at sheep on a hillside wondering how we would ever find a mechanic! We figured it out, even with the German language car manual.

Probably the worst travel nightmare experience we have ever had was at Frankfurt Airport. We were on flights from Athens to San Francisco with a connecting flight in Frankfurt. We had been on a wonderful cruise through the Adriatic, the Greek Islands, and Turkey. Our plane was delayed taking off from Athens, supposedly for bad weather, and yet we had enough time to get to Frankfurt for our connecting flight to San Francisco. Arriving in Frankfurt we ran to our plane only to find it sitting there, but they would not let us board. The door had been closed, and as we learned about FAA standards, they cannot open it again, no matter how much we begged them. Subsequently we presumed they had given away our seats even though it was the same airline in which we were making the connection and they should have known we were arriving within time.

This started an odyssey of travel trauma I would not wish on anyone. We were directed to a 'reassignment line', that literally snaked around the airport for a mile. Apparently, we were not the only ones having missed a flight. An Australian family was behind us and we got to know them well, because we waited nine hours. Yes, nine hours, and I did not think I could stand that long. The Australian family's two little children napped on coats on the floor and got yelled at by airport security guards for doing so. I called our travel agent in the States who assured me we were assigned a new flight; yet we were not.

Noticing that they were taking others before us, primarily Germans just arriving, the line turned into bedlam. People had enough. I finally left the airport to see if I could rebook outside, and that was to no avail. By time another hour passed we had left and re-entered the airport a dozen times and had more German entry stamps in our passports until we were getting strange looks at security. Going to the first class lounge we insisted to stay until the situation was settled and we were warned security would throw us out before midnight.

We finally found an agent willing to help us and he booked us on a flight the next morning, early. He also gave us vouchers for a hotel and cab rides back and forth. It was two in the morning at that point and the plane would leave at ten. We went to the hotel anyway, in a nearby town called Dreieich, which we dubbed 'dry ice'. Giving us just enough time to rest for an hour and take a shower the hotel was gracious enough to get up earlier than usual and have a breakfast for us. I think they saw our pain and felt sorry for us.

Meanwhile no one back home knew we were in Dreieich and not back in the United States by then. It was still dark when a cab came to take us back to the airport. The driver was a bit disgruntled and wasn't happy with our voucher, and to avoid a conflict I offered to pay him in *euros* if needed. He was Iranian and not liking us too much; and wasn't shy to show it. He took us on a drive that frightened us to the core, down dirt roads and obviously not the way we had come. Coming to a gate, he opened the barrier blocking the road ahead, and continued down another dirt road. Both Ed and I were simultaneously convinced it was not a good situation. Ed looked at me, and I at him, and without words indicated we were in trouble. I could tell from his look that Ed figured this guy might kill us both. Ed began looking around for a weapon to use.

While discreetly searching I glanced up and saw the lights

of the airport ahead of us; and hit Ed's arm to also look. Soon we were getting closer, and a big relief came over us. This guy apparently took a short cut, and we later figured perhaps to avoid a train track we had seen coming into the town. Whatever it was we could not get out of the car quick enough and gave the guy some *euros* and the voucher, yet still he was somewhat angry for whatever reason.

We had at least six boarding passes for different flights at this point, and we found that they did not matter one bit if you did not have a seat assignment on them. Lesson learned. They just gave us boarding passes to appease us. By time we got to our gate we found the boarding passes we got were bogus, no seat assignment. Another woman, Monica, who we just met from Marin County in California was in the same situation and was furious. She insisted on getting on the plane and would stand all the way to San Francisco if she needed to do that. Security finally took her away. I got so unhinged, and totally unlike me, I went through a security gate, not sure why, and set off all the alarms. Fortunately, they did not take me away.

Ed and I were upset with frustration and went back to the reassignment station again. We were told all flights were fully booked for the next three days! I decided we should go to another airline, one that was a part of the Star Alliance system. We got to the booking agent and pleaded our case, finally saying, 'we will take any flight getting us to North America'. The woman, who I believe was pitting us, found a flight to Denver leaving in a few hours. BINGO. We took it. Flying to Denver we were relieved and knew we could just drive back to California if needed, but when we arrived there, they booked us on another flight, home. The most amazing part was when we got to San Francisco, our bags arrived with us. Miracles never cease and we had no idea how that happened; and were not intending to find out.

Another little airline travel tidbit I learned is the following. While on a trip to Los Angeles I was booked on a return flight. When I got to the airport, I found the flight was delayed back to Oakland, first by thirty minutes, then an hour, then two hours, then three hours, then five hours, then seven! I was supposed to leave at 6pm and it was finally rescheduled for 1am. I could drive in less time. I went to the booking agent for any flight between then and my new departure time as there were hourly flights, but I was told all were booked. I then headed for the next departing flight and asked to be put on a waiting list. I was told it was useless as it was overbooked, but I insisted. I saw she had a Russian name, and I said some words in Russian to her. She lit up and put me on the list. The plane boarded and I was the only person remaining in the waiting area, certain I had no luck, when she called my name. Astonished she told me I could board, there was one seat left, but I couldn't take my carry-on bag with me. No problem. I boarded the packed flight and there was one middle-seat way in back between a very frail elderly Asian woman who needed to be lifted out with assistance and a 'Goth' guy at the window. It was a very uncomfortable flight, especially when the guy started picking skin off his arm and flecking it my way; but luckily it was only for an hour. I did swear to never fly again once I arrived.

What I learned from that experience is that the airlines do not know who will be on board until the plane has fully loaded. Even though some people confirm they might not show up, for whatever reason. That is why they take a head count right before take-off. In a panic, there is every reason to insist on getting on the wait list.

On a lighter note, Ed and I have had a tradition of surprising each other for our birthdays, usually with a trip. The birthday person does not know where he is going up until that day, or even upon arrival. It makes packing a little difficult, but clues are given to help. Tropical? Cold climate? Lots of walking? Bathing suit or formal wear? That sort of thing.

It is always fun and full of surprises. Ed once got me on a flight to New York and we had a wonderful time. Sometimes, we go to some reclusive area renting a house to just chill for a few days or a week; often on the ocean. There was one surprise birthday trip, for Ed's fiftieth that was particularly interesting. I was able to get him to the airport without him having any clue where he was headed to go. At check-in I told him to stand back, and I went to the counter with his passport and told the clerk that it was a birthday surprise, and he did not know where he was going. She looked at me like I had lost my mind, but eventually went along with it giving me our boarding passes. Perhaps being in Business Class helped the situation.

I was even able to get him on the plane without any awareness of the destination; and informed the flight attendants who went along with it. It became a guessing game for them too since we were connecting to another flight, so they teased him the entire way trying to make him figure it out. When we got to New York City I called the contact I told him was arranging things, a woman named Monique. Really, I was calling a group of friends meeting us at the gate unbeknownst to him. I left enough time between flights for us to have a celebratory dinner together. He was totally caught off guard when several people approached with big signs announcing his birthday!

During dinner I revealed to him that we were headed to France. He had never been to Paris, and I wanted him to see it, lopped on a tour of the Loire Valley with chateaux visits, a trip through Normandy and then a seven-day boat trip down the Seine to Paris where we would stay for several days. His actual birthday would be in Normandy. What he also did not know was that other friends were meeting us in France to tour with us.

It was a fabulous trip with lots of adventures, good food, and exploring different regions, including seeing some magnificent towns along the Seine. One of the best meals we had was in a tiny village restaurant near Charles de Gaulle Airport.

In Normandy we visited the American cemetery and randomly left flowers at a grave of a fallen WWII D Day soldier. We took a photo of the grave and later looked him up, a soldier from Iowa who was killed in the boat also carrying Theodore Roosevelt's son.

In Paris we had a glorious time and I wanted Ed to see all the landmarks I had loved in previous visits. We experienced one of the best travel experiences ever during one of our last days. We explored the Right Bank neighborhoods and happened upon a little corner café serving cous-cous, just that day, so we sat outside and ordered it. Three heaping bowls of cous-cous, vegetables and broth were brought to us, and we had the best meal, including the most incredibly delicious carrots, ever. It was truly memorable.

Walking back toward the Louvre we passed shops selling all types of food goods, a bakery, fish monger, cheese shop, specialty stores and it was quintessential Paris. Arriving at the Louvre near dusk we decided to watch the sunset in the courtyard near the glass pyramid. As the sun set the lights of the city came up and it was the most magical evening one could ever imagine. We had decided not to see any museums on that trip, but we could clearly see some of the beautiful works of art in the windows as the lights of the Louver came on.

It was a time right after Paris had a series of rainstorms and it was warming up and people were sitting on the bridges and other places on blankets with wine and picnics out to enjoy themselves outdoors. The atmosphere was quite congenial and fun. We walked around further along the Seine until it got to around midnight and we headed back to the hotel. What impressed me most was a lone older woman in a fur coat just strolling comfortably along the quay. I thought that was a civilized place where an older woman could walk securely at night along the river, completely in her own thoughts, without a care in the world, or fear.

A couple of years ago after visiting family outside Munich Ed and I took a train trip through Austria stopping and staying in Salzburg and Vienna. It was tremendous fun, and the trains were wonderful. We got to see so much countryside and even ate some good meals on board too. Both cities were beautiful, and it was a relaxing trip full of landscapes, gardens, architecture, art, and music. We saw the Klimt paintings in Vienna, as well as an evening concert at the Musikverein, a magnificent concert hall with superb acoustics. We grabbed some delicious bites of food at the outdoor Naschmarkt, and I was really impressed by some of the Successionist architecture we saw. Our apartment was a classic old apartment with high ceilings, large windows looking onto the Danube, full of character, fashionably decorated. We were told to try out McDonalds Cafe and scoffed at it; but did so at the train station before we left. The experience was nothing like that in the United States, superior quality, and service beyond anything we have even seen at a McDonalds back home.

Last year we took a trip for Ed's sixtieth birthday, by ship, to England. I will describe the sea voyage later, but the prime purpose of the trip was to explore the English countryside and see the Chatsworth estate near the Peak District that Ed had been interested in and had read a lot about over the years. The owner of the small stone cottage we rented nearby gave us a private tour of the first rooms at Chatsworth and told us some wonderful stories of the house that aren't usually noted. We decided to not set foot in London on that trip, so visited Bath, The Cotswolds, the Peak District, York (for his namesake), Lincolnshire and leaving from Gatwick Airport back home. We visited the towns where Ed's family was from originally in Northamptonshire and from where they left for America in the mid-1600s.

What surprisingly impressed us during that trip was an unexpected visit we had to make to the doctor as Ed had some bug bites on this face that appeared infected. Although in a rural area of Lincolnshire with small villages we found a clinic. Within an hour Ed saw a doctor, got the bites examined and diagnosed, and a prescription right on the spot; and when we offered to pay with British pounds or a credit card, they refused. It was free. It nearly knocked us over, as in the United States just getting to a doctor that quickly would not be possible, especially for a foreigner.

I have had many trips by trains, planes, and automobiles and each is memorable in its own way. Each has been an experience that has expanded my life. It is a wonderful world, a place we should cherish, and protect in every way possible.

CHAPTER 21

A potpourri of attachments

Our lives are a labyrinth of connections, friendships, and relationships. I am often amazed at how small the world can be when I meet someone who knows someone else I know. Then too I have been mistaken for someone else more times than I care to imagine. Attachments are made, sometimes planned and sometimes spontaneous. Sometimes these attachments last a lifetime and other times it is more fluid, and people come and go.

Family, friends, and neighbors are the center of our lives. Occasionally our 'family' are blood relations and other times created with people we bring together. None of it is any less in importance to us.

A friend I have known the longest, Jean-Pierre, is someone I have never met. He lives in Belgium in the same town he has lived in all his life. We came together through a US-European pen-pal exchange program in the 1960s. During those early days we wrote extensively about our lives and how we lived in our respective countries. I would wait diligently for his airmail letters to arrive. Over the years we have kept our communication alive and today we use email. Although our lives have evolved, we still are bonded in friendship, and one I sincerely appreciate. It is our hope that we will meet one day.

During my youth and upbringing family was important, and

every holiday and major celebration we spent it with family members. Each year my father's aunt and uncle in White Plains, New York gave a huge Fourth of July backyard party for all those relatives on that side of my family, the Rodamers. I cherish looking back on how everyone came together from far and wide.

Ed's family similarly had a yearly reunion of family members on the Olympic Peninsula in Washington State, and I always looked forward to attending. The first years I attended there were over two hundred people. There was an abundance of food, including the best salmon you could ever imagine. As the older family members passed away fewer and fewer came to the reunion, and unfortunately it eventually faded away. Yet what a wonderful way for generations of family to come together for one day and be together.

One of my dearest family members was my father's cousin, Dorothy Johnson. Dorothy was a meaningful attachment in my life. She lived in Mt. Kisco, New York and was married to a man well established in that part of Westchester County as his family had been there for generations. They didn't have children, although he had from a previous marriage. They treated me like a son, and we were very close. Dorothy had been married before, well before I was born so I never knew him; but I heard he was quite wealthy and treated her very badly. She went to Florida for the divorce.

She was very encouraging of my education and was pleased seeing me do well in school. While I was at college I would sometimes come home and find an envelope on the desk in my bedroom that she had given to my parents for me. She did not want or expect any acknowledgement of it, or discussion, but inside the envelope was typically five thousand dollars in cash. All I would do is say 'thank you' when I saw her next and she would merely smile and nod. She was very generous in that way, and yet very humble too.

I have lived in neighborhoods where the neighbors became friends, and often those friendships fade away once one moves on. The proximity is what brought those people together, and although we might think of one another occasionally, we do not usually see each other again; especially if there's considerable distance after a move.

A neighbor I had in Connecticut was a girl my age named Paula Davis. Paula became a good friend. She was born with a severe heart condition and had several open-heart surgeries early in her life. It was debilitating and she was unable to do many things other kids our age could do. Yet, Paula had a heart of gold. She had older siblings who were grown and out of the house and a younger brother. Her father did not necessarily treat her very well and often dismissed her for her illness.

The kids in school treated her badly as well, harassing her and calling her names because her lips would turn a deep purple color due to her heart condition. We became friends and I did my best to support and encourage her, and not let her fall into a quagmire of sadness. Her limitations really frustrated her. I admired her strength of character, and I believe she appreciated that I treated her like an ordinary person, neither an invalid; nor someone who needed to excel.

Her death came while she was in her twenties, and I was extremely saddened. She was one of those attachments who is a loss; but lives on in memory; and will so forever.

I have had many lessons from illness and death over the

years and how it affects our attachments in life. My stepson, Matthew, is one of those people who has lasted in my memory. I have mentioned him before and he was an inspiration to me. He had muscular dystrophy, nearly totally paralyzed. Matthew had a quest for life that I greatly admired. He often lived for the moment. Yet, I knew he had a certain loneliness in his life too. Sometimes people were very callous and perhaps unknowingly rude. We were on an elevator in a hotel in Chicago with Matt in his wheelchair when a well-dressed middle-aged couple got on. The man stared at Matthew and looked at us and said, 'So what's the boy's problem?'. What does one say to that? We matter of fact told him.

Matthew loved to play chess with my father when he visited, and it was heartwarming to watch their enjoyment and engagement. Matt would typically sit outside our apartment building in San Francisco for sun and socialization. Except, no one would talk with him. A young man in a wheelchair must be a bit of a barrier for most people; hard to know. We did learn one day that a person who lived down the block made a point to every day come and talk with him. It was Bobby McFerrin, the well-known musician. I was most impressed and pleased by that, and when Matthew passed away, I left Bobby a note and thanked him for being a friend to Matthew. He sent back a very cordial response of sorrow for the loss.

There is a common theory that death comes in threes, and to some extent that has played out in my life. One year, within a couple of months, my mother's brother, Willy, died; and then my father's Aunt Betty, and finally the woman I considered a second grandmother, Mary Skalandaitis.

That was followed up by another triade in Ed's family. First his sister-in-law, Linda, passed away from cancer, and it was a terrible loss as she was so very much loved by all of us. Then Ed's brother, of esophageal cancer. Finally, the year my mother dies Ed's mother, Rolleen, died too. It was sad as she was taken to the hospital and never knew she would never return home. Ed suffered through days of back and forth with her health; and putting her on and taking her off life support. It was a horrible time and quite agonizing. All of them were attachments cherished and gone, but never forgotten.

All these deaths do take a toll, and perhaps when it happens in threes, that makes it even worse.

Getting back to neighbors. Ed and I lived in a very elegant apartment in the Pacific Heights neighborhood of San Francisco. The building was built in the 1920s and the rooms were enormous, with high ceilings and lots of detail and moldings. It was a classic apartment built in an era when the market was attempting to lure people from houses into a different style of living. Some of the apartments had maids' quarters.

The one-bedroom apartment we had was the size of most suburban houses. Our entry hall was the size of a standard bedroom. The apartment had a large formal dining room with a brass chandelier and built-in cabinets across one entire wall. There was a half bath totally clad in a sensual brown marble with a Murano light fixture, with a vestibule. An impressive fireplace dominated a living room that was large enough for three seating groups that included an area with shelves for a library. The building was family owned and occupied, well preserved and taken care of over the years.

We lived there during the turn of the new Millennium – the year 2000. We slept on the floor in front of a raging fire in the fireplace, waking on occasion to watch the celebrations at various places around the world. There was supposed to be a huge event, called the 'Y2K', that supposedly would shut down all the computers in the world, or some such thing; and it never materialized other than some wacky conspiracy theory that took off in people's fears.

We became friendly with several of the other residents, and especially liked the building manager, Ann.

One evening while Ed was working in his office in Vallejo, I sat reading on the loveseat in the bedroom when I heard a deep, strange voice outside on the sidewalk below. The voice said a number of things like, 'death comes to all of us' and 'the spirits of the world walk amongst us.' Looking out the window I saw a man, totally dressed in black holding a lantern with a candle. He had on a top hat and his garb was that of a nineteenth century undertaker. He was pointing to the Victorian mansion across the street. One of the family members there had died on a trip to the South Pacific decades ago and apparently was delivered home in a barrel of brandy, and supposedly his ghost still lurked around the house. When I looked further there was a group of six people listening intently. I went outside to see what it was about, and the man introduced himself as he was conducting a 'ghost tour' of the neighborhood and gave me his card. Ed and I took that ghost tour sometime later and got to know the gentleman conducting it. It was a very well-devised, interesting tour and took over an hour walking several blocks.

We had a couple of unfortunate neighborly attachments there too, that shows that not all attachments are necessarily good ones. Although we got to know most of the other residents and we are quite friendly with them, we had one woman move in who was a 'trust fund baby' and very problematic. She was unreasonably noisy; and seemed at times manic. We tried our best to be accommodating but it was quite upsetting. After she moved a young man moved in who had just sold a business and done quite well. He did not need to work. He often created disturbances, and knew it, leaving us gifts to make amends. We tried our best to be friendly as he seemed earnest and nice enough, but it was also somewhat strained.

One night, very late, we heard an explosion. I went to the apartment, but there was no answer. I called as I had his phone number, but no answer. Getting back to bed there was another explosion, followed by a series of loud noises that literally rocked our apartment. Again, no answer to the phone or at the door.

The next day, in the afternoon, I heard someone go into the apartment and I went over to ask if everything was alright. A poised middle-aged woman answered the door, not the resident or anyone I had seen before, and I introduced myself. She seemed upset and asked if I would come inside, which I did. She took me into the bedroom and the man was on his bed flailing and sweating profusely. I tried to talk with him, but he was barely coherent. I told the woman to call 911 and get him to a hospital, but she insisted he would not go. It seemed to me a drug overdose, but I don't have much experience in that. She got a stack of his credit cards and I dragged him to my car in the garage and drove him to the emergency room a few blocks away. The woman told me he was having a turbulent time in his life and did not know what to do. She said he was trying to lift suitcases down from the uppermost part of the closet during the night and when they fell those were the 'explosions' we heard. I left them in the hospital. He disappeared thereafter, and I must say that it was an attachment that was one of the rather unpleasant ones.

After we moved into our house in Oakland, we found a very open, inviting neighborhood of a variety of people from different backgrounds and places, some living there for some time and others more recent. Oakland can be described as the Brooklyn of San Francisco, diverse, culturally varied and a place people go for its proximity to the big city, especially smaller businesses, and restaurants to escape the high rents across the bay.

One of our neighbors, a long-time couple who lived in the neighborhood for many years, introduced a concept of creating neighborhood attachments and cohesion from an oceanfront community where they have a second home. There an older resident started what are called 'flag parties.' She would put out a flag on a Friday afternoon to indicate that neighbors could come and gather in her yard, bring your own bottle, and share some camaraderie together.

Our neighbors tried it in our own neighborhood, and it was a tremendous hit. On a Friday afternoon someone would put out a flag and everyone knew they could stop by, usually after work, with their favorite alcoholic beverage and gather for some neighborly chatter. It came that we typically met in the driveway of the home flying the flag so others in the neighborhood would see the activity and feel welcomed to join it. Those parties became a mainstay event. Usually, the person intending to hang the flag gave a heads up in advance so people knew, and word would spread.

Ed and I love dogs and would have one if we did not travel so much. Dogs are another type of companion, an attachment, as any pet can bring joy and pleasure to our lives. I consider Ed to be a 'dog whisperer' as he can detect the personality of any dog by just looking at it. He really understands animals and dogs love him.

As a child I did not have a dog as my parents did not believe in having one in a large urban city, saying that it wasn't good for the dog. My father had a one-hundred-gallon fish tank instead with a beautiful array of fish, and I had a turtle, named Speedy, but that was about the extent of my pets.

Ed and I often take care of dogs while their owners go on vacation. There are two dogs we love to have stay with us, Charlie, a very loving Poodle mix, and Jax, a terrier mix. Charlie is adorable and a dog who wants to be admired and loved, very well behaved and a wonderful companion. Jax on the other hand is somewhat neurotic and edgy; but loving too. We always welcome them into our home.

If we ever had a dog of our own Ed and I always said we would call it something unique, for example '*Ach du Lieber*', or the German language equivalent of 'Oh my goodness', 'Oh my gosh', or 'Oh, dear'.

I returned home from work one day and was about to drive into the driveway when a small black dog stood defiantly in my way half-way up the driveway. I got out of the car and Ed came out to tell me that it was our dog! Alright, when did that happen?

The story goes that the dog had been abandoned and was wandering the neighborhood haphazardly. It wasn't uncommon for an unwanted dog to just be tossed into the street and left on its own. A neighbor took it in, and their own dog did not like this new intruder at all, so it got passed to the next neighbor, who's dog also did not like this dog. Posts went out to try and find the owner, to no avail.

Finally, Ed ended up taking in the dog, getting it bathed and cared for. The dog had a beautiful black shiny coat and was a dachshund mix. A male dog he was somewhat skittish, and it was hard to know how long he had been abandoned. We took the dog to the vet, got it everything it needed, including shots, and we decided to foster it for as long as possible.

And he took on the name '*Ach du Lieber*'.

What was endearing was the neighborhood children came to love him and looked for him when we took him on walks, and he was great with kids too. I laughed one day when leaving the house and the two little girls across the street were yelling '*Ach du Lieber*'! '*Ach du Lieber*'! Only a German would understand the ironic humor in that!

'Ach' became a part of our household and we did all we could to care for him. There was one problem, however, a very inconvenient one… he could not be left alone without totally freaking out. It may have been partly due to his apparent abandonment. We got doggy gates to put in the doorways to keep him in the kitchen, but whenever we would go out, we would come home to find him hoping up and down in the living room window. And he would go berserk when we walked in the door. It became difficult go out anywhere and leave him alone.

We alternated taking him to work with us; and tried our best to always keep him in sight. He was becoming adjusted, but he needed someone with him, all the time, to feel comfortable.

One day we heard a crash and I walked into a room to find a one-thousand- year-old Chinese plate smashed and broken on the floor. Ach had seen a squirrel out in the yard and jumped up on a breakfront barking at it while pushing the plate off onto the floor. I said that plate survived war and famine, but not Ach. We knew the dog did not mean it, but nonetheless we were becoming to fear that he was not fitting our lives too well either.

Ed posted an ad in a local paper and a young couple in San Francisco contacted us as they were interested in adopting a dog. They had a young daughter. We brought the dog over for the family to meet Ach. It seemed to work well and Ach did not seem too terribly disturbed by being with them. We decided to take another step and leave him overnight, and subsequently for a weekend. Both times the stays went very well, and the family was becoming attached to Ach.

Their daughter, around six years old, was suffering from severe seizures that happened multiple times a day. It was amazing as she came to bond with Ach and the dog with her, even during these short visits. Ach would stay close to her and apparently try and comfort her during the times that the seizures came. It was simply amazing. The couple had a friend who was a dog trainer and met the dog and felt it suitable for the family, and willing to take on training Ach some too. They adopted Ach and it became a win-win for all of us.

A few weeks afterwards we visited the family to check in and much to our pleasure Ach had found a true home. He and the girl were nearly inseparable, and he would follow her around, and continued comforting her in her bad moments. It was very endearing, and we felt he found a loving home too, one where he now had a job that was fulfilling to his needs as well.

Attachments come in many forms, yet they touch our lives in sometimes unimaginable ways. Those who enter our lives, even unexpectedly, become a part of us and who we are in life.

CHAPTER 22

Finding America

I am sure at one time or another, or perhaps more often, many of us question our own ability to be prejudice, even if it seems suppressed or not so apparent.

My awakening occurred while living in New York City during the late 1970s. One day on the subway from work in Manhattan to my home in Forest Hills, Queens I realized that I did not hear one word of English in all the voices in conversation that I overheard. It wrangled me to be annoyed by it. Wasn't this America, The United States, where English is the official national language? Why did I hear so many foreign voices, and NO ENGLISH?

It was a startling eye opener for me. Constantly being around various ethnicities was certainly wonderful, but I had to question how much is too much. In my two architectural offices in New York there was a Bulgarian man, a Romanian woman, a Thai man, an Asian Indian man, a Chinese man, and a man from Jamaica with a wife from Suriname.

All of them enhanced and brought wonderful things to my life in knowing them. I recall the man from Jamaica best, Tony, as he was approximately my age and we had similar aspirations. We became good friends. He often remarked how shocked he was by the opposition to interracial marriage in the US. His comments were followed by his noting that it is not an issue in

Jamaica. And frankly race relations in the US had been abysmal for decades, for generations.

Prejudice comes in many forms. When I was living in an upscale apartment building in Forest Hills, Queens the demographic was primarily white and overwhelmingly Jewish. I believe my wife and I were the only two Christians among the sixty households residing there. My wife had a very good friend, an African American woman, Mona, who was an exceptional professional dancer with the ballet and some well-known dance companies in New York City. Mona was visiting us once and walked in the building with my wife, past the doorman, and got on the elevator followed by two older women who were residents. One woman seemed frazzled and annoyed, looked at my wife and said, 'You should be careful who you let on the elevator!'. Looking at Mona she then said, 'there is a service elevator in back!'. As my wife told me of the incident I was shocked beyond comprehension, and Mona was extremely offended.

So, prejudice exists. It's real.

I saw this again at the Community Planning Board meetings in that same community. Forest Hills had started as a planned community for the working class in the 1920s and rapidly transformed into one for the upper middle class instead. Fine stately homes surrounded a beautiful Tudor style commuter train station with central mixed-use buildings including a hotel and restaurant. Beyond were streets of typical retail and then a community of smaller homes and many finely designed apartment buildings built between the 1920s and the 1960s. It was an extremely desirable place to live. It's national, if not international claim to fame, was its renowned tennis stadium.

The original covenants of the community in the 1920s limited residents to Christians. No one else was welcomed or allowed. This prevailed until WWII when Forest Hills, not unlike many other upscale New York communities, became predominantly Jewish. The original covenants of the community were disputed and pushed aside, essentially outlawed as discriminatory.

During one very infamous Community Planning Board meeting I attended in Forest Hills there was a measure being voted on to allow a group home to be opened in the neighborhood for 'mentally-handicapped' individuals. It was highly contested by local residents. After much testimony and comment a resident came to the microphone and said that she wanted everyone in the room to recall the days when Jews were not allowed to walk the streets of Forest Hills, and prejudice prevailed. The audience went completely silent. She said it very eloquently and directly and it hit home. As I recall the group home was approved.

America, and its multifaceted environment of many peoples does indeed challenge us. There is no 'true, pure' America... Native Americans being the closest to it, yet it is diverse, and it should be, as that is what makes it so wonderful and unique in the world.

I have had my prejudices questioned too. I am someone who believes I am not prejudice, yet at times it does surface.

My wife's friend, Mona, confronted me once over it. An elegant, educated, sophisticated black woman I was telling a story of enjoying Popeye's Fried Chicken in New Orleans, but to find the best you had to go to 'the really black neighborhoods.' Well, that obviously bristled Mona who looked at me directly and said emphatically, 'So, am I just black or *really* black?'. She went on, 'Explain to me, what is a *really* black neighborhood?' 'And, why they'd have better fried chicken there?' She continued, 'And how about you? Are you just white or *really* white?' I was stunned, but she was correct. I was expressing a type of inherent prejudice in my words, and thoughts, yet did not recognize it.

Facing one's own prejudice is tough.

It's interesting in that a man I knew growing up, who I will fully introduce later, named Vince, was profoundly a bigot, in the style of 'Archie Bunker' from the TV show, *All in The Family*. A truck driver, he knew all the ethnic slurs and derogatory terms and name calling; and used them frequently. As he was a long-time family friend, and hard to dismiss, my mother would always tell me after a visit, 'please don't listen to him, and never use those words as they are demeaning and bad.'. The interesting thing was he was the most kind, caring person you would ever want to know... *if* you were of the same race and ethnic background as he.

Another fascinating thing in my finding 'America' was learning it is more complex than simple. Getting back to people speaking English, I was on the Haight Street bus that I took home nightly in San Francisco for some time. There were always tourists on the bus, many foreign tourists, heading to Haight Ashbury, and I would try to identify them by listening to their languages. Quite different from the New York subway where I was annoyed by not hearing any English, I came to appreciate the variety of languages I heard, but also understood they were just visitors. I enjoy languages and often could correctly identify what country they were from, and I would ask to confirm my guess. One evening, however, I just was totally stumped by two young men engaged in conversation. I could not decipher their language, or country of origin, at all. Out of curiosity, I finally asked them. They were Scottish and speaking English! So much for my little game at trying to identify influences on America through foreign language.

My mother sometimes would say she thought I would end up, 'a man without a country'. Perhaps I criticized the United States too many times. I have had two times that I attempted to leave. A college friend of mine, Greg, and I once applied for a work visa in Germany. We thought it would be fun to live there after we graduated. We filled out all the application necessities and were so proud of ourselves, submitting it to the German authorities. We were both rejected. Then around 1982 I became extremely frustrated with the state of this country under Ronald Reagan, wrote him a pointed letter, and sent in an immigration application to Australia. It was returned, 'rejected'. The explanation was there was no work for architects in Australia.

During the 2020 election I yelled at the television as the election results came in late at night. I would not stand another four years of the Trump administration and after a bottle of wine I swore I would leave the USA for good. A friend who was texting me during the result count asked where I intended to go, and I commented back, 'French Polynesia'.

I am still in America and now, perhaps, I accept more than ever that I have found America, and it is what it is, a melting pot of diversity.

CHAPTER 23

The Immigrant experience

Everyone in the United States is from somewhere else, immigrants, whether acknowledged or not, and some here longer than others. These immigrant roots are very powerful and tie us together in a myriad of ways. The newer immigrants are the most resilient in sticking together and creating community.

I found this on both sides of my family, my maternal Lithuanian side, and paternal German side, although the Lithuanian side was much more recent.

There have been people in my life that are not blood relations, but certainly are considered such. Often, I did not know how they came about, or entered my family picture, but they were significantly there.

I will dwell specifically on the Lithuanian side as they were truly the immigrants in my life; and the most influential was the Skalandaitis family. They lived in Maspeth, Queens, in New York City in a decidedly Lithuanian enclave. There's a large Lithuanian Roman Catholic Church there, Transfiguration, that is very important in the community.

Vince Skalandaitis was approximately fifty years older than me; and was a close 'family' member, although there was no actual relation. Vince was the 'bigoted' person I wrote about earlier. His parents were Lithuanian immigrants and his father had died before I was born. His mother was quite elderly, frail, and infirmed when I was a child and I called her '*Teta*', or 'Aunt' in Lithuanian. Vince was essentially equal to being an older cousin to my mother. He called her 'Dottie' and had known her since she was born.

I believe the connection was with my maternal grandmother and that the Skalandaitis family may have cared for her after her sister's returned to the old country and left her here alone at a very young age. I never asked about it, and that is the only logical thing I have determined. The Skalandaitis family had bought and owned a middle-class house in Maspeth and had a rental unit with a long-term tenant, the Whippers, who occupied it for years. Vince was an only child and was tasked with totally taking care of his mother. As a truck driver he drove a truck for an ice company, Knickerbocker Ice.

Although stereotypical to the Queens working class man, Vince was a gentle soul and someone who truly was generous. Every Sunday he would drive a few of the older women in the neighborhood to church, although he called them 'flannel mouths' as he felt they gossiped too much. He called the woman who made pizzas down the street 'hot lips.' He had a nickname for nearly everyone. I was 'Dennis the Menace'.

Vince always kept a bottle of Four Roses Scotch in a hall closet and would often pull it down for a quick swig. He was also enormously humorous and had a fantastic sense of humor, although often at someone else's expense. I was just about the only child he had contact with and he treated me extremely well, and with care. When my parents had a wedding or some event to attend, I would often spend the night with Vince and Teta at the house and they indulged me in every way. Vince always made sure to have snacks and ice cream, and the first thing he would do is drive me to the toy store and say I could pick out anything I wanted… and he would automatically buy it for me. I was always 'spoiled' when around him, yet I always knew to be respectful and not overdue the kindness offered.

Part of every visit was my sitting with Teta in her bedroom and telling her about what I was doing. She spoke both Lithuanian and English, but preferred the former, of which I knew little to none. Yet she always smiled and looked kindly to me. At the end of each time, she would ask me to open her dresser drawer and get her purse. She would open it and hand me five dollars. My mother would balk at her doing that and she would sternly correct my mother in Lithuanian, saying 'young men need money!'. When getting confused in the language exchange, Vince always translated for me.

As far as I can remember Teta never left the house and primarily stayed in the bedroom, although she was pushed around the house in a wheelchair too. What I enjoyed most is that she liked sitting in the living room and watching wrestling, boxing, and Roller Derby on television. It was quite something to see this old, frail woman get excited over watching people get beat up.

In truth I knew nothing of her background, how she came to the United States or anything about her past.

They kept a ruby colored candy dish of small, wrapped Hershey chocolates in the dining room china cabinet. I knew it was there but always waited until Vince or Teta offered for me to get some. I would slowly open the glass door with the key that always sat in the keyhole and took a chocolate or two. My favorites were the dark chocolate ones, or the ones mixed with 'Rice Crispies'.

Vince encouraged me to get good grades in school, and emphatically told me to stay away from drugs and alcohol. He was always dressed well, even when working. When President Kennedy was shot, he took me aside and said, 'Tommy, do not ever become President. It isn't worth it'.

During a visit when I stayed with them Vince drove me down to the 'ice-house' in lower Manhattan. Now a vestige of the past, it was amazing. A large ice palace with large pallets of ice, and bitterly cold. Frequently these blocks of ice were delivered to places like Cartier Jewelers for ice sculptures at events or parties.

There was another time I remember well when we drove to the train yards between Queens and Brooklyn; and waited. It was a virtual wasteland with a multitude of train tracks going every which way. After some time, a very expensive looking car drove up and an elegantly dressed man and woman got out of the car and went to talk with Vince. He had me wait by his car while he had a discussion with them. I have no idea what it was all about, but the woman wearing a full-length fur coat came to talk with me. She asked my name and spoke kindly while asking me questions, then opened her purse and took out ten dollars to give me. Do you get the impression that people were always handing me money! They did, and I never complained; or refused.

There was once when Vince decided to join us on a vacation, to Niagara Falls. He drove, his large Plymouth automobile, and we had a blast. Teta stayed home with an attendant. Although I was young, I remember the trip well as he added a new dimension of humor and fun to it all.

When Vince was sixty years old, or so, he decided to marry.

There was a woman, Mary, who he knew in his youth and apparently was quite fond of her. She was living in Washington State with a daughter, son-in-law, and grandsons. By telephone they rekindled a relationship and she decided to come visit. I remember we all went to the airport to pick her up after an arduous thirteen-hour flight from Seattle, and it was the first time I met her. She was a very kind and a loving person, and it was nice to see her and Vince together, as they obviously cared about each other even after so many years apart.

Not long after Vince proposed marriage to Mary while on the phone to her in Washington and she flew back, permanently, to marry him and live together as man and wife. Vince's mother was not that pleased about the arrangement, but endured, somewhat. They had a simple wedding ceremony at Transfiguration Church and my parents were their Best Man and Maid of Honor. My recollection was that it was a marriage of happiness, except that Teta did not treat Mary very well. At times Teta was abusive, yelling 'Marija', or Mary, in Lithuanian and insisting she do things for her, without much appreciation, as though she was a servant. She also told Vince that Mary would go down to the bar and drink as soon as he left for work, which was totally fabricated and downright nasty. Vince got annoyed with her attitude.

Mary became a part of my life and essentially a second grandmother to me. I knew, too, that she terribly missed her family back in Washington as the distance was so far. We did a lot together as my parents were very close with them.

Teta died while I was upstate New York at my uncle's summer house, and Vince shortly thereafter developed Parkinson's disease. He would shake profusely and would always apologize for it, which I found totally unnecessary. He died while I was away at college and unfortunately, I could not attend the funeral, yet his memory lasts with me. He may have been a bigot, but he had a whole other side to him too.

After I graduated college Mary offered to have me come stay with her to find a job in New York City. I stayed about two weeks and we had a wonderful time together having long talks and sharing lots about our lives. She was very devout in her spirituality, and very blunt in her views. We cooked together and I helped with chores around the house, heading by bus to Manhattan every day to look for work. Mary was very specific in the ways she did things; and taught me how to scrub a kitchen sink properly. I so enjoyed my time with her, and we had a good time together during that time, and I was forever grateful for her hospitality.

It is another example of the immigrant experience. Helping those with specific ties to you, although not through relations, in helping one get set up and going in a new life.

Mary eventually moved back to be with her family in Washington State and I never saw her again. I had met one of her grandsons when he visited her in New York, and the other was the well-known race boat driver, Chip Hanauer. The last time I saw her was in 1980. She passed away in 1997 in her nineties.

Then there were those from my immigrant past who were family, actual blood relations. My maternal grandfather's sister married a tobacco farmer in north central Connecticut, Windsor Locks. Many folks associate tobacco farms with North Carolina not knowing that they exist in somewhat unlikely places, Connecticut and Wisconsin being two of them.

The offspring of that family all took on being 'American' but did occasionally talk of the older family members and their 'ways'. They were good people, led ordinary lives; yet were products of their ethnic upbringing.

Perhaps one of the most memorable immigrant connections was my godmother, Aunt Marie. Again, not a blood relation yet connected through the Lithuanian community. She knew my mother's family well, and her mother who lived in Maspeth was close with the Skalandaitis family. It was all somehow intertwined.

Aunt Marie was a former New York fashion model, very colorful, and my own *Auntie Mame*. Outspoken, impeccably dressed and quite vivacious she always commanded the room. She had incredibly good taste and most impressive was her New York apartment that I remember as a child decorated quite professionally with mid-century blond wood furnishings.

She was married to Uncle Bill, a quintessentially 1950's *Mad Men* type person who wore good suits and had a pencil moustache. His ethnic background was Hungarian. They had two sons and the family lived primarily in Germany during my youth as he worked for the federal government. My aunt loved living life abroad. She would send us beautiful gifts, and one year I even got a pair of lederhosen, which my mother forbade me to wear. In the late 1950s it still had raw associations with Germany's not too distant past.

They moved often and for a period lived on Long Island and then New Jersey. When they lived in New Jersey I was in college. At the end of a semester my college friend, Mark, and I drove back from New Orleans, and he dropped me off at her house as he lived nearby. We got to the front door, and I introduced Mark. She looked at him, shook his hand, and said quite defiantly, 'how can you live in this hell hole of a place, called New Jersey?'. I was quite embarrassed, and I hoped Mark just took it in stride.

Her brother, Joe, was a Monsignor in the Catholic Church and the man who baptized me at our family church, St. Aloysius, in Great Neck on Long Island. I was told that when he was baptizing me, he said I would grow up to be a Bishop. Well, that never happened, but a nice gesture, nonetheless. He was the head of a parish in Pueblo, Colorado and would come visit us in New York on occasion. During holidays we would speak with him by phone, and he would sing 'Old Man River' to me in a booming baritone voice.

Aunt Marie's mother did live near the Skalandaitis family and visited them often. One evening we got a call from Vince that we should come immediately. Aunt Marie's mother visited and had dinner with them, then went to sit in the living room while Vince was cleaning up; and died on the sofa. There was a crowd of people on the sidewalk when we arrived as word travels quickly in those close-knit communities, and there were several police and an ambulance present. We went upstairs and my Aunt Marie was already there. Out of the corner of my eye I saw a sheet over a body sitting upright on the sofa. As they lifted the body out Vince looked at my mother and said, 'why did she have to come here to die!'.

There's little semblance of my immigrant roots left in my life. A Lithuanian restaurant opened in Oakland for a few years, and I took great pride in it. It was the only one west of the Rocky Mountains, and surprisingly many non-Lithuanian people enjoyed the home cooking type meals.

I do know that my roots did influence who I am as a person, but interestingly as we move further along, they become a further memory too.

Chapter 24

The kids down the block

Because Astoria was so diverse, along with the proximity to Manhattan, there were many interesting folks from varied backgrounds who lived there during my youth. For one it was a magnet for up-and-coming artists and actors who blended in with everyone. Several well-known celebrities were born there including Ethel Merman, Tony Bennett, Maria Callas, Cyndi Lauper, and many others. My mother's hairdresser was Tony Bennett's brother.

This produced a good number of interesting and unique kids in the neighborhood, sons and daughters of immigrants, schoolteachers, actors, and everyone else you can imagine. 'Billy Bam', a child advertising TV 'star' from the Welch's grape juice commercials of the 1950s lived down the next block. He was just like any other kid, but also took on a certain persona of being a celebrity to us kids.

My own block of Crescent Street, between 35th and 36th Avenues, on the border of Astoria and Long Island City, included a wide array of kids my age, and we all hung together. We ignored and avoided the gang members down one end of the block who just called us names as we walked by on the sidewalk. We all had 'street smarts' and knew where not to go and what was safe or not so safe.

We identified ourselves by our ethnicity, even though most

of us were born in the United States, yet not far beyond the immigrant experience. I was the 'German' kid, primarily due to my last name, yet my Lithuanian roots were not much removed from that. I was the sole 'German' in my network of school mates. My other good friends were Irish, Italian, Puerto Rican, French, Serbian/Yugoslavian, Polish, British, and Jewish. In Astoria being Jewish was considered an identifiable ethnic 'heritage' group while not necessarily linked to a specific country. All were white or Hispanic, and I do not remember many black 'African Americans' around the neighborhood, although they certainly would be welcomed.

My Catholic elementary school had kids who had just arrived in the U.S. One boy, about fourteen years old from Italy, was placed in my third-grade class with nine-year olds. He was taller than anyone and barely fit in the desk. They put him there because his English skills were poor, and they thought this would help get him up to speed. I am not sure it ever did. He was out of place, and I felt sorry for him. Another girl, who just arrived from Colombia, was not treated well and often teased. The kids called her 'banana box' as she was overweight. I never sensed the teachers had a grasp on what went on with these types of things.

For some unknown reason most of the kids on my block were girls. Cathy, a girl whose Italian immigrant parents lived two houses down from me, followed me everywhere and it was quite annoying. She always seemed to know when I was coming or going as though she constantly watched out the window. Another girl, Diane, lived several houses down in the opposite direction. We would frequently walk to school together, about eight blocks away. She once accused me of pushing her and breaking her front teeth when she fell on the sidewalk. He mother, Cookie, was livid and insisted on a meeting with me and my father. We went and there was an interrogation to establish the truth. Diane finally admitted she lied about me pushing her, and her mother slapped her right across her bruised and scared face. That shocked both my father and me. I was relieved, however, as I knew I had not done it, but I also do not remember us having much interaction afterwards.

Some people would occasionally say to me that it was unfortunate that I was an only child, and frankly I never understood the sentiment. I had plenty of friends and cousins around my age and it seemed a better situation than having siblings. The others went home after we had been together, and they weren't around continually to bother me. Being an only child also made me fiercely independent. When no one was around I certainly could keep myself occupied without feeling lonely. Besides, I have observed a good number of siblings who did not get along with each other.

It was a close-knit neighborhood, and everyone seemed to have a relative nearby. Very often, as with my own family, three or four generations lived in proximity, if not in the same household.

One of my closest friends was Joey Agresti. He lived a block away and his family had emigrated from Italy. He had one younger sister. His grandmother lived with them and she could not speak English yet was a kind, nurturing person. Joey and I spent a lot of time together, playing, riding our bicycles, and just becoming a part of each other's family. His mother, Marcella, made the most incredibly delicious Italian lunches and dinners; and I was often invited. Our families came to know one another well, and Joey's mother became friends with mine. We went to the same school and were typically in the same classes.

One day Joey came to me, nearly in tears, and let me know that his father had decided that they would return to Italy, for good. It was devastating to him; and shook me up too. I, and a group of his other friends, were determined to think of a way for him to stay, yet all pipe dreams. His father, a carpenter, thought he could do better back in their homeland. It all happened very quickly, and after he moved, I never heard from him again.

I also belonged to the Boy Scouts during this time, Troop 230 from Queens, and we met at St. Patrick's School where I attended elementary school. The boys were from all over the neighborhood and not necessarily associated with the school, some of other faiths, and others were public-school kids. The Scout Masters were a motley crew of men who just wanted to do something good for us, and I could not fault that; but they never seemed to have their hearts into it either.

We went on many camp outs. I hated them. All too often they were during winter when it was cold and the weather not very conducive to being outdoors. A couple of times it snowed, and we slept in what were called 'lean-too' structures with an open side. I once remember waking up with snow all over my face. We did have insulated sleeping bags to keep us warm in those conditions, but it was still miserable. There was one time, as a 'tenderfoot', when the older scouts had us go to another camp to get 'elbow grease'. A couple of us diligently went and came back with a plastic bag of jelly, thinking it was really elbow grease! We didn't know the difference.

At one camp in New Jersey, it snowed so hard that we were stranded. I had to be back in New York for a building dedication, so I and a couple of the other scouts hiked up to the road and tried to hitch a ride. No one stopped, until finally a hearse drove up and was heading for the city and offered to take us. The three of us hopped into the back of the hearse with our backpacks and sleeping bags and were snug as anything, quite thrilled to be riding where the casket typically rested in its final journey. To this day I will never forget the face on the toll-booth attendant when we stopped to pay our fare and our three heads bobbed up from the back of the hearse to look at him. We did make it back to the city in time!

I got very little out of the Boy Scouts and it got very little from me. One thing I did learn was that I absolutely did not enjoy camping, and all those knots I learned... who cares.

When I was about four years old my mother decided to provide day care for another child in the neighborhood whose parents were working while also giving me a companion. We were the same age and it turned out the boy who came to be with us daily was Ron Howard, the actor and director. His father would drop him off every morning and pick him up after work. Ron spent each day at our house, and we would play together, either inside or in our backyard. Our families became close, and our mothers socialized by going to theater productions together as both of Ron's parents were in acting and had access to tickets.

My mother was very fond of Ron, and she often was pleased that he especially enjoyed her home-made vegetable soup.

After some time, Ron and family moved on to Los Angeles to launch his career and to continue his parents' own careers.

Agents were telling them that the prospects in the acting industry were much better out west. I remember so well the last time I saw Ron in our Astoria house, in the entry hall, when his father, Rance, came to pick him up for the last time. I was sad. My mother and his mother, Jean, maintained a life-long correspondence and got together whenever circumstance allowed.

When I saw Ron on television, primarily the *Andy Griffith Show*, where he acted in the role of 'Opie', it was somewhat troubling to me. There was this kid I played with for all that time suddenly on TV, seeing him remotely on the screen as opposed to daily in my home. I didn't quite know what to make of it. My mom sensed it and sat me down one day and told me that Ron hadn't changed, that he still ate with forks and spoons, just like me.

When my parents lived in Florida, Ron was making the movie, *Cocoon*. His mother was there and went to my parent's home to visit, while another day they spent on the set watching the movie being made. My parents were so excited about the opportunity; and especially seeing all the stars in the movie.

In 2000 when both my mom and I were living in California, we arranged to visit Jean and Rance in Los Angeles. We were to have lunch together, but after we arrived Rance called me to say that Jean had been taken to the hospital. Arrangements were made for us to go visit her there, although she was in the ICU, and our visit would have to be limited. We arrived at the hospital and both Jean and my mother were just beaming with delight to see one another. Jean asked me if I was OK if she referred to me by the nickname she always knew me by, 'Tommy', and I said certainly.

It was such a good visit, and it went on for a couple of hours even though we had been limited to only half an hour. The nurses, who checked on Jean frequently, said that she was in such good spirits over seeing us that they did not want to limit her enjoyment. It was fascinating to listen to the two moms sharing their years of knowing one another while reminiscing about their time of going to New York performances along with other tidbits. I was so surprised when at a point Jean looked at me and told me that Ron had always considered me his, 'first best friend'. I guess I was honored, as we were so young. We said our goodbyes, and that was the last time we would see her as she passed away shortly thereafter.

After our visit we went to the Howard's house. Rance met us and said that Ron was at the studio and would like to see us, so we went. Universal Studios is a fantastic and amazing place, and we went directly to Ron's office, in one of the quaint backlot cottages. It was interesting to see the parking spaces marked for each of the stars, and Rance entertained us by imitating Jimmy Stewart as we drove down the street named for him. When we arrived, Ron had just returned from a meeting with Steven Spielberg.

After some time talking with Ron in his office, he offered to take us on a tour of the studio, and to show us his favorite places and sets. The four of us got into a golf cart and Ron drove us around. We had a very enjoyable tour and saw so much of what otherwise might not be seen on a tour, plus the commentary from Ron's perspective. What was fun was we passed a couple of open-air tour buses and the people on board went crazy when they spotted Ron, yelling and waving, cameras out. The interesting part was that they did not identify or call out to him as 'Ron', but rather 'Opie'. I smiled recalling my days of seeing him in that role on television.

He took us to the editing studio where he was putting the finishing touches on his movie, *How the Grinch Stole Christmas*. We sat in comfortable theater type seating and he asked us to critique various scenes, anything that stood out as not being quite right. I noticed Jim Carey's skin exposed slightly near the neck of his tee shirt in one frame, when it should be the green 'Grinch' color. We felt like 'studio people', and it was such a privileged treat.

We had a wonderful time connecting with the Howards and it was truly nice for my mother to see Jean again, especially before she passed away. The movie, by the way, was dedicated to Ron's mother, as she loved Christmas.

CHAPTER 25

Being Enlightened

It is amazing the things I have been exposed to over my lifetime thus far. One thing I attribute it to is my inherent adventurous nature, and my lust of travel. I have serious 'Wanderlust'. Travel is a great educator, especially if you open your mind to the diversity and cultures of our vast world, sometimes jarring and uneasy as was my trip to India. I understand completely why the Grand Tour was such an important part of a young man's education in eighteenth century England.

Over time my enlightenment of what can occur and how to handle it has come in various ways. One transpired in New Orleans when a group of us guys decided to go downtown to get coffee and beignets after working late in the architecture studio. It was past midnight, and it wasn't unusual we would do that, including a typical stop to a place called Picou's Donuts. In a particularly dangerous part of town, we'd go to get fresh donuts when they were first baked early in the morning. Another regular stop was a bar called Nick's, a local well-known watering hole. Nick's bar was a longstanding New Orleans institution. Located in a rather lack luster part of the city it was a run-down shed type building packed full of liquor boxes that became the seating. The bar was long, and they had crazy named drinks like the 'War Eagle', 'Naked Lady', and 'Between the Sheets'. For a special treat it's best to order those last two together. The drinks came in creamy or clear. One thing was certain in that they were colorful and very strong. The place would pack in the evening with longshoremen, debutants, college kids, and businessmen. It was a complete mix of the New Orleans citizenry. Nick was an incredible, generous man who actually paid for several college students' tuition.

Once I had too much to drink and Nick's wife, who was elderly yet spry and incredibly short, was mixing drinks. After one drink too many I looked up at the bar and all I could see was her chin and head resting on the bar. It was surreal.

So those were our late-night hangout places, but this one evening it was Café du Monde for the coffee and beignets. This night, however, was also different. We were driving back past Lafayette Square, windows down, when we heard screams. Out of the park came a young woman running frantically and hysterical. We stopped, opened the back door so she could get in and she kept saying, 'He's got a gun. He's going to kill me!'

We hightailed it out of there and I remember there were four of us in the car and she sat in back with two of us. I also recollect mascara running down her face with her tears.

Being the days before cell phones we tried to figure out where there was a police station, but nothing came to mind. We did not particularly pay much attention to those places. When we could not think of anything else, we drove immediately over to the Hyatt Hotel, not far away. Pulling up we asked the doorman for a security person and that person came and escorted her inside. We went inside too. After a bit of time the police did come, and the manager of the hotel asked us why we brought her there? Good question. It happened to be the first place we thought of that might be safe.

Later we got back to campus and when I got to my room the phone rang. It was the police chief. He said he would be calling each of us separately but wanted us to know that he was very proud of our heroism and helping the woman out of a bad situation. It seemed to be an attempted rape.

However, he also made it very clear, and warned me, to never do what we did again, by putting her in the car and taking off. He said that she very well could have claimed we were the perpetrators and tried to rape her. We would have been booked. That never occurred to me at all, but wise and enlightened advice. He did not exactly say what we should do in a case like that. Yet, we were at least happy we did what hopefully was a good deed.

I am not a huge believer in the paranormal; but have had some very interesting unexplainable events occur in my life. Those who do believe say that children perceive paranormal events more than adults. If that is so I do believe our house in Astoria was haunted. When we lived there, I frequently had dreams of lights being turned off when no one was around, and that scared me. More than once, I thought for certain that I woke up and saw the apparition of an old man with a white beard standing at the foot of my bed. The mechanical room gave me the creeps and I hated going into it and did not very often. And a large room downstairs, which was my playroom, had a certain eerie quiet and coldness to it. I am quite certain someone or something shoved me down the stairs one time knocking the wind out of me so I could not breathe while gasping for air.

All very odd, yet the one time I remember best was when my parents and I were sitting in the yard one very warm evening and my mother asked me to bring out some iced tea. I ran into the kitchen and to my astonishment the stove, a gas stove, raised up in the air and lifted out onto the middle of the floor. I stood there totally stunned. It then lifted upward and back into place. I got the tea and was scared to death, reluctant to tell my parents about it, and I don't think I ever did.

Some years later I got into reading about Hanz Holzer, a noted ghost hunter, on Halloween. The stories were seemingly very real. It was in Madison, Wisconsin and while I read my neighbor suddenly pounded on the back door. Three apartment buildings behind my house were on fire and burning rapidly. I grabbed our dog, and we ran across the street to a neighbor's house watching the inferno and the firefighters doing their best to extinguish it. They doused and saved my house as embers came down on it, and I never read another ghost story on Halloween again after that.

Probably the most profound paranormal event occurred during a visit Ed, my mother and I made to Kauai. We had rented a house near the ocean on a bay and the road leading to it was about a mile or more long to get to it from the main road. Ed and I went to get Thai food one evening and while driving home I slammed on the breaks abruptly while going down the road to the house. Before us on the road were two tall figures, a man and a woman, in old fashioned clothing walking down the road. If I hadn't slammed on the breaks immediately, I would have hit them. Looking at them for a second the most amazing thing occurred. They slowly raised up from the road in unison, floating up into the air and disappeared, vaporized! I looked at Ed sitting beside me, looking stunned, and asked if he had seen anything. He told me what he saw, and it was precisely the same thing. We did not tell my mother.

When we got back to the mainland, I decided to email the woman we rented the house from to ask if she ever heard of such occurrences, promising we were not drinking, smoking, or snorting anything when we saw what we did. She responded back, 'no, never', and she then felt frightened to drive down the road after hearing of it; but more so was concerned we had not written anything into the guest book about it. She did tell me of the natives' legend of dwarfs, the Menehune, who supposedly came down from the mountains, along with the myth that you should never go through a tree while carrying pork. I am not sure any of it related to our actual experience.

Our enlightenment came in the form of having some awareness of things beyond our understanding.

So, what was the one event that I believe was the enlightenment that forever changed the course of my life? It was brought about by Mrs. Robinson, my Kindergarten teacher at PS 112 in Astoria. The school stood one block away from my house and was the most convenient place for me to attend elementary school.

I do have memory of my Kindergarten days in that school. The rooms were an adjunct to the prime building and the windows large with lots of natural light. There were probably thirty of us in the class. What I remember of Mrs. Robinson was that she was tall, slender, and very much in command, yet kind. Every morning we started class by singing the National Anthem. I hated that, and often just mouthed the words. It was a fun class and obviously not very heavy on intensity or homework at that stage.

My mother often would walk down the block during the winter at the end of the class period, which I recall as being half days, to help Mrs. Robinson dress the kids into their snow suits and boots. They apparently bonded over this activity, and Mrs. Robinson must have appreciated the help.

There was some point when she took my mother aside and told her very directly to get me out of that school. From what I know she claimed I would have a much better education elsewhere than going through the NYC public school system. My parents heeded the advice for change and enrolled me in a Roman Catholic parochial school, St. Patrick's Elementary School, run by the Sisters of St. Joseph several blocks further away.

The affiliated parish Church had been founded around the mid-1800s and at the time I attended was predominately immigrant based, Irish and Italian.

Although in no way was St. Patrick's an elite private school of superior quality it certainly had a definite way of teaching and instilling discipline, ethics, values and responsibility in a child. The nuns, although in most cases elderly Irish immigrants themselves, were committed to excellent teaching and the work.

The priests of the parish were well intentioned, and very diligent in their work to guide parishioners. Some were a bit wackier than others. One priest would stand in the second-floor window of the school and toss coins into the school yard to watch the kids run, scramble and fight for a coin. Today, I question the sanity of such an action, but it did happen.

Father Variele was the Pastor, a very proper, dignified looking man of Italian descent. When his mother died all of us school children were required to attend her funeral in another parish.

A bit strange as none of us had ever met or seen the woman.

One priest who stood out was Father Faye, a younger priest with a lot of enthusiasm, and a newcomer. Being an altar-boy he asked a couple of us to show him around the parish to give him some insight from our perspective. A time that stood out was when he took the altar boys on a bus trip to Pennsylvania to see Amish country. While at the bus station one of the boys went to get a candy bar. He returned with a story about a 'black woman' he had encountered. Father Faye asked why he had to characterize her race, and why not just say a 'woman'. In retrospect that was very insightful for 1966, but that was just the type of man he was as a mentor.

There were, however, some very bizarre theories and teachings told to us kids by the nuns. One was that should we receive communion without going to confession and still be in sin, we would immediately explode when receiving the communion host, and would be responsible for killing everyone around when it happened.

The school had no gym, science classrooms, or cafeteria, and a meager library. The only outdoor space was an asphalt yard surrounded by a high, black wrought iron fence. The Church, Rectory and Convent were all part of the complex. Going to Mass regularly was expected. Many of the kids had never been outside of their neighborhood, or at the most the Borough of Queens. It was telling in that the teachers had cue cards to teach the first and second graders about animals by displaying pictures of them on the cards as most students had never seen these animals.

I will never forget the day my teacher asked me to take the class records to the principal's office. I was considered trustworthy, for whatever reason. On the staircase my curiosity got the better of me and since my name began with a 'B' I knew my record would be toward the top of the pile, so I took a quick look. What I saw shocked me. Boldly written and underlined in red it said 'One parent is Protestant. This child should be watched'. I never told anyone at the time, including my parents, because I did something bad by looking at it.

By becoming an altar boy, it taught me discipline, the value of ritual and organization, and patience. As was required I learned and memorized the entire Latin Mass and subsequently never used it since Vatican II at the time changed the rules to institute English, or any native language, as acceptable for Mass. That right there tested my patience.

Every week a piece of paper was placed in the rear Sacristy door with the altar-boy assignments for the week. I have no idea if it was random selection, or what, but you just did whatever was assigned to you. Weddings and funerals were included. I absolutely cringed and hated when I was selected to be 'Master' or head altar boy at a funeral. I dreaded it.

Along the way of my serving as an altar boy there were some mishaps.

As funerals did upset me, remembering my grandfather's, I usually did something unintentionally bad. I dropped the bible on the floor in front of the altar once, and my all-time favorite was when I accidentally went the wrong way during the incense procession around the casket and met the priest head on with the incense burner flying toward me. He gave me a rather stern look.

The one most memorable time, however, was Easter eve service!

I was chosen to carry the crucifix on a tall wooden pole to lead the procession around the interior of the church. It was an enormous honor. My mother, of course, was proud. I was a bit nervous and became increasingly so when I started down the aisle and all the elderly Italian and Irish women either bowed or genuflected as I passed. It felt sincerely weird. I stayed focused on looking ahead with this enormous pole above me.

Totally unexpected because I wasn't looking or paying attention above me, but I slammed the crucifix into a metal grillwork above one of the archway openings. It hit very hard and the metal hitting metal created a resounding reverberating clang throughout the interior of the church. I had whacked Jesus extremely hard into the grill! There was a sudden gasp all around me and the procession stopped cold. I looked over to my mother and she was hanging her head downward. So evenly and slowly I lowered the crucifix and tucked it under the grillwork and continued the procession, totally mortified. No one ever mentioned it, yet I am sure to be one step closer to being sent to hell for being so callous and not paying attention to the honor bestowed upon me.

It taught me stamina and fortitude. I was further enlightened.

My religious journey has been a rather uneven experience. As a 'half breed', with a Catholic and a Protestant parent, it started the irregular road, yet my Catholic elementary school existence seemed to set the course somewhat straight, perhaps. I still had questions and was totally disillusioned, more confused, by the Church's change of course through Vatican II. What seemed so absolute and required then had loosened. So many of the rules seemed to bend, and I recalled vividly in the fifth grade when I respectfully asked my teacher, a nun, if it was permissible for me to attend Mass on a Saturday, instead of Sunday, to go fishing with my grandfather. It was answered with a stern slap across the face for even suggesting such a thing. This is post-Vatican II and just before the Church said it was permissible to attend Church on a Saturday in lieu of Sunday! What type of impression does that leave on a child trying to figure all of it out?

The other bomb came when I went to marry a Protestant woman, one who grew up believing Catholics were bad people, and to have the ceremony in a Catholic Church in 1978. That was not to happen, forbidden; so then how about having a Catholic priest officiate elsewhere. Well, that led to all types of bad situations, including being totally rejected by the parish Catholic Church we attended weekly and contributed to in Connecticut.

Finally going to neighboring parishes of friends we were also met with hostility. One priest asked my wife-to-be the religious denomination she intended to bring up our children. She responded that we would teach them about both our faiths and let them decide in later life. The very pointed response from the priest was 'Oh, and I suppose you'll let them decide when they get bathed too?' It did not end well.

The strangest and most bizarre, however, was the Bishop of the Diocese got wind of our search and wrote a letter to all the parishes of our search and instructed that no priest should marry us. Some days later we got a call from the priest at the local Federal Corrections Institution who said he would agree to marry us in defiance; and yes, he would do it in a Protestant Church, and he did. We were forever grateful. He co-offici-ated with the minister in a Congregational Church. The only controversy was the giving of Communion that ultimately was decided to forgo over the differences in teachings. All went smoothly beyond that. Except, that several minutes before the ceremony the priest came to me with a paper that I needed to sign in which I would attest to raise our children Catholic. It was unbelievable, so tongue in cheek I signed the paper without much intent to observe it.

My own mother once surprised me with her own staunch Catholic upbringing and her reversal of thinking over the years. She was confronted in a phone call once with the son, Richard, of one of her best friends. She was calling her friend and the son answered. She asked how he was doing as she had known him since birth. He said fine, but that he wasn't Richard any longer, he was now Rachel. I was so amazed and proud of my mother as she apparently did not flinch and just went on to say how happy she was for HER, and undoubtedly important to Rachel to hear that too. Rachel went on in life living with her wife who she had married as a man and raising their child.

Subsequent discriminatory actions by the Catholic Church against gays, especially after I came out, made me reconsider my affiliation and I decided to convert to be Episcopalian. I did, and I went through instruction during 1988 and 1989 to be confirmed in Grace Cathedral, San Francisco, by the Bishop of Seattle in the latter year. It was a breadth of fresh air in my spiritual life and my partner and I became regular members of Trinity Episcopal Church in San Francisco attending every week with our children.

When my partner and I ended our relationship the priest from Trinity, Father Cromey, was very caring and supportive of us individually to be sure we were doing OK, and I sincerely appreciated it. Being two gay men raising children was rather unique at that time, but both children were also grown at that point.

It was at this time that I also learned something that totally turned me off to organized religion. Not to go into details to avoid pointing fingers needlessly but a friend showed me information about a person within the Episcopal Church not adhering to any of the tenants of the Church and making statement that 'all religious bend the rules.' That about did it for me, until I became involved with the St. Anthony Foundation and the Franciscans renewed my faith in the religious orders again.

Having the St. Anthony Foundation come into my life was quite remarkable. I was working on a building for them, the 'New Madonna' residence for indigent women when I came face to face with a remarkable San Francisco institution that is over fifty years old. Founded by Fr. Alfred Boeddeker to feed the poor and hungry he witnessed in San Francisco's poorest neighborhood, the Tenderloin, he established an organization that provides free food, health care, clothing, mental health support, technical skills, and rehab programs for those most in need. Learning about St. Francis and Franciscan values was awe inspiring, and frankly the basics how we all should live, regardless of religious affiliation. It is essentially about stewardship of the earth we inhabit and share.

What impressed me most is they survive solely on donations; and take no public monies. It is quite amazing and admirable, yet purposeful too. While working on the building I was asked if I wanted to join the Board of Directors, and I agreed. You may remember from an earlier chapter that I had an association with the friars back in New York City when my mother took me to Mass at St. Francis of Assisi for holy days in mid-town Manhattan. Joining the Board was inspirational, and the people involved, from many faiths, were truly dedicated to the cause. Several have now become lifelong friends.

The work done at the Foundation is simply miraculous. Several thousand meals a day are served with dignity, providing sustenance and hope. It also broke through some misconceptions, prejudices, of my own, believing the 'guests' were probably addicts, bums, or just lazy. Sitting and talking with them is a learning experience, as many, including families, seniors, and veterans, just cannot make ends meet, some with full time jobs. They are not as I would have imagined, at all.

Then I was elected Chair of the Board, a four-year tenure that challenged me in many ways. First the organization was imploding with all it was trying to do. The financial situation was tenuous, and they were strongly depending on bequests, which seemed onerous at best. The friars always said, 'God will provide', and you know God always did! We squeaked by, yet we had to make cuts to survive, and it was painful. I am happy to say that we did so with dignity and without giving up supporting the need. I always say I have the dubious distinction of being the Chair during the time we cut programs, laid-off staff, and even sold the farm! The organization had owned a large farm in Petaluma that was wonderful, but a 'cash cow' to operate as an organic farm.

Then suddenly the Executive Director, a religious person who had done wonders in his work, was elevated to a higher Provincial position. We had to develop a plan to find someone new, in little time. It all worked out.

I was also challenged being a gay man in a Catholic

organization, yet not only did I feel welcomed and safe, but I had a renewal of my faith that I had lost in anger years beforehand.

It has been quite the road through the world of organized religion and today I merely call myself 'spiritual'. Yet, I also experienced enlightenment.

One last interesting tidbit. When I visited Argentina, I attended Mass at the Cathedral in Buenos Aires. Against all the prescribed rules I received communion as I found it was within my spirit to do so. I recall looking into the face of the priest giving me communion and locking eyes. I wondered if he sensed my disloyalty, yet his look seemed kind and nurturing too. Many years later that priest would become Pope, Pope Francis, and when I saw his face on television, I recognized it immediately as the priest who gave me communion! And I did not explode or evaporate for doing something supposedly bad!

Pope Francis was the third Pope I saw in my life in person. The first was Pope Paul II when he visited the U.S. in the early 1960s, the first Pope to do so. His motorcade was to drive nearby my Catholic School, St. Patrick's; the nuns insisted we go and stand by the roadside to greet him. We waited hours and finally his motorcade came across the bridge where we were standing, near Queens Plaza. The bridge went over a railroad yard and we later found out there was a rumor of a bomb planted there. When the Pope passed it seemed as though all the girls screamed on top of their lungs lunging forward to wave, like he was a rock star. It was quite the spectacle, but we did see the Pope in an enclosed car.

The second Pope I saw was John Paul II when he visited New York City. His motorcade went by my office on West 40th Street and we ran downstairs to see him pass is his 'Popemobile', a big glass enclosure around him. Then I again saw him in Rome some years later as he greeted the crowds from the Vatican balcony. Again, I waited hours to that too.

So, Pope Francis is the third one I have seen.

In essence, none of this would have happened without the advice of my Kindergarten teacher, Mrs. Robinson, to my parents, in enlightenment to them and me, and I do believe in the long run I benefited. Mrs. Robinson's advice changed the course of my education and future.

I've often said that in retrospect it would have been possible in the overall working-class environment of Astoria that I could have ended up being a beer- guzzling delivery man without much education or insight, yet things in my life altered that.

Thank you, Mrs. Robinson.

Chapter 26

Out to sea

Being at sea is one of the joys of my life. The fresh sea air, the water, the waves, the movement of the ship, the beauty of being out in the middle of nowhere. All of it is fantastic. I have always been drawn to ships, and the sea. Most of my experiences have been enjoyable, but one in 2001 is not to be forgotten.

Ed and I were on a luxury cruise ship in Alaska during the 9/11 attacks and crisis. It was utterly surreal. We woke up to a beautiful day outside Sitka and had a 'room service' breakfast. Whales and dolphins were in the water just off our veranda. It was the one morning we did not turn on the TV to watch some news as we were preparing to go on shore.

When we got to the gangway to disembark a ship's crew member immediately pulled us into an office. In a heightened sense of anxiety, he wanted to know where we were from. We said California and he said, 'Oh good, not New York'. We were thrown off guard when he proceeded to tell us in a strained, emotional voice what was occurring in New York. Planes had hit the side of the two World Trade Center Towers and, 'they were DOWN', he said in a near frenzy, 'like totally destroyed, collapsed'. He continued, 'tens of thousands may be dead!' We stood in complete shock while taking it in.

It came to pass that terrorists had commandeered four US

planes that left early that morning from the East Coast, taking select ones with long flights and lots of fuel. The perpetrators broke into the cockpits and took over the planes crashing two of them into the twin towers. Another hit the Pentagon, and a fourth crashed in a field in Pennsylvania.

We exited the ship, and the somber atmosphere of Sitka was unmistakable. Even so far from New York you could feel uncertainty in the air. People walked around shell shocked and in total disbelief everywhere we looked. It all seemed silent.

Most bizarre was finding a stream with rapidly moving water, and thousands of dead salmon. It was nearly prophetic and symbolic of what was happening around us.

Getting back to the ship all passengers were asked to assemble on the upper deck. We were advised of the current state of affairs and told to return to our cabins as each cabin was going to be inspected. In the uncertain times there were precautions in the event a bomb may be on board. While waiting in our cabin the sense of insecurity became all too real. We had passed those passengers who wanted to leave and fly home immediately although all flights were grounded at that point.

The news channels were reeling with images of the Towers collapsing and thousands of people fleeing lower Manhattan on foot, most covered in debris and soot.

There was a knock on our cabin door and a crew member apologetically came in while we stood aside. It was nearly comical how disinterested and unprepared he was to check our cabin for a bomb. He moved some cushions, opened the closet, and gave us the 'all clear'.

Later that afternoon it was announced there would be a memorial service for those who had been killed. Ed was reluctant to go, but out of respect we did. The theater was packed with people, and it became disquieting for us as the emphasis was on a Christian service with singers emphasizing 'Jesus'. It seemed disrespectful as it was not respecting other faiths, or even those without faith.

The rest of the voyage, another three days, was sobering at best. No one was jovial or happy and passengers and crew just moved around somber and silent. People were concerned about how they would get home without any air travel. It was literally a mess.

When we docked in Seattle for a day the place was eerie. Ed and I visited the Titanic exhibit that was currently on display there, yet another disaster. It was a diversion, and everything just appeared to stand still.

When we finally disembarked in San Francisco I just recall getting home to our apartment on California Street and feeling somewhat secure again.

9/11 was a tremendously significant and earth-shattering event, for the world and in particular for the U.S. Many of us never felt so vulnerable. It was unimaginable and on the scale of Pearl Harbor. Thousands were indeed killed. In my mind it was inconceivable. I had this very sheltered idea that the U.S. had never been attacked and could never be attacked; well, that got dispelled rather quickly in this event.

In March 2002 I was invited to a reunion of all the people who had worked for my first firm, Russo and Sonder, in New York City. I discussed it with Ed, and he encouraged me to go, and unfortunately, he could not join me because of his 'tax season' underway. I had not been back to New York in twenty-two years and it was a bit emotional for me since I had totally written it off as a place I cared not to ever return. But, I went, and was so glad I did.

Taking a red eye overnight Jet Blue flight, I landed early at JFK airport and took the bus to Grand Central Station. I stayed at the Roosevelt Hotel directly next to it. My room was small and dark, but it did not matter because I was set on exploring Manhattan. So many memories flooded back as I explored the streets and places I remembered best.

The reunion was at an Upper East Side restaurant and was most delightful, especially seeing all these people I had worked with nearly a quarter century beforehand. We all seemed the same, just older.

I was only in New York for three days and got together on one day with my dear friend, John Lorenc. He provoked me to go visit the 9/11 site with him and I adamantly refused. I did not want to go. I had such vivid memories of those towers being built, and although they were indeed ugly, more so I remembered the times spent dining and having tea at Windows on The World, the magnificent restaurant on the top floor of one of the towers with designs by Warren Platner, an architect I greatly admired.

The restaurant was so popular when it first opened that when I visited with my wife we snuck through a back area and just sat down at an available table as though we had been shown there by the maître d. It worked. Another time I was taken for lunch by family friends of my wife who were visiting from Texas, sailing on the QE 2 from Florida to England with a stop in New York. We were invited with another young couple they knew from the New York area. It was a delightful lunch, the view unbelievable, as though you were flying above the city.

Yet, what I remember most was the young pompous sommelier who thought he had hooked some tourists. He described a very expensive wine he wanted to sell us and went on to describe it like 'rainbows rippling across the tongue'. He also noted that a previous guest had given him a glass of his own to enjoy. Well, our host did not buy the scam and ordered something else.

I had many memorable meals there, and now the place was gone, destroyed.

Another memory of the towers was taking my grandmother there to see them when first completed. She could not believe the size and scale, and recall she was born in that city in 1891. Standing at the base of one of the towers I had to hold her while she leaned herself back to look up to the top, in total astonishment.

John prevailed and took me to the ravaged site. It was indeed emotional. We passed the historic church nearby where people had posted photos of lost friends or relatives on the metal fence post that went on seemingly forever. Hundreds of images of lost people. It was six months after the disaster but when we got to the giant holes in the ground, with debris everywhere, the crews were still lifting bodies out of the rubble. Each body received a silent procession of work men carrying the carnage on gurneys and stretchers. As each was removed silence permeated the air as all work apparently stopped.

John walked me many blocks away to show me offices that were still closed, and it was apparent large amounts of ash were on interior furnishings. He pointed out inlets of storefronts where ash was still piled inches high in corners. It was alarming as we had walked a considerable distance from the disaster site and still saw that. The final and most profound thing was at a nearby fire station where the garage doors suddenly opened and along one long wall were hanging all types of mangled telephones the firefighters pulled out of the wreckage. They had made an art statement, a memorial, of what was left of this equipment.

I revisited the site in 2019, an entirely different experience. Now entirely recreated the area has become a living museum of the tragedy. Two large fountains make up the footprint of where the Towers stood flanked around the perimeter by the names of those who died. It is very somber and moving. The buildings around have been restored or newly built. There is a transportation terminal building designed by the architect, Santiago Calatrava, that is quite impressive.

The cruise at that fateful time was only one of many cruises Ed and I have taken together over the years. Being at sea is something both of us enjoy tremendously. There is nothing more refreshing to us than having a formal dinner in our tuxedos and venturing out on deck afterwards to stroll and feel the sea air while looking up at the sky full of stars. Being away from urban light the stars are certainly remarkable at sea in total darkness. That alone is worth a sea voyage.

Ed was the first person willing to take an ocean voyage with me, as it was a lifelong dream of mine. As a child and youth in New York I saw many grand ocean luxury liners leave the piers, primarily for Europe. There was The France, Queen Mary, Queen Elizabeth, The United States, and countless others lined up on the West side of Manhattan and in Brooklyn. We were invited to many bon-voyage parties on-board, and they were indeed memorable.

In those days there was such a flurry of activity at the pier before embarkation. Anyone could go on-board and there were flowers, carts of hors d'oeuvres and drinks moving about everywhere, into suites and private parties. Often the ships were divided by class, first, second and tourist. Near the time of departure, a staff member would walk the corridors with a chime and say, 'all ashore going ashore'. It was the signal to get moving and disembark if you weren't a passenger.

Crowds of people would line the pier for the ship's departure and the passengers would stand three deep at the edge of the decks to wave goodbye. Streamers would fly from the ship to land on the crowd below, and a band could always be heard playing. I recall seeing people crying as they waved, and I distinctly remember one teenage girl, with her family, crying as she waved from the deck to a young man standing next to me. It was quite the scene, but the entire thing was exciting and endearing. Eventually the whistle would blow loudly, and the ship would slowly and methodically leave the pier.

Once we went to see some acquaintances leave on The United States, bound for Europe. It was always a dress up event as that is what one did when seeing-off passengers, and my mother and a friend were photographed by the ship's photographer as they walked along the pier to the gangplank. The energy was noticeable, and everyone seemed in both high spirits and an excited mood. More than anything I wanted to explore every inch of the ship as luxury liners greatly interested me.

Another time, in 1979, we saw some people off on the newer Queen Elizabeth II, or QE2 as it was called. That time we were not allowed on the ship because security had changed the regulations. It was still exciting but not being able to go on board was frustrating too. As the ship pulled out into the

Hudson River it seemed majestic as it glided along with people waving from the decks.

While I was in New Orleans in the 1970s, and after I had returned from my Soviet Union trip, my friend, Richard, had a relative who was head of the Port. A Soviet Russian luxury liner, The Odessa, had come into port and he got us a waiver to go on board and have a tour. It was obvious the standard and quality were much different, much less, than the liners I saw in my youth. It seemed very stark and basic, little embellishment or luxury.

In retirement my parents took many cruises on liners, primarily to the Caribbean and South America, during the 1980s. They had endless stories of their adventures on-board with friends.

When Ed and I were first together it was finally my turn, in May 1999. He had been on liners before and said that we had to do the very best, first class, so we booked on a one class five-star luxury line, Crystal, from Lisbon to Rome for ten days on the Crystal Symphony. I was ecstatic. We spent some time in Germany and Lisbon before the cruise and when the ship arrived in port I could not wait to run down and see it. We boarded the next morning and I was like a kid in a candy shop. I wanted to explore every inch of the ship and did not waste a minute.

The cruise was everything I hoped for, and the lectures, cuisine, activities were top notch; plus, we saw Gibraltar and Tangiers from the ship, and visited ports in southern Spain, France and finally in Italy. We disembarked for a day in Villefranche on the French Riviera and went to Monte Carlo, Monaco one day and to Nice the second. The Grand Prix and the Cannes Film Festival were both happening simultaneously, and the place was full of visitors. Because the trains were so crowded, we ended up walking many miles on the beautiful Corniche from Nice back to the ship in Villefranche. We laughed as we were hoping to see the ship at every turn, but it took quite some time to see it. Another port we liked was Portofino, well worth a visit and quite idyllic.

After that trip I was sold on ocean travel and cruises. We booked another shortly after, on a new ship with Regent, another luxury line, and took a cruise to Alaska; the one I noted at the beginning of this chapter. What became apparent, and something I wondered over, was whether I'd get seasick. It turned out that neither Ed or I get seasick at all, and in fact like the rolling and rocking of the ship when the waves get going strong. We often book toward the front of the ship for that very reason, you can feel the movement more up there. Only once, in the North Atlantic, did it get so bad one night that things came crashing off the shelves.

Being interested in ship design I carefully study every detail of the ship's layout. We both favor sea days when there is no port-of-call as they are so carefree and enjoyable, and just really enjoy sitting in lounge chairs on the cabin verandah sipping wine and watching the water, seeing the endless horizon, and reading a good book from the ship's library. We are not much into the show productions; but attend occasionally. We do enjoy the lines that have strict dress codes, especially formal nights were tuxedos are required. We have both black and white tuxedo jackets, depending on whether it is a cold or warm weather route.

We have sailed on all the three Crystal ships, the Harmony, Symphony and Serenity. We have traveled the Mediterranean from Portugal to Turkey; the North Atlantic from England to New York visiting places like the Faroe Islands, Iceland, Greenland, and Newfoundland; San Francisco to Ft. Lauderdale through the Panama Canal; and the South Pacific from San Diego to Tahiti.

On one trip, a Mexico trip, it was the last voyage of the Harmony. On board was Mary Tyler Moore and her husband, as she was the 'godmother' of the ship having christened it. We got to meet her, and she was a delightful person. We once ran into her spontaneously when an elevator door opened and there she stood with her husband. What do you say to Mary Tyle Moore when not prepared? It was very cordial, and she later autographed a book for us. We have pictures of her doing so. One evening we were at a cocktail party in one of the lounges and a woman said to us that she heard Ms. Moore was on board but hadn't seen her anywhere. We discreetly pointed as Mary was standing right behind her.

We have been to Hawaii and back twice from San Francisco and that is the most relaxing excursion imaginable. Five days at sea, either way, with ports in Hawaii. The last trip we witnessed Kilauea Volcano erupting. It was a once in a lifetime event, and the ship appeared to get too close to the lava flow as the temperature of the water exceeded one hundred degrees and we immediately left the area.

On the main Island, Hawaii, we went ziplining. I doubt I would ever do it again. Fun at first there was a course of approximately eight different lengths and difficulty. The last was a hum dinger! When our van arrived at the last zipline there was total silence. In front of us was a platform, about three stories high, that we would need to climb up and jump off, going a thousand feet or so across a deep gorge and waterfall. You literally could not see the platform at the other side. I did jump and hated every minute of it. I am not one for jumping into the air with nothing but vastness beneath me.

After having flown several times in and out of Honolulu Airport we took the opportunity on our first cruise to the Islands to explore it. We found it to be a wonderful place, full of history and energy and enjoyed it immensely. We wondered why we had just past it up all the previous times there.

There was a moment when we were on the ocean headed for the South Pacific, when we had been at sea for several days, and I looked at a map and realized that there was no land within thousands of miles of us! That is a very daunting feeling. What was amazing was to see birds on deck on occasion. How could they be so far from shore? Well, we had a lecturer on board who explained that some birds can fly for a year away from land and that they had filtration systems within their systems to drink the ocean water and survive. Simply amazing. On one voyage Ed found what appeared to be a sickly bird resting under an outdoor staircase. Being 'St. Francis' who he emulates in his care of all animals big and small, including tiny spiders, he brought it pieces of bread to nurture it back to health. When we went back to check on its wellbeing, it was gone, hoping it got better and flew away.

We met many people, interesting people, on these voyages and some have become good friends. One woman we met on a trip was particularly fun, named merely 'EJ', her initials. We never learned her full name. At cocktail parties she regaled us with stories of places she visited over the years. She was very feisty and energetic. Having been on several world cruises, she noted that Africa was one of her favorite places. When we arrived in New York we saw her waiting at the curb for a vehicle, perhaps a taxi, with many pieces of fine luggage. We felt sorry for her just standing there, and were going to help her, either hail a cab or something to assist. As I started over to her a limousine pulled up and a driver got out to open the door for her and take her bags. A crew member told us that was her own car and chauffeur taking her back to her estate on the 'Main Line' in Pennsylvania.

A most memorable time we had on a ship in port, however, was going in and out of St. John's, Newfoundland. We were one of the first luxury liners to come into that port, and a maiden port call for our ship. You enter the port through a narrow passage of high cliffs, called 'The Battery'. It feels as though you can touch each landmass side, they are so close together. It is an awesome experience. We arrived right at dawn, and we noticed lots of flashes going off on the cliffs. We later learned it was from people taking pictures of the ship entering the port, even in the dark! The residents were so excited about our visit, and they had volunteers all through town in vests to help get us to interesting places to see. They were extremely hospitable. As I left the ship, I was even greeted by an enormous Newfoundlander dog, who wanted to lean against me, nearly knocking me over. But the most memorable time was when we were leaving the port and exiting through The Battery again to go out to sea. Hundreds, if not thousands. of people appeared at the top of the cliffs to wave goodbye. It was simply amazing; and reminded me of those earlier days sending a ship off to sea.

Our last voyage, for now anyway, was on the Queen Mary 2, from New York to Southampton. It is the last true ocean-going luxury liner, and it was phenomenal; just like I remember from years ago. One of the few ships remaining with a class system we stayed in a suite so had the privileges of certain areas of the ship off-bounds to others. We discovered the delight of a real English high tea; and we were in a private dining room where we had a table exclusively for ourselves the entire voyage; coming and going as we pleased. We typically had drinks in the upper-class lounge and the waiters even came to know and address us by our surnames after the first visit there. The ship is enormous and super elegant in every way imaginable.

We were fortunate as that voyage had very special passengers onboard, the last surviving US veterans of D-Day who were able to travel and return to Europe for the Seventy-Fifth Anniversary memorial events. All in their nineties they were a spirited, fun group who deserved lots of attention thanks to their everlasting bravery. One of them said that he had only two messages for today's world, amazing ones at that. First is that we should never go to war ever again, as no one ever really wins; and second to never hate your enemy for they are just honest people doing their duty just like they did.

There is something quite amazing about being out in the open ocean, seeing the beautiful stars at night, and especially arriving and departing from ports. You see a place in an entirely different way coming into a port as opposed to flying into an airport. Both are fascinating but watching the land slowly engulf you from the sea as it gets closer is mesmerizing. When Crystal ships leave port, they play two songs on the loud-speakers, 'It's A Wonderful World' by Louis Armstrong and a Norwegian classical piece, 'Out to Sea'. Both make the experience even nicer and more memorable.

Chapter 27

Barbara

Barbara Hoffman is my father's first cousin and my all-time hero. Living her life in Boston she created an enviable existence that revolved around activism. She was passionate about it and lived it to the max.

Barbara often said that she and I were alike, both of us an only child, and full of 'Wanderlust' or the need to discover, explore, learn, and find out about the far reaches of our world. She was right. A psychologist by profession Barbara was an inspiration to discuss personal issues and help resolve whatever the problem of the day. She was thoughtful, insightful, smart, compassionate, independent, and very caring. She was also a lesbian activist.

Barbara's father was my grandmother, Ollie's, brother. They lived in Deep River, Connecticut on a large property on Main Street. Barbara's father, my Uncle Yank (Frank) and her mother, Aunt Helen were endearing people who I loved greatly and knew well in my formidable years. I learned later through Barbara that she did not get along too well with her mother, and especially that she despised the small town of Deep River.

Her parents were exceedingly kind and a part of my life in that they visited often when we lived in Connecticut. I found them not only loving people but a lot of fun too. My Aunt Helen was born in Astoria, as was I and my father, but to a

Czech rather than a German family. She had a very unique and endearing accent.

Barbara looked very kindly on her many relatives and always sent a box of chocolates to her aunts for the holidays. Although a somewhat tumultuous relationship with her mother, from her discussions with me, she did hold her parents near to her heart, yet did not let them totally into her life either.

In a private moment I asked Barbara how she had told her parents that she is a lesbian. She made it clear she never told them and doubted they would have ever understood. The entire concept of homosexuality she said was in her estimation beyond their comprehension, although she said ironically, they regularly played cards with a male couple; she was sure were gay. Then I also asked her if she ever suspected I might be gay when she visited us in my early years. She said absolutely she did and even mentioned it to her partner at the time, although once I got heterosexually married, and she did attend my wedding, she just assumed she had been wrong. Well, she was not.

She did have a partner, an African American woman, in the 1960s; but truthfully, although I supposedly met her, I do not remember her at all. Barbara said that she and her partner visited my family in Connecticut in my teenage years, most likely with her parents. What I do remember of the visit was her very lively recollection of renovating her Boston townhouse, especially a humorous account of laying the bricks for a patio in the back yard not knowing what they were doing.

Barbara was indeed very sophisticated compared to many of our family members, yet she never looked down or dismissed anyone. I respected and admired that so very much in her.

She was always clear and articulate with her thoughts.

Although her Deep River upbringing seemed limiting Barbara was ambitious. She was never going to let anything stop her from achieving her goals, very much like myself. When she first applied to Radcliffe, they apparently turned her down merely from being from Deep River, a small backwater town of no consequence as she told it. She attended another college for a year to prove her value and academic abilities and was accepted to Radcliffe on her second try. It meant a great deal to her, and she achieved getting to Cambridge and Boston.

Barbara also attended Boston College and eventually got her PhD in Psychology much to the pride of her parents. She settled in the South End of Boston and bought some town-houses where she lived for over fifty years. At the time she bought those houses, in tandem, in the 1960s that part of Boston was predominantly black and bordered on nearby Roxbury, considered the 'ghetto' of Boston. The dynamic was what drew her to this part of town, and she loved and cherished it, and lamented the eventual gentrification.

For a tall, blond Caucasian woman with pronounced staunchly New England features Barbara in turn was embraced by the community. Barbara was gradually exerting her lesbian activism and during this time compiled a huge list of nearly every gay and lesbian person in Massachusetts. Her goal was to coalesce the gay community and push for civil rights. Her home became a center of that activist endeavor. Many stories have been told of her having dozens of people over to lick and stamp envelops to send out to everyone she could get interested in the cause of gay rights. She became a political powerhouse in her own right, although somewhat introverted and quiet in her own way, there was no stopping her.

Once the *Boston Globe* ran an article about the prejudice among black people toward gays and lesbians. Barbara was incensed. She immediately contacted the press to right the wrong, and the specific example she gave was of the black lesbian couple living in the neighborhood. One of those women had died and the black community supported and rallied around the grieving partner. Barbara made it clear that blacks were not prejudice toward gay people.

One of her greatest achievements, of many, was to take on Harvard University. For this I will be forever proud of her. Harvard did not have inclusive language for gays and lesbians in their policies, especially the protections, and Barbara made specific note of it. When Harvard said that it was not necessary since it was not an issue there, she took it head on. She and a group of friends took a survey of every person on campus, from students to staff to administrators, to even the janitors. Turned out that the survey showed that Harvard had a great need for such inclusive language. She presented the results to the President and Provost of the University, and inclusive language was added.

To all of you Harvard folks out there, you can thank Barbara Hoffman.

Barbara's family name was Rodamer. Hoffman came from her marriage to a Harvard man in 1954, the year I was born. I do know from an obituary that he was accomplished man of the arts and from a 'Main Line' Philadelphia family. The details of that marriage, which did not last long, are shrouded in history. Barbara spoke very little about it except I had heard that he was a musician. I acquired her wedding album after she passed away and I look at those photos with great amazement.

Of course, she was to attend my own wedding in 1978, under similar circumstances. We both eventually 'came out'. The only time she ever spoke of her husband to me was when he tried to get her to agree to an annulment some years later so that he could marry in the Catholic Church. Barbara who was a complete atheist, or at least believed in a 'goddess', despised the Catholic Church in general, so she apparently ignored the request. Yet she did rant about it to me.

What I know of Barbara is her warmth, kindness, determination, and passion for her beliefs. I think she may have seen a bit of herself in me. Friends told me when I came 'out' to her in a letter, around 1990, she was elated. It created a very strong bond between us, and she took me under her wing, and we synergized together in many wonderful ways.

When I married Ed, in 2008, she said she had called our remaining family members to tell them the news! I asked if she told them I had married a man. She screeched out 'OF COURSE, my dear'. She did not attend our wedding as she informed me the trip would be too arduous for her as she was aging. She did gave us lots of advice. Barbara did not believe in marriage, although advocated for same-sex marriage, and said, 'if someone is crazy enough to want to get married then they should at least have the right to get married.'.

Visiting Barbara was always a treat. We stayed with her once in her second-floor guest room. Her master suite was one floor above. She insisted not to be woken before noon. We always just snuck downstairs and made ourselves comfortable. Her kitchen was enormous and the hub of her house. Her 'perch' was at a table and chairs placed at the windows looking into her rear yard and beyond. During that stay I made a video and have some wonderful footage of the various things we did together, including Barbara preparing a true New England style lobster dinner for us. Our first night she made an incredibly tasty miso soup and the next day we watched her diligently canning tomatoes, for her Bloody Mary's, as she chortled. So carefully and diligently she used a food mill to crush out the tomato juice. Barbara was indeed an excellent cook and was widely known among her Boston friends for her holiday feasts.

Barbara also gave an exceptional tour of LGBTQ+ sights in Boston and outlying areas. If you ever were fortunate to have her private insider tour it was most rewarding.

She helped found the Wooster Street Garden, a neighborhood collaborative of vegetable plots located behind her house on land that used to be a mews for stables back in the days of horse drawn carriages. She loved that garden and maintained three individual plots herself. The participants also sold their produce and canned goods at the local farmer's market. Barbara was never without fresh produce she had gown herself.

The aforementioned lobster dinner was quite momentous, and one of our fond memories of our time with her. She wanted to know where we would like to visit and we said Salem and Newburyport, so off we went on a drive. Barbara's driving was that of a true Bostonian and resident of Massachusetts. You merely buried your head in your hands while she drove to avoid seeing her very precarious maneuvers over the road. It was a fun trip nonetheless and we stopped by the beach at one point for a short stroll and photos.

Two very poignant stories emerged from this trip. I told both at her memorial service while giving a eulogy.

First, we were walking in Newburyport going to Barbara's

favorite historic ice cream parlor. At an intersection while waiting for the light to change an extremely handsome man rode by us on a bicycle. Both Ed and I discreetly ogled the man passing us as Barbara belted out 'Eyes FORWARD, boys!'. Did we laugh. Nothing escaped Barbara.

Second, on our drive back she stopped at her favorite seafood-lobster depot to pick up three huge succulent lobsters for our dinner. She picked each out from the tank, still alive of course, and I was surprised to see one nip the finger of the vendor even though the claws had rubber bands over them. He put them in a paper bag and off we trundled back to Boston.

Near her house Barbara careened the car to park in the middle of the street, something many people do there, and told Ed to run into a small grocery store and get a bag of potato chips and a bottle of Chardonnay. She made it apparent we needed both to go with lobster. While he was crossing the street, Barbara yelled out the window, 'get TWO bottles!'. Ed got the stuff and off to her street we went to park. She had a typical parking space in the alley behind her townhouse but decided to park across from the front of her house this time.

The entire way back to Boston I heard the lobsters stirring in the bag and trying to get out. I lifted the bag off the floor and started walking across the street when the bag broke with the lobsters falling to the street; and beginning to run off in every direction. I was literally stunned and yelled out, 'just let them go!'. In total disgust Barbara reached down and put each one in her arms and looked at me and said, 'You gay boys are ALL alike.' 'Scaredy cats!'. Again, we laughed.

We ate the lobsters by candlelight, along with the potato chips and Chardonnay and she was right about the pairing, as she carefully told us how to disassemble the lobster to eat it correctly. Such a treat, and it made for a very memorable day and meal.

Another time when we visited there was a gubernatorial race underway. I cannot tell you the year or any details other than Barbara was very well known in Democratic politics. As we passed the State House, and she was telling us about the many times she 'wore out the sidewalk' in silent protests, she saw the Democratic candidate giving a press conference on the front steps. She grabbed my arm and tugged me up the stairs, pass the press and walked me right up to the candidate in the middle of his speaking. He looked surprisingly as he was interrupted, and said, 'Well, hello Barbara'. She looked at him and in return said, 'Hello. I want you to meet my GAY cousin from California and his partner'. There we were with press cameras rolling and reporters all around. We shook hands, and Barbara turned us around and back down the stairs we went. I made Ed agree that we would not watch the news that night.

Barbara always said I was the 'historian' in the family, always researching our past and the family. I think she was indifferent.

For the holidays she would send us some of her wonderful homemade jams and preserves made primarily from the Wooster Street Garden. What I loved was her quince jam, and she always did her best to include a jar.

When she retired, she spent nearly six months traveling through remote parts of Indonesia and Australia. She told me once she cried when she saw Indonesian money with a woman's image on it.

The morning her attorney, a good friend of hers, called me to tell me she had passed away I was at my office, and I cried hearing the news. I would miss her many lengthy phone messages in her low gravelly voice sounding like Bette Davis with a cocktail in one hand and a cigarette in the other. She loved both, especially while gossiping or talking of the politics of the day.

The last winter of her life in Boston was tough. It snowed beyond anyone's previous recollection, and she was very much confined to her townhouse. I believe it took a toll, as did her friends. She was already suffering from health problems, installed an automated chair to take her up the narrow stairs from floor to floor, and was gradually diminishing.

Barbara left the bulk of her estate to the ACLU and a women's shelter in her neighborhood which pleased me greatly. Her papers were donated to a LGBTQ+ archive which I appreciated a great deal. Her friends did an awesome task of closing out her estate. I had the distinct honor of inheriting the contents of her townhouse. When I went through it there were only some family pieces that I remembered most that I had sent to me, mainly of sentimental value. I also received all her many certificates and declarations she was awarded from various entities, including the State of Massachusetts and the City of Boston. Her friends were most helpful in arranging everything, including her memorial service near her home, and I sincerely appreciated their help.

Her friend, the attorney, told me a cute story about Barbara. He once went to visit her to have her sign some papers and brought along a young attorney from his firm with him. When they walked into Barbara's kitchen, her social hub, she was sitting at a table cleaning a gun, undoubtedly with a cigarette hanging from her mouth. The gun belonged to her father. Her friend told me that the young attorney tried to be polite but was utterly terrified seeing it, yet her friend knew that Barbara was harmless. I was also offered that gun after she passed; but declined.

Her friends and I scattered her ashes in a secret place she loved dearly. She had made her mark on Boston and was a trailblazer for LGBTQ+ rights. Her photo is in a book, *Improper Bostonians*, about the history of LGBTQ+ folks in Boston, and she was proud to have been included, as she should be.

CHAPTER 28

My life at Tulane

Before I left for college at Tulane University in New Orleans my mother took me aside and said she was going to teach me how to sew a button and how to cook a simple meal. She made it quite clear that every man should know how to do those basic things and not run around trying to find some girl on campus to do it for him.

My dad on the other hand subsequently took me aside and talked with me about using protection should I have sex.

Both were rather awkward conversations, but rather necessary for a young man heading out on his own in his new world of independence.

I left for Tulane from our home in Connecticut in August 1977. The week before my parents and I diligently watched the PBS Masterpiece Theater series, *The Eight Wives of Henry VIII*. The last episode was the night before I left. It felt weird to know after eighteen years I would be leaving the fold and heading out. No doubt it was difficult for my parents, too, as I was an only child.

Yet I was packed and ready to go!

My education to this point was interesting, and perhaps somewhat lopsided. Going to elementary school in a socially economically challenged neighborhood to a more affluent high school environment presented challenges, yet I overcame them.

It did make me stronger in character. College was my step into independence and adulthood. It was a time I looked forward to with great anticipation.

When I started high school in Connecticut, I came with a heavy New York accent. A couple of the teachers made fun of me in class imitating the way I said 'fur' instead of 'for'. An English teacher told me I would never succeed if I did not lose the accent, and I trained myself to diminish it, although I can readily go back into it again, if I try.

In high school I knew I wanted to be an architect and geared my entire coursework around it. Somewhere along the way I got misinformed into believing that taking German and Calculus was required. I did both, but neither proved beneficial. I was good at both Physics and Trigonometry which were helpful. Chemistry was a complete bore, and could have been helpful, but between disliking my teacher and not liking it much I pretty much sat it out. Besides, they had placed me in Advanced Chemistry which was even more painful.

In the late 1960s and early 1970s major corporations were moving out of New York City and establishing themselves in the suburbs. During high school, the AIA in Westchester was reaching out to those students interested in architecture to promote the profession. They held a conference at the new IBM headquarters in Armonk, NY to talk about being an architect, and of course, I attended.

My introduction to Tulane happened months before I went, shortly after I was accepted, and about six months before I first attended. First, I was invited to a Tulane event at the Biltmore Hotel next to Grand Central Station in New York. I took the train from Brewster NY and arrived a bit early so went to the men's room to freshen up to look my best. What I remember best was the attendant who came to brush off my suit jacket as I washed my hands, and hand me a towel. Something I wasn't too accustomed to; yet seemed very adult like. The event, a luncheon, was in the ballroom and there were speeches and presentations on the school. Bea Field, a noteworthy Newcomb-Tulane alum spoke. I met several administration folks, including Dean Turner from the School of Architecture who would be the head of the department during my time there.

Next, I was invited to a party at a home in Connecticut on Long Island Sound owned by the publisher of *Architectural Record*. His son was in the School of Architecture, and they were recruiting for a fraternity. Oddly, the fraternity was only for students from Connecticut. I was 'rushed' but never joined as it was not of interest to me to be in a fraternity.

Getting on a college campus was overwhelming at first; and figuring out where classes were became the first hurdle, yet it all seemed to fall into place. I enjoyed the amenities, the libraries, student center, and a variety of places to hang out or study. The warmth of the weather in New Orleans was such a nice break from the winters of the Northeast, although during my first final exam, Architectural History, I was sitting in a window seat of the architecture library and looked out the window and saw it was snowing. Snowing on palm trees and large southern oaks with Spanish moss!

When I arrived in 1972 the architecture department was moving into a new building, Richardson Hall, that had been the medical school. The building was under renovation and not quite ready to occupy so I spent my first semester in the older existing school building, Stanley Thomas Hall, the engineering building. We were located up in the garret and although a somewhat interesting space with the sloped ceiling height it was temporary quarters. The August and September spent up there, without air conditioning, was brutal at best. The heat was unbelievable, and we would bring towels to put under our elbows and arms to catch the sweat from going on our drawings.

During one of our first meetings the Dean brought the First Year together to tell us about our education, the outlook for what to expect, and our further lives as budding architects. It was a frightful, daunting speech. He outlined as architects that we should expect to work holidays, have minimal vacations, and not make much money. The hours in school and in the studio lab would be intense. We lost about fifteen people that first week, either leaving or transferring to another major. The committed diehards stayed, and I was one of them.

One of my first professors was a kindly young man, Michael Dobbins. He was a confirmed communist, and whenever his wife and child visited, they seemed untidy, as if they were living a hippie-like lifestyle. He was a good professor, caring, and I learned a lot; but very different from what I experienced from teachers in suburban Connecticut.

After that first semester in the Stanley Thomas building, the Richardson Memorial building was ready enough for us to move into it. The classroom studios were spacious and bright with huge windows to the outside. It was such a pleasant change and there was air conditioning too. We each got a desk-drafting table with a locker in which to store our drafting equipment.

There were still some medical experiments in jars with

formaldehyde in the basement of Richardson Memorial. That was truly disgusting, and we did everything to avoid going down there, but it did provide some workspaces too.

At one point I was placed down there in a room with two of my friends, Jose and Greg. It was nice because we could lock the room without putting our things away, and it did have a large window we could open to the Quad, so you could walk through it as if it were a door to the outside; but it was still the basement. One evening we encountered one of New Orleans ubiquitous cockroaches walking across the floor. It was the biggest one I had ever seen and before long all three of us were standing on our desks to avoid encountering it. Eventually it went behind a file cabinet and I slammed the cabinet several times against the wall to kill it. Relieved, we all got down off the desks when suddenly the roach appeared again! I had to eventually spray glue it to the floor, and that did kill it. We disposed of it immediately. We had hoped it wasn't from a time of living around those medical experiments.

As an architecture major, we had little say in classes and electives. Everything was prescribed and regulated. Usually, we were allowed only one elective per semester. It was also a five-year course work for a professional degree, a Bachelor of Architecture, over the usual four year.

The times were tumultuous, too, as it was near the end of the Vietnam War. There had been riots on campus just a year or so before my attending. My first year I came very close to being drafted if the war had not ended. One day a bunch of guys sat listening to the radio as the draft pick called out the sequence of draft allocations based on birthday. I turned out to be number eight, which was an absolute first draft. There were no exemptions at that time. My father, a staunch WWII vet who had been awarded a bronze medal for 'liberating the Philippines', shocked me by claiming I wouldn't go and that we'd move to Canada if needed. Fortunately, the war did end.

Having fellow students from all around the country, and internationally too, was great and helped expand my education. I appreciated the various points of view, and the varied backgrounds. My friends came from all over the United States with a common goal of getting a university degree and launching into life.

I also encountered things I had not been accustomed to from my own upbringing. One time while sitting in a dorm room with friends one of the guys called his father and demanded a new car, as others had them. I could not imagine what my father would have done, probably hung up the phone on me. It was also interesting to see some students who came from small cities, or more rural areas, whose parents were quite affluent in their areas and thought they were the tip of the heap only to learn that there were many others far more affluent than themselves, if that counted at all.

Newcomb College was the women's division of Tulane and strangely some classes, like freshman English, were segregated. A true vestige of a past era. Tulane men were permitted to take courses at Newcomb, and I had some very good ones, including Modern Art, and even Social Dance. Newcomb had an unfortunate reputation of being a 'finishing school' for southern women, and some did seem to be there to find a husband… in medicine, law, business, but certainly not in architecture.

The other, more disturbing, thing for me was the remnants of the 'Jim Crow' South that still existed. Tulane was essentially a white institution at that time. Most of the black people on campus were janitors and service workers. They were the people who cleaned our dorm rooms, emptied the trash, and were expected to stand aside if one of us came down the hall. It really bothered me and friends from the South informed me that it was greatly diminished compared to what had existed just a few years previous.

There were two black students in my class.

The classes and education were indeed rigorous, yet I enjoyed all of it. There were challenges to meet schedules and deadlines, and the jury reviews were intense.

There was one guy in my class who was really a character, fun and sincere. He had been adopted and whenever his parents came into town there would be a feast at some major culinary restaurant as his father knew and owned restaurants. Everyone tried to get on the guest list for those dinners as they were quite memorable, from the Caribbean Room at the Pontchartrain Hotel to Brennan's.

Tulane football is a big deal, as is football in the South in general. Tulane Stadium was an enormous edifice that held nearly 50,000 people and was also the site for the yearly 'Sugar Bowl'. The stadium would pack for games, and I went to most as students got to go for free, and it was entertainment. When the crowd roared you could hear it for blocks away. The team has never been that good, but I was in attendance when they won their nemesis team, LSU, for the first time in twenty-five years. The crowd went wild, stormed the field, and pulled down the goal posts. A lot of drinking went on too.

One yearly special event was the Beaux Arts Ball. It was not only for architecture students, but for all the architects and artists in New Orleans. It was a big deal and as is customary in many New Orleans events, a costume event based on a theme. Held in a downtown ballroom the Ball was always well attended and had a lot of hype generated around it. As students we were always looking forward to it and I believe I attended every year I was at Tulane.

One year the theme of the Ball was 'It's Against the Law'. I dressed as a gangster and my date dressed as my 'maul'. A friend went as my sidekick bodyguard with his 'slum raised girlfriend' chewing gun, dressed to match the part. We were thrown out of the Royal Orleans Hotel when we stopped by before the Ball to use the bathroom as security thought the girls looked like prostitutes, and I was a bit too Mafia like for their lobby. The costumes and creativity of the participants at the Ball were amazing and my favorite was the group who came as 'Assault and Battery' wearing costumes that had some in salt-shaker costumes and others in costumes resembling batteries.

At another Ball people came dressed as buildings and amazingly the Curtis and Davis architectural firm came in segments of their newly designed Superdome, and at times brought the segments together to form the complete stadium.

I once went as a 'Tacky Tourist' wearing gaudy tourist garb, Hawaiian shirt and shorts, flip flops and holding a potted aloe plant. In another year, and I do not remember the theme, we needed particularly flashy costumes. A girl in my class had an aunt, Aunt Gaunky, who lived nearby and had a Mardi Gras room in her large house, where costumes were stored from past celebrations. We went and four of us picked out outrageous outfits to borrow. Wearing them to the Ball we were chastised for looking too much like Mardi Gras, a sacred time for New Orleanians, when it was not that event at all. Oh well, we had fun, nonetheless.

I enjoyed my education immensely and very much appreciated the professors. Some were far more severe than others. One infamous professor, James Lamantia, was widely known for being extremely tough. He would do things like just rip drawings off a table in front of a student and tear them up in front of everyone. He was a definite force, yet a very good teacher, especially if he saw some talent in a student. He had very little patience for incompetence.

Interestingly I got to know him socially once I had graduated and moved to New York City, where he had a second residence. He was quite different from his hard-nosed self of my school years; and was much more fun and sociable once you broke past the veneer.

Thesis year, the fifth year, was probably the most intense, and I still sometimes have dreams and nightmares over it. I had a few friends drop out then, which seemed so unfortunate to be so close to the goal, the Degree, yet the stress at times loomed larger. Most finished in a following year.

Graduation did not come too soon for me. I was ready to move on into a career. I lamented to my thesis director, Georgia Bizios, that I feared not being hired and she smiled in a reassuring manner and told me I should not worry about it, I'd find one. And I did, back in New York.

In 2004 I received a Master of Architecture degree, and the following year Katrina devastated the city. For decades everyone knew a storm of that magnitude was inevitable, yet no one really prepared for it. In 2007 I joined the Dean's

Advisory Board of the Tulane School of Architecture that brought me back semi-annually for the next ten years. It was a great experience and reconnected me to the University and the School.

The Board was made up of not only former architecture graduates but notable residents of the city with a penchant for architecture, the essence of New Orleans. One of these people was the Grammy award winning musician, Irvin Mayfield. I was once invited to his home for a concert, and it was one of my most remarkable times. Being there with just a small group of people and hearing him play the horn with accompaniment was awesome. I sat near the fireplace with his Grammy on the mantle.

One of my favorite memories of this time was quite impromptu. I had to attend a Board meeting and unfortunately Ed could not join me on this trip, so I invited my childhood friend, Andrea, from Mexico to come stay with me. She did and unbeknownst to us it was the time for the French Quarter Festival in New Orleans. We had a blast spending our days wandering the Quarter to listen to a plethora of free music by extraordinary musicians. It was truly magical. The energy of the city was alive at its best.

Post Hurricane Katrina New Orleans had transformed itself after the catastrophe, and the city was reinvented in new and exciting ways. New entrepreneurship, and in particular young people looking for opportunity, infused a whole new energy into the culture of the city. A multitude of new restaurants came on board and the city took a new direction in facing a future. Unlike its stagnant ways of the past, it seemed to be gaining vitality and momentum in very positive ways. It was exciting to see it. Renting a 'shotgun' house each Board meeting Ed and I revisited the city enough to have an appreciation of its wonderful existence and grew to love it dearly, as we do Tulane as well.

CHAPTER 29

Work!

I started working at age fifteen, yes, essentially child labor; but it meant making money. One of my priorities in life, so all is good.

My mother having been a governess was very particular about good manners, and to my benefit taught me appropriate behavior in work and social environments. She was careful to teach me about proper table manners, and to never use words like 'yeah' or 'nah' but always 'yes' and 'no', and even the correct side to walk with a woman on the sidewalk, always curb street side for the man. Her bit of training actually paid off well in my work life as it gave me good skills for socializing.

In elementary school I thought I might like to be an attorney, but quickly pushed that aside; and then I focused my interest on becoming a career diplomat. I always was good at diplomacy; and having just visited the United Nations I was intrigued, yet that was short lived as I did not even know how to approach it. Being an architect came to me around age twelve or thirteen and I stuck with it. If one thing stands out in my personality, if I am determined I will pursue it wholeheartedly.

When I was in high school, and during some of my summers thereafter, I worked at my father's place, Alpex Corporation. My job was in the blueprint room, called 'Document Control', where five others worked, primarily middle-aged women. There was a lot of good times, and drama too. It was run by a man named, Seymour Sinuk. Once during a college summer break, we went out together for bowling after work. I left early when they all went out to a bar afterwards. The day after no one was talking to anyone else. I soon found out that one woman claimed that another had hit on her boyfriend, which was totally untrue as I later realized she was probably a lesbian.

There was a kindly older gentleman who worked there, Walter O'Connor. He took me under his wing, and it seemed odd he'd be working in the blueprint room with a bunch of middle-aged women. Always nattily dressed and very proper he appeared somewhat of an English gentleman, although he was very American, although also an Anglophile. I learned that in his career he had been a journalist for the *New York Times*. He told me that after many years he got burned out and needed to leave his writing profession, and just do something that did not require much thinking. He seemed content. Yet, it did make me ponder getting burned out in a professional career and ending up there. Always talking with me about history, and his particular interest in English history, I knew more about the year 1066, and its significance in British history, than probably a scholar in that area after listening to him. His wife had died a few years before and it was obviously he adored her, although they had no children together. She was from a British family that owned drug stores in the UK.

My interest in architecture fascinated him and he was behind it one hundred percent, encouraging me the entire time. For some unapparent reason he had a love for Calgary and went every year for a vacation. During my time working with him at Alpex he set me up corresponding with a well-established architect in Palm Springs he knew, after learning I did not have any architect connections. That architect was a tremendous mentor, and I could kick myself as I did not save his letters, or do I remember his name.

At one point, Walter spoke with my father privately about his serious desire to adopt me and send me to the university in Calgary for my education, which he offered to pay entirely. My father thought that was rather bizarre and it never went very far.

I also worked at another place I got through an employment agency, called Topstone Rubber. I worked in the stock room. They made Halloween masks with fake blood and other seemingly scary items. I was quite good at organizing and keeping pace with product, so the stock room was a good fit for me. Whenever the truckers came in to pick up or deliver a pallet of materials they would inevitably ask if I could give them some condoms. They always seemed to think that Topstone Rubber made condoms, not Halloween masks. They usually left embarrassed and disappointed after I explained.

There were a few times when a worker was out sick, and they would put me on the production line. I had never heard of 'piece work' as a form of payment, but that is what they did; and I learned the premise very quickly. There were a group of older women who worked the assembly line, and they were very motherly and protective of me. They knew that I generally worked the stock room. All of them would say to me, 'get that college education or you'll end up in a place like this'. It was truly revealing to me; and made an impression.

I spoke previously of my summer work at National Semiconductor in another chapter, but I had one other summer job that lasted one day. Looking for work I went to a temp agency, and they put me to work at a factory that made lipstick container tubes. My job was to take dozens of these containers and put them into an oven for the containers to bake. The oven was at some ungodly temperature of heat. I found I could accidentally get locked inside as you needed to push a cart all the way into it. That was not worth the risk, at minimum wage.

I also worked briefly at an ice cream parlor, and they said I could eat whatever I wanted but that wore off after a couple days of gorging. They smiled having seen it done before. The cheesecakes they also served came from a special bakery in New York City, and the owner always gave me the leftovers to bring home as they got new ones every day. My mother asked me to stop after a week of proudly carting them home for us to eat.

There were also a couple of diversified jobs in high school, one teaching a boy in our neighborhood mathematics being recommended by our school, and another being a babysitter for a boy and girl for a nearby family when the parents went out for the evening.

One gig I did during my college years was to design a rectory for the Russian Orthodox Church in Danbury, Connecticut. It was basically a single-family house to be built next to the church, and I did it totally pro bono to get the experience. It was built, blessed by the bishop and the one priest of the parish lived there. Right after it was built one of the icons in the church started to tear, and it was thought to be a miracle. People came flocking for miles to witness it. One afternoon, when no one was there, my friend, Paul, who was a member of the Church and Mary Ruth, my friend visiting from New York, went to see for ourselves. They had placed a couple of cotton swaps at the base of the icon to catch the tears. There was an obvious liquid stain from the one eye of the icon image down to the cotton, but no signs of actual tears. Paul, the joker he is, claimed that the only reason it cried was because of my rectory design. Nice guy. Nothing really came of it, and eventually the entire miracle went to the waste side without any proof, or true reality.

I was well versed in the various types of work, mainly menial jobs, out there when I finally settled down to find a real job after college.

New York City, New York

After I got my architecture degree in New Orleans, I returned to New York to find my first professional job. I returned to New York for a variety of reasons. It was my true 'home', my parents were nearby in Connecticut, my girlfriend who'd soon be my fiancé was there, and I always wanted to live in Manhattan as an adult. Being it was 1977 the times were not good, especially for architects.

There was very little work available anywhere, and New York was particularly in a doldrum. But being young and determined nothing was going to hinder me, so I launched forward in my search. Back in those days before the internet I merely ripped the pages of the architectural firms out of the yellow pages and started my pursuit of gainful employment through cold call visits. I had tried sending out resumes but never got responses.

My days walking from firm to firm with my resume and portfolio were exhausting. What I soon found was a total lack of any available employment, especially for a rookie just out of school. Firms were down to skeleton staff and those that typically had one hundred or more architects were down to a handful. The most telling thing to me was walking into a high-rise office building, having a doorman see me with my portfolio of drawings under my arm, and shaking his head that I was wasting my time. I did have some interesting encounters along the way. I got on the elevator to go to the office of Johnson Burgee in the Seagram Building, only to get on the elevator with Burgee. There was no advantage in that impromptu opportunity as he seemed totally disinterested in chatting. Then I went to offices of Paul Rudolph, who was in his prime at that time, and when the elevator door opened, he was sitting right there working in front of me. Looking up at me I was totally speechless. We spoke some, and he interviewed me on the spot and told me not to expect much. I never heard from him again. More on that later.

Along the way I found again and again architects who showed me some pity referred me to one person, and one person alone, for possible employment; a Mrs. Wallack at New York State Unemployment. She only handled architects and engineers and I was told that if she liked a person, and saw talent, that person would get a job, and if she did not, you should consider leaving town immediately. I could not believe one person held such power, but I heard stories of prospective candidates bringing her flowers, candy, anything to gain her approval.

I made an appointment with Mrs. Wallack for the following week and contemplated my fate.

In the meantime, I kept visiting architectural firms. People were friendly enough, but it was still looking dire. On the Friday of my second week of continual visits I was exhausted, plus it was steaming hot weather. At around 5pm on that Friday

I got on the elevator at 111 West 57th Street, the Steinway Building, whose major tenant was Metropolitan Life Insurance, to visit a firm on the top floor. I threw my portfolio down on the floor rather worn out and disgusted, sweating profusely from the heat, and thought after this one I would call it a day. A man got on the elevator and asked where I was going. I told him while he pressed the elevator button for me. I thanked him and then went into a rant about how I was probably wasting my time, it is ridiculous, and the firm I was going to undoubtedly had no work.

The man looked at me and smiled, getting off at the same floor. He was one of the head architects at the firm. Inviting me into the conference room he interviewed me, and then called in a couple of other people to talk with me as well. Shaking my hand, he gave me no assurances and wished me well. The firm was Russo + Sonder and they primarily did hospital design work.

Early the next week was my appointment with Mrs. Wallack. I did everything to look my best and as confident and professional as possible. She sat in an open room with many other employees of New York State Unemployment and just had a chair for guests next to her desk. We talked, I told her my story, and she asked me lots of questions. I could not get any read if she was feeling positive, or not. But it became obvious she was no novice at this game. She reviewed my resume and portfolio, tugged over her Rolodex, and began making phone calls while I sat there. It was most impressive as she knew many of the top architects of the day by first name; and spoke immediately to them when she called. She had connections, and with each made an inquiry while I sat attentively. I felt somewhat reassured that she was trying, so I inevitably made a favorable impression.

Not having much success, she looked at me and reiterated the fact I knew, getting work was difficult at that time. She had one last person to call, a man called Seymour Herbst. He wanted to interview me, and she set up an appointment for that Friday. A sole practitioner in Riverdale, The Bronx, I was not totally enamored with being out of Manhattan, but I was not going to turn anything down either. What I did know was that Mrs. Wallack did in fact like me, which was wonderful, and she wished me well asking me to confirm the outcome of my interview.

I continued looking and visiting firms but that Friday I went to the Riverdale offices of Mr. Herbst. A kindly, middle-aged gentleman, quite professional, he interviewed me for some time. I was lucky in that I had a full set of working drawings that I had done in school. To be productive at that time it was really what was needed most at my level of career; and gave me an edge over others at my stage. He decided to hire me, although with the caveat that I 'would be somewhat of a burden' in that he would have to do a lot of mentoring to get me up to speed. My salary would be slightly over five thousand dollars, a year. He had three other 'draftsmen' and I would be the junior. Nonetheless I was ecstatic to get work, any work.

Right after learning I had accepted the job my parents sat me down and told me to always remember that someone gave me my first opportunity, and that later in life when I would be hopefully successful to hand that down to someone just coming up in their career as well.

I never forgot that wisdom.

That weekend I began looking around the Riverdale area for an apartment. Deciding to wait a week before taking anything I at least found what types of places were available. On Monday I started, introduced to everyone, and got a desk at the back of the office. Seymour handed me two specification manuals and told me to compare them and note any differences. I diligently buried myself into the task.

Tuesday morning when I was finishing up the task a person I had not met came into the office and went directly into Seymour's office, closing the door. One by one each of us were called in, and I was last. It was Seymour's son and he had come to tell us that Seymour had passed away during the night and the firm was now defunct. I sat in the chair totally speechless, and he reassured me that I could use Seymour's name on my resume and to use his contact information. Well, one day of employment. Although not much good I did appreciate the thoughtful gesture.

Wednesday was Seymour's funeral on the Upper West Side, and I went. The other draftsmen were very complimentary of my attending, but I only thought it respectful and the right thing to do. I felt as though I was grieving as much for Seymour as was his family. After the service there was a reception line to extend our condolences to the family. Going up to his wife, who I obviously had never met, I was at a loss as to what to say. Still a young woman she had lost her husband, and it was just sad. I introduced myself and told her who I was. She smiled and said that Seymour had talked about me and was very happy to have taken me on. That was very nice to hear, and then she took my hand and said, 'you know, we have both lost a very good friend'. I was so moved by that, a widow with a sudden and perhaps totally unexpected death to be so well poised and kind. I will never forget her, or her words.

I drove back to Connecticut after the service, mournful the entire way, and yet happy I had not got an apartment. I could only think of calling Mrs. Wallack. When I pulled up in the driveway my mother was gesturing me to come to the phone immediately, someone was calling me from New York. It was the man I met on the elevator, at Russo + Sonder; his name was Cal, and he was offering me a job, and at a much higher salary than Seymour had offered me. I was beside myself with elation and became a believer in miracles at that point. Of course, I accepted; and I promptly called Mrs. Wallack to tell her the news and to thank her. She had heard of Seymour's passing and was glad it worked out for me, especially since I got the new job on my own.

That Monday I started at Russo + Sonder. The environment was much different than Seymour's office, many more architects and a real hierarchy of staff. Joe Russo and Rick Sonder owned and ran the firm; and were very well known in the hospital design world. They had even designed hospital room furniture, the Kangaroo Chair. The firm was quite active, unlike many in the city, and had a good amount of work. I would do junior design work and drafting, starting on a hospital renovation and addition for Booth Memorial Hospital in Queens, a Salvation Army institution.

The firm was made up of a variety of folks, all very interesting in their own way. One architect was the heir to an olive oil fortune and lived on Park Avenue, and another a gay man who had been in Andy Warhol movies. There was an outgoing man from Bulgaria, and a Jewish woman from Romania whose family had fled their country leaving everything behind; both fun yet very different. Another man was from India and complained constantly to me about how American architects are treated so poorly when in India he would have a car and driver given to him. An architect from France had a wife who was a major fashion model, and was always posing when I saw her, as though ready for a photo shoot. There were also architects with seemingly very unique and distinguished names. One woman's name was Xiena, which I found very exotic. Another asked me if I played polo. At one point I thought they may have hired me for my last name mistaking it for Brunning, a prominent New York family who owned a major blueprint enterprise. Nonetheless it was a really great group of people, and I learned a lot.

Another man who worked at the firm, about my age, was also an accomplished portrait painter, John Kelley. I commissioned him to paint a nearly full-size oil portrait of my wife and myself for our first anniversary. He was quite an extraordinary realist portrait artist, and it was an honor for him to do so.

I worked primarily with Cal Kiffner, the man who hired me, and a woman who had recently made Associate, Jean Mah. Both were truly good people and great mentors.

There were a couple of other recent hires, my age, one of whom, Bob Miller, became a good friend. His parents lived in a penthouse on the Upper East Side, and they had a summer house in the same town where my parents lived in Connecticut. Bob and I did a lot of things together after work. Another classmate of mine from Tulane also came to work there, Robbie, whose family had vineyards and a winery in Virginia.

Robbie had started work with Paul Rudolph but left after

a few months as the pay was so low that he could not sustain himself and his wife living in New York. They were renting a condo on the Upper West Side, owned by our professor James Lamantia, barely making rent with the salary Rudolph paid him. That was not uncommon in the high-profile offices of well-known architects where people were willing to work for little money, sometimes less than minimum wage, just to get the firm's name on their resume. I was very happy I did not end up working for Rudolph.

I had gone to see Robbie at Rudolph's office before he left it and I was surprised to find a secured glass enclosure when I arrived, unlike when I had been there looking for work. Robbie told me that Rudolph had to add it for security protection since having an open office from the elevator proved unwise. Rudolph had placed his wallet on his desk, and it had been taken, most likely by a delivery person.

There were others from Tulane who ended up in New York too, a couple pursuing advanced degrees at Columbia. Although older than myself my favorite Tulane, Newcomb College, grad at Russo + Sonder was the Marketing Director, Frances Shaw. A wonderfully kind and motivated person she watched over me as well; frequently reminded me in her southern accent that I really did not ever live in New Orleans, I had just been there on a 'sojourn'. She was a native. Very much involved in New York's art scene she owned a beautiful brownstone house on the premier street of the Park Slope neighborhood of Brooklyn. Her parties were legendary.

We worked hard and sometimes put in overtime to meet deadlines, and I very much enjoyed the vibe. I worked primarily on the Booth Memorial Hospital project and the Hospital for Joint Diseases, a new hospital on the Lower East Side. Joe and Rick were very generous with their employees, and when I was getting married the firm gave me a big party, lots of gifts, and Joe gave a very eloquent and fun speech about the foibles of marrying an architect.

Right after starting in the firm and getting to do some design work, I was invited to a team meeting in Joe's office. I was so excited to be participating in a meeting with the Partner of the firm reviewing the work. Sitting next to him on a bench I felt rather proud and important being there when suddenly he started to twitch, sometimes violently. I became concerned. Then he stood and started shouting profanities. I was shocked and quite worried our team was failing to meet his expectations. No one else seemed overly anxious. He told us all to get up and go to the window to admire the beauty of the city and said that we should replicate it. The meeting then ended abruptly. Later that day I learned his outburst had nothing to do with our work, but rather his affliction, Tourette's Syndrome. There would be times on the crowded elevator when he would have a sudden burst of fits. I wondered how the client's reacted to sudden outbursts, and I also wished someone had told me in advance of that first meeting.

My first Christmas was very exciting, and there were lots of parties and events to attend. New York was totally decked out for the holidays, and it was great fun to just wander the streets looking at decorations and experiencing the liveliness. This was also a time when major manufacturers of architectural products needed to unload some cash reserves, probably for tax purposes, so they would give big bashes and invite their constituents. I got invited to one at the ballroom of the Plaza

Hotel. It was quite elaborate with a wonderful dinner, fine wines, and lots of liquor. I was placed at a table with twelve people, all strangers to one another, yet the conversation was spirited. Six of the women alternately seated amongst the men were very elegant, poised and quite fashionable. After about fifteen minutes into the conversation, I became aware that they were high-priced prostitutes providing the 'entertainment' for the evening. I had wondered why they were so overtly friendly. I did not partake in their additional, seemingly available services, beyond chatting.

About this time, I started taking my architectural licensing exams too. Four full days of exams culminated in a twelve-hour design component where the candidate needed to design a building from a set program given to you when you arrived for the exam. Mine turned out to be a fire station. What I remember most was exiting the subway with my drafting table and tee square, plus drafting tools, with twelve hundred other candidates doing the same thing. An amazing sight to behold. It was given at the New York Coliseum that once stood on Columbus Circle, now the Time Warner building. Most disconcerting was when some of the people around me who were taking the test would just get up and leave halfway through it. Miraculously I passed the design test the first time.

After a year and a half, which then seemed like a long time, I was getting restless and decided that in the long run I was not cut out for the hospital design world as the projects seem to just move at a terribly slow pace. I started looking for new work; and went back to Mrs. Wallack who welcomed me back. I think she still felt sorry for me over Seymour's untimely demise. She grabbed her Rolodex again and started making calls; this time I had some experience under my belt, with a good firm. After a couple of calls she landed me an interview with a firm, Leibowitz, Bodova & Assocs., Architects, on West 40th Street, just off of 5th Avenue and across from Bryant Park.

I wasn't very good at quitting and leaving Russo + Sonder and was very nervous about it, including giving up such a good first opportunity. Although I would be paid more at Leibowitz, Bodova & Assocs., and doing more varied work, from transportation to retail buildings, I was still somewhat loyal. I completely botched telling the bosses at Russo + Sonder I was quitting and at one point one looked at me and said, 'well are you quitting, or not?'. I did.

Some twenty plus years later, in 2002, there was a reunion of all past Russo + Sonder employees after the firm had closed and both Joe and Rick retired. I flew out from California to attend and it was the first time I had been back in New York since 1980. It was all bittersweet, and really none of us had changed except for aging.

Leibowitz, Bodova & Assocs. was located on the 16th floor, the top floor, of an older classic building and we had a sweeping view above the trees of Bryant Park, which was quite seedy in those days, the late 1970s. I saw several drug deals there and it was not a place you would linger or spend much time. There were also cardboard set-ups for 'three-card monte' gambling on the sidewalks. It is so different now.

Leibowitz, Bodova & Assocs. was a somewhat smaller firm than Russo + Sonder with approximately twenty people employed there. Rene was a very feisty and fun receptionist who sat at the center of all the activity. She kept us all in line. Again, there were an interesting group of architects and I enjoyed all of them. One man, a Thai immigrant, was very amusing. He came back once from a lunch break to ask Rene about lesbians, as he did not know what they were. Rene laughed and gave him an explanation and then asked why he wanted to know. He had heard something on 42nd Street, that was quite gritty at that time, about them and was curious.

There was another man, younger, who had moved from France. He disappeared after taking a vacation and no one could reach him. Finally, one day the elevator door opened, and he walked in totally drenched from the rain and insisted on talking with the bosses. He claimed it was impossible to work in the drafting area and needed a special place set up for him in the men's room. That obviously was not going to happen. He went over to one of the oversized windows, opened it, and sat on the ledge rocking back and forth. The police had to be called to get him to come down. About a week later an older woman came to the office and said she was his wife and they had just been married during his vacation, and she had come to pick up his things. I heard several similar stories of architects just 'cracking under pressure'. One had gotten on a plane to Africa, unbeknownst to his family, and was not heard from again.

I worked on many airport buildings, primarily at JFK and Newark airports. There was a variety of building types, functions, and it was fascinating, including the cargo buildings that were vast structures with offices included. KLM Royal Dutch Airlines was a major client, and it was my task to get them theater tickets whenever they came into town. I must have purchased dozens of tickets to *A Chorus Line* with David Leibowitz's credit card. I also had to deliver them to the client's hotel. One time I ran into a guy making quite a spectacle of himself in the lobby of a midtown hotel. It was the new pop singer, Boy George. It was simply amazing the little side jobs that the junior designer got to do at a firm.

I also worked on a few retail centers, new shopping malls. They were more routine than the airport buildings; yet learning the 'ins and outs' of retail was interesting. There was a string of fast-food establishments I worked on, and even airport car rental places. I learned the specifics about tire slashers; and even got to detail them. Again, junior designers didn't often get glamorous tasks.

The big design project of my time there was a new $400 million Transportation Center for Atlantic City. Atlantic City was revived by new casinos and entertainment venues, so they needed the infrastructure. The new Center would have a large train station, bus terminal, hotel, office building and a 'DPM', a 'Downtown People Mover', a monorail that could bring people from the Center to the various casino and hotels. It was a very exciting opportunity for a young, inspiring architect.

I worked directly under the head designer, a Chinese architect, who was quite creative but also overly dramatic. He brought diva status to a whole new level. We did enjoy working together and I just rode the wave of his ups and downs. The plans were quite spectacular, and it looked like a contemporary glass palace. I was also charged with overseeing the building of an enormous scale model of the complex. A professional model maker was employed, and I spent a couple of late nights supervising and helping to build the various pieces. Seeing how a building was created in miniature by professionals was an education by itself.

New York always had unexpected, impromptu happenings. *Saturday Night Live*, the comedy TV show, was taking off and one of the skits included a little figure made of puddy called 'Mr. Bill'. 'Mr. Bill' was always being squished, or some equally awful thing happened to him. One day when leaving the office someone on the corner of W. 40th and Sixth Avenue yelled out in the rush hour crowd, 'Oh no! MR. BILL!', a typical saying from the TV skit, as if the character was being run over in the traffic. Suddenly dozens of people started yelling the same thing. It was utterly bizarre and truly a New York moment.

I spent nearly two years at Leibowitz, Bodova & Assocs. quitting to move to Wisconsin. No one could quite believe I was doing that, but nonetheless that was the plan.

Madison, Wisconsin

It seems unlikely that an architect would head off to Madison from New York in search of work unless there was a connection there, or a very specific reason. I came for my wife to attend UW for her doctoral degree and to be in a new environment, and I considered it a challenge. There are only a handful of firms in Madison, and most are sole practitioners or two and three person operations doing single family houses, renovations, and commercial remodels. At the time there were probably five firms of over twenty employees. I knew nothing about any of them, and my resume with a $400 million Transportation Center in my portfolio was not going to do much good.

In surprisingly little time, however, I found work with a larger firm, HSR Associates, that was headquartered out of LaCrosse, Wisconsin, a sleepy mid-sized city to the north on the Mississippi River. As I recall there were probably seventy total employees across both offices with about twenty in Madison itself. One of the Partners was from New York, and I think may have taken a liking to me, partly for that reason. After I was hired, he mentioned to me that they rarely see employment candidates arrive for an interview in a three-piece suit. It made an impression.

HSR did a considerable amount of housing and had a major client doing affordable, non-profit type housing throughout Wisconsin for low-income individuals, both families and seniors. I was put in charge of some smaller housing projects to start, some no bigger than ten to fifteen apartments on an acre of land. Much of it was senior housing in small towns. I enjoyed the work and it enabled me to move up in my experience, including dealing directly with the clients.

I worked with one county housing authority that took me out to very rural areas, designing apartment buildings for small towns and communities that maybe had no more than five hundred people living there. The sites were challenging, but that made it more fun. Most were one story wood stick framed buildings. I did my best to add some design flare to each, even under tight budgetary constraints. This work also allowed me to present to housing authorities and local planning boards, if one existed, and building departments. The most shocking thing was having the head of a county housing authority tell me that they needed to be careful where they advertised the new housing. He said if they advertised too close to Milwaukee, then they might not like the 'type' of people they could get applying for the housing. I was aghast at such blatant discrimination and prejudice, and reluctantly did not respond to the comment as I knew it wrong and probably illegal.

I also was given another commission that absolutely delighted me, especially from my ancestral background- designing a new brewhouse for the G. Heileman Brewing Company. They made the famous label 'Old Style' beer. Located in LaCrosse, it would be the largest brewhouse ever built in the United States, and the best perk was being given the ability to visit all the brewery companies in Milwaukee to research other operations. Already knowing some basics of the brewery operation helped, but I learned a great deal more during my tours.

The site, next to the existing brewery, was directly on the Mississippi River. The brewing equipment was to be manu-factured in England and transported over by ship. I worked directly with the representatives of that British company who also participated in looking over the development of the plans. Most interesting was that the walls of the brewhouse had to be designed to fall out of the building in case of an explosion, as that did happen on occasion. An accident like that severely injured my great-grandfather decades before in New York City leaving him with burns over most of his body. The exploding walls were a safety measure to let the blast escape and not internalize it, mitigating some of the impact. It required careful detailing.

The brewhouse was successfully built and it was exciting to see the brewing equipment lifted from the ship on the Mississippi into the side of the building, then enclosed within it.

LaCrosse had an annual Oktoberfest that is well known in those parts. My wife and I went and spent a couple of days to join in the celebrations. The Oktoberfest event was dazzling in scale with nearly the entire city attending and included music by the Guy Lombardo band. There were more polkas, beer and sausage than one can ever imagine. This area gets very cold in the winter, so this is a nice way of saying goodbye to Fall for the upcoming start of that season.

Many riverside cities along the Upper Mississippi are caught in a time warp and have changed little over many decades, yet the locals don't lack enthusiasm and energy. LaCrosse is very much like that.

The HSR Partner, Greg, from New York took a liking to me and we did things socially with he and his wife. The first year in our new Wisconsin home he offered to take us to a Christmas tree farm with his family to cut down a tree. I had never done that before and was quite enthused, a city kid out cutting down a tree! We arrived at the farm, and I immediately grabbed a saw and cut down the first eight-foot spruce I saw, which was met with a roar of laughter. Examining the trunk, it was extremely crooked, and the Partner told me that looking at the trunk first was rather important because I would have one heck of time getting it to stand upright in a stand. I did my best when I got home, with a bit of a list.

Winters in Wisconsin were brutal, far worse than anything I experienced on the East Coast. Many days below freezing, or even below zero were relentless. There were warnings against having any exposed skin when outside for fear of frostbite. A couple of times in severe snowstorms I walked the five miles to work and back just to be able to keep working. I looked like Dr. Zhivago in Siberia, with snow and icicles on me, as I trudged through the snow.

While at HSR I also got involved in a blend of several

interesting project types as a Project Architect. We were engaged by the city to do a study for a downtown firehouse that included the feasibility of renovating the existing historic one; and evaluating three other sites. I did designs and analysis for all four locations, and it was decided to build a new building on a new site. I learned a great deal about fire stations and the operations, especially it being the design problem for my licensure exam in New York when I knew relatively little.

Then I got to design a couple of ice cream parlors at mall locations in Madison and Kissimmee, Florida. Those were fun, mainly interior design exercises. Also, concurrent with that I worked with the head designer for the firm to do a new retail-commercial building for Madison's prime retail corridor, State Street. It was quasi post-modernist, but in a restrained and dignified way. Lastly, I got to work on my first mixed use development, Capitol Square, a two block, double high-rise in downtown Madison. That was an incredible opportunity to design a mix of housing, both senior and family, with commercial, including a major supermarket and hardware store and an allocation for parking. As they were all-brick buildings, I learned the economy and value of using 'king-size' brick, including patterning it.

About that time, 1982, the US economy was beginning to wane, and times were getting tough for architects. There was a series of layoffs at HSR, and the firm dropped from a total of around seventy-five people to under twenty. The Madison office was decimated, and I remember only five of us remained, including two Partners and a Receptionist. Our major housing client had stopped doing work, and we were down to bare bones. I remember so well going into work one day and putting my nose to the drafting table working on details like crazy to look busy. That afternoon, September 1, the boss taped me on the shoulder, took me into the conference room and let me go too. I was devastated. I had a wife in a doctoral program and a mortgage and a lot to worry over.

I was out of work for nearly four months, and it drove me insane. Not that I was bored, just concerned about keeping our heads above expenses. I did everything to find a way to make money, including baking dozens of cookies to see if I could sell them. Turned out to be a loser for profit. Any home-based industry would work, but it isn't easy developing a profitable one. I also further immersed myself into neighborhood and city politics with the extra time I had on my hands.

Never forgetting the stress of that period, as it has lasted with me a long time, I hated to ever have a layoff for those who worked for me later. I remembered the pain all too well.

Finding another job prospect in Madison was not going to be easy, but after the holidays, in late January, I got a call from a firm, Strang Partners, inviting me to an interview. I jumped right on it, and they hired me. It was such a relief, and after working there for a couple of months they gave me a good-sized raise as they thought I was worth more than I had asked originally. It felt like I found a really great place to work, I liked the culture and the people. The firm employed about twenty-five people. Fortunately, they had an active book of work, so that was great.

One of my first projects was to design a retail center for a neighboring town, Middleton. I really enjoyed it and it gave me a great opportunity to express my design abilities. The client and partners were quite pleased. Rick Parfrey, the nephew of the Alan Strang who founded the firm in 1935, was the head Partner and President of the firm. Strang, himself, was well known for his 'International- Style' house designs. Rick and I shared a good synergy in working together, and he became both a mentor and a good friend. Working with him was amazing and he gave me a lot of latitude. He was a perfectionist in many ways, and he detected my diligence to create good design.

Strang also had an engineering division, so we did our own electrical and HVAC design as well as architecture. Another partner was a structural engineer as well, as was one at HSR. The people were great to work with and we had fun as well as doing some really good design work. One of Rick's design philosophies, that I fondly admire, is that the foundation walls of a building should extend out from the base to plant it firmly in the ground, an illusion of rising from the ground. Most often it tapered out from the earth, and it looked very effective.

I worked on a variety of projects, mainly in the Madison area. One major renovation and addition I did was for an existing commercial insurance company building on Lake Monona, 'Lake Terrace'. Purchased by a prominent real estate developer for his corporate offices, and for other rental spaces, it was a prize of a project. Rick and I worked closely on it, including doing all the interior design for the offices. At one point into the final working drawings for construction the client called us in and gave us one million dollars to acquire art for his space. It was exciting to participate at that level, and off we went to buy art. One special piece was commissioned for outside the front entrance, a sculpture by internationally known artist, Tony DeLap from Los Angeles. He created a beautiful piece entitled, *Levitation of an Enchanted Princess*, that you walked under and into the main entrance.

We got a commission to renovate a large State office building for the DMV and I was put in charge. Part of the program was to make the spaces more efficient, so we employed the newly launched systems furniture approach. I spent a lot of time in Chicago at the Merchandise Mart learning about systems furniture and employed some very interesting space conserving layouts using it. The State also wanted me to use CAD software, which had only come out in the mid-1980s. Moving from drafting board and tee square was daunting, but it was part of our contract. Since Strang did not have the technology, the State had me trained at their own computers. Supposedly our fee would be lower because using CAD was considered a time savings, and in the long run it was, especially for making revisions.

I was also tasked with designing a new cafeteria for them, and that was a fun design exercise, including separating the smoking from non-smoking areas effectively. When the construction documents were completed and going out to bid, I had a phone call from someone at the State unknown to me. He was very irritated and upset and insisted I come present the design to him. I learned that he was supposed to be included on the design review team but was overlooked by the State, and he was furious. I reviewed the design with him, and he insisted on major design changes; I suspected to be obstinate over his omission. We were paid another fee to completely revise the design to his liking, and frankly the modified design did not match in character what was originally done, unfortunately. It seemed watered down to me. But it taught me a further lesson in politics.

At this point in my career, I also went to a few fun junkets from various manufacturers. A carpet manufacturer sent me to Williamsburg, Virginia to see their factory and to spend some days, at their expense, at historic Williamsburg and the 'Grand Illumination'. Steelcase flew me on their private jet to Grand Rapids, Michigan to their factory and touring that town. A stone quarry, Valders, flew me by private plane to their quarry in northern Wisconsin to see the quarry and sent me back with a slab of stone for a tabletop.

Oddly enough we started getting a lot of work for attorneys, including the State Bar Association, so I became Project Architect for those too. My own attorney hired the firm to do a major renovation of a building on Capitol Square and Rick and I did a design competition with each other, ending up combining elements of each. I did some interior projects for law offices, build-outs, and worked directly with the partners. A couple of them had me design their new houses on the side. I recall negotiating one agreement with an attorney for a new house for his family while sitting in his car. It was all very rewarding and enjoyable.

A non-profit housing client of ours wanted to enter a design competition for a surplus parcel of land in my own neighborhood. I was put on that and did a cutting-edge design incorporating a very unique property allocation that also included moving four old abandoned, yet historic, mansions from an adjacent neighborhood on to the site, and rehabbing them for apartments. We won the competition, but unfortunately the project was never built.

It was also at this point that I recognized the friendly competition among firms. With limited work every firm was out to get a share, so strength of design, character, trust, and value were all important keys to success. I also saw the importance of working in a firm with a good employee culture. With that we had some amazing and very creative parties, including holiday ones that will stand out in my memory forever.

Probably the best break in my career was one day when Rick came to my desk and placed several client folders on it, telling me he and his wife were going on vacation to France and I was in charge while he was gone. I felt overwhelmed with the challenge, but I was not going to refuse it. I knew very well that Rick did not do that sort of thing lightly, including putting he and the firm at risk. He also asked that I watch after his house while they were gone, something his partners found amazing. I worked myself relentlessly to do a good job and got some valuable experience at being in charge while working directly with clients on a variety of projects. Rick came back quite pleased.

I came to work on churches of various denominations while at Strang. They were everything from Mormon temples to Methodist churches. With the Mormons I had to sign an affidavit that I would not smoke, consume alcohol or caffeine while working on the projects. They had specific building products we had to employ, including a grey brick.

The one major church I did for a Madison Methodist congregation had a retired partner from Strang on the Board and I had to present to him and the review committee. I was pleased that he was complimentary of the work I did for them.

Two of my final projects with the firm were a new Madison Children's Museum which was a renovation of an existing basement space in a commercial building. That was very interesting, especially since the first exhibit, which I helped design, was a mock architect's office, child sized. The other was a small credit union building, a pavilion type structure, for a new banking machine, the ATM. After I left the firm and came back to Madison, I unexpectedly drove down a street and there it was, the exact design I did for that credit union structure, and I was quite pleased.

I quit Strang in 1986 and it was extremely bittersweet. Going through a divorce, coming to terms as a gay man, something I did not divulge directly to them until later, and wanting to move on to a new life, I decided to relocate to Des Moines, Iowa. Rick was not happy with that choice, although not knowing the full specifics, and we had a somewhat distant relationship thereafter, which greatly saddened me. We did keep in touch, but nonetheless I believe he thought after mentoring me I had an obligation to remain with the firm, and not leave it.

Des Moines, Iowa

Amazingly over a matter of a couple of days, over the Labor Day holiday, in 1986, I was hired by the firm of Englebrecht & Griffin, a firm that primarily did large CCRC, Continuing Care Retirement Communities, across the United States, with the main office in Des Moines, and satellite offices in Newburyport, Massachusetts, and in Boca Raton, Florida.

It was a good career move for me as I was very interested in senior design evolving from my housing experience, including the non-profit world. Englebrecht & Griffin was very corporate in image and culture, yet I settled in just fine. It was the first place I worked with a total open office plan, no private offices. It also had an interior design division.

The firm had one major client, a retirement community developer, out of Boston. They were doing some incredibly large retirement communities across the entire country, and I worked with them on ones in Georgia, Massachusetts, Illinois, Florida, New York, and Arizona. I worked on design for a location in Manlius, upstate New York, that was enormous in scale. I designed the main community building, that resembled a classic country club, and worked on a couple of mansion sized villas for the owners.

Both Englebrecht and Griffin were extremely talented and intelligent men, and Englebrecht taught architecture classes at the university too. The people in the firm were friendly, professional, and very serious about the work. We were producing some very good designs, and nationally noteworthy. Working directly with an Associate, Kate, I learned a great deal and appreciated the opportunity to learn more about senior design from her.

Many of the drawings were ink on mylar, a very tedious and precise drafting technique, and we used these crazy, difficult templates called 'Corbu', for Le Corbusier, templates, and smaller ones for lettering to make it uniform. The drawings were beautiful but there was little margin for blunders as it was hard to revise.

I did get to work with city and state agencies for approvals; and learned a lot about skilled nursing code requirements in various places, including the agencies that regulated them. I made a few visits to the state agency in Springfield, Illinois flying there from Des Moines while doing a skilled nursing facility design in that state. Learning my way through the codes

I was able to secure permits and apply for necessary allowable exemptions. All of this was valuable experience.

Seeing some of these communities constructed was incredibly fulfilling and I took pride in the ways I contributed to them. They seemed to go through the channels and get built far quicker than what occurs today. Perhaps it was because they were constructed in locations in more semi-rural settings without much bureaucracy.

I also spearheaded a couple of miscellaneous projects that were a bit out of the norm for the firm, like an interior remodel for an investment firm in a downtown high-rise. The reception room was elliptical in shape and the entire suite had high end finishes while employing very beautiful and expensive wood surfaces. One of the partners was into Remington figures and we had to make shelves throughout the suite for the collection. Overall, it was an interesting endeavor in luxury Class A type office space and in fine detailing.

In 1989 I resigned and headed for California.

The San Francisco Bay Area, California

I have written earlier about my arrival in San Francisco, and I will focus here on my career change.

Arriving in town after having sent out resumes and having a few interviews lined up, times were booming in the Bay Area. I got some offers right away and came to be interviewed by HKIT Architects, aka Hardison, Komatsu, Ivelich & Tucker Architects. The firm was founded in 1948 by Don Hardison, and joined by Richard Komatsu, but they had retired by time I arrived.

I had three interviews with the firm, all because the partners, four of them, were not there at the same time. I seemingly passed muster to get invited back to meet with the others, and the final was with a man I came to greatly admire, Richard 'Dick' Banwell. An extremely intelligent, professional, and talented architect he had his own firm at one time, but through unfortunate circumstances lost it. Education and schools were something he did know very well and did some high-profile schools in the Bay Area.

My interview with him was one I will never forget. He was a reviewer for the state licensing exams, so he was well versed at asking questions. California had a requirement for every person to be licensed to have passed an oral exam specific to the state, and Dick was one of the reviewers. When I arrived for my interview the first thing that he did was to tell me to loosen my tie and just relax, it would be a casual conversation. I was amazed at how adroit he was at getting to the bottom of one's knowledge base, asking very strategic questions about design and architectural practice.

While touring the firm one thing stood out, the culture seemed well suited for me; exactly what I sought and what I had known in previous firms where I enjoyed working.

When I got the phone call offering me a position I accepted right away. HKIT would be the firm I'd work for the next thirty-plus years, taking me through the rest of my career to retirement.

My first assignment was working on a large retirement community on the Peninsula in the Bay Area and my past experience was helpful. There were three teams, and I was put on the Health Care building including Assisted Living and Skilled Nursing residences.

After I started Dick took me aside and gave me the most valuable advice of my career. He said that no matter what, under any circumstance, I should never lose my cool or temper. In his estimation any architect who does that forfeits his or her professionalism. At times when it was difficult advice to follow, yet extremely wise, I did my best to abide by it. Whenever I was confronted by a situation and tested Dick's words would return to me loud and clear, and I am forever grateful for it.

I worked directly under Dick until he decided to retire a few months after I had been employed. I assumed his work-load which entailed a lot of construction administration work. He had become frustrated and weary of how the construction world had gone; and had enough of the frustration. It turned out I was quite good at construction administration, having done it before, and the partners figured that was a good place for me. My diplomacy of working with various factions on a construction site, including with the clients, worked well. I learned about construction specifics and techniques helping to make me a better architect. I enjoyed conversing with the subcontractors about best practices, and they appreciated that I was interested in their work.

I now believe that every architect should spend considerable time in the field to gain well-rounded proficiency. The other thing I proved good at was making instantaneous decisions to keep the work moving along. If it meant crawling through a tight space to see if ductwork would need to be rerouted to make fit, then I did it; and then I gave the contractor the details in the field, right then and there. I could make quick design decisions and the firm came to trust my judgement in doing so. Contractors liked that as opposed to returning to the office to figure it out and delaying the work progress. I had one project in Reno, Nevada and flew there every other week, so decisions had to be timely.

I worked closely with another man at HKIT who primarily did construction administration and very good at it too, Linton. He and I became good friends. As an openly gay man he immediately made it clear that I should never hide my sexual orientation. San Francisco was not Des Moines, Iowa. I truly appreciated his advice, and it was a breath of fresh air of freedom for me.

There was an Administrative Assistant, Sue, who was amazing in her job, and I came to greatly appreciate her value to the firm. She was the 'eyes and ears' of the business and knew everything, all the clients, and all the major issues at any given time. Not many people can emulate her professionalism and wisdom on the job. She has a lovely British accent that the clients often remarked to me as sounding very distinguished on the phone when they called.

Bob Tucker, George Ivelich, and Dennis Okamura all had distinct personalities, and styles of working, yet ran the firm well. Working with each of them I greatly appreciated their talents and knowledge. I had the opportunity to see exactly how they worked with clients; and learned quickly that getting work meant keeping strong relationships, something they each did very well.

Seven months into my employment the great earthquake of 1989 hit the Bay Area. It was devastating, and I thought my new-found home in San Francisco might be at an abrupt end. It pulled together quickly, however, as the firm managed to maintain its workflow and we soon moved to a new location in the SOMA neighborhood, to the resistance of many employees because it was 'no man's land' at that time.

I had some unique, and interesting experiences in doing on-site construction administration work. We had a non-profit senior housing building in Stockton, California that I worked on and during the time of final construction, when doing the 'close-out', I decided to stay overnight since it was a two-day effort. The contractor strongly advised me to not stay downtown. It was indeed seedy. I was amused when the client, from a religious order, came in one day to the job trailer to say he was so pleased by how friendly some women were waving to him from an adjacent street corner as he drove by. We did not have the heart to tell him they were prostitutes.

Against the advice of the contractor, I checked into a downtown motel for the night as it was the most convenient for me. About two in the morning, I was awaken by the police activity outside the motel. Soon after I heard gunshots. What soon became apparent was someone in the next room to me was shooting at them, and the police advising everyone by megaphone to shelter in place. I crawled under the bed and just stayed there. There were more gunshots and after about an hour the person was apprehended. I did not sleep the rest of the night and the contractor noticed my bleary eyes the next morning. He asked if I had had a late night out drinking, or merely stayed downtown. I owned up to the latter.

Once while driving back from meetings in Silicon Valley on I-280, a relatively new highway and not very well traveled in the early 1990s, a police car pulled me over. That car was then accompanied by another two police cars as I pulled on to the shoulder of the road. To my amazement and shock six policemen got out with drawn guns pointed at my car. I sat stunned when one of them came and tapped on my window, telling me to get out slowly. I did, nearly shaking in fear. I asked what I had done. The officer pointed to my car and said, 'tinted windows'. WHAT? Yes, I was stopped for tinted windows. My parents in Florida had just given me another Crown Victoria as they had bought a new car. All the windows were tinted dark black, in apparent violation of California law. When the officer noted the windows, I asked if all the drawn guns were necessary. He responded that since they could not see in the car, it was indeed necessary.

I protested the ticket because I had just registered the car in California and a DMV Inspector looked over the car and said nothing about the tinting. I certainly did not know. I was required to bring the car to a police station for verification the tinting, in the front windows only, was removed. When I sent in the proof, I got a response that the ticket was dismissed, with a smile face drawn at the bottom of the letter.

There was one rather seemingly unscrupulous contractor who did work for the school districts. They gave a Chinese Banquet for invited guests at a restaurant on the 'Avenues' in San Francisco. I was invited so I went. It was quite the experience. When I arrived, they handed me a tumbler of cognac, which they did with each guest. A tumbler! There was a bottle of cognac at every table for a refill. The banquet was exquisite, and I had foods I have never had before, all delicious. Some had what I'd consider unusual animal and fish parts to consume, but fortunately I did not know the details. I was seated with the head of the San Francisco Building Department, his wife, and several others. At one point the mayor stood to toast the contractor and drank the entire tumbler of cognac in one gulp. I sat there in total amazement as he seemed to do it with little effort.

This was the beginning of my attending many banquets, parties, events, and other functions over several years. It became a part of my professional life, and a way to build relationships. I had what I called a 'Spring Social Season' and a 'Fall Social Season'. The parties also ramped up during the holiday season. I greatly enjoyed the socializing and met many people along the way. I look back to my parents who were wonderful at socializing and taught me valuable lessons that proved well during this part of my life, including my mother's insistence on knowing proper etiquette. I could hold my own at an event with homeless shelter folks or at the higher echelon of the Pacific Union Club.

Events came in all types and for many reasons. Our firm often gave toys to needy children for the holidays. Once the head of a non-profit residential building asked if I would be Santa Claus to distribute the gifts to the kids. I gladly agreed. They had a Santa outfit for me to wear, which was far too big for me. Much to my shock when I bent down to pick up some gifts my Santa pants fell to my ankles. I did have pants underneath, so avoided a crisis, but the head of the non-profit whispered in my ear, 'keep it clean Santa, this is a family event!' I burst out laughing and pulled up the pants and continued with giving out gifts. These are moments one never forgets. It is amazing what one will do for a career.

I became friends socially with some of clients and enjoyed that engagement a great deal. I carefully learned to balance the business vs. personal social side of knowing people. One of these people was a man named Richard Flower, a retired researcher at UCSF, who I admired a great deal. As the head of a board of a retirement community I worked on he supported my ideas when others thought I was merely creating a 'Taj Mahal' for myself. After the Health Care addition was built, Dick, as I knew him, sent me notes of complimentary comments he overheard from residents, staff, and guests about the building. It was very kind of him, and I got to know him personally as very intelligent and forthright person. He eventually built a house on property he owned in Carmel, and I would stop and visit whenever in the area.

After almost a decade at HKIT I was invited to be one of the third generation of partners of the firm. It was a tremendous honor, and a whole new phase of my career, running a firm and a business. I was named with two others to continue the legacy of the firm and we took it on with complete intent on succeeding. The responsibility of leading and keeping a firm alive, and knowing one is responsible for not only keeping many employed, but also feeding their families, is not to be taken lightly. Life does change after becoming an owner and partner in a business.

We did succeed and moved the firm forward in many ways. I was at the forefront of establishing us as a noteworthy firm in senior living design. I started a Design for Aging Committee locally within the American Institute of Architects that grew to have one hundred and fifty participants. It was a time that I attended many conventions and conferences all around the country, speaking and presenting at sessions at nearly every one of them. I got to see cities in the US that otherwise I many have never visited, Austin, Nashville, Savannah, Columbus, Charlotte, and others. I did, however, come to dislike air travel as the years progressed as it was never pleasant with overpacked airports and planes. I was fortunate as my husband, Ed, often accompanied me to these things and willingly participated in the socializing too.

At one convention we got to have dinner at the house of a prominent member of San Antonio society, a Mrs. Steves. She lived in a classic contemporary house designed by O'Neil Ford, a well-known architect in that part of Texas. We were given free rein to explore the house, a sprawling ranch, and it was stupendous and elegantly designed. Meeting Mrs. Steves was incredibly enjoyable. She had a phenomenal sense of humor and was the consummate host. She showed us the part of the living room where she sat with friends, 'to tell secrets', and when I complimented her on her impressive Mexican folk-art collection, she looked at me and said, 'give me a dollar and I'll go to the border and get you a collection of your own!'. There were no thresholds at the exterior doors and when someone asked how she kept out the 'bugs' she said, while sidestepping and pretending to squish something, 'well, you just look the other way'. She told us that Lady Byrd Johnson, a good friend of hers, was there when she made the remark. It was times like that that made an adventure of these visits to other cities so amazing.

At one of the retirement communities where I had done a considerable amount of work, I had a call from one of the residents asking me to come meet with him and another resident to discuss a building addition he wanted to sponsor and donate. He was a retired Marine General and the thought of that alone put a chill into me, hoping I would be respectful and competent enough to meet his expectations. He hired me and I met several times with him. Each time he would establish the day and time to meet, and I would receive a formal message confirming it with something to the effect of 'you will appear to meet with me on such and such a date at a designated time', always in military time. After a couple of meetings, and my getting over my anxiety of his former position, he turned out to be a very down to earth likable man. He had written a book of his time in WWII, and he graciously gave me a signed copy. It was enlightening to see someone of his stature being so human.

It is difficult to condense thirty plus years in one firm into a short synopsis. There were many highlights and probably the lowest points were having to let an employee go, never easy. I did a lot of volunteer work along with my professional life and can look back with pride at the accomplishments.

I was always so proud of our staff at HKIT and in their dedication in their work. Many came to us specifically because of the type of work we did in the non-profit realm of affordable housing, education, and senior living. I worked with both architects older and more experienced than myself, and those just out of school. One man I especially appreciated working with, and admired, was an architect named Tom Oakes. We worked so well as a team, and he was always so thoughtful, wise, and talented in many ways. He also made it known to me that being a Principal, or Partner, was of no interest to him. Sometimes when the work was in a rough spot, he would say to me, 'well, that's why they call it work!'.

The enthusiasm to create well designed, enduring, sustainable architecture in every person at the firm was very inspiring.

Going into retirement in January 2020 I had just finished

up design work on two amazing and cutting-edge senior communities to culminate my career, 'Viamonte' in Walnut Creek and 'EnsoVillage' in Healdsburg. That latter was a joint venture client of the San Francisco Zen Center and Kendall, a Quaker senior living group in Pennsylvania. Both of those were marvelous projects and I am most proud to have been a part of creating them.

The utmost highlight and honor of my entire career was being elevated to be a 'Fellow' in the American Institute of Architects (AIA), an incredible honor. Only five percent of all architects receive that distinction. I was invested at the annual AIA Convention at the Denver Opera House in 2013. I could, with pride, use the designation 'FAIA' after my name. Most folks outside the profession would not know the meaning of it, but for me it was the climax of a career I embraced with fondness. It was recognition amongst my professional peers acknowledging my accomplishments, in a career that I had dreamt about since a teenager.

CHAPTER 30

Paradise found

I was born on an island, Long Island, and although in the Borough of Queens as a part of New York City it is still an island, albeit lost in the urbanity of it. Islands have always held a fascination for me, and I especially take pleasure in the tropical islands I have visited over my life.

There is a certain splendor and richness about tropical islands, and I have seen many from Aruba, Hawaii, Bermuda to French Polynesia. In French Polynesia I have visited Nuku Hiva in the Marquesas Islands, Rangiroa, Bora Bora, Moorea, and Tahiti. All distinctly different and all hugging the ocean and water like being a part of it, while the beauty of these places is incomparable and unmistakable. Truly paradise. They are living, thriving places that are also evolving. Growing out of the ocean over centuries they eventually return to the ocean. Once knowledgeable you can detect the age and stage of evolution in an island's life.

I especially appreciate the Pacific Islands, Hawaii, and French Polynesia, for the culture and history. Decimated by Explorers and Westerners the culture is once again surfacing in wonderful ways. I was amazed to learn that unemployment in French Polynesia is extremely high, yet it's unimportant to them. Unlike Western culture based on money and earning power everyone in French Polynesia watches after everyone else, everyone has a purpose, and no one goes hungry. Some educated in the best schools and universities in France, England, and the U.S. return to the simple island life they always have known. The people also do not have the hang-ups and taboos we possess. Men are permitted to dress like women if they want, and no one looks askance at them, or chides them. Everyone is respected for their individual choices. I saw several men dressed as a woman and they blend perfectly and seamlessly into society.

Island life moves slower, there is no need to rush or hurry. People are friendly, wave and smile. We had a taxi driver in Papeete, Tahiti who was so entertaining and friendly that by the conclusion of our ride she invited us to her daughter's graduation party.

The fact that Hawaii has no snakes and indigenous flora and fauna found nowhere else, and on Rangiroa grape vines grow on coral that is then made into a unique wine is both miraculous and incredible.

Learning about the navigation abilities of the peoples of Polynesia is remarkable. For centuries they could travel hundreds, if not thousands, of miles in small boats, and they did.

To find a private, secluded beach is one of life's great pleasures, in my view anyway. When in Bermuda a guide gave us information about a secluded beach that Ed and I then went to visit. No one was there, we were able to change into swimsuits and the coral-colored pink sand was extraordinary. We jumped into the clear aquamarine colored water and tossed around and swam, and it was like heaven on earth.

If possible, I would visit every tropical island on this earth, and I am certain that each would be an adventure. The natural light is more intense. The lushness of the landscape is awe inspiring.

CHAPTER 31

Our built environment

There is an elegant and simply designed pocket park on East 53rd Street, just off Fifth Avenue known as Paley Park, designed, and built in 1967 on the location of the former Stork Club. It is absolutely my favorite urban space anywhere in America. Tranquil and ever so restful, an oasis away from the energy of the city, it is tucked away yet has all the elements to appeal to the senses, from the gentle smell of the trees, hearing the cascading waterfall, a place to relax and taste a lunch, or just to sit in peace.

As a child in New York City, I was impressed by the beautiful classically designed buildings such as Grand Central Station, The New York Public Library, The Museum of Natural History, and The Plaza Hotel; public buildings that exude an elegance and grandeur with stone, magnificent staircases, and incredible detailing. As impressive to me were the modernist buildings I admired, the Seagram building, the United Nations, and even the Art Deco Chrysler building. They all amazed me and had an impact on my understanding of the built environment. Then too, I was fascinated just by the fabric of urban design and the intertwining of spaces, including the subways and their stations and how people moved around functioning in a city.

When visiting any city take some time and walk around, look around, explore. What you may discover is a treasure trove of urbanity with extraordinary details in buildings. Look up at the windows, the parapets, the lines, and details. Soon one realizes the time, effort, and ingenuity in creating our built environment.

There is no doubt we have overdone it a bit, including when the suburbs sprawled out in the 1960s and 70s. Sustainability has become a buzz phrase, yet an important one. We all must conserve, and our buildings need to be responsible to the environment. We have lost some ground, but we can regain it again, for generations to come.

I am impressed with the younger generation, especially the younger architects that worked in my office, as they had a different view of sustainability. To them it was not a question, but an essential necessity. Although in some ways seemingly entitled in cocky youth, they really do focus on a better world, and I admire that. They also come with a new lingo, acronyms, apparently derived from texting and other social media. It took me awhile to determine that 'WFH' meant 'work from home'. I mentioned to one woman of a younger generation about my recent trip on the Queen Mary 2 and to my surprise she asked if I had purposely done that to minimize the travel carbon footprint by not flying. I had not even considered it.

Like in fashion, styles in architecture come and go, some more enduring than others. Timeless buildings last, the buildings of ancient Rome or Greece, or even Egypt, created in inventive styles yet look beautiful and inspiring centuries later. Man can create amazing things with the creative mind. With the invention of the elevator and steel, we could go to whatever heights and expanses we choose. There are future innovations yet to come.

Habitation is an essential right, yet so many do not truly understand the concept of space and use, especially here in the U.S. Look to places like Japan where space is a constrained, well designed, and how creatively, elegantly, and responsibility people live quite comfortably with less.

When arriving in New York, Paris, Shanghai, or Istanbul one cannot be too unaware of the magnificence of our built environment. It is my hope we continue to create and make built environments in which we can thrive, be engaged and inspired, while still respecting our planet.

CHAPTER 32

Community

I parked on my usual side street to go to Kaiser Medical Center in Oakland one morning. When I walked to the intersection, at the top of the hill, this older lady appears, quite well dressed and confident looking.

She walked right up to my face and clearly barked at me, 'Peace or War?'

I was kind of taken aback and uncertain what to do.

She stared fiercely at me.

I finally said 'Peace'. She smiled and put out her hand to shake mine and said, 'Thank you, young man. Right answer'.

She continued, 'Now it's your job to put an 'e' at the end of human to carry it out to the world'.

I wondered. Religious fanatic? Wanting money? Crazy? It is Oakland. Nope, none of it.

Seriously, I nearly slapped my face to see if I was dreaming the whole thing, but nope, it was real.

Then she grabs my arm, puts hers through mine, and wants to walk with me.

This is when I got a little concerned. Dementia? No, not really. She was obviously alert.

In my usual paranoia, I'm focused on my wallet. I am a New Yorker, after all. I could just see me running and screaming after this old woman after she robs me!

We get to the next corner, and she seems perfectly content and chatty, so I told her about the WWII vets on my recent voyage on the Queen Mary. Especially how pleased I was for their appeal for world peace.

Well, she was just so delighted with my story, and said so.

I told her I had to go to an appointment, so she let go and said, 'Thank you for making my morning walk a bit more special. This is what living is supposed to be like, as opposed to today's crazy world. Take care, sweetie'.

So, I went on to my appointment while wondering what that was all about!

It was quite heartwarming, and very much a *Tales of the City* moment.

This is what community is all about. Connections, yes, even with those new to us.

It is about engagement, with those around us. No one should be isolated or segregated. Everyone has something to offer, we just need to reach out for it. As with my time living in Manhattan you can be with millions of people around you and still live isolated.

Ed tells of an experience he had in San Francisco when he had an office on Market Street. He would wait for me on a street corner in SOMA for me to pick him up on my way from work to take us home. One evening he observed a large garbage dumpster on the street next to the curb. Out of the corner of his eye he noticed a man standing up in it while eating a sandwich he had obviously taken from the garbage. Ed was in shock and their eyes met. The man said to him, 'Look, I don't want to be here but I'm hungry'. Ed offered to take him into the fast-food burger place behind them and the man agreed.

While waiting in line the guy told Ed he was just down on his luck, homeless, and desperate for anything to eat. Ed bought him a meal and left to come out to wait for me. That to me is what community is all about, helping a stranger in need. No one should be hungry.

I once had a small apartment in the Presidio Heights neighborhood of San Francisco. It was small yet ever so comfortable. A building with six apartments some of us got to know one another well. I used the living room for a bedroom and the bedroom, on the street with a nice bay window, as my living room. I adapted the space to my desires and needs. Sitting in that bay window connected me with community. From that same bay window, I also watched a Buddhist monk do his ritual prayer and meditation on his balcony across the street each day and I shared the meditative silence. That is community.

What is neighborhood, but the people who inhabit it, the community. Surely it has boundaries, imaginary or established. It is the residents and personalities that bring it together. I knew a man in New York who I would ride home with on the subway. He had a game where he would identify each passenger and the subway station that they would exit at based on how they dressed, spoke, and generally looked and conducted themselves. He was never wrong. Some would say that is profiling or stereotyping; but is it? It seems like it might be establishing commonality, or community. It is the uniqueness of each that makes neighborhood and identity.

Visiting Washington State for Ed's father's milestone birthday he rented a house on Puget Sound so the entire family could come and celebrate. Next door was a beautiful large stone house owned by an Indian tribal leader whose tribe owned a local casino. Concurrent to our celebration they were having their own. A visiting native tribe from Hawaii was being hosted by them. We could hear the beautiful chanting and music during the days we stayed there, and their children became friendly and spent time with us when we sat outdoors, often bringing food they had prepared for us to try. Their communities became a part of our community, and the blending was truly wonderful. One of the young girls memorized each of our names. She came back one evening to say that the tribe had discussed me, for whatever reason, and had bestowed a tribal name on me, 'Talking Tom'. I thought Ed's brother was going to fall off his chair laughing. Nonetheless we came together as community, and I was brought into the fold and frankly honored.

San Francisco has no cemeteries, except for a military one in the Presidio, a national park. All the cemeteries were moved out of the city in the 1930s to a city to the south of it, Colma, 'The City of the Dead'. The only way you can be 'buried' in San Francisco is to be cremated and interred in a columbarium. My final resting place will be in Grace Cathedral on Nob Hill with my family in that columbarium. If you go there, and it is generally not open to the public, you'll see a different type of community. There are hundreds of plaques lining the walls of those who once lived here, in final community together. There is an amazing cross section of people interred there, and each has a story of their life. I have heard some of the stories and, trust me, they are fascinating. Look through the book of the names of those who are interred there, in calligraphy, and each name takes on a part of communal history.

Like in an existentialist story by Jean-Paul Sartre I imagine those folks in the columbarium laughing and enjoying being together and relishing the afterlife, perhaps looking down on the living and remarking on what we are doing. They know that someday we will join the fold.

As humans we exist best in community, and we need to get along, even when times are tough, and we may not be alike.

Respect is honorable. Understanding is essential.

No one truly lives alone. Even the hermit, recluse or cloistered person lives with someone within their soul.

Think about it, you are community, and the adventures of your life contribute to the person you are, now and forever. And the more we explore, experience, and understand the world the more we will come to appreciate it.

Conclusion

Undoubtedly, you have learned that I am a gatherer of life's experiences. I like to explore, try new things, meet new people, and appreciate the ones I have, savor life's special moments along with enduring the periodic trials and tribulations that happen; and lastly, I recognize love is a beautiful thing.

This brings us back to Cousin Daisy's cabinet, where this all began. Life is like a series of cabinets. What we encounter may appear locked, but we can persevere to open and discover what lies within it. As we yearn to open and find what it holds for us, and once we do, it may be full of treasure or completely empty and discouraging. Either way, what matters most is the *adventure* of having it, pondering it, and eventually the reality of unlocking and learning from it.

We never know how or when our last breath will be taken, but in the meanwhile make the most of the time you have, to enjoy everything the world has to offer. Unlock it. Do not be discouraged with an empty cabinet, as another will come along. It may be empty again; or hold treasure!

Also, care for others, engage and contribute, and embrace community…

Explore, take chances and risks, learn, listen, and relish every second of life!

Gather your life's experiences… and share them.

THE END

Acknowledgements

Dorothy and Charles Brutting, my parents, for inspiring me in many ways; and many good people- Gloria Reynolds, Jean-Pierre Van Autreve, Andrea Tutrani, Paul and Claudia Nickolloff , Joe Walker, Alan Karchmer and Sandra Ann Benedum, Jack Siebert and Nato Flores, Hilda and David Kuter, John Lorenc, Dennis Rocchio. Mary Ruth Quinn, Julie Barrow and JoAnn Semones, Nila Rusnell Oakes, Marv Johnson, Dave Latina, Anne Burns Johnson, Dara Youngdale and Steve Lovell, The Gridleys, Soher Youssef and Celinda Cantu, the Wasserman family, the Watsons, the American Bruttings; Ollie, Barbara, Cynthia, Marilyn Day and Tom Oakes who are now gone; the Brütting family in Germany; Ed's family who welcomed me in; plus countless people I've met along the way in life including Ambassador John Withers II who inspired and encouraged me to write this book; and of course, Ed York Jr., my husband, friend and companion who listens to so much of my rambling on, and on.

Furthermore, I am extremely grateful for the very professional guidance of James Essinger at The Conrad Press who helped in many ways to make this book possible.

Finally, with gratitude to Charlotte Mouncey, who produced the book cover design and typesetting with her noteworthy talent.